Praise for *Wendell Berry: Life and Work*

"Trying to keep up with the prolific writings of farmer-poet-essayist Wendell Berry leaves one both grateful and breathless. This rich and varied assembly is the next-best thing to Berry's own work and will send the reader eagerly back to the original poems, stories, and essays. Here many skilled voices diagnose, extend, celebrate, and affirm a whole range of his art and ideas—and illuminate the striking example of his life as well. Berry's moral and agrarian vision is taking an ever deeper hold in America, and this book will help it happen."
—Ronald Jager, author of *Eighty Acres: Elegy for a Family Farm*

"This volume is of great value and importance. What emerges from these various writings (which include telling personal memories) is the greatness of this man, good and wise at the same time. His talents as a writer and poet include those of a historian and a prophet. More and more Americans—entire generations—ought to hear his voice and read him."
—John Lukacs, author of *At the End of an Age*

"Though the 'characters' herein are real people, there is magic in this book that rivals the best of Wendell Berry's writings. Over and over we see solitary readers grappling with Berry's art and thought amid struggles and in places unknown to the author."
—David James Duncan, author of *God Laughs and Plays: Churchless Sermons in Response to the Preachments of the Fundamentalist Right*

"This book welcomes into community all who read Wendell Berry's work habitually and with mounting desire for a sane culture. It is good to have neighbors who share the gratitude and even affection we feel for a man whom most of us have not met. These writers confirm our sense that reading Berry is one of the most important things we do."
—Ellen F. Davis, author of *Wondrous Depth: Preaching the Old Testament*

"This is a superb collection. Berry is one of America's greatest social critics, essayists, and poets, and the grand simplicity and unity of his life and thoughts emerge from the fascinating details of his personal history, captured beautifully in the words of his friends."
—David Ehrenfeld, author of *Swimming Lessons: Keeping Afloat in the Age of Technology*

Praise for *Wendell Berry: Life and Work,* continued

"What a joy to read *Wendell Berry: Life and Work,* a rich collection of personal stories, literary critiques, and thoughtful reflections about Wendell Berry's life and work—all essays written by friends who know him best. It is all here in this wonderful collection of essays."
—Frederick Kirschenmann, Distinguished Fellow, Leopold Center, Iowa State University

"Wendell Berry has revitalized American agrarianism with his uncompromising good sense, quiet urgency, and graceful style. This generous collection of reminiscences, insights, and storytelling from the who's who of American agrarianism ably demonstrates the power of one person to influence an entire generation. *Wendell Berry: Life and Work* is worthy of the man it honors.
—William Vitek, coeditor of *Rooted in the Land: Essays on Community and Place*

Wendell Berry

Culture of the Land: A Series in the New Agrarianism

This series is devoted to the exploration and articulation of a new agrarianism that considers the health of habitats and human communities together. It demonstrates how agrarian insights and responsibilities can be worked out in diverse fields of learning and living: history, science, art, politics, economics, literature, philosophy, religion, urban planning, education, and public policy. Agrarianism is a comprehensive worldview that appreciates the intimate and practical connections that exist between humans and the earth. It stands as our most promising alternative to the unsustainable and destructive ways of current global, industrial, and consumer culture.

Series Editor
Norman Wirzba, Georgetown College, Ky.

Advisory Board
Wendell Berry, Port Royal, Ky.
Ellen Davis, Duke University, N.C .
Patrick Holden, Soil Association, United Kingdom
Wes Jackson, Land Institute, Kans.
Gene Logsdon, Upper Sandusky, Ohio
Bill McKibben, Middlebury College, Vt.
David Orr, Oberlin College, Ohio
Michael Pollan, University of California at Berkeley, Calif.
Jennifer Sahn, *Orion* Magazine, Mass.
Vandana Shiva, Research Foundation for Science, Technology & Ecology, India
William Vitek, Clarkson University, N.Y.

Wendell Berry

LIFE AND WORK

Edited by Jason Peters

THE UNIVERSITY PRESS OF KENTUCKY

Publication of this volume was made possible in part by a grant from the
National Endowment for the Humanities.

Copyright © 2007 by The University Press of Kentucky
Scholarly publisher for the Commonwealth, serving Bellarmine University, Berea
College, Centre College of Kentucky, Eastern Kentucky University, The Filson Historical
Society, Georgetown College, Kentucky Historical Society, Kentucky State University,
Morehead State University, Murray State University, Northern Kentucky University,
Transylvania University, University of Kentucky, University of Louisville, and Western
Kentucky University.

Editorial and Sales Offices: The University Press of Kentucky
663 South Limestone Street, Lexington, Kentucky 40508-4008
www.kentuckypress.com

11 10 09 08 07   5 4 3 2 1

Library of Congress Cataloging-in-Publication Data

Wendell Berry : life and work / [edited by] Jason Peters.
     p. cm. — (Culture of the land)
 Includes bibliographical references and index.
 ISBN 978-0-8131-2442-1 (alk. paper)
 1. Berry, Wendell, 1934– I. Peters, Jason, 1963–
 PS3552.E75Z96 2007
 818'.5409—dc22
 [B]   2007005962

Manufactured in the United States of America.

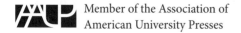 Member of the Association of
American University Presses

For Tanya and Wendell Berry

Contents

Foreword

IN *THE PRESENCE OF THE PAST* Sheldon Wolin has a wonderful essay titled "Tending and Intending a Constitution: Bicentennial Misgivings," which provides categories that make clear the significance of Wendell Berry's work as well as these essays in this book. Wolin suggests that "tending" and "intending" characterize two persistent modes of thinking about politics that confronted one another during the ratification of the American Constitution. A politics of "intending" Wolin describes as one shaped by the language of contract in which a system of power seeks to ensure a future by bringing all life under a single rational order. A politics of intending comes fully to fruition in our time by the development of the "science" of administration that legitimates the expert as the power behind the throne of those who rule us.

In contrast, a politics of "tending" is best identified with what we do when we look after another, as in tending the sick or a garden. Tending requires "active care of things close at hand." To "tend" is to care for objects whose very being requires that they be treated as historical and biographical beings. Such a politics requires the existence of a political culture comprised of shared beliefs, habits, practices, and memories that define the particularity of a place and determine how the future will be negotiated. Wolin suggests that in such a setting politics is best understood, not as something practiced separate from the ordinary, but rather as a form of cultivation analogous to tending fields or flocks.

Wendell Berry obviously exemplifies a politics of "tending." That he does so, moreover, helps us understand why his life as a farmer, husband, father, and friend, and why his poems, novels, and essays, are of a piece. Berry farms as he writes and he writes as he farms. Each word is cultivated just as each row is carefully plowed. As many of these essays witness, he cares for friends the way he writes, and he writes with the care demanded by the love of friends. Yet each friend, just as each field of his farm, requires different "tending." Moreover, as is clear from these essays, Berry depends on being befriended by friend and land because he recognizes he can give only because of what he has first received.

I call attention to Wolin's account of intending and tending in order to anticipate an oft-made criticism that Berry's agrarianism is utopian. But if Wolin is right about the politics of tending, and if the essays in this book rightly describe Berry, then it is clear Berry's life and work are not utopian but as real as the dirt he farms. That Berry's work has ever been considered "unrealistic" is surely because of the unhappy dominance of the politics of intending in our time. Berry's politics is as real as the next poem he writes, the meal Berry and Tanya share with friends, and the crop soon to be harvested. Indeed, this book itself is testimony that Berry and his friends cannot be dismissed as "idealist," if for no other reason than their determined "earthiness," which is prominently displayed by the sense of humor that pervades these essays.

I suspect that Berry will at once be a bit embarrassed by this book but also be grateful to learn the joy his work has given his friends. These are celebratory essays that make the reader happy. That a book of essays can do that in our day testifies to the extraordinary power of Berry's life and work. I often think that Berry's novels do what is next to impossible in our time, and that is make goodness compelling. I usually hate sweetness because it always threatens to become sentimentality, and sentimentality is, I think, the enemy of the good. But *Jayber Crow,* for example, like so much of Berry's work, is a sweet story about goodness wrought from the hardness of life. What a remarkable achievement rightly celebrated by almost every essay in this book.

When a book of this sort is published, the subject of the book—I speak from personal experience—cannot help but think, "They must think I've come to the end of the row. I have nothing else to say. I may even be dead." But everyone who writes in this book does so with the knowledge that Wendell Berry is anything but dead. Berry's unrelenting attack on the abstractions that underwrite the current war in Iraq are a sure sign that he has not come to the end of the line. Indeed, these essays help us know better how alive Berry is.

Those who have written these essays have tended to Wendell Berry's "tending." Therefore these essays will help inscribe on our hearts the habits of tending. Read this book slowly. Read this book joyfully. Read this book again. In doing so you will discover the essays do what they were meant to do; that is, after having read these wonderful, joyful essays you will discover you cannot wait to read more Wendell Berry. I take this to be a tribute to the tending to Berry these essays so richly exhibit. We live in a world dominated by the "intending," which means we need not only Berry's work but the work that Berry's work makes possible. What a hopeful book this is.

Stanley Hauerwas
Gilbert T. Rowe Professor of Theological Ethics
Duke Divinity School, Duke University

Acknowledgments

I'M GRATEFUL FOR the assistance I received from the Academic Initiatives Fund and the Center for Vocational Reflection, both at Augustana College. Thanks also to Connie Ghinazzi, Nick Barrett Stirrett, Mary Sutherland, Norman Wirzba, Bill Kauffman, Jeremy Beer, Ron Jager, George Core, and Barry Lopez. I'm happy to acknowledge the help, advice, and friendship of Paul Schellinger, Dave Crowe, Mike Nolan, Tom Thompson, Scott Sanders, and especially Steve Wrinn. Thanks to Guy Mendes for providing the excellent photographs reproduced here, and to my friend the monk Zosimas (né Miles Belcher) for introducing me to Wendell Berry's work. For their contributions untold and untellable, I thank my parents, Janet and Richard Peters, and especially my wife, Kristin. For their many kindnesses to me, I thank Tanya and Wendell Berry, to whom this volume is dedicated.

"You are a hero among those who have been wounded and offended by industrial living and yearn for a simpler and more natural and more feeling relation to the natural world. I should add that you wouldn't be as good a man as you are if you were not a member of Tanya, and she of you."—Wallace Stegner, "A Letter to Wendell Berry"

Photograph by Guy Mendes from Light at Hand, *reprinted by permission of Gnomon Press*

Jason Peters

Introduction

> I desire to speak somewhere *without* bounds; like a man in a waking
> moment, to men in their waking moments; for I am convinced that I
> cannot exaggerate enough even to lay the foundation of a true expression.
> —Henry David Thoreau, *Walden* (1854)

> Though I have had many of these ideas consciously in mind for several years,
> I have found them extraordinarily difficult to write about. . . . But they are
> ideas of great usefulness, and I am eager to have a hand in their revival.
> —Wendell Berry, *The Long-Legged House* (1969)

IN 1862 EMERSON said that "no truer American existed than Thoreau." In
context the remark was instructive, for it followed fast upon the punning observation that Thoreau "had no talent for wealth" and that "he knew how to be
poor without the least hint of squalor or inelegance."[1]

But out of context—next Friday at happy hour, for example—the remark
is inscrutable. We Americans apparently have talent for little else. We seldom
depart from the script written for us by the Magic Hand of the "free" market.
We don't excel at any form of consumer restraint, to say nothing of dissent. If
advertising were a virus, most of us would be dead, taking to our graves the
suspicion that Thoreau was seditious and unpatriotic—a true crackbrain but
not a true American. For Thoreau, also punning, admonished us to "cultivate
poverty like a garden herb, like sage." He warned us "of enterprises that require new clothes, and not rather a new wearer of clothes." He said, "A man is
rich in proportion to the number of things which he can afford to let alone."[2]

That such advice portends disaster for the unassailable gross domestic
product hasn't inhibited one of Thoreau's worthiest heirs from repeating it.
Wendell Berry says plainly that we "must achieve the character and acquire
the skills to live much poorer than we do." He says that "virtually all of our
consumption now is extravagant, and virtually all of it consumes the world."
He reminds us that "to have everything but money is to have much."[3]

This is more seditious and unpatriotic talk; it offends against the unim-

1

peachable moral code known as the American Way. And yet one contributor here says in Emersonian fashion that Berry is "perhaps our greatest patriot"; several others see in Berry a reinvented Thoreau.

Neither Thoreau nor Berry suffers damage by the comparison. One went to the woods to live deliberately; the other went home to live defensibly. Both built small domiciles out of reused lumber, one on the ground beside a pond and the other on stilts alongside a river. As writers both are keen to etymological impertinence: "Of a life of luxury the fruit is luxury," Thoreau says, "whether in agriculture, or commerce, or literature, or art"; "we are acting out the plot of a murderous paradox," Berry says, "an 'economy' that leads to extravagance."[4] Both require mindfulness with respect to food: Thoreau says, "It is hard to provide and cook so simple and clean a diet as will not offend the imagination"; Berry says, "I dislike the thought that some animal has been made miserable in order to feed me."[5] Both attend to food in its many cultural, imaginative, and intellectual associations: so Thoreau, in pursuit of higher laws, says that "the gross feeder is a man in the larva state; and there are whole nations in that condition, nations without fancy or imagination, whose vast abdomens betray them"; and Berry, in pursuit of higher sense, says, "There is nothing more absurd . . . than the millions who wish to live in luxury and idleness and yet be slender and good-looking."[6]

But, although neither man believes that we live by bread alone, both reject the cheap grace that religion often grants itself. Thoreau: "What avails it that you are Christian, if you are not purer than the heathen, if you deny yourself no more?" Berry: Christianity as it is currently practiced is a "comforter of profitable iniquities"; it has made its "peace with 'the economy' by divorcing itself from economic issues."[7]

There are of course differences between the one who said "simplify" and the one who says "complexify." These contrarians are often stylistically and rhetorically as distant as Massachusetts is from Kentucky. Thoreau: "The greater part of what my neighbors call good I believe in my soul to be bad"; Berry: "I suffer very comfortably the lack of colas, TV dinners, and other counterfeit foods and beverages."[8] But then not always so distant. Thoreau: "To be awake is to be alive. I have never yet met a man who was quite awake. How could I have looked him in the face?" Berry: "I knew a man who, in the age of chainsaws, went right on cutting his wood with a handsaw and an axe. He was a healthier and saner man than I am. I shall let his memory trouble my thoughts."[9]

And you don't necessarily have to begin with *Walden* in particular to sustain the comparison, for Berry participates in the enduring strain of Thoreauvian civil disobedience: arguments against a standing army "deserve to prevail," says the one; "Ceaseless preparation for war / is not peace," says the other.[10] Politicians fare poorly in the judgment of both: "For eighteen hundred years," says Thoreau, "the New Testament has been written; yet where is the legislator who has wisdom and practical talent enough to avail himself of the light which it sheds on the science of legislation?" "It is now . . . merely typical," says Berry, "that a political leader can speak of 'the preciousness of all life' while armed for the annihilation of all life."[11] Berry's indefatigable judgment of an economy predicated on competition—that it not only facilitates but also encourages the accumulation of wealth and power into fewer and fewer hands—accords with that sentiment in Thoreau that unites his naturalism and his political grumpiness: "They who assert the purest right, and consequently are most dangerous to a corrupt State, commonly have not spent much time in accumulating property."[12] And if Berry affirms that the lost disciplines of domesticity—the husbandry and wifery of making do—have the possibility of enriching our lives and making us glad, he has Thoreau's precedent, also from *Civil Disobedience:* "The opportunities of living are diminished in proportion as what are called the 'means' are increased. The best thing a man can do for his culture when he is rich is to endeavor to carry out those schemes which he entertained when he was poor."[13]

For back of everything, these great dissenters behold similar maladies: one, looking out upon his pond, wonders why we should "be in such desperate haste to succeed, and in such desperate enterprises"; the other, looking out upon his river, wonders at the boaters

> speeding by as if late
> for the world's end, their engine
> shaking the air, breaking
> the water's mirrors.

Perhaps the only difference that matters is contextual: in Thoreau's time the mass of men led lives of quiet—in Berry's they lead lives of noisy—desperation.[14]

I don't intend to exaggerate a comparison that I am by no means the first to make, nor by hyperbole to make more of Emerson's "no truer American" than the remark warrants. But it is not irrelevant at this moment in American letters when, as Berry says, *the* story line is the breaking of faith,[15] that Berry himself, so like that true American of whom Emerson wrote, answers variously to his many and disparate forebears in the literary tradition: to John Cotton, who required that every man "live in some warrantable calling"; to Benjamin Franklin, who observed that "he that by the Plough would thrive, / Himself must either hold or drive"; to Thomas Jefferson, who held that "small landholders are the most precious part of a state"; to John Wannuaucon Quinney, who lamented a Mohican land that had "never been purchased or rightly obtained"; to William Apess, who complained that the colonists thought "it no crime to go upon Indian lands and cut and carry off their most valuable timber, or anything else they chose"; to Melville, who said no writer can "soar to such a rapt height, as to receive the irradiation of the upper skies" if he does not also possess "a great, deep, intellect, which drops down into the universe like a plummet"; and to Hawthorne, who said there is "folly [in] tumbling down an avalanche of ill-gotten gold." In noting that nature "does not tolerate or excuse our abuses," Berry reminds us of Emerson himself, who said "she pardons no mistakes."[16] In speaking of "economic nonentity"—"a condition that people grow extremely tired of, and when tired of it become extremely dangerous"—he reminds us of Langston Hughes, who gave us the festering, stinking, and at last exploding "dream deferred." [17] In wondering long ago whether Port Royal, Kentucky, could produce the kind of poet he hoped to become, he reminds us (as he reminded himself) of the precedent in Paterson, New Jersey, where William Carlos Williams engaged the "unceasing labor of keeping responsibly conscious of where he was," speaking in his poems not "as a poet but as a man."[18] And when, recalling Saint Paul, Berry says that "a healthy community is like a body, for its members mutually support and serve one another," he returns us—shorn of the embarrassing social and economic disparities—to John Winthrop's call aboard the *Arbella,* nearly four hundred years ago, for a community of members held together by love, which is that "bond of perfection."[19]

True enough: "true American" is not a category. But if Berry's voice seems an anamnesis of the oracle of *Walden,* it also resounds within a richly varied tradition, and his critique reaches further and sustains an urgency greater than anything Thoreau ever attempted: for above all this, Berry, more than any living writer, certainly more than any commander in chief, has defended —without a standing army—*actual* American soil. Having understood the necessity of "food production that pays its debt to the soil," to use Steven Stoll's useful phrase, he has seen agriculture—again in Stoll's words—as "a delicate system of return, powered by the sun and managed by cultivators who [see] soil as the totality of matter passing through their hands."[20] If your average American is voracious in appetite and profligate in spending, consuming what he does not own and mortgaging a future that cannot be his, he is anything but *true*—whether in the Emersonian sense or not—for he keeps no troth. But *fidelity,* the keeping of faith, has been Berry's enduring theme, our dominant and countervailing storyline notwithstanding.

All of which is to say that the question J. Hector St. John de Crèvecoeur once posed in *Letters from an American Farmer*—"What is an American?"—is endlessly interesting, and its answer endlessly relevant. Is an American a man who cultivates poverty or debt? Is she wary of enterprises that require new clothes, or does she build more closets to placate that fickle tyrant Fashion? Can he resist sales talk, or does he leave nothing alone that's for sale—especially if it obviates the need for any bodily exertion not specifically copulative? The answer to "what is an American?" goes some distance in explaining why the Joneses and those who keep up with them live not as Thoreau did, nor as Berry does, but as bundles of unacknowledged contradictions: they have treadmills in their basements and riding lawnmowers in their garages; they drive to gyms across town (and over rivers) to ride stationary bikes (and use rowing machines). These exemplary citizens have been "educated" to be self-reliant and resourceful in schools funded by state lotteries and casinos.

Berry has aimed his sharpened pencil at dumb game of this kind exactly—nature lovers (he calls them "nature consumers"[21]) who want pristine places through which to run their recreational vehicles, students who want a good "education" so long as it is easy and fun, parents who want good neighborhoods but not the burden of being good neighbors, citizens who expect honesty from their political leaders but not from the advertisers and corporations that flatter them, politicians who talk of "homeland security" but secure no actual land, legislators who support the powerful but expect gratitude from the weak, health-conscious consumers who want chemical-free food but not the responsibility of growing or preparing it, environmentalists who expect moral behavior from industries that thrive in an economy predicated on moral turpitude, and above all the economy's cheerleaders—those most superstitious and credulous of creatures, shortsighted if not short-skirted—who assure us that infinite appetites can be infinitely satisfied in a finite place and who, as Herman Daly says, treat "depletion and pollution as 'surprising' external costs."[22]

For such fools was satire invented; around them a whole fraternity of splenetic writers might rightfully gather. But however much we may need a Swift or a Mencken now, Berry, though capable of ridicule, has never been the sort of essayist merely to vent his spleen upon the incorrigible and unsuspecting. Beneath the severity and sometime anger of his most polemical work there abides a love for this great house long since turned into a den of thieves. It is this love—and a tender but not sentimental affection—that even in this dark world and wide stirs Berry at the start of his eighth decade to say, "The work that I feel best about I have done as an amateur: for love. But in my essays especially I have been motivated also by fear of our violence to one another and to the world, and by hope that we might do better."[23]

And it is to this cause, to this wheel of love, that the writers here assembled have put their shoulders. We intend, all of us, either to commence an accurate biography or to inaugurate a careful consideration of Berry's place in American life and letters. Several essays here take up Berry the man, often mistaken as dour by readers who have either ignored his fiction or, like so many trained critics, have read it with their eyes shut. These essays paint a man with a prodigious capacity for laughter and conviviality, and they come from the pens of those who have had the great honor to know Berry's friendship. Other essays consider Berry's expansive practical, imaginative, and intellectual labor: his work on a hillside farm, his work in three genres, his knowledge of or interest in economics, politics, theology, education, technology, peace. We endeavor, that is, to treat him as he is: a complex man of place and membership, of domestic, of intellectual, of filial and fraternal talents. If for a few hundred pages we divert attention from Berry's own work, we may yet help readers by indirections find directions out.

So this collection considers Berry as a writer of many parts (as one contributor calls him) and, in a manner of speaking, a farmer of one: a novelist, poet, and essayist, Berry has given his life to tending a small hillside in his native Kentucky county, writing there by hand and farming by hand- and horse-labor.

In eight novels and far more short stories, Berry tells with humor and affection the story of a small farming community, Port William, as it struggles to preserve its traditional ways against predation from without and disaffection from within. In more than ten volumes of poetry, he likewise celebrates (among other things) "the world of nature despite its mortal / dangers" in a "language that can pay just thanks / and honor for those gifts." In more than twenty collections of essays, and in an idiom clear and uncompromising, he diagnoses our besetting ills, chief among them a blind faith in science (self-mitred, self-crowned), addiction to labor-saving devices ("We would use a steam shovel to pick up a dime"), and dependence upon an extractive economy (it "takes, makes, uses, and discards" and moves therefore "from exhaustion to pollution").[24]

Born in 1934 to John and Virginia Berry, Wendell Erdman Berry confessed some delight in pretending, as the son of a prominent lawyer, to aspire to a career as a bootlegger. (John Sr. was in fact one of the principal architects of the Burley Tobacco Growers Cooperative, a program formed in 1921 to help tobacco growers in five states deal with volatile markets.) In high school Berry attended Millersburg Military Institute—or rather "waged four years there in sustained rebellion against everything the place stood for, paying the cost both necessarily and willingly"[25]—the main consequence of which seems to have been the making of a confirmed and talented contrarian. After earning AB and MA degrees from the University of Kentucky (1956, 1957), Berry went as a Wallace Stegner fellow to Stanford University, where he met, among others, Ken Kesey, Ken Babbs, Ernest Gaines, Larry McMurtry, and Nancy Huddleston Packer. He spent a year in Italy on a Guggenheim Fellowship (1961–62) and then, from 1962 to 1964, taught English at New York University before deciding to return to Kentucky. "At a time when originality is more emphasized in the arts, maybe, than ever before," he says, "I undertook something truly original—I returned to my origins."[26] Berry then taught at the University of Kentucky (1964–77, 1987–93), all the while improving the farm on which he and his wife, Tanya, still live and work.

But it is a mistake, Berry says, to characterize this story as a return to the simple life. It is a story of return, to be sure, and it is one of the oldest and most instructive in the Western tradition, but there is nothing simple about it. Berry returned, he says, to a far more complex life, a life that he sustains and that in turn sustains him—not by easy purchase and haste but by difficult work and patience, not by mindless acquiescence to a centralized economy but by careful attention to local ways and wisdom.[27]

This commitment to local ways signals a salient theme in Berry's work; that our lives must be built, and our problems reduced, to the scale of human competence. Cities must not be so large that local agriculture cannot sustain them. The economy must consist of smaller, local economies that attend to local needs and capacities. Citizens must act according to what they can know not in the abstract but in concrete particulars. If they cannot act in a manner commensurate with their capacity to know and to do, if they give themselves over to abstractions—which, Berry says, always conduce to abuse—they will necessarily abuse the sources they live from: water, soil, and air.

For Berry, there are no better examples of this abuse than strip-mining and large-scale farming. In both cases, distant but powerful corporations—whether in mining or agribusiness (the difference is negligible, for the methods are indistinguishable)—impose their "advice," their whims, and finally their will on vulnerable regions from which they extract profits, in which they destroy fertility, and to which they return waste. Berry has criticized these government-sanctioned practices in, among other works, *The Long-Legged House* (1969) and *The Unsettling of America* (1977)—both in a sense wartime books inasmuch as they uncover from the temporal vicinity of Vietnam the similarities between military and economic aggression: in the former book he says that "the idea of controlled destruction [in strip-mining] may be as much a rationalization, as potentially a delusion, as the idea of limited war"; in the latter he says that "the people who make wars do not fight them. The people responsible for strip-mining, clear-cutting of forests, and other ruinations do not live where their senses will be offended or their homes or livelihoods or lives immediately threatened by the consequences. The people responsible for the various depredations of 'agribusiness' do not live on farms."[28] The ongoing systematic destruction of hillsides, farms, and farmland—the destruction, that is, of the soil and the cultural institutions that attend it—is a failure of knowledge, of character, of moral strength, of intellect, of policy, of many things, which Berry is careful at each turn to clarify and by example and instruction to correct.

Among the many correctives Berry has proffered, two recur frequently: the acquisition of skills, not money, and the practice of restraint, not extravagance. But he believes that neither of these is possible apart from "culture-borne" instructions. Nor does he believe our ecological crisis is a crisis of knowledge only: "Rats and roaches live by competition under the law of supply and demand," he says; "it is the privilege of human beings to live under the laws of justice and mercy."[29] Berry adumbrates the complexity of this moral vision and the difficult demands of his own code when, in *The Unsettling of America,* he makes bold to say that we will certainly use clean energy poorly, could we ever adopt it, because we are not good enough to know how to use energy well and not smart enough to know what it is for.[30] To the quantifying utilitarian mind, to the mind rendered impervious and invincible by unconscious, systemic errors, this claim can only increase the inveterate confusion. And yet this is precisely the kind of gospel that the current mind, so incapable by now of turning suspicion on itself—and in ways perhaps unprecedented—needs.

Berry's politics, closely tied to his economic critique and his distrust of organizations, are complicated by the fact that America's two major political parties increasingly resemble each other. He calls himself a Jeffersonian and a Democrat. He is a Jeffersonian inasmuch as he supports decentralization and the proliferation of as many small landholders as are possible, and he is a Democrat inasmuch as he was born into, and comes out of, the New Deal. He holds that a responsible government will protect small businesses and craftsmen against the ravages of the "free" market, which, far from being free, gives the wealthy and powerful easy permission to become richer and stronger. He does not believe democracy can survive apart from a well-informed citizenry that heeds the available moral instruction. But he has been clear on many occasions that he speaks for neither the liberals nor the conservatives as they currently understand—*if* they understand—themselves. Both are beholden to an economy intent on destroying whatever it can in its effort to support a standard of living that destroys whatever is.

As for his religious sympathies, Berry admits that Christianity, "for better or worse," is the religious tradition he is heir to, but he also confesses a debt to other religions—Buddhism, for example—that provide useful correctives to our most grievous faults.[31] He seems less and less likely to countenance claims of religious singularity, given the pattern of warfare that follows from such claims. Nevertheless, Berry has consistently declared fealty to the literary and religious tradition to which Dante, Spenser, Shakespeare, and Donne—among others—belong.

All of these concerns—agrarianism, politics, religion, economics, literature—and many others are the objects of inquiry here, and the essays that treat them range from the scholarly to the personal. If I depart from the formalities of an introduction and forgo the tiresome task of summarizing each essay (and I do), I do so because each of these splendid pieces speaks clearly and elegantly enough to its topic. This collection testifies to the breadth and depth of Berry's work, and it recommends his exemplary and difficult life as an alternative to the desperation, whether quiet or noisy, of our own.

Whitman, in a moment of characteristic exuberance, said that "the proof of a poet is that his country absorbs him as affectionately as he has absorbed it." Thoreau we have affectionately absorbed, I think, though we've hardly heeded him. These essays suggest in what manner the country may absorb Wendell Berry, a man whose life and work have been an affectionate defense of land not only worth defending but much in need of affection—affection for local, knowable, defensible places—apart from which "national defense" reduces to abstraction, and topsoil continues to roll toward the Gulf of Mexico, there to rest in the hypoxic zone.

Berry has rightly stated that "Emerson's spiritual heroism can sometimes be questionable or tiresome, but [that] he can also write splendidly accurate, exacting sentences." A few of them occur in that same piece on Thoreau from 1862: "He chose to be rich by making his wants few, and supplying them himself"; "I have repeatedly known young men of sensibility converted in a moment to the belief that this was the man they were in search of, the man of men, who could tell them all they should do."[32]

Notes

1. Ralph Waldo Emerson, "Thoreau." This was originally published in *Atlantic Monthly* in August of 1862. Citations here are from Henry David Thoreau, *Walden and Civil Disobedience: A Norton Critical Edition,* ed. Owen Thomas (New York: Norton, 1966). See 269, 267.

2. Thoreau, *Walden,* 217, 15, 55.

3. Wendell Berry, *What Are People For?* (San Francisco: North Point, 1990), 201, 177, 159.

4. Thoreau, *Walden,* 9; Wendell Berry, *Home Economics* (San Francisco: North Point, 1987), 128.

5. Thoreau, *Walden,* 143; Berry, *What Are People For?,* 151.

6. Wendell Berry, *The Unsettling of America* (San Francisco: Sierra Club Books, 1977), 12.

7. Thoreau, *Walden,* 147; Wendell Berry, *Sex, Economy, Freedom and Community* (New York: Pantheon, 1992), 100; Berry, *What Are People For?,* 95.

8. Thoreau, *Walden,* 6; Berry, *What Are People For?,* 196.

9. Thoreau, *Walden,* 60–61; Berry, *What Are People For?,* 196.

10. Thoreau, *Civil Disobedience,* 224; Wendell Berry, *Given* (Washington, DC: Shoemaker and Hoard, 2005), 28; see also Wendell Berry, *The Long-Legged House* (1965; Washington, DC: Shoemaker and Hoard, 2004), 78–87.

11. Thoreau, *Civil Disobedience,* 242; Berry, *Sex, Economy, Freedom and Community,* 124.

12. Thoreau, *Civil Disobedience,* 234.

13. Ibid., 234; Wendell Berry, *Citizenship Papers* (Washington, DC: Shoemaker and Hoard, 2003), 51.

14. Thoreau, *Walden,* 215; Berry, *Given,* 63; Thoreau, *Walden,* 5.

15. Wendell Berry, *Life Is a Miracle* (Washington, DC: Counterpoint, 2000), 133.

16. Berry, *What Are People For?,* 209; Ralph Waldo Emerson, *Nature* (1836) in Donald McQuade, ed., *Selected Writings of Emerson* (New York: Modern Library, 1981), 22. Preceding quotations in this paragraph come from Cotton, "A Christian Calling"; Franklin, *Poor Richard's Almanac;* Jefferson, Letter to James Madison, Oct. 28, 1785; Quinney, "Quinney's Speech"; Apess, "An Indian's Looking Glass for the White Man"; Melville, "Hawthorne and His Mosses"; Hawthorne, preface to *The House of the Seven Gables.*

17. Wendell Berry, *The Hidden Wound* (San Francisco: North Point, 1989), 123; Langston Hughes, "Harlem."

18. Berry, *The Long-Legged House,* 140; Wendell Berry, *A Continuous Harmony* (1970; Washington, DC: Shoemaker and Hoard, 2004), 55, 57.

19. Berry, *Sex, Economy, Freedom and Community,* 155; John Winthrop, "A Model of Christian Charity," 298; "All the parts of this body being thus united are made soe contiguous in a speciall relacion as they must needes partake of each others strength and infirmity, joy, and sorrowe, weale and woe" (299).

20. Steven Stoll, *Larding the Lean Earth* (New York: Hill and Wang, 2002), 5, 7.

21. Berry, *The Long-Legged House,* 30–42.

22. Herman Daly, "Sustainable Economic Development: Definitions, Principles, Policies," in *The Essential Agrarian Reader,* ed. Norman Wirzba (Lexington: University Press of Kentucky, 2003), 62–79, 66.

23. Wendell Berry, *The Way of Ignorance* (Washington, DC: Shoemaker and Hoard, 2005), x.

24. Berry, *Given,* 28; Berry, *Life Is a Miracle,* 18; Berry, *The Long-Legged House,* 47; Berry, *Home Economics,* 124.

25. Berry, *The Long-Legged House,* 123, 124.

26. Ibid., 177.

27. See Berry, *Way of Ignorance,* 47–48.

28. Berry, *The Long-Legged House,* 23; Berry, *The Unsettling of America,* 52.

29. Berry, *What Are People For?*, 135.

30. Berry, *The Unsettling of America,* 13.

31. Berry, *Sex, Economy, Freedom and Community,* 95.

32. Emerson, "Thoreau," 268, 272.

Ed McClanahan

Ain't They the Berries!

WENDELL AND TANYA BERRY have been my friends for over fifty years. Wendell and I got to know each other in graduate English classes at the University of Kentucky in Lexington in the fall of 1956; Tanya Amyx, his fiancée, was a senior English major. I had made a false start at graduate school at Stanford the previous year and had come home to Kentucky in the spring of '56, chastened for my hubris, and, in a last-ditch attempt to avoid the military draft, had enrolled in a couple of graduate-level summer-school classes at UK. To my draft board's amazement (not to mention my own), I aced them both, and was suddenly a bona fide candidate for an MA.

"I had gone west" (I would write many years later, in my book *Famous People I Have Known*) "the blandest perambulatory tapioca pudding ever poured into a charcoal-gray suit, and I came home six months later in Levi's and cycle boots and twenty-four-hour-a-day shades and an armpit of a goatee and a hairdo that wasn't so much a duck's-ass as it was, say, a sort of cocker spaniel's-ass. . . . I'd been Californicated to a fare-thee-well, and I'd loved every minute of it."

Such was the sorry-looking article that Wendell was confronted with in the first meeting of old Dr. Brady's grad-school class in bibliography in the fall of 1956. Wendell, on the other hand, was—oh, my—*formidably* straight. Treetop tall and as sober as an undertaker, he scared the pee-waddin' outta me at first; it was like the young Abe Lincoln had just walked in and caught me pretending to be the young Tony Curtis. And young Tony was three years *older* than young Abe!

Still, however warily, Wendell and I liked each other right away, and it wasn't long till I discovered the gleeful, goofy Wendellian grin that lurked behind all that exterior gravitas.

We've had some grand times together over a lot of years.

Like the 1958 Kentucky Derby party where, during a walk in the country after what could have been his fourth (my sixth) mint julep, the coltish young Wendell undertook a six-foot broad jump over an eight-foot creek and landed up to his argyles in backwater.

Or our glorious four-day canoe trip down the Kentucky River a few weeks later that same spring, and the night we spent along the way in the old fishing camp that, a few years later, would provide Wendell with the title of his landmark book of essays, *The Long-Legged House*. Or another four-day boat ride we took up the Ohio in 1961 on my father's towboat, the *City of Maysville*. (We put in a great deal of time in the wheelhouse, where the pilot, a burly, whiskey-voiced old scapegrace named Cap'n Bill, regaled us with highly improbable tales of his sexual prowess. "You know how much I get?" he'd growl, with a piratical squint. "All I can stand!")

Or the time in San Francisco when, after an uproarious martini-enhanced dinner at a big Fisherman's Wharf restaurant, we were crossing the Golden Gate Bridge and Wendell said to the guy in the tollbooth, as he forked over the toll, "Thank *you*, sir! This certainly is a mighty fine bridge!"

Back in 1956, when Wendell and I first met, I was under the spell of a thick, purple-covered paperback titled *Mysticism*, by Evelyn Underhill, which I carried everywhere and ostentatiously peered into with great frequency, in the hope that anyone who noticed my choice of reading material might also get a glimpse of the sensitive youth who peeked out from behind my thuggish imported-from-California outer brute. But try as I might to get my mind around the whole Dark Night of the Soul thing, I couldn't quite manage it—which is probably why I was always squinting like old Cap'n Bill when I actually attempted to read the book. My new friend Wendell, amused by the struggle I was having with all that endless goddamn purple claptrap, suggested that it should've been titled "Misty-cism."

Dr. Brady was an endearingly punctilious, excruciatingly boring old gent who was said never to have surrendered a single A in his bibliography class, abiding as he did by the principle that none of us is perfect, nor ever shall be, Amen, B+. His class was a real grind, one of those grad-school boot-camp courses designed to weed out the unworthy. We were remanded weekly to card-catalogue hell to solve the research problems he assigned us, such as, "How much was Byron paid for the initial publication of 'Beppo'?" (Answer: 2,600 quid, cash on the barrelhead.) And we were obliged to produce, in lieu of a term paper, an immense bibliography, typed to inflexible perfection, mapping some remote, arid, uninhabitable area of literary scholarship.

(I submitted a forty-five-page behemoth lyrically titled "The New Critics vs. Robert Browning: 1945–1950," chronicling five years of assaults carried out by my then literary heroes, those intrepid New Critics, upon the reputation of the Great Poet, who, being thoroughly deceased, was in no position to defend himself. Unhappily, I exceeded the one-inch-margins rule by a couple of letters here and there, and therefore garnered, for all my colossal labors, the inevitable B+.)

And finally we had to survive a ruthlessly exacting final exam, rife with bolt-from-the-blue surprise questions, among them one requiring us to list all the works in English literature of which concordances have been compiled. (For the uninitiated, a concordance is an alphabetical index of all the words—every single goddamn word!—in a given text or body of texts. In the days before computers, putting together one of these bibliolatrous enormities was virtually a life's work, so there weren't all that many of them.) Anyhow, on the final, everybody in the class came up with Shakespeare, of course, and then Chaucer, and then Milton, but after that it grew murkier. Donne? Dr. Johnson? Matthew Arnold? Trollope, with his forty-seven novels, fer crissake? Who knew?

Wendell did. He listed the King James Bible, by God. (That's an attribution, not an expletive.) The answer tickled Dr. Brady's hitherto undetected funny bone, and he gave Wendell what was reputed to be his (Dr. Brady's, not Wendell's) maiden A.

Years flew by. Wendell (lucky dog!) won a Stegner Fellowship in Creative Writing to Stanford in 1958, and went west—as did I, that same autumn, not to Stanford but to what I like to call Backwater State College in Backwater, Oregon, where I was to teach four gigantic sections of freshman composition. Over the next few years, while I languished in the wilds of Oregon, teaching prescriptive grammar to wave after wave of invading ignorant freshmen armies, Wendell landed himself a Guggenheim, took Tanya abroad for a luxurious year in the fleshpots of Europe, and then scored a cushy teaching gig at New York University and sublet Denise Levertov's apartment in the very heart of wicked Greenwich Village! If I was ever going to hate the rascal, that would've been the time to start.

But Wendell returned to Kentucky after only a couple of years in New York, first to work on the family farm in Henry County (and to continue writing, of course); he subsequently became for many years a valued member of the English department faculty at the University of Kentucky in Lexington, and published more or less as many books as Anthony Trollope, as everybody knows. Along the way, he bought an exhausted, overgrown little hillside farm in the Henry County community of Port Royal, on the banks of the Kentucky River, and resolutely set about restoring it to respectability and productivity.

Meanwhile, I snagged my own Stegner Fellowship in 1962 and then stayed on to teach at Stanford, clinging by my fingernails to a visiting lectureship until 1972. I filled in for Wendell at UK when he went on sabbatical in 1972/73, then took my visiting lecturer act to the University of Montana, in Missoula, where I hung on till 1976, when I found myself out of work, out of luck, and out of money. My second wife, Cia, and I, after a feckless cross-country adventure pursuing a book about, of all the elusive subjects we could've chosen, honkytonks, had decided that the pluperfect best spot we'd parked ourselves in, briefly, during our rambles was a little tumbledown abandoned tenant house on the farm of Jim Perry, Wendell's uncle, on the banks of the Kentucky River, just down the road from Wendell and Tanya's own house. So when all else had failed, we bounced, like a couple of bad pennies, right back to Port Royal and presented ourselves on their doorstep.

Omigod, it's the McSquatleys again!

During the five years my burgeoning second family and I lived next door to Wendell and Tanya in Uncle Jimmy's sweet little house, Wendell and I logged countless hours of working side by side—housing tobacco, bucking hay, fencing, killing hogs, forking manure, and even (the juxtaposition is intentional) teaching college English. Best of all, though, were the wintry days we worked with Wendell's team of Belgian draft horses, cutting firewood in the woods up Cane Run lane.

The winter of '77 was especially bitter and protracted; we had snow upon snow upon snow, weeks and weeks of relentless cold. First the ponds froze, then the creeks, then the Kentucky River, and before the siege had ended there were ice-skaters on the broad Ohio for the first time in almost sixty years.

Three or four afternoons a week, Wendell and I would take our chain saws and the Belgians and Wendell's little border collie, Zip, into the woods, where we'd fell the trees we wanted and limb them, and then use the horses to drag the logs into the clear to be worked up into firewood. Following those great gorgeous Belgians as, snorting and farting and straining at the traces, they tramped through the picture-perfect snowy woods, the little black-and-white dog nipping at their heels, their breath coming in puffs of white vapor as though they had steam engines inside them. . . . Well, it was better than taking an afternoon stroll through a Currier and Ives print—unless you persuade Messrs. Ives and Currier to put Wendell Berry in the picture with you.

Not even counting all I've learned from him about writing and literature, Wendell has been my mentor in a thousand ways. (I daresay I've taught him a thing or two as well, but we needn't go into that.) Almost daily, as we worked together, he showed me or told me all manner of stuff I desperately needed to know about trees and plants and farm animals, about the ways of weather and the seasons, about handling tools, about stringing fence and building rock wall—and along the way he generously clued me in on the history and the mores of the community he'd lived in all his life, into which I was striving to insinuate myself.

(Here's the very best story he ever told me: There once was an irascible old Henry County doctor whose patient was a lady not recently conversant with the amenities of soap and water. The doctor agreed to examine her, on the condition that she first step into the ladies' washroom and freshen herself up a bit. When she came back, the doctor asked, "Well, did you wash?" "Why yes, Doctor," she said, "I washed as far as possible." "Goddamn it," cried the doctor, "'possible' was what I wanted you to wash!")

Under Wendell's tutelage, I became that prized commodity in farming communities, a Pretty Good Hand. ("Y'know, Wendell," I told him one blistering August day while we were hanging tobacco in a ninety-eight-degree barn, "my dad always wanted me to learn to do this kind of work, but I don't think he meant for me to start when I was forty-five years old!") The knowledge he imparted sustained me and my family for years, and I'm eternally grateful for his enduring—some would say persevering—friendship.

As for Tanya, everybody knows what a beautiful, gracious, warm, caring person she is, so here's a flashback that reveals a side of her that her countless more circumspect admirers will never mention:

Once, during our long-ago days at the university in Lexington, Tanya and I and a grad-school pal of mine named Charlie Mahan (now long since gathered unto his fathers) were having lunch together at the Paddock, a student hangout just off the UK campus. Tanya had to eat and run in order to make it to her one-o'clock class. As she was hurrying off, Charlie turned to me and murmured, almost wistfully, "Damn, she's sexy!"

Acknowledgment

"Ain't They the Berries!" is adapted from an essay that originally appeared in *My VITA, If You Will: The Uncollected Ed McClanahan* (Washington, DC: Counterpoint, 1998).

Bill Kauffman

Wendell Berry on War and Peace; Or, Port William versus the Empire

> I think the first thing that made me dislike imperialism was the statement that the sun never sets on the British Empire. What good is a country with no sunset?
> —G. K. Chesterton

THE FIRST CASUALTY OF war is not truth—that expires during diplomacy—but the country.

Wendell Berry, the exemplary countryman, a man of place in a world run by the placeless, has chronicled the ways in which war and the preparation therefor drain the countryside and feed the hypermobility that is the great undiagnosed sickness of our age.

War devastates the home front as surely as it does the killing fields. Soldiers are conscripted, sent hither and yon to kill and maim or to be killed or maimed; their families relocate, following the jobs created by artificial wartime booms. War is the great scatterer, the merciless disperser. How you gonna keep 'em down on the farm when Mom and Pop and Sis have found Elysium in Detroit?

Nothing of nobility, perhaps even nothing of necessity, dignifies foreign wars in Berry's world. When, in *A Place on Earth,* Ernest Finley returns a cripple from the Great War in 1919, he finds his parents dead, their home sold. He is staggered by "the implausibility of the fact that something so vast as a war had picked out and defeated so small a thing as one man, himself."[1] The sun also rises, but this doughboy does not.

The First World War, that maiden voyage of the U.S. military across the oceans to "make the world safe for democracy," in President Wilson's ringing phrase, is but an adumbration of the Second in Berry's fiction: "It was 1916 and a new kind of world was in the making on the battlefields of France, but you could not have told it, standing on Cotman Ridge with that dazzling cloud lying over Goforth in the valley, and the woods and the ridgetops looking as clear and clean as Resurrection Morning," we read in the story "Watch with Me."[2] A clan of eccentrics is Port William's first war casualty:

> There had been a time when a Proudfoot almost never worked alone. The Proudfoots were a big family of big people whose farms were scattered about in the Katy's Branch valley and on Cotman Ridge. They liked to work together and to be together. Often, even when a Proudfoot was at work on a job he could not be helped with, another Proudfoot would be sitting nearby to watch and talk. The First World War killed some of them and scattered others.[3]

The childless Tol Proudfoot, last of his era, dies, appositely, in 1941. His world soon follows.

In Berry's fiction, the Second World War is the great climacteric. By 1942, says Hannah Coulter,

> A great sorrow and a great fear had come into all the world, and the world was changing. I grew up, it seems to me, in the small old local world of places like Shagbark and Hargrave and Port William in their daily work and dreaming of themselves. . . . But then, against the fires and smokes of the war, the new war of the whole world, that old world looked small and lost. We were in the new world made by the new war.[4]

Hannah marries her first husband, Virgil Feltner, "as war spread across the world."[5] *A Place on Earth* (I quote from the 1983 revised edition) opens in that bleak first winter of the war, as fathers and uncles, including Mat Feltner, Virgil's father, play cards in Frank Lathrop's empty store, minified by "their sense of helplessness before an immeasurable fact."[6] For what is there to do at home during war but wait and work, tormented by absence?

According to Croesus, "In peace the sons bury their fathers, but in war the fathers bury their sons." Mat is deprived of even the meager solace of such an interment. Virgil is reported missing in action at the Battle of the Bulge; he is never to return. As his wife explains in *Hannah Coulter*, Virgil would "disappear, just disappear, into a storm of hate and flying metal and fire. . . . Virgil was missing, and nobody ever found him or learned what happened to him."[7]

Tom Coulter, whose grim job it is to bulldoze the anonymous dead into mass graves, precedes Virgil in death. As Hannah says, "One day we knew that Tom Coulter was dead somewhere in Italy. Nothing changed. There was no funeral, no place to send flowers or gather with the neighbors to offer your useless comfort."[8]

Tom's brother Nathan, who will marry Hannah after the war, fights in but rarely speaks of the Battle of Okinawa, in which, his wife surmises, the soldier "lived inescapably hour after hour, day after day, killing as you were bidden to do, suffering as you were bidden to do, dying as you were bidden to do."[9] It is no life for a man, as the author makes clear in "Manifesto: The Mad Farmer Liberation Front," wherein he counsels, "As soon as the generals and the politicos / can predict the motions of your mind, / lose it."[10]

War, kens Hannah, "is the outer darkness beyond the reach of love, where people who do not know one another kill one another and there is weeping and gnashing of teeth, where nothing is allowed to be real enough to be spared."[11] The reach of love, a frequent Berryan trope, might extend to eastern Kentucky on a good day but never, ever, to Europe. Or even Washington.

The deaths overseas are not explicable; they are as senseless as the drowning of little Annie Crop in *A Place on Earth*. Nathan Coulter pithily describes the Battle of Okinawa as "ignorant boys, killing each other."[12] (This is not to say that Port William boils with antiwar anger. Old Jack Beechum carries around a newspaper picture of FDR, exhorting the president: "Go to it. By God, we're for you, sir."[13] These are yellow-dog Democrats, even as their community is riven by a Democratic president's war.)

According to Hannah Coulter, "I think this is what Nathan learned from his time in the army and the war. He saw a lot of places, and he came home. I think he gave up the idea that there is a better place somewhere else. There is no 'better place' than this, not in *this* world."[14]

It was a conviction never again shared by U.S. policymakers.

The instruments of American displacement have been various, but Berry quite rightly—and courageously—locates many of them in what has come to be known, at least among those who did not fight in it, as the "Good War."

Conscription is the least of these deracinating forces: after all, the draftee, if he is lucky enough to survive, may come home. But to what does he return? To a land denuded by the great exodus of rural southerners, black and white, to the industrial cities. More than 15 million Americans, or 12 percent of the civilian population, resided in a different county in March 1945 from the one they resided in on December 7, 1941—and this doesn't even count the more than 12 million who were wearing Uncle Sam's khaki.

The border states were especially hard-hit: as an anti-hillbilly joke of the 1940s went, America lost three states during the war: "Kentucky and Tennessee had gone to Indiana, and Indiana had gone to hell."[15]

The diaspora of rural southern blacks was no less tragic. Uprooted and urbanized blacks found otiose those skills that had been necessary to country life. Some were consumed by the vast industrial armies that, for a time, promised steady and remunerative employment; others fell into welfare. The verdant countryside of black farmers that might have been was eclipsed by urban moonscapes of sullen slum-dwellers. (In my home county of Genesee in New York, the Good War swept able-bodied farming men into the army or the factory, creating an absence in the fields that was filled by migrant workers: people from away, people who had no stake in the land, in the region.)

In Berry's fiction, the Second World War is a watershed in so many ways: it rends, it depopulates, it mechanizes, it destroys. So do its offshoots.

Hannah Coulter refers to "The interstate highway that transformed everything within its reach."[16] The people-scattering National Interstate and *Defense* (my italics) Highway System was conceived during World War II by top-down planner extraordinaire Rexford G. Tugwell and made concrete by an itinerant general named Dwight D. Eisenhower, who had admired Hitler's autobahn and got one of his own.

Tugwell, chief ideologist of the New Deal, had defined the American farm as "an area of vicious, ill-tempered soil with a not very good house, inadequate barns, makeshift machinery, happenstance stock, tired, overworked men and women—and all the pests and bucolic plagues that nature has evolved . . . a place where ugly, brooding monotony, that haunts by day and night, unseats the mind."[17] To Tugwell and the highwaymen, the interstate over which the benighted peasantry might relocate to a Cincinnati suburb was no mere ribbon of road: it was a lifeline.

Since those who write books and make movies and TV shows are distinguished as a class by their mobility, we seldom get an honest reckoning of the cost of modern nomadism. If anything it is celebrated as the flowering of the human spirit.

Nor do we often assess the domestic effects of militarism, or should I say militarism's effect on domesticity? The cost of war might be measured not only in body bags, in returning boys without legs, arms, eyes, faces, but also in divorce, dislocation, novels never written, children not fathered. During World War II, the divorce rate more than doubled, normal patterns of courtship were disrupted, daylight saving time was imposed nationwide over the objections of rural America, and the subsidized day-care industry was born via the Lanham Act, which sponsored three-thousand day-care centers to incarcerate the neglected children of Rosie the Riveter. (To be fair, the war did prove a boon to the moving and storage industry.)[18]

The Second World War, says Hannah Coulter, changed the ideal "descent of parcels," which is "for every farm to be inherited by a child who grew up on it, and who then would live on it and farm it and care well for it in preparation for the next inheritor."[19] Hannah's three children would leave home, forfeit their membership; we are told this in some of the most heartbreaking prose Berry has written.

This was by no means a generational fracture limited to the rural South; John P. Marquand, in his novel of the World War II home front, *So Little Time* (1943), calculated a similar domestic cost in the Northeast: "There was no use thinking any longer that someone who belonged to you might live in your house after you were through with it."[20]

Burley Coulter, in the story "The Wild Birds," expresses it this way: "I thought things would go on here always the way they had been. The old ones would die when their time came, and the young ones would learn and come on. . . . And then, about the end of the last war, I reckon, I seen it go wayward. Probably it had been wayward all along. But it got more wayward then, and I seen it then. They began to go and not come back . . . the young ones dead in wars or killed in damned automobiles, or gone off to college and made too smart ever to come back."[21]

To be fair, Burley, the place to which they did not return was not the place they had left. "The days before the war were 'the old days,' sure enough," admits Hannah Coulter. "The war changed the world. The days when Nathan and I were little, before we had electricity and plumbing and tractors and blacktopped roads and nuclear bombs"[22]—all the conveniences of the modern world—were perhaps beyond reclamation.

"There was no TV then,"[23] she recalls, which is to say that vital regional cultures might exist. But then almost every healthy manifestation of local culture was smothered—terminated—strangled—by U.S. entry into the Second World War. The Iowa poetry renaissance. The efflorescence of upstate New York fiction. The regional theater movement. Hell, even North Dakota cornhusking contests. (Don't believe me? See Gordon L. Iseminger, "North Dakota's Cornhusking Contests, 1939–1941," *Agricultural History,* winter 1997.)

War nationalizes culture; it exerts a centripetal force that shreds what it does not suck in. A cold war would follow, logically, the abandonment of traditional American neutrality in the two world wars; its policy fruits, besides the aforementioned interstate, included the acceleration of school consolidation, a profoundly anticommunity movement conceived by progressives of the Big Is Beautiful stripe that was given wings by the militarism of those allegedly halcyon 1950s, when the chimera of well-drilled little Ivan Sputnik was used to regiment the comparatively anarchic American educational system. Schools were centralized, which eliminated local idiosyncrasy, local accents, removed parents from the daily life of the schools, and finally led, in this age of Bush II, to the virtual nationalization of the curriculum. Consolidation made war upon the school as a repository of shared memory, as a physical manifestation of community culture. No Coulter girl will ever again be graduated as valedictorian from Port William High School. For there was no place for Port William High in the "changed world."

Yet a homeplace remains central to any possibility of a good life. In "Making it Home," a story from *Fidelity,* Berry describes one of the lucky ones—a revenant: a soldier who has his place to which he can return.

After three years as an expendable cog in a military machine, Art Rowanberry, a member of Port William, returns—alive. Art travels homeward by bus as far as Jefferson—a town name pregnant with meaning. He hoofs it the rest of the way, as the fetters of the myrmidon fall off, for "whatever was military in his walk was an overlay, like the uniform."[24]

Over there, Art was unmoored, "trusting somebody else to know where he was," marching without aim or knowledge of his surroundings. Walking home, he is now separated from his place, his anchorage, by "only a few creeks that he knew by name" (83).

Art Rowanberry "had been a man long before he had been a soldier, and a farmer long before he had been a man" (84). The armed services had no use for farmers and little more for men. "From a man used to doing and thinking for himself, he became a man who did what he was told" (92). Appraising the "fine brick farmhouses" by the roadside, Art muses that the illusion of their permanence had been shattered by the army: "We wouldn't let one of them stand long in our way" (84). "Farms, houses, whole towns—things that people had made well and cared for a long time—you made nothing of." Coming home from killing, from "the unending, unrelenting great noise and tumult" of death and the slaughter of strangers, from "little deaths that belonged to people one by one" (86), Art is once more made whole by his gradual reabsorption into his Kentucky ground.

"Making it Home" is rich in the language of incompleteness: "We blew them apart and scattered the pieces so they couldn't be put back together again" (86–87). Art sees his war as "the great tearing apart," after which "nothing was whole" (88), and of course the same is true, in its way, of the home front the men left behind. War blows communities apart, scatters the pieces, and even Port William would not be put together again, not really.

Taking his leave of Uncle Sam, Art is the cussed independent, the "insubordinate American" in which Robert Frost placed his trust: "The government don't owe me, and I don't owe it. Except, I reckon, when I have something again that it wants, then I reckon I will owe it."

That due bill would come a generation later, when the government drafted the sons of Art Rowanberry's generation for a war that no one in power even bothered to declare.

Of Art, Berry writes, "It pleased him to think that the government owed him nothing, and that he needed nothing from it, and he was on his own. But the government seemed to think that it owed him praise. It wanted to speak of what he and the others had done as heroic and glorious. Now that the war was coming to an end, the government wanted to speak of their glorious victories."

Art Rowanberry, it appears, would never fall for any of the Greatest Generation hokum of a half century later. One doubts his acquaintance with the Collected Works of Tom Brokaw's ghostwriter. "They talk about victory as if they know all them dead boys was glad to die. The dead boys ain't never been asked how glad they was" (91), muses the veteran. Nor were the dead boys consulted beforehand. The Department of War (which would be euphemized to the Department of Defense in the infancy of the Cold War) requested their presence; they complied.

Having been separated from home, Art, like so many of his coevals, might well have been cut adrift forever, dying slowly of inanition brought on by residence in the WildeWood Lanes of suburbia or on the nineteenth hole of Myrtle Beach. For a melancholy moment he is struck listless with "aimlessness, as if, all his ties cut, he might go right on past his home river and on and on, anywhere at all in the world" (94). But he presses homeward, taking refuge and nourishment in an empty church, and in the bright morning "he was in his own country now, and he did not see anything around him that he did not know" (99).

He will come upon his father and brother and nephew plowing, and if a fatted calf is not repast at the reunion, nonetheless his father rejoices, prodigally, telling Art's nephew, "Honey, run yonder to the house. Tell your granny to set on another plate. For we have our own that was gone and has come again" (105).

Sounding like the old Populists, Art Rowanberry notices that "the government was made up of people who thought about fighting, not of those who did it" (91). The former, who except for that rara avis bred in Washington are a rootless bunch, send the rooted to die. But it was not until the next generation of young men marched off to war that the people who did the fighting would, in any appreciable numbers, stand up and say no.

Since the Spanish-American War, the South, despite its status as a conquered province, has been much the most hawkish region of the country. The Georgia populist senator Tom Watson might ask of the Spanish-American

War, "What do the people get out of this war? The fighting and the taxes."[25] But southerners fought for the Union in 1898 with all the dash and bellicosity with which their grandfathers had fought to sunder it in 1862.

They were, in the main, every bit as hawkish in the twentieth century's two world wars. Diplomatic historian Wayne S. Cole notes that "in no section of the nation did the America First Committee encounter such uninterrupted, vehement, and effective opposition as it met in the South."[26] The subsequent war might decimate their country, but southerners as a whole supported it with a fervor rivaled only in New York City.

The pattern of southern (and border-state) enthusiasm for war held during Vietnam, cooked up by the graduate-degree-stamped products of the northeastern ruling class but fought in disproportionate number by denizens of hollows and hamlets never dreamt of by McGeorge Bundy.

When Wendell Berry delivered "A Statement Against the War in Vietnam" on February 10, 1968, to the Kentucky Conference on the War and Draft, he adverted to the ambient martial mood: "I am a Kentuckian by birth, by predilection, and by choice. There are a good many people in this state whom I love deeply. And of all those perhaps only four believe that I should be speaking here today—and one of them is me."[27] Berry speaks only briefly to the particular case of Vietnam, finding it an Orwellian entanglement:

> We seek to preserve peace by fighting a war, or to advance freedom by subsidizing dictatorships, or to "win the hearts and minds of the people" by poisoning their crops and burning their villages and confining them in concentration camps; we seek to uphold the "truth" of our cause with lies, or to answer conscientious dissent with threats and slurs and intimidations (68).

He asks where in the Gospels, the Declaration of Independence, or the Constitution the leaders of our ostensibly Christian and democratic nation find authorization for such actions.

But Vietnam, while perhaps an especially unlovely canker on the body politic, is only a symptom of "a deadly illness of mankind" (66): that unholy mélange of selfishness, violence, placelessness, and greed against which Berry has tilted his lance these forty years.

In this speech, Berry reveals himself to be a pacifist, or very nearly so. "I have come to the realization that I can no longer imagine a war that I would believe to be either useful or necessary" (65), he says. Due in part to the technological enhancement of the weaponry of war, its unimaginably vast potential for slaughter, "I would be against any war" (69). (Except, one suspects, a war to repel an armed invasion of Kentucky.)

He recognizes war's collateral damage: the curtailed civil liberties, the despoiling of the land and its bounty, the hypertrophied bureaucracy, the erosion of national character that is inevitable as we "become a militarist society" with "a vested interest in war" (72). He denies "absolutely the notion that a man may best serve his country by serving in the army": the uniform that Art Rowanberry wore a generation earlier connotes, in 1968 and maybe 1945 as well, servility, not service.

But Berry's preponderant reason for opposing war—*any* war, not just Vietnam—is located in the innermost of those concentric rings of citizenship: his family.

> As a father, I must look at my son, and I must ask if there is anything I possess—any right, any piece of property, any comfort, any joy—that I would ask *him* to die to permit *me* to keep. I must ask if I believe that it would be meaningful—after his mother and I have loved each other and begotten him and loved him—for him to die in a lump with a number hanging around his neck. I must ask if his life would have come to meaning or nobility or any usefulness if he should sit—with his human hands and head and eyes—in the cockpit of a bomber, dealing out pain and grief and death to people unknown to him. And my answer to all these questions is one that I must attempt to live by: *No* (75).

Berry says much the same thing in his Cold-War-era poem "To a Siberian Woodsman":

> There is no government so worthy as your son who fishes with
> you in silence beside the forest pool.
> There is no national glory so comely as your daughter whose
> hands have learned a music and go their own way on the keys.
> There is no national glory so comely as my daughter who
> dances and sings and is the brightness of my house.
> There is no government so worthy as my son who laughs, as he
> comes up the path from the river in the evening, for joy.[28]

Berry descants on this theme in "Some Thoughts on Citizenship and Conscience in Honor of Don Pratt," an essay inspired by a University of Kentucky student who would spend two years in federal prison for refusing induction into the U.S. Army—or, in the invidious phrase of the day, dodging the draft. (Berry would elsewhere propose raising the draft age from eighteen to forty, a deadly serious piece of whimsy earlier suggested by William Jennings Bryan, among other antiwar populists.)

"My devotion thins as it widens," explains Berry. "I care more for my household than for the town of Port Royal, more for the town of Port Royal than for the County of Henry, more for the County of Henry than for the State of Kentucky, more for the State of Kentucky than for the United States of America. But I *do not* care more for the United States of America than for the world."[29]

This last sentence divides Berry from the antiwar isolationists, with whom he otherwise has much in common on matters of foreign policy. Like them, he abhors militarism and foreign wars; unlike them, he sees peaceable potential in cooperative international agreements.

Wendell Berry is no nationalist:

I sit in the shade of the trees of the land I was born in.
As they are native I am native, and I hold to this place as
      carefully as they hold to it.
I do not see the national flag flying from the staff of the
      sycamore,
or any decree of the government written on the leaves of the
      walnut,
nor has the elm bowed before monuments or sworn the oath of
      allegiance.
They have not declared to whom they stand in welcome.[30]

Berry shares the spirit of the great literary anarchists of the American tradition: Thoreau, Edward Abbey, William Saroyan, even Edmund Wilson. He sounds Concordian notes in his Pratt essay, lamenting that "the state is deified, and men are its worshippers, obeying as compulsively and blindly as ants."[31]

He desires neither alms nor arms from the state, averring that "the government cannot serve freedom except negatively—'by the alacrity,' in Thoreau's phrase, 'with which it [gets] out of the way.'"[32]

Still in the Thoreauvian vein, he asserts: "I wish to testify that in my best moments I am not aware of the existence of the government. Though I respect and feel myself dignified by the principles of the Declaration and the Constitution, I do not remember a day when the thought of the government made me happy, and I never think of it without the wish that it might become wiser and truer and smaller than it is."[33]

This is Wendell Berry the rural anarchist, the reactionary radical, the lover of his country and contemner of its government. As he adjures in "Manifesto: The Mad Farmer Liberation Front":

Denounce the government and embrace
the flag. Hope to live in that free
republic for which it stands.[34]

If he is usually assigned to the left pen of our hopelessly inadequate and painfully constrictive political corral, that is because by the 1960s conservatives had largely renounced peace and stewardship—once cornerstones of a broad movement capacious enough to include Senator Robert Taft and the authors of the southern agrarian manifesto *I'll Take My Stand*—and embraced finance capitalism, development *über alles,* and a promiscuously interventionist foreign policy.

"The great moral tasks of honesty and peace and neighborliness and brotherhood and the care of the earth have been left to be taken up on the streets by the 'alienated' youth of the 1960s and 1970s,"[35] writes Berry in *The Hidden Wound* (1970). If he aligned himself—provisionally, with many stated reservations—with the Left, it was because the Right objurgated peacemakers as unpatriotic. Yet Berry understood the New Left, or at least the spirit thereof, as an essentially "conservative" movement, as we were told at the time by sources ranging from Paul Goodman to SDS president Carl Oglesby to *Easy Rider.*

Wendell Berry in the 1960s marched under no banner, stood for nothing larger (or smaller) than what he stood on. His touchstone was not Karl Marx or Herbert Marcuse but Thomas Jefferson, the political figure most often quoted by Berry in essays and poems. Like Jefferson, the polymathic planter "with his aristocratic head set on a plebeian frame,"[36] in Vernon Parrington's phrase, he insisted that "the small landholders are the most precious part of a state."[37] Like Jefferson, who opined that "our General Government may be reduced to a very simple organization and a very inexpensive one, a few plain duties to be performed by a few servants,"[38] Berry scorned the massive state. And like Jefferson, he is an anachronism in postrepublic America. Among the tragedies of contemporary politics is that Wendell Berry, as a man of place, has no place in a national political discussion that is framed by Gannett and Clear Channel.

Apropos Don Pratt, Berry wonders whether he ought to feel "great shame in going free while good men are in jail because of their goodness."[39] Thoreau, after all, did his time, hard as it wasn't. But Henry David was a bachelor, dependentless as he was independent, while Berry is a husband, a father, a farmer, and these blessings entail obligations that a political prisoner cannot fulfill. Again, Berry's boy trumps politics, the state, the outer—the more distant—world.

These remote and impersonal institutions are undeserving of loyalty anyway. It is simply not possible to pledge allegiance in any meaningful way to an entity as large and abstract as the nation-state.

"My country 'tis of the drying pools along Camp Branch I sing,"[40] Berry hymns in the poem "Independence Day." His country is that which is within the range of his love, his understanding: not a bloodless (if bloodthirsty) abstraction at the other end of a TV tube but rather the dirt of his backyard.

In the acronymical argot of our day this praiseworthy sentiment, this love and active cherishing of home, is derided as selfishness, as NIMBY—not in my backyard—by those who have no backyards.

Yet it is only in defense of one's backyard that a "cause" achieves justness. Without "land under us / to steady us when we stood,"[41] a political movement, even one so putatively well-intentioned as the anti–Vietnam War coalition, is doomed to a formless rage that is as ugly, in its way, as the McNamara-Rumsfeld cold calculus of death. As Berry writes in "A Standing Ground," "uprooted, I have been furious without an aim."[42]

Behold the anger of the deracinated, who know what they hate but not what they love, whose motivation *is* hatred, never love. Berry warns that the peace movement must not "become merely negative, an instrument of protest rather than hope." He cautions, prophetically as it turns out, against "self-righteousness and disillusionment and anger."[43]

The life of the professional protester, the chronic placard-carrier and slogan-shouter, is desiccated and desolate. "The political activist *sacrifices* himself to politics," Berry writes in "Some Thoughts on Citizenship and Conscience in Honor of Don Pratt"; "though he has a cause, he has no life. . . . Unsubstantiated in his own living, his motives grow hollow, puffed out with the blatant air of oratory."[44]

The itinerant activist of the '60s was every bit as placeless as Richard M. Nixon. Credit-card-carrying members of the "nation of transients"[45] could not credibly protest the war because they rested their case upon the defense of . . . nothing. To combat nomadism, one must make a home; to combat violence, one must embrace peace, and that peace is more, much more, than the mere absence of war.

Berry was never one of those inveterate petition-signers and microphone-hoggers, the frenetic engaged intellectual ever attaching himself to Worthy Causes That No Person of Intelligence and Goodwill Can Gainsay.

> I am not bound for any public place,
> but for ground of my own.[46]

Like charity, dissent begins at home—*with* a home.

Homeways lies renewal. Berry ends his essay on Don Pratt and war by proposing, not a change in administrations, not a get-out-the-vote drive or a march on Washington, but rather the reclamation of rural places, a restoration of the class of "independent small landowners," à la Jefferson. Such a move would, he envisages, "restore neglected and impoverished lands, and at the same time reduce the crowdedness of the cities. They would not live in abject dependence on institutions and corporations, hence could function as a corrective to the subservient and dependent mentality developing among government people and in the mass life of the cities."[47]

Though the etiology of the maladies be remote, the cure is at hand. As Berry poetizes in "February 2, 1968":

> In the dark of the moon, in flying snow, in the dead of winter,
> war spreading, families dying, the world in danger,
> I walk the rocky hillside, sowing clover.[48]

It sure beats napalm.

There was about Vietnam a whiff of missionary liberalism, at least at first, as John Kennedy's best and brightest sought to reproduce the Great Society in Southeast Asia, in Hubert Humphrey's hubristic threat. The idealistic among the war hawks were consumed by the "gleeful imperialism of self-righteousness,"[49] to use a Berry term, not unlike those church missions that always travel to remote and allegedly benighted climes, so much more exotic than the shantytown down the road. The Lord seems to call an awful lot of Christian missionaries to Kazakhstan and Bolivia but precious few to the trailer park on the edge of town.

A kindred Marine-borne uplift virus is detectable in President George W. Bush's campaign to "rid the world of evil," starting in Mesopotamia. For reasons both quintessentially American and unmistakably his own, Berry is out of sympathy with Bush's neo-Wilsonian plan to rescue the world for democratic global capitalism—whether the world wants rescue or not.

In "A Citizen's Response to 'The National Security Strategy of the United States of America,'" Berry finds in the Bush strategy, with its assertion of the right to preemptive attacks, "a radical revision of the political character of our nation." The executive is now the supereminent branch of a national state that grows more secretive and expensive, for the "war on terrorism" is "endlessly costly and endlessly supportive of a thriving bureaucracy."[50]

In his essay "The Failure of War" Berry wonders "to what extent the *cost* even of a successful war of national defense—in life, money, material goods, health, and (inevitably) freedom—may amount to a national defeat." Randolph Bourne's aphorism has become an unassailable truism: War is the health of the state. As Berry writes, "Militarization in defense of freedom reduces the freedom of the defenders. There is a fundamental inconsistency between war and freedom."[51]

Once more, Berry, as a patriot of his place, assays the domestic consequences of a foreign conflict. How will this war change life as it is lived in one's home place? (Not "homeland," an un-American locution foreign to our vernacular and which, prior to the ascendancy of George W. Bush's speechwriters, was redolent of Nazi Germany and Soviet Russia.)

Because—unlike the makers of policy and manufacturers of punditry—Berry has a home, he is trenchant and refreshing on the "homeland security" con:

> Increasingly, Americans—including, notoriously, their politicians—are not *from* anywhere. And so they have in this "homeland," which their government now seeks to make secure on their behalf, no home *place* that they are strongly moved to know or love or use well or protect.[52]

The root cause of the new U.S. imperialism is the lack of roots.

Wendell Berry is no world-saver. He admonishes "you easy lovers and forgivers of mankind," those lovers of disembodied Men but despisers of particular specimens of the race,

> My love must be discriminate
> or fail to bear its weight.[53]

Loving all equally, the humanitarian universalist loves none especially. He will raze a village in order to save it, jail the opposition in order to preserve freedom, and order boys from Port William into combat and death to prove with what value he endows all human life.

The architects and archons of Empire, of the subordination of Port William to the needs of what Clinton's secretary of state Madeleine Albright so memorably called "the indispensable nation," fit Berry's description of the "'upwardly mobile' transients" who wage war upon our places: "They must have no local allegiances; they must not have a local point of view. In order to be able to desecrate, endanger, or destroy a *place,* after all, one must be able to leave it and to forget it. One must never think of any place as one's home; one must never think of any place as anyone else's home. One must believe that no place is as valuable as what it might be changed into or as what might be taken out of it. Unlike a life at home, which makes ever more particular and precious the places and creatures of this world, the careerist's life generalizes the world, reducing its abundant and comely diversity to 'raw material.'"[54]

The arsenal of epithets that the publicists of the War Party use against their opponents is revealing: provincial, parochial, isolationist. For the most honest and compelling antiwar impulse comes from the love of the particular. In cherishing Port William—or Port Royal—one disdains to bomb Baghdad.

If Wendell Berry is not quite pacifist enough to suit the precisian—one has little doubt that he would use force to deter the mad rapist-killer of so many philosophical challenges hurled at the pacific—he will not countenance acts of war by the nation-state. He asks in "The Failure of War": "How many deaths of other people's children by bombing or starvation are we willing to accept in order that we may be free, affluent, and (supposedly) at peace? To that question I answer pretty quickly: *None.* And I know that I am not the only one who would give that answer: Please. No children. Don't kill any children for *my* benefit."[55]

Once more we espy the Siberian woodsman. The "enemy"—who has never done or even contemplated doing the least bit of harm to Port William—has a face. His children live in Novosibirsk, Baghdad, Hiroshima, Hanoi, Teheran, Atlanta. "Thou shalt not kill" means us, too.

So where do we go from here?

Home, perhaps? Once there was a way to get back home. Art Rowanberry found it. We can, too. For as Hannah Coulter says, "We all know what that beautiful shore is. It is Port William with all its loved ones come home alive."[56]

Notes

Epigraph as quoted in Jay P. Corrin, *G. K. Chesterton and Hilaire Belloc: The Battle Against Modernity* (Athens: Ohio University Press, 1978), 9.

1. Wendell Berry, *A Place on Earth,* rev. ed. (San Francisco: North Point, 1983), 32.

2. Wendell Berry, *Watch With Me* (New York: Pantheon, 1994), 134.

3. "The Solemn Boy," in *Watch With Me,* 95.

4. Wendell Berry, *Hannah Coulter* (Washington, DC: Shoemaker and Hoard, 2004), 41–42.

5. Wendell Berry, "Fidelity," in *That Distant Land* (Washington, DC: Shoemaker and Hoard, 2004), 402.

6. *A Place on Earth,* 10.

7. *Hannah Coulter,* 31, 58.

8. Ibid., 46.

9. Ibid., 169.

10. Wendell Berry, "Manifesto: The Mad Farmer Liberation Front," in *Collected Poems, 1957–1982* (San Francisco: North Point, 1985), 152.

11. *Hannah Coulter,* 168.

12. Ibid., 5.

13. *A Place on Earth,* 50.

14. *Hannah Coulter,* 83.

15. John W. Jeffries, *Wartime America: The World War II Home Front* (Chicago: Ivan R. Dee, 1996), 83.

16. *Hannah Coulter,* 175.

17. Edward S. Shapiro, "Decentralist Intellectuals and the New Deal," *Journal of American History* 58 (March 1972): 949.

18. For more on the deracinating effects of the U.S. military, see Bill Kauffman, "Doesn't Anybody Stay in One Country Anymore?" in *With Good Intentions? Reflections on the Myth of Progress in America* (Westport, CT: Praeger, 1998), 103–16.

19. *Hannah Coulter,* 135.

20. John P. Marquand, *So Little Time* (Boston: Little, Brown, 1943), 93.

21. Wendell Berry, "The Wild Birds," in *The Wild Birds* (San Francisco: North Point, 1986), 135.

22. *Hannah Coulter,* 113.

23. Ibid., 45.

24. Wendell Berry, "Making It Home," in *Fidelity* (New York: Pantheon, 1992), 84, hereafter cited in text.

25 C. Vann Woodward, *Tom Watson: Agrarian Rebel* (1938; New York: Oxford University Press, 1972), 335.

26. Wayne S. Cole, "America First and the South, 1940–1941," *Journal of Southern History* 22 (February 1956): 43.

27. Wendell Berry, "A Statement Against the War in Vietnam," in *The Long-Legged House* (1969; Washington, DC: Shoemaker and Hoard, 2004), 64, hereafter cited in text.

28. Wendell Berry, "To a Siberian Woodsman," in *Collected Poems,* 98.

29. Wendell Berry, "Some Thoughts on Citizenship and Conscience in Honor of Don Pratt," in *The Long-Legged House,* 77.

30. "To a Siberian Woodsman," *Collected Poems,* 97.

31. "Some Thoughts on Citizenship," 78.

32. Wendell Berry, "Discipline and Hope," in *A Continuous Harmony* (New York: Harcourt Brace Jovanovich, 1972), 129.

33. "Some Thoughts on Citizenship," 79.

34. "Manifesto: The Mad Farmer Liberation Front," 151.

35. Wendell Berry, *The Hidden Wound* (1970; New York: North Point, 1989), 18.

36. Vernon Parrington, *The Colonial Mind,* vol. 1 of *Main Currents in American Thought* (New York: Harcourt, Brace, 1930), 343.

37. Berry quotes this Jeffersonian maxim in "The Mad Farmer Manifesto: The First Amendment," in *Collected Poems,* 153.

38. Thomas Jefferson to Gideon Granger, August 13, 1800, in *The Political Writings of Thomas Jefferson,* ed. Edward Dumbauld (Indianapolis: Bobbs-Merrill, 1955), 97.

39. "Some Thoughts on Citizenship," 81.

40. Berry, "Independence Day," in *Collected Poems,* 116.

41. "The Mad Farmer Manifesto: The First Amendment," 154.

42. Berry, "A Standing Ground," in *Collected Poems,* 116.

43. "A Statement Against the War in Vietnam," 73.

44. "Some Thoughts on Citizenship," 83.

45. Ibid., 86.

46. "A Standing Ground," 116.

47. "Some Thoughts on Citizenship," 89.

48. Wendell Berry, "February 2, 1968," in *Collected Poems*, 108.

49. *The Hidden Wound*, 66.

50. Wendell Berry, "A Citizen's Response to 'The National Security Strategy of the United States of America,'" in *Citizenship Papers* (Washington, DC: Shoemaker and Hoard, 2003), 4.

51. Wendell Berry, "The Failure of War," in *Citizenship Papers*, 23.

52. "A Citizen's Response," 6.

53. "The Mad Farmer Manifesto: The First Amendment," 154.

54. Wendell Berry, "Higher Education and Home Defense," in *Home Economics* (San Francisco: North Point, 1987), 51.

55. Berry, "The Failure of War," 29. The pacifist poet William Stafford made the same point in his journal: "Save the world by torturing one innocent child? Which innocent child?" William Stafford, *Every War Has Two Losers*, ed. Kim Stafford (Minneapolis: Milkweed Editions, 2003), 39.

56. *Hannah Coulter*, 62.

Scott Russell Sanders

Words Addressed to
Our Condition Exactly

IN THE FALL OF 1971, seeing that I was floundering, a veteran teacher who'd floundered himself when he was twenty-five gave me a book by a writer he knew down in Kentucky. "You might find some guidance here," he said, handing me *The Long-Legged House.*

It was a paperback edition, small enough to fit in a coat pocket, printed on cheap paper, unassuming, not the sort of book one would expect to confirm or change the course of a life. The cover illustration showed a cabin perched on a steep riverbank, with a view across the stream toward green ridges fading away into the distance; a curving flight of stone steps led to the uphill side of the cabin, which rested on the ground, while the downhill side rested on poles, evoking the long legs of the title.

The author's name, Wendell Berry, was unknown to me, but his photograph on the back recalled men I'd known while growing up in rural Tennessee and Ohio. He wore a work shirt unbuttoned at the throat, with a T-shirt underneath and striped coveralls on top; beneath a billed cap, his face lay in shadow, the mouth slightly open and jaw set as if he were catching his breath in the midst of sawing or plowing. In the faint background of the photograph, instead of the usual desk littered with papers or shelves of books, there were blossoms, as of hollyhocks or fruit trees in flower. The biographical note identified him as a teacher and farmer, as well as the author of three collections of poetry, two novels, and the slender book of essays I held in my hand.

I was floundering that fall of 1971 because I had just returned to the United States after four years in England, where I had earned my doctorate at Cambridge, where I had helped organize protests against the war in Vietnam, and where I had begun to write stories. I knew my writing was clumsy and shallow, but that knowledge only made me determined to go deeper and write better. When my wife and I chose to decline the offer of a teaching position in England and sail home to America, our friends told us we were fools. Why give up a career in the motherland of English and return to a land bitterly divided over a war, smoldering with race riots, rife with political corruption and corporate greed? I was all the more a fool, our friends assured me, for choosing to settle in the godforsaken Midwest and for imagining I could find anything worth writing about in the hills of southern Indiana, where I had accepted a job.

Didn't I know that for generations the most talented writers born and reared in the Midwest had moved away as soon as they found their traveling legs? Mark Twain, Theodore Dreiser, Sinclair Lewis, T. S. Eliot, F. Scott Fitzgerald, Willa Cather, Hart Crane, Sherwood Anderson, Ernest Hemingway, Langston Hughes, Kenneth Rexroth, Wright Morris, Theodore Roethke, Wallace Stegner, Kurt Vonnegut Jr., and sundry others had left. What writers of note had stayed? Saul Bellow, I suggested. Sure, my friends conceded, but he lived in Chicago, a cosmopolitan city immune to the deadening effects of the provinces. Whereas I would be lost in the boondocks, my friends warned me, and if I did manage to write books, nobody would care to read them.

My wife and I shared our friends' dire view of what America had become during the Vietnam War, but that seemed all the more reason to return from exile and lend our hands to mending what was so grievously broken. I felt my own misgivings about settling in the Midwest. I had been reared on the back roads of Ohio, where I'd met little encouragement for the life of the mind. A scholarship carried me to an Ivy League college, where the Midwest, if mentioned at all, was spoken of as a vast expanse of corn and beans and hogs, a region topographically and intellectually flat. Another scholarship carried me from New England to graduate school in old England, where the Midwest hardly figured in anyone's imagination, except as another one of those forbidding hinterlands, like the frozen wastes of Siberia, the Australian outback, or the South African veldt.

For my wife, a biochemist, the move was less troubling. Given adequate laboratories, one could do good science anywhere. She had been reared in Indiana; her parents, grandparents, and most of her aunts, uncles, and cousins lived there still. As teenagers, she and I had met at a science camp in the very town where I was going to teach. We both felt at home among the forested hills and limestone creeks; we knew the birdsongs, the burly clouds, the teeth-rattling thunderstorms and sudden snows, the flash of fireflies and rasp of cicadas; we knew the habits of speech, the shapes of churches and barns; we knew the smells of thawing soil in the spring and hard frost in the fall; and those were all good reasons for moving there.

But moving to Indiana was a far milder step than deciding to settle there, to rear a family and make a life and ground my writing in this unfashionable place. I gained the courage to put down roots largely from reading books by writers who had chosen to settle in other seemingly out-of-the-way places. And for me, the most encouraging of these writers turned out to be the man whose publicity photo showed him wearing coveralls and a feed-store cap. Unlike Thoreau, Faulkner, Eudora Welty, Flannery O'Connor, William Carlos Williams, Gary Snyder, and other deeply rooted souls, Wendell Berry lived in my home region; the water that rolled off his hillside farm in northern Kentucky, like the rain that drummed on my roof in southern Indiana, flowed into the Ohio River. His home state came in for as much scorn from literary potentates as did Indiana, yet he had defied those opinions to gaze at the world from the banks of the Kentucky River and to publish, so far, six books about what he had seen. His example inspired me to imagine that I might become a writer and a useful citizen in the hills of southern Indiana as well as anywhere else. And that imagining began with my reading of *The Long-Legged House*.

I don't need to recollect the look and feel of *The Long-Legged House* in its paperback edition, for I am leafing through the book now, thirty-four years after it was given to me. From my several readings, passage after passage has been underlined, and the margins have been riddled with comments, all in ink, for the paper is too soft to record the marks of pencils. Tape holds together the cracked spine. The pages have turned yellow and brittle. I can't help sensing an affinity between this battered book and my own body, now on the verge of sixty. I can't help reading *The Long-Legged House* with a dual perspective— part of me my present age, author of some twenty books, firmly committed to my midwestern home ground; part of me still the young man wondering how and where and if to become a writer.

What struck me most vividly when I first read *The Long-Legged House* in 1971 were the confidence, clarity, high aspirations, and moral passion of the voice on the page. The aspirations had to do not with making a name or a fortune but with leading a meaningful life: "My aim is to imagine and live out a decent and preserving relationship to the earth."[1] The moral passion showed in the narrator's willingness to condemn behavior he saw as destructive—strip mining, aimless mobility, war—but even more so in his efforts to clarify and act on his own values: "If one disagrees with the nomadism and violence of our society, then one is under an obligation to take up some permanent dwelling place and cultivate the possibility of peace and harmlessness in it" (89). While admitting that a perfectly harmless and peaceful relation to place might be impossible, the narrator stood by his ideal: "It is a spiritual ambition, like goodness. The wild creatures belong to the place by nature, but as a man I can belong to it only by understanding and by virtue. It is an ambition I cannot hope to succeed in wholly, but I have come to believe that it is the most worthy of all" (151). I could have imagined such words coming out of Emerson, Thoreau, Whitman, or some other nineteenth-century American sage, but I was surprised and thrilled to hear them coming from one of my contemporaries.

Berry had written most of these essays when he was in his early thirties, only about half a dozen years older than I was on first reading them, and yet he spoke with the authority of an elder. Thus he could say about a strip mine in eastern Kentucky: "Standing and looking down on that mangled land, one feels aching in one's bones the sense that it will be in a place such as this—a place of titanic disorder and violence, which the rhetoric of political fantasy has obstructed from official eyesight—that the balance will finally be overcast and the world tilted irrevocably toward its death" (28). He could respond to the roar of motorboats on the Kentucky River by pronouncing judgment on our industrial way of life: "Man cannot be independent of nature. In one way or another he must live in relation to it, and there are only two alternatives: the way of the frontiersman, whose response to nature was to dominate it, to assert his presence in it by destroying it; or the way of Thoreau, who went to the natural places to become quiet in them, to learn from them, to be restored by them" (42).

Even back in my twenties, eager for a clear diagnosis of the world's ailments, I realized there were more than two ways of relating to nature; yet I relished such decisive proclamations. I welcomed a narrator who could bluntly denounce the Vietnam War: "We say that America is a Christian and a democratic country. But I find nothing in the Gospels or in the Declaration of Independence or in the Constitution to justify our support of puppet tyrants, or our slaughter of women and children, or our destruction of crops and villages and forests, or our herding of civilians into concentration camps in Vietnam. We do these things because we have forsaken our principles and abandoned ourselves to the inertia of power" (70). In an age of cynicism, here was an Ohio Valley neighbor who spoke with utmost seriousness about principles, virtues, and spiritual ambition. In an age of irony, here was a man who spoke with the solemn indignation of the Hebrew prophets.

Indeed, biblical cadences and allusions ran through the book: "The most exemplary nature is that of the topsoil. It is very Christ-like in its passivity and beneficence, and in the penetrating energy that issues out of its peaceableness" (204). Such prose rhythms and sentiments were utterly out of keeping with the most celebrated nonfiction of the day, which I read carefully in my search for literary models. Norman Mailer's *The Armies of the Night* (1968), Tom Wolfe's *The Electric Kool-Aid Acid Test* (1968), and Hunter S. Thompson's *Fear and Loathing in Las Vegas* (1971)—to choose three distinctive examples—featured brash, hip, slangy, irreverent narrators preoccupied with drugs and deals and politics. One could not imagine them brooding on the fate of the biosphere, let alone the fate of hillside farms, nor could one imagine them citing the Bible to illustrate their points or speaking forthrightly, as Wendell Berry did, of our need for reverence: "We must abandon arrogance and stand in awe. We must recover the sense of the majesty of creation, and the ability to be worshipful in its presence" (196). The narrators created by Mailer, Wolfe, and Thompson were urban and secular, not so much hostile to rural communities and religion as oblivious to them. Speaking in a swaggering first-person singular, each of these narrators seemed to strive for an idiosyncrasy of voice that would make him stand out in the crowded literary marketplace.

By contrast, the narrator of *The Long-Legged House* was formal, dignified, and reserved. He showed no inclination to display his personality, or to reveal more about his private life than was necessary to explain his principles. What little he had to say about cities was mostly a lament over the estrangement of urban people from nature. Instead, his points of reference and his sympathies lay in the countryside, among people who worked with their hands, among plants and animals both wild and domestic. His framing vision was ecological and moral, rather than political or technological: "I must attempt to care as much for the world as for my household. Those are the poles between which a competent morality would balance and mediate: the doorstep and the planet. The most meaningful dependence of my house is not on the U.S. government, but on the world, the earth" (79). He showed no interest in the culture broadcast on television, on radio, or in cinemas, but he cared deeply about the culture embodied in the skills and lore of farming communities.

When this narrator employed the first-person singular, he did so in a spare, measured, almost impersonal way: "I had been a native; now I was beginning to belong. There is no word—certainly not *native* or *citizen*—to suggest the state I mean, that of belonging willingly and gladly and with some fullness of knowledge to a place" (167). He also deflected attention from himself by using the indefinite pronoun: "Knowing this valley, once one has started to know it, is clearly no casual matter. . . . Its wonders are commonplace and shy. Knowing them is an endless labor and, if one can willingly expend the labor, an endless pleasure" (33). And often he used the first-person plural, as a way of speaking not just about himself but about all of us:

We have lived by the assumption that what was good for us would be good for the world. And this has been based on the even flimsier assumption that we could know with any certainty what was good even for us. We have fulfilled the danger of this by making our personal pride and greed the standard of our behavior toward the world—to the incalculable disadvantage of the world and every living thing in it. And now, perhaps very close to too late, our great error has become clear. It is not only our own creativity—our own capacity for life—that is stifled by our arrogant assumption; the creation itself is stifled (196).

On first reading such passages back in 1971, I admired the boldness and reach of this narrator, who was always gesturing beyond himself, toward our collective fate and our shared planet. I was smitten by his voice. The elegant balance of his periodic sentences, the gravity of his diction, the reticence about private matters, and the prophetic tone set him apart from his flashy contemporaries and linked him to such predecessors as Jefferson, Lincoln, and Thoreau. Amid so much writing that seemed petulant and perishable, Wendell Berry sounded like a grown-up, like someone whose words would last.

Although I still value the clarity, confidence, and fervor of this voice, what I perceive more clearly now, as I look back on *The Long-Legged House* from the neighborhood of sixty, is the narrator's uncertainty, his emotional and intellectual struggle, and his search for literary ancestors. I notice the young man's effort to persuade himself, along with the reader, that what he has chosen to do with his life is honorable and sensible. I hear him acknowledging his doubts, as when he confesses "the suspicion that pursued me for most of my life, no matter where I was, that there was perhaps another place I *should* be, or would be happier or better in" (199). I see how wary he is of appearing to be "something of an anachronism" (173), as when he concedes that the ideas he is advocating have been "allowed to grow old-fashioned, so that in talking about them now one is always on the verge of sounding merely wishful or nostalgic or absurd" (91). I sense the grief that weighs on him constantly: "The pristine America that the first white man saw is a lost continent, sunk like Atlantis in the sea. The thought of what was here once and is gone forever will not leave me as long as I live. It is as though I walk knee-deep in its absence" (190).

Having become a father—and recently a grandfather—I read the few references to Berry's own children with a piquancy I could not have felt in my childless twenties: "I am the father of two young children whose lives are hostages given to the future. Because of them and because of events in the world, life seems more fearful and difficult to me now than ever before. But it is also more inviting, and I am constantly aware of its nearness to joy" (198). And I see more clearly now the scars left by passages in Berry's own childhood, such as his having been sent away from home at the age of fourteen to attend a military boarding school: "The highest aim of the school was to produce a perfectly obedient, militarist, puritanical moron who could play football. That aim, of course, inspired a regime that was wonderfully vindictive against anything that threatened to be exceptional. And having a lively and independent mind, I became a natural enemy of the regime" (126).

Having made my break with the metaphysical claims, as opposed to the ethical instructions, of Christianity, I now see Berry himself wrestling with the shadow side of the religious tradition he invokes. While he acknowledges that his thinking and rhetoric have been shaped by the Bible, he also challenges much of what passes for "religious": "I am uneasy with the term, for such religion as has been openly practiced in this part of the world has promoted and fed upon a destructive schism between body and soul, heaven and earth. It has encouraged people to believe that the world is of no importance, and that their only obligation in it is to submit to certain churchly formulas in order to get to heaven" (199).

And having sought for more than three decades to make sense of things from a home base in southern Indiana, a place that many people consider a backwater, I now see the narrator of *The Long-Legged House* striving to justify his decision not merely to live and farm beside the Kentucky River but to reflect on America, indeed on the earth and the universe, from that vantage point: "Against a long-standing fashion of antipathy, I will venture to suggest that the best model we have of a community is still the small country town of our agricultural past" (63). Here and elsewhere, in words such as *venture* and *suggest,* behind the voice of authority I now hear a defensive note.

In one of the book's most eloquent passages, Berry describes the impact of watching, on a slough near his cabin, a pair of blue geese stopping over on their way south from Hudson's Bay:

> They made me realize that the geography of this patch of riverbank takes in much of the geography of the world. It is under the influence of the Arctic, where the winter birds go in summer, and of the tropics, where the summer birds go in winter. It is under the influence of forests and of croplands and of strip mines in the Appalachians and it feels the pull of the Gulf of Mexico. How many nights have the migrants loosened from their guide stars and descended here to rest or to stay for a season or to die and enter this earth? The geography of this place is airy and starry as well as earthy and watery. It has been arrived at from a thousand other

places, some as far away as the poles. I have come here from great distances myself, and am resigned to the knowledge that I cannot go without leaving it better or worse. Here as well as any place I can look out my window and see the world. There are lights that arrive here from deep in the universe. A man can be provincial only by being blind and deaf to his province" (164).

That is beautifully said; but no young writer who lived in New York, say, or Chicago, San Francisco, London, or Rome would have felt the need to say it.

Before settling on his hillside farm, Berry had tried out some of the certified literary places. He had studied for two years as a Stegner fellow at Stanford, lived for a year in Italy, and taught for two years at New York University. When he decided to give up his job at NYU and return to Kentucky, his friends and academic mentors greeted the decision with incredulity, reflecting

the belief, long honored among American intellectuals and artists and writers, that a place such as I came from could be returned to only at the price of intellectual death; cut off from the cultural springs of the metropolis, the American countryside is Circe and Mammon. Finally, there was the assumption that the life of the metropolis is *the* experience, the *modern* experience, and that the life of the rural towns, the farms, the wilderness places is not only irrelevant to our time, but archaic as well because unknown or unconsidered by the people who really matter— that is, the urban intellectuals (176).

During his time away from Kentucky, he admitted, "I had been enough influenced by the cultural fashion to have become compulsively suspicious both of my origins and of myself for being unwilling to divide myself from them" (177). Only a writer who has made a home in the provinces—which means anywhere outside the great cities and beyond the ken of travel brochures— needs to defend himself against the charge of being provincial. Only such a writer would assert the relevance of his home place by appealing to the migratory patterns of birds and the wheeling of stars.

The narrator of *The Long-Legged House* knows that if he is to avoid "intellectual death" in the provinces he must face what is most shameful and paralyzing in the history of his province: "I am forever being crept up on and newly startled by the realization that my people established themselves here by killing or driving out the original possessors, by the awareness that people were once bought and sold here by my people, by the sense of the violence they have done to their own kind and to each other and to the earth, by the evidence of their persistent failure to serve either the place or their own community in it" (179). Indeed, this brutal history goes a long way toward explaining the "long-standing fashion of antipathy" that questions whether "the small country town of our agricultural past" can be a worthy model for community.

To make matters worse, the few predecessors who had written about any portion of Kentucky had either ignored or sentimentalized this legacy of slaughter, slavery, selfishness, and waste: "My problem as a writer, though I didn't clearly know it yet, was that I had inherited a region that had as a literary tradition only the corrupt and crippling local colorism of the 'Kentucky' writers. This was both a mythologizing chauvinism and a sort of literary imperialism, tirelessly exploiting the clichés of rural landscape, picking and singing and drinking and fighting lazy hillbillies, and Bluegrass Colonels. That is a blinding and tongue-tying inheritance for a young writer" (140).

About his own portion of Kentucky, no one had written at all, a blankness that posed challenges of its own:

> And this place I am related to not only shared the state's noxious literary inheritance, but had, itself, never had a writer of any kind. It was, from a writer's point of view, undiscovered country. I have found this to be both an opportunity and a disadvantage. The opportunity is obvious. The disadvantage is that of solitude. Everything is to be done. No beginnings are ready-made. One has no proof that the place can be written about, no confidence that it can produce such a poet as one suspects one might be, and there is a hesitance about local names and places and histories because they are so naked of associations and assigned values—none of which difficulties would bother a poet beginning in Concord, say, or the Lake District (142).

Bereft of local models, he drew encouragement from American writers who proved that an unheralded place could be written about, as William Carlos Williams did in Paterson: "I saw how his poems had grown out of his life in his native city in New Jersey, and his books set me free in my own life and my own place as no other books could have. . . . Reading them, I felt I had a predecessor, if not in Kentucky then in New Jersey, who confirmed and contemporized for me the experience of Thoreau in Concord" (143).

More clearly now than on my first reading of *The Long-Legged House,* I see that Thoreau is the pervasive influence behind the book, not merely as someone who chose to make his native place the lens through which he viewed the world but as a prose stylist and contrarian thinker. Many of the sentences might have been written by Thoreau: "It was fishing that paid well, though not always in fish" (136). "Does the hope of peace lie in waiting for peace, or in being peaceable? If I see what is right, should I wait for the world to see it, or should I make myself right immediately, and thus be an example to the world?" (74). "It is certain, I think, that the best government is the one that governs least. But there is a much-neglected corollary: the best citizen is the one who least needs governing. The answer to big government is not private freedom, but private responsibility" (58). As Thoreau apologizes on the opening page of *Walden* for speaking in the first person, so Berry defends his own right to offer a personal vision: "I am writing with the assumption that this is only one of several possibilities, and that I am obligated to elaborate this particular one because it is the one that I know about and the one that is attractive to me" (90).

In tracing these resemblances, I don't mean to suggest that the writer from Kentucky merely imitated the writer from Massachusetts, but that Berry found in him an essential predecessor. Thoreau was the prime example for Berry, as Emerson was for Thoreau, of someone thinking and writing about fundamental questions in a place with no literary history. In subsequent books, Berry would have his quarrels with the philosopher of Walden Pond, and would go beyond him in significant ways, but in *The Long-Legged House* Thoreau is still his tutelary spirit, one who blesses a chancy endeavor.

Any writer could be proud of having written *The Long-Legged House* as a culminating book, let alone as a first collection. Knowing what Wendell Berry has accomplished in the four decades since writing those earliest essays, one might be tempted to imagine, as I did when I first read them, that his triumph was inevitable. But of course it was not; he might have failed, might have sunk into silence, as many aspiring artists have done, defeated by geography or lack of talent or loss of hope. Instead, he has gone on to write many more essays, poems, novels, and stories, gradually building up a comprehensive vision of what is wrong with our present way of life and what a finer, fairer, more reverent, and more enduring way of life might be. By way of some forty books, his hill farm, the nearby town of Port Royal, and the lower Kentucky River now find their place on the American literary map, along with Concord, Paterson, Mark Twain's Mississippi River and William Faulkner's Mississippi, Flannery O'Connor's Georgia, Willa Cather's Nebraska, and John Steinbeck's California.

Even as Berry's thought has grown more complex over the years and his style more assured, his work has shown remarkable consistency. Open any of his dozen or so books of essays, and you will recognize a distinctive voice pondering a distinctive set of concerns, and you might conclude that neither voice nor vision has changed much between the earliest published essays from the 1960s and those appearing in the first decade of the twenty-first century. And yet, a close reading of *The Long-Legged House* reveals that there is more searching, more testing, more trying out of ideas—in short, more *essay*ing—

in the early essays than in the later ones. There is a freshness here, a sense of discovery, as he glimpses possibilities that would later harden into certainties; and there is a disarming candor, as he questions the adequacy of his cultural inheritance and of his own powers for the great task he has set himself, that of challenging the industrial worldview and rethinking our whole way of life.

I still read everything Berry publishes, because I never tire of watching this fine mind grapple with the central questions of our time—as in the magisterial *Citizenship Papers* (2003), in which he confronts terrorism, biotechnology, the latest American wars, and the decay of democracy. But I'm stirred more deeply by the early essays, where the young man was still trying to find his way. His marriage was new; his two children were young; he had only recently convinced himself to settle down for good in his native place, and the possibility of making significant art there was still unproved, as was the relevance of his agrarian worldview. His ideal of achieving "a more indigenous life" (206) was still an aspiration and not yet an accomplishment. This first gathering of essays tells more poignantly than any of the later ones the story of his wandering and his settling down—what he calls "the myth of my search and my return" (213)—and this overarching myth is as crucial to Berry's self-understanding as the tale of escape from Egypt and wandering in the desert and return to the Promised Land was for the Israelites.

Wendell Berry's story, in turn, helped me begin to understand my own. *The Long-Legged House,* this gift from a wise older teacher, came into my hands precisely when I needed it. Distraught over what had become of my country during the Vietnam War, wary of settling in the Midwest, uneasy about my rural and religious upbringing, uncertain how to lead my life, I found in this book a clarifying intelligence. It confirmed my anguish and my hope, calling to mind the promise Thoreau offered in *Walden*: "There are probably words addressed to our condition exactly, which, if we could really hear and understand, would be more salutary than the morning or the spring to our lives, and possibly put a new aspect on the face of things for us. How many a man has dated a new era in his life from the reading of a book."[2] *Walden* has been such a book for many readers, as I suspect Thoreau devoutly hoped it would be. *The Long-Legged House* has been such a book for me.

Notes

1. Wendell Berry, *The Long-Legged House* (New York: Ballantine, 1971), 83, hereafter cited in text.

2. Henry David Thoreau, *Walden,* ed. J. Lyndon Shanley (Princeton: Princeton University Press, 1973), 107.

Donald Hall

The Best Noise in
the World

THE FIRST TIME I met Wendell Berry, it was 1963 at a literary cocktail party on Riverside Drive in Manhattan. He was young, skinny, wore a dark suit and a necktie—and never smiled. It was during his brief time teaching at an uptown campus of New York University, and I found him intimidating. With his sober stern face, I felt that he was judging us all, and we weren't coming off well. Maybe I was right, but it is more likely that he was wishing not to be wearing a dark suit with a necktie in a flat over the Hudson but wearing overalls and feeding a draft horse in Kentucky. A year later I read *The Broken Ground,* his first book of poems, and bought copies to mail to friends. I had found the writer, the poet. Later I found the man, thank goodness—the farmer who wrote books that I loved—novels, poems, stories, essays—and whose smile and laugh were incomparable. Jane Kenyon said that Wendell's laugh was the best noise in the world.

By the time I gave up teaching and moved back to the family farm in New Hampshire in 1975, Wendell and I were beginning to know each other, writing letters. Wendell taught at the University of Kentucky and commuted hours to Port Royal, to farm as much as he could. He had read a prose book I wrote, *String Too Short to Be Saved,* about my childhood summers haying with my grandfather in New Hampshire. When he heard I was leaving the academy to move back, he wrote me from Kentucky advising me "not to put in too many acres at once." I could answer Wendell quickly and firmly: "Don't worry about a thing." I would raise cats and one dog, not sheep, with maybe some beans and carrots and corn across the road. (The vegetable garden lapsed when a local farmer opened a produce stand and grew better tomatoes and parsnips than I did.) Once somebody in a book referred to Wendell and me as two farmer-poets. He was half right.

We were not farmers together, but we became fast friends. We are two people left in the world who love to write letters, and our correspondence is vast. Early on, we started to exchange manuscripts and help each other out with our poems. Wendell sent me his "Sabbaths," the Sunday poems that make up some of his best work. I also read his stories and novels in manuscript. The quality and quantity of his work dazzles me, essays and fiction and verse, as multiple and fruitful as D. H. Lawrence—as passionate too, and as candid. In letters, Wendell let me know that the university weighed on him. As I remember, he told me that at faculty meetings the professors kept agreeing with everything he proposed, and then voted down his recommendations. He stopped commuting to Lexington and concentrated instead on land and language.

My letters to Wendell were dictated, a practice that is relaxed and natural for me, and which I have practiced for forty years. Wendell's letters for the most part arrive in his clear firm hand, nothing ever scratched out. (In recent years, he has taken to dictation sometimes, and these letters sound a little more formal.) We also visit each other's places. Here, Wendell can muse over the pitchforks and scythes that Wesley Wells and I employed back in the 1940s. There, one time, I read my poems at the University of Kentucky, and Wendell drove me afterward to Lanes Landing Farm, the next day all the way to the Cincinnati airport—giving us much opportunity for extending ourselves in car talk.

Another thing we had in common was good, solid, loving, and companionate marriages. On one of our car trips, I complained over the useless, trivial hyperactivity of my eyes gazing at women. At any conference, or in an airport on the way, I find myself continually checking out the beauty of young women, dwelling on figures and faces. It disturbed me that I wasted time and energy evaluating quarries I would never mine. Wendell agreed explosively, as if he had been waiting for someone to bring up the subject. He suffered from this idle habit himself, and found himself in lecture halls doing inventories of the female audience. One day, he told me, he saw one face that was absolutely perfect and irresistible to him. It was a few seconds before he realized that his eyes had lighted on his wife, Tanya.

Jane and I visited the Berrys together, driving out from Louisville, staying at Lanes Landing Farm. I accompanied Wendell as he did his chores, which is exhausting companionship. Wendell tends to horses, cattle, and sheep not only with dexterity but faster than the speed of light.

Early on, there was a memorable occasion when Jane and I met Wendell elsewhere. Our friend Bert Hornback, who taught at the University of Michigan, arranged a reading for four friends of his: Galway Kinnell, Seamus Heaney, Wendell, and me. (It was a private poetry reading using Michigan buildings, on a January Saturday night just before the Super Bowl, and Bert sold out Michigan's largest amphitheater, which he had rented. People scalped tickets outside, at zero.) After the reading, we recovered in Bert's house, reciting Thomas Hardy to each other, as Jane and Bert listened. After a while Bert asked Jane to say a poem. She had not yet published her second volume, and Wendell has written that he had not yet read her because he liked her and didn't want to be disappointed. Jane said "Twilight: After Haying," and Wendell realized what he had been missing.

In December of 1993, a month before Jane was diagnosed with leukemia, Wendell and Tanya flew to the farm so that the four of us could visit here. Since Wendell hates to fly, Jane and I understood the tribute they paid us by flying from Kentucky to New Hampshire. As at Lanes Landing Farm, we talked late into the night, drinking not Jack Daniel's (even in Kentucky) but single-malt Scotch. We laughed loud enough to wake the dead cows in the barn. Many months later, when they were in New England for a lecture, Wendell and Tanya drove to see Jane at the Dartmouth-Hitchcock Hospital, but she was very sick. Since then, when we visit we entertain an absence.

"In his strongest work, he has told us as much about our life and our minds as any of his contemporaries and much more than most."—Robert Hass, "Wendell Berry: Finding the Land"

Photograph by Guy Mendes, courtesy of Ann Tower Gallery

Kimberly K. Smith

Wendell Berry's Political Vision

FOR MILLIONS OF Americans, the terrorist attacks of September 11, 2001, ushered in a new world—a world in which security, power, and control must necessarily take precedence over our other civic ideals. To me, however, the events of that day were not transformational. I had just finished my book on Wendell Berry when I heard about the attack on the Twin Towers, and I witnessed with the rest of the country the tragic results. But Berry's vision affected my interpretation of these events: they did not change the world, I thought, so much as force us to confront the world we were already living in. As Berry would later put it, the terrorist attacks destroyed the illusion that "we were living in a 'new world order' and a 'new economy' "[1] of unending prosperity. The lesson of September 11 was for Berry an ancient one, and one that permeates all his writings: the world is not and never will be a safe place. We must learn how to live a fully human life in a dangerous and unpredictable environment—not by seeking godlike control over the conditions of our existence but by cultivating those virtues (moderation, prudence, propriety, fidelity) that allow us to live gracefully in the presence of fear.

This is, I believe, a particularly relevant lesson for those of us interested in the state of American politics. Indeed, seeing the attack on the World Trade Center from Berry's point of view brought home to me how deeply he is concerned with man's *political* condition: not our ultimate, transcendent destiny but how we humans (who are neither beasts nor gods) make a home for ourselves in the mutable, transitory, secular world. Granted, that political concern isn't always apparent on the surface of his writings. Berry is notoriously disdainful of the major political parties and generally avoids too close an association with any organized political movement or policy agenda. In fact, it's tempting to interpret his writings as discouraging public engagement in favor of a solipsistic retreat into private domesticity.[2] For more than three decades Wendell Berry has been debating and critiquing the fundamental values of American society, and a careful reading of his essays confirms what his career of critical engagement suggests: Berry has never been apolitical. He has simply pursued a vision of citizenship deeply at odds with conventional American politics. His writings offer a consistent and coherent picture of what citizenship would consist of in his ideal republic—a picture made even more relevant by the events of September 11.

Wendell Berry's political values resemble in many respects Thomas Jefferson's. Both men envision their ideal America as an agrarian republic: a community of honest laborers pursuing a modest life of virtue, seeking peace, commerce, and honest friendship with other nations. Political power in this republic is decentralized, economic policies favor farmers and small-scale enterprises over large corporations, and freedom is guaranteed by a watchful and active citizenry. But Berry's vision is shaped also by the intellectual currents informing the twentieth-century environmental, sustainable-agriculture, and peace movements. He is, for example, a more thoroughgoing pacifist than was Jefferson (who famously declared that "the tree of liberty must be refreshed, from time to time, with the blood of patriots and tyrants"[3]). And Berry's agrarianism (unlike Jefferson's) is shaped by his concern for sustainability and environmental integrity. Jefferson hoped a republic of yeomen farmers could avoid the political corruption stemming from concentration of wealth. Berry hopes that a republic of *good* farmers (and other responsible citizens) will sustain the environmental conditions necessary for a fully human life.[4]

And that, for Berry, is the fundamental business of any political community: to preserve the land and culture on which it depends. "A viable community," he argues, "is made up of neighbors who cherish and protect what they have in common"; it "protects its own production capacities." Politics under this view is an act of stewardship: it is part of the work of making a home for ourselves in a world not entirely hospitable to human purposes. Patriotism, in turn, is "a knowing, intelligent, sustaining, and protective love"—not for "the nation" as an abstract concept but for the land as the physical foundation of our lives. To be patriotic is, first and foremost, to protect the land's beauty, health, and productivity. It is an act of fidelity to place.[5]

Industrial capitalism poses many threats to the land and to this fidelity, and most of Berry's writings about agriculture, economics, and nature aim at identifying those threats. Like Jefferson, however, he is also concerned about threats to liberty—particularly the threat posed by the concentration of power in the executive branch of federal government. Political freedom for Berry is essential to community and responsible stewardship, and the chief danger to political freedom lies in the power of the president and his modern ministers—the federal bureaucracy.

Berry's suspicion of bureaucracy has been a persistent theme in his writings since his earliest essays criticizing the effect of federal welfare programs on Appalachian communities. He worries in part that welfare fosters dependence, but his deeper concern is that bureaucrats do not properly *value* the people they are trying to help. Bureaucrats may be well-intentioned, he concedes, but they necessarily treat people impersonally, as members of a class rather than as individuals. "An agency or bureau or institution cannot exercise taste and judgment, cannot be motivated by love or compassion, cannot value a man for his industry or his art or his pride," he warns. "They are abstractions themselves and must deal with people as abstractions."[6] But "it is not just or merciful or decent to treat people as abstractions." Indeed, "if one is going to destroy a creature, the job is made easier if the creature is first reduced to an idea and a price. Reduction, that is, facilitates manipulation or use without affection, and use without affection is abuse." He applies his point more generally: the land, too, is at risk of abuse by those given to thinking abstractly and categorically. According to Berry, particular knowledge of a place is essential to proper land stewardship, but "the particular knowledge of particular places is beyond the competence of any centralized power or authority." Bureaucrats— most of whom come from outside the local community—live and think in a world of abstractions. Out of touch with local conditions and unfamiliar with the people they are supposed to be helping, they are not likely to treat citizens or the land with respect, fairness, and sensitivity.[7]

This complaint about the dehumanizing effect of bureaucracy sounds more like Max Weber and his progeny than like Thomas Jefferson, of course. But President Bush's response to the terrorist attacks highlighted for Berry another, more Jeffersonian, worry about the executive branch: the potential for tyranny inherent in the president's national security powers. The president's decisions concerning national security, according to Berry, are the least subject to the public's critical scrutiny, and therefore the greatest threat to citizens' freedom. He points, for example, to the president's September 2002 statement that the United States has a right to act unilaterally and preemptively against terrorists. To carry out such action, Berry reasons, the president must "plan in secret and execute his plan without forewarning." The policy therefore precludes public debate; it depends on "the acquiescence of a public kept fearful and ignorant, subject to manipulation by the executive power, and on the compliance of an intimidated and office-dependent legislature."[8] Thus there is no effective check on this executive power.

According to the original constitutional design, of course, the legislature is supposed to serve as a check on the president and his ministers; even preemptive attacks could in theory be subject to congressional deliberation. But

Berry has little faith that the legislative branch will effectively represent the country's true interests. The professional politicians who staff our legislatures, he argues, develop a narrow and specialized perspective that puts them out of touch with their constituents and impairs their ability to understand the broad context of public policy issues. Our representatives inhabit a kind of intellectual ghetto, "not necessarily made up of groups living in the same place," but composed of people having "the same assumptions, the same sort of knowledge, the same mentality, often much the same experience." These professional politicians are "insulated specifically against the claims of responsibility" and "answerable only to the requirements of their specialty" (that is, getting elected).[9] Popular elections are supposed to correct such narrow perspectives and hold our representatives accountable—but elections, according to Berry, have become little more than ad campaigns, composed of "catch phrases, slogans, clichés, euphemisms, flatteries, falsehoods, and various forms of cheap wit."[10] It's hard to see how a legislature so constituted could provide meaningful representation, much less an effective safeguard against executive tyranny.

In short, Berry identifies the chief dangers to our liberty as a strong executive and an excessive bureaucracy, neither of which is checked by our unresponsive, unaccountable legislature. Happily, however, he has a Jeffersonian solution to these Jeffersonian problems: a robust concept of citizenship. Citizens, for Berry, are the most important check on government power: "An inescapable requirement of true patriotism, love for one's land, is a vigilant distrust of any determinative power, elected or unelected, that may preside over it."[11] Jefferson undoubtedly would agree—but Berry's concept of citizenship is again somewhat different from Jefferson's. Indeed, Berry's list of civic virtues is quite distinctive and perhaps the richest dimension of his political vision.

To begin with, citizenship requires patriotism—but patriotism in Berry's distinctive sense of the word: fidelity to the land. Such fidelity gives citizens the motive to serve their community and resist destructive exercises of government power; it gives them a "home *place*" that they are strongly moved to know and love and use well and protect.[12] But love for the land is not sufficient to guide civic engagement; Berry also demands a high degree of rationality from his citizens. Rationality in fact holds equal weight with patriotism in his concept of citizenship—but not rationality as conventionally understood.

For Berry, rationality does not imply the narrow sort of economic or scientific reasoning common in policy analysis. Indeed, he is a vocal critic of the ascendancy of economic (cost–benefit) analysis in political decision-making. "The cost–benefit ratio is limited to what is handily quantifiable, namely money," he argues. It therefore does a poor job measuring emotional and other hard-to-quantify harms. More generally, economic and scientific reasoning reduce their objects to abstractions, while citizens, according to Berry, must deal with concrete, particular things and people and places. To do so intelligently, they need a "sympathetic mind"—an embodied, responsive mind that understands the limits of human knowledge and the proper place of both reason and sentiment in decision-making.[13] Rationality thus understood should grow out of and complement a passionate love for the land. On the other hand, it does require a critical attitude toward government and society: citizens must be willing to subject not only the decisions of the government but the fundamental values of their society to "strenuous," "principled and serious" public debate.[14]

Ever sensitive to the limits of human reason, though, Berry does not count on rationality alone to ensure sensible decision-making. On the contrary, citizens must also be mindful of both the power of modern nation-states and the responsibility the government owes to the citizens, the rest of the world, and future generations. This mindfulness is captured by the classical virtue of *sophrosyne*—the counterpart to the classical vice of hubris or arrogance. Sophrosyne is sometimes translated as humility, but it also denotes self-control (moderation, temperance), prudence, and good management. In classical thought, sophrosyne was the virtue proper to the good husbandman and the *vita rustica;* Plato associated it with order and harmony more generally, thus linking it to justice.[15]

Berry does not mention sophrosyne by name—he uses cognates such as humility and propriety—but it permeates his moral vision. It is perhaps the paramount civic virtue, the virtue needed to counter the arrogance and hubristic overreaching represented by both modern industrialism and American foreign policy. Our technology and wealth give us tremendous, undreamed-of power—but "people are not gods," he warns. "They must not act like gods or assume godly authority. If they do, terrible retributions are in store. In this warning we have the root of the idea of propriety, of *proper* human purposes and ends."[16] Sophrosyne is a particularly important civic virtue for citizens of the most powerful nation on the earth; it reminds us of the restraint and moderation we need to exercise such power wisely.

Restraint and moderation do not imply passivity, however. Citizens also must be active. They have a duty to make serving the public's interest an integral part of their lives. Indeed, our most serious social and environmental problems, according to Berry, are rooted not in government policies but in our daily lives. Ultimately "our country is not being destroyed by bad politics; it is being destroyed by a bad way of life." Thus "we must go to work" to build a better economy and better communities. If we are serious about peace, for example, "we must work for it as ardently, seriously, continuously, carefully, and bravely as we have ever prepared for war."[17] What he has in mind is not, however, the sort of political activism represented by the mainstream environmental movement. Berry worries that professional environmental activists are subject to the same forces that cause politicians to get out of touch with their constituents. Activists, too, tend to adopt the narrow perspective of specialists. "The political activist," he complains, "*sacrifices* himself to politics; though he has a cause, he has no life; he has become the driest of experts."[18] And, as experts in environmental policy, activists tend to embrace the same assumptions as their opponents. Sharing the "pinhole vision of the industrial intellectuals," they "are not comprehensive enough, they are not radical enough." Instead of delegating one's civic responsibilities to such movements and activists, Berry wants citizens to focus on realizing their political ideals in their daily lives—to "think and act in consideration of [their] responsibilities" not only in their conventional political activities but also in their work and play, in what they eat and how they interact with their neighbors (human and nonhuman).[19]

In sum, Berry imagines republican citizenship as intelligent, practical, responsible activity aimed at building sustainable communities and motivated by our attachment to particular people and places. It is hardly a revolutionary vision; its roots lie in long-standing American political and moral traditions. But it is deeply opposed to the values driving contemporary American politics: our faith in technology, our pursuit of economic growth instead of sustainability, our attempts to achieve peace through war, our desire to control the conditions of our existence. According to Berry, these values—embodied in the prevailing ideology of American nationalism—are the ones most in need of radical critique from a responsible citizenry.

Against this misguided nationalism, Berry proposes a civic ideal of *localism*. A citizen's primary loyalties, he contends, are and should be local. Meaningful political action for Berry is "an action which one takes on one's own behalf, which is particular and complex, real not symbolic, which one can both accomplish on one's own and take full responsibility for." Such action, he suggests, can grow only out of an attachment to one's locality, to a place that one knows concretely and intimately. Expressions of nationalism, in contrast, are "most apt to be fanatic or brutal or arrogant."[20] Based on an abstraction ("the nation"), nationalism promises to lead citizens into the same insensitivity, injustice, and carelessness he sees in bureaucrats and professional politicians.

This localism, however, requires careful qualification. His point is not, I think, that citizens shouldn't be involved in national and even international policymaking. Indeed, that would be hard to reconcile with his democratic principles. Nor does he suggest that most substantive policy should be in the hands of local government. That position would be hard to defend in light of the global dimension of many environmental problems (not to mention our vulnerability to global terrorist networks). Surely such global problems call for international coordination; Berry's argument for local civic engagement is probably not intended to discourage such national and international political organization. Rather, his aim is to describe the conditions necessary for meaningful political action. His point is that if we are to engage meaningfully in national and international politics, we must preserve a sense of the concrete and particular—the things, people, and places we are governing, and the ties of affection and belonging among them. That sense of the concrete and particular is best cultivated at the local level.

Nevertheless, Berry's recent writings make it clear that he understands citizenship to involve membership in an international as well as a national and local community. To be sure, he opposes the militant internationalism represented by the current administration's post–September 11 decisions to invade Afghanistan and Iraq (actions that were justified, in part, by the internationalist goal of creating stable democracies in those regions). But his opposition to those actions derived not from isolationism but from pacifism. He opposes the use of violence for *any* reason, on the grounds that it inevitably leads to more violence. "If violence is 'just' in one instance . . . why, by a merely logical extension, might it not also be 'just' in another instance, as determined by an individual?" What leads to peace is not violence but "peaceableness, . . . an alert, informed, practiced and active state" of building community and cooperation.[21] He thus advocates a *cooperative* internationalism: "We cannot hope to be secure when our government has declared, by its announced readiness 'to act alone,' its willingness to be everybody's enemy." The world is a "community of all the creatures, a community which, to be possessed by any, must be shared by all." Therefore, a civilized nation should "conduct [itself] as a responsible citizen, honoring the lives and the rights of others."[22] In short, the United States ought to be a good citizen of the global community, displaying the same virtues of rationality, moderation, prudence, and constructive engagement he expects from individual citizens. And the only way to accomplish that end is for individual citizens to involve themselves, deeply and critically, in public debates over foreign policy.

A foreign policy of cooperation does not necessarily mean acquiescence in a global free-market economy, however. His opposition to economic globalization stems in part from his suspicion of the claim that it will promote prosperity; the definition of "prosperity" used by proponents of globalization seldom considers its effect on the environment and local communities. But he also challenges the other shibboleth of those proponents: the belief that economic interdependence among nations promotes world peace. Their argument is that as the economies of individual nations become more dependent on international trade, their leaders will be reluctant to go to war and suffer the resulting economic impacts. Therefore, economic globalization increases the incentives for peace. This theory, of course, relies on a number of assumptions that may not hold true in particular cases: that a given war would actually harm the economy, for example, and that the nation's political system is responsive to economic forces. But Berry doesn't challenge those assumptions; rather, he points out that such reasoning, even if it was once correct, doesn't take into consideration the recent rise of terrorist networks. These networks are not under the control of any nation and do not have the same economic incentives that nation-states do. On the contrary, they may well benefit from disruptions of international trade and depressed local economies. "How nations . . . are to shape and protect themselves within this 'global economy,'" he notes, "is far from clear."[23]

Berry points out that economic globalization makes our economy more dependent on global communication and transportation systems—systems that are very difficult to protect from terrorists without "a hugely expensive" worldwide police force. In fact, dependence on these transportation and communication systems might draw us *into* war, in order to protect them.[24] He insists that he does not oppose international trade per se. But as a matter of national security, nation-states should not promote international trade at the expense of economic self-sufficiency—and particularly *local* economic self-sufficiency. "At the very least, a nation should be able sustainably to feed, clothe, and shelter its citizens, using its own sources and by its own work."[25]

This point brings him to the national-security implications of agricultural policy. Local self-sufficiency, for Berry, is particularly desirable in food production, because it ensures that we will be able to feed ourselves if global trade is disrupted. In fact, agriculture "is the economic activity *most clearly and directly* related to national security, if one grants that we all must eat." His position thus revives an old theme in American agrarianism: the argument for food security. Depending on another nation for food, the argument goes, gives it power over us. "How are we going to defend our freedoms . . . when we must import our necessities from international suppliers who have no concern or respect for our freedoms?"[26] Such reasoning is of course a familiar support for efforts to reduce American dependence on foreign oil; it may sound less compelling when applied to agriculture, given the productivity of American farmers. But Berry suggests that such confidence may be misplaced. Our food security rests not only on the productivity of farmers but on a complex distribution and processing system, as well as an increasingly degraded ecosystem—all of which are quite vulnerable to disease and terrorism.[27] Self-sufficient local economies could serve as a safety net in case such systems fail.

Still, Berry's argument for local self-sufficiency is less satisfying than his argument for local civic engagement. After all, local economies are vulnerable as well, from natural disasters like hurricanes to economic crises like local bank failures—and we are as likely to suffer abuses and injustices at the hands of our neighbors as at the hands of international terrorists or corporations. Ties to the global economy give communities and individuals some protection from those dangers. Even more problematic, this argument for self-sufficiency doesn't quite fit within his larger philosophic framework. A central principle of that framework is that we can never escape from "the whole network of interdependence and obligation" in which human lives necessarily unfold.[28] So why should we try to escape the interdependencies and vulnerabilities of the global economic system? Isn't local self-sufficiency just another misguided bid for an illusory sense of security?

I suspect that this argument from security is somewhat opportunistic. Although Berry has discussed food security in earlier works,[29] his recent emphasis on it seems to be taking advantage of the post–September 11 milieu. His writings taken as a whole suggest another reason to support local self-sufficiency: not that it makes us safer but that depending on our friends and neighbors and our own efforts requires *more* from us—more conscious effort, more awareness of our duties toward one another, and more active involvement in the life of the community. In other words, promoting local self-sufficiency makes us better citizens, local *and* global. Seeking local self-sufficiency is after all nothing more than preserving the community's productive capacities—which is for Berry the very definition of patriotism.

Wendell Berry's political vision is a provocative alternative to the vision guiding most of his fellow citizens and lawmakers in the post–September 11 world. Against our national ideals of security, autonomy, and economic and military ascendancy, Berry advocates humility, community, and restraint. No amount of power, he warns, will make us completely safe; we cannot through technological advance escape our responsibility for and dependence on the land and each other. A meaningful life consists in embracing these dependencies and fulfilling our obligations as best we can with our limited capacities.

This may seem a strangely discordant, even un-American, message, uncomfortably out of tune with conventional American optimism and self-confidence. But Berry's political vision is also a native species, derived from long-standing and deeply rooted American traditions. We shouldn't be surprised that these old visions and values should find such an eloquent spokes-man, even after September 11. The world, after all, has not been remade. Like Jefferson's generation, we are still embarked on a vessel amid the conflicting elements of a troubled world—vulnerable, interdependent, and responsible. Berry's critical perspective on American society does not promise us a safe harbor, but it may help to clear our vision and chart our course.

Notes

1. "Thoughts in the Presence of Fear," in *Citizenship Papers* (Washington, DC: Shoemaker and Hoard, 2003), 17.

2. "American Pox," *Nation*, Nov. 4, 1968, 457; Foreword to *Another Turn of the Crank* (Washington, DC: Counterpoint, 1995), ix–x. See also Kimberly Smith, *Wendell Berry and the Agrarian Tradition* (Lawrence: University Press of Kansas, 2003), 183. Berry has become more active in electoral politics recently and publicly endorsed a presidential candidate (Ralph Nader) in 2000 for the first time.

3. Letter to Colonel Smith, Nov. 13, 1787, in *The Life and Selected Writings of Thomas Jefferson,* ed. Adrienne Koch and William Peden (New York: Random House, 1993), 403.

4. Berry explicitly embraces the Jeffersonian mantle. See, e.g., *Another Turn of the Crank,* 49 ("In my own politics and economics I am Jeffersonian"). However, such statements should be read with care. Berry, like many of Jefferson's self-proclaimed intellectual heirs, has reinterpreted that legacy in important ways. See *Wendell Berry and the Agrarian Tradition,* 14–35.

5. "The Total Economy," in *Citizenship Papers,* 75; "A Citizen's Response," in ibid., 10; "The Loss of the Future," in *The Long-Legged House* (1965; repr., Washington, DC: Shoemaker and Hoard, 2004), 49; "Some Thoughts on Citizenship and Conscience in Honor of Don Pratt," in ibid., 77.

6. "The Tyranny of Charity," in *The Long-Legged House,* 9.

7. *Harlan Hubbard: Life and Work* (Lexington: University Press of Kentucky, 1990), 33; "Nature as Measure," in *What Are People For?* (San Francisco: North Point, 1990), 210; *Sex, Economy, Freedom and Community* (New York: Pantheon, 1992), 152–53.

8. "A Citizen's Response," in *Citizenship Papers,* 2.

9. "The Loss of the Future," in *The Long-Legged House,* 50.

10. "Discipline and Hope," in *A Continuous Harmony* (1975; repr., Washington, DC: Shoemaker and Hoard, 2003), 92.

11. "A Citizen's Response," in *Citizenship Papers,* 5.

12. Ibid., 6.

13. "Going to Work," in *Citizenship Papers,* 36, 37–41; "The Two Minds," in *Citizenship Papers,* 85–105.

14. "A Citizen's Response," in *Citizenship Papers,* 13–14.

15. See Helen North, *Sophrosyne: Self-Knowledge and Self-Restraint in Greek Literature* (Ithaca: Cornell University Press, 1966).

16. "The Gift of Good Land," in *The Gift of Good Land* (San Francisco: North Point, 1981), 270.

17. "Think Little," in *A Continuous Harmony*, 75–76; "A Citizen's Response," in *Citizenship Papers*, 50.

18. "Some Thoughts on Citizenship and Conscience in Honor of Don Pratt," in *The Long-Legged House*, 83.

19. *The Unsettling of America* (San Francisco: Sierra Club Books, 1977), 23–24; "In Distrust of Movements," in *Citizenship Papers*, 45.

20. "The Reactor and the Garden," in *Gift of Good Land*, 167; "The Loss of the Future," in *The Long-Legged House*, 49.

21. "The Failure of War," in *Citizenship Papers*, 20, 25. Berry frequently cites a familiar pacifist tradition that draws on the Bible, Gandhi, and Martin Luther King, but I believe his pacifism is based also on a moral vision informed by the classical virtues. Violence against persons, for Berry, is hubristic—it is an attempt to seize more power than is appropriate to humans. See Smith, *Wendell Berry and the Agrarian Tradition*, 136–40.

22. "A Citizen's Response," in *Citizenship Papers*, 8, 9–10.

23. Ibid., 9. On the connection between globalization and peace, see Michael Doyle, "Kant, Liberal Legacies, and Foreign Affairs," *Philosophy and Public Affairs* 12 (1983): 26–27.

24. "Thoughts in the Presence of Fear," in *Citizenship Papers*, 18–19; "The Total Economy," in ibid., 71.

25. "A Citizen's Response," in *Citizenship Papers*, 10; "Thoughts in the Presence of Fear," in ibid., 19; "The Total Economy," in ibid., 75.

26. "A Citizen's Response," in *Citizenship Papers*, 12 (emphasis added); "The Failure of War," in ibid., 28. On the food-security theme in American political thought, see Drew McCoy, *The Elusive Republic* (Chapel Hill: University of North Carolina Press, 1980), 141, 217, 227–28.

27. "A Citizen's Response," in *Citizenship Papers*, 14.

28. "Two Minds," in *Citizenship Papers*, 103.

29. E.g., *Home Economics* (New York: North Point, 1987), 125.

David Kline

How Wendell Berry Single-Handedly Preserved Three Hundred Years of Agrarian Wisdom

I WAS BORN and grew to adulthood in a community that has never relinquished the agrarian ideal and that chose in the first quarter of the twentieth century to stay with animal traction for field work, a decision that ensured a community of small farms, worked by families and their neighbors, that was thus largely shielded from the single-minded rush toward mega-agribusiness promoted by the land grant colleges and the mainstream agricultural publications.

Coming from a family of readers, I read everything that crossed the threshold into our home—a daily newspaper called the *Cleveland Plain Dealer*, farm periodicals such as *Successful Farming, Farm Journal, Hoard's Dairyman*, the *Farm Quarterly, Everybody's Poultry Magazine, Ohio Farmer*, and I'm sure there were others from time to time. Even though I was taught that technology should be our servant and not our master, I absorbed enough information from the farm magazines during the late 1950s and the early '60s that I became a believer in technology as the answer for agriculture. Get rid of the old and ring in the new.

I had questions—did I have questions. Why weren't we keeping up with the latest in confinement housing of animals—cages for hens, crates for sows, elevated pens for pigs? Why didn't we clip teeth, dock tails, remove beaks, install slatted floors for cows, replace the bull with artificial insemination? And in the fields—why the archaic rotation of crops? Why not more fertilizers, high-powered hybrids? Why bother with oats (a necessity in a horse economy), why not more silos, 2–4D, and atrazine instead of cultivating? The ag magazines said we needed to rise above groveling in the dirt, that modern farming is a breeze, and that there would be money to live a life of leisure.

But above all else, I questioned the stupid decision to stay with the out-dated and slow horse when we could use that beautiful golden (usually green or red) calf of modern agriculture, the tractor, and farm many more than our 120 acres.

These questions still nagged me when I ended my two years of alternative service during the Vietnam War and returned to the home farm. I struggled but still read the farm magazines and attended the annual Ohio Farm Science Review, an agribusiness version of Woodstock. In the late 1960s and '70s American agriculture was rounding the far corner and entering the home stretch toward full industrialization, cheered on by the battle cry "get big or get out!" The young tigers of the early '70s got big, and then they got out. Somewhere in those years I came to the realization that my dad was brilliant, and then something else happened to show me why I walked the low-tech path I did.

In 1974 I bought two hives of bees from a neighbor who had sold his farm and moved to another community. Of course, I had read everything I could about bees, and Dad had kept bees (as did my two grandfathers and my schoolteacher) several decades before, so he helped me get started. But I needed to get the bees inspected, and that is when fortune smiled on me. About the third inspector to check on my bees was a simple-living sort of hip-pie named Phil; we'd find shade from the summer sun and have great discus-sions on the direction American agriculture was heading. One day Phil told me, "You have to read Wendell Berry's book *The Unsettling of America*." I was somewhat familiar with Wendell's writings in *Organic Gardening* and *Farming* magazine, but I wasn't prepared for *The Unsettling*.

That was in 1980, three years after the book was published. Emerson wrote that a man standing in his own field is unable to see. That was me. Wendell took me by the shoulder, turned me around, and led me—with words so profound and powerful that they kept me awake long into the night—to where I could see the whole picture. Here, at last, were answers to the many questions and doubts I had about farming on our scale.

In my heavily underlined copy of *The Unsettling* I began to understand my dad's philosophy of farming when he insisted on the traditional and prov-en methods over the newfangled and community-destroying ways of the new. On page 4 I marked,

> Time after time, in place after place, these conquerors have fragmented and demolished traditional communities. . . . They have always said that what they destroyed was outdated, provincial, and contemptible. And with alarming frequency they have been believed and trusted by their victims.[1]

Now I could begin to see that the decisions my dad and others before him had made were meant to preserve an agriculture and community that would endure and survive the damages of the cheap-oil-addicted industrial agriculture. I read, "The exploiter wishes to earn as much as possible by as little work as possible; the nurturer expects, certainly, to have a decent living from his work, but his characteristic wish is to work as well as possible." [2] I read, "Once the revolution of exploitation is under way, statesmanship and craftsmanship are gradually replaced by salesmanship," which Wendell defined as "the craft of persuading people to buy what they do not need, and do not want, for more than it is worth." [3]

I was taught to be a nurturer. The goal my dad set for himself was to leave the farm in better condition for the next generation than it was in when he got it. He succeeded. Twenty years before Dad started farming our farm, it was sold at sheriff's sale because of unpaid taxes. There were gullies too deep to farm across, but they were gone by the time I returned in 1968. The farm's fertility was restored with the annual rotation of crops, seeding of grasses and forage legumes, and countless manure-spreader loads of straw-based manure from the diversity of livestock on the farm.

I began to understand what Dad was teaching, often nonverbally, when I read,

> The best farming requires a farmer—a husbandman, a nurturer—not a technician or businessman. A technician or businessman, given the necessary abilities and ambitions, can be made in a little while, by training. A good farmer, on the other hand, is a cultural product; he is made by a sort of training, certainly, in what his time imposes or demands, but he is also made by generations of experience. This essential experience can only be accumulated, tested, preserved, handed down in settled households, friendships, and communities that are deliberately and carefully native to their own ground, in which the past has prepared the present and the present safeguards the future. [4]

I was being handed generations of agricultural experience and knowledge and wisdom. And I thought it outdated and irrelevant until I began to see it in *The Unsettling of America.* I began to understand that it need not be "inevitable" that every farmer and every community follow the path of destructive agriculture promoted by the agribusiness conglomerates.

Wendell showed me that my three hundred years of agrarian heritage—dating to the time when my ancestors left the alpine meadows of Switzerland because of religious persecution and moved to the Alsace region in France following the Thirty Years War and the Treaty of Westphalia (1648)—had much more value than I thought.

Being a cow-culture people, they took with them on their late 1600s pilgrimage some improved dairy cattle, the knowledge of animal husbandry, and the motto of *Arbeit und Hoffe* (work and hope). After thirty years of war a countryside tends to become depopulated, so our ancestors were invited to lease, usually long-term, the estates of the lords and the princes. At the time, the local farmers in Alsace were following a three-year rotation of wheat or rye, followed by oats or barley the second year, and then a fallow third year.

This rotation of crops was slowly mining the soil; it was not replenishing the necessary soil nutrients needed for plant growth. Grain yields were only five to eight bushels per acre. My ancestors saw opportunity in turning those tilled fields into improved meadows. They introduced clovers and lucerne (alfalfa) to the region, much to the ridicule of the local farmers; but, with the legumes' ability to take nitrogen from the air and convert it to plant food, the meadows flourished.

The legume and grass meadows produced enough forage that hay could be cut and dried and stored in the barns for winter feed. Before the latter part of the 1600s there were no hayfields. Up until then little stock could be overwintered—what the Germans called *Überwinterungsmasstab*—for want of hay. With the increase of animals there came an increase in manure—that absolute essential for improving a farm and an essential we've been accused of worshipping. That constant recycling of nutrients allowed the Swiss "guest workers" to prosper in the new land.

A member of the French ministry of interior said, "Almost all the milk in Saint Marie comes from farms the Swiss Anabaptists lease. And during the evenings and mornings of every season, people see the young Anabaptist dairymaids come down from the mountains into the valley and liven up the streets of the town."[5]

The interior minister went on to say, "An Anabaptist named Gingerich moved in twenty-eight years ago and brought the means of growing clover to Alsace; solely by this method he brought a degree of perfection to agriculture heretofore unheard of in this country. The soil of his land, although not particularly fertile, is always covered in rich cereal crops. . . . Gingerich is the best farmer in the province and perhaps in the entire republic."[6] In all modesty, I note that my paternal grandmother was a Gingerich.

The intense application of solid manure and the profitable advantages made possible by man-made meadows ended the practice of letting land lie fallow. Vladimir G. Simkhovitch, a professor at Columbia University, wrote of this period in his historical study "Hay and History" (1917), "The introduction of grass seed and clovers marked the end of the dark ages of agriculture. It is the greatest of revolutions, the revolution against the supreme law, the law of the land, the law of diminishing returns and of soil depletion."[7]

In order to speed up the cutting of larger tracts of hay, the Anabaptists introduced the scythe to replace the hand sickle, a transition that was again ridiculed and resisted by the local farmers. The locals did not accept the scythe for more than a hundred years.

They also introduced "real" Belgian plows to replace the inferior steel-plated wooden plows then in common use. The Belgian plow was loved by the plowmen after its first test in the field. Afterward they argued as to who should have the honor of using them regularly.

This is the agricultural knowledge my ancestors brought to this country in the 1700s and early 1800s and applied to the fertile soils of Pennsylvania and later the Midwest. It is the knowledge they flourished by, a knowledge and wisdom I was ready to throw to the winds of agricultural change until Wendell Berry showed me the error of my ways. Thank you, Wendell. I'll be forever grateful.

As Wendell says, "the care of the earth is our most ancient and most worthy and, after all, our most pleasing responsibility. To cherish what remains of it, and to foster its renewal, is our only legitimate hope."[8]

There is no greater pleasure for an agrarian than to show a fellow farmer, who fully understands and appreciates what you are doing, your farm. I had the pleasure in the early 1980s of showing Wendell Berry our farm.

Then several years later Wendell showed me his farm. It is on much steeper land than ours. He does have some bottom ground along the Kentucky River, which has to be managed differently than hill land. And he was doing both very well. As we walked the bottom fields we agreed that, along with the fertile silt (we also have creek bottomland) that arrives with flooding, a host of weed seeds gets a free ride downstream to our farms. He showed me giant ragweed, Jerusalem artichokes, jimsonweed, and others that are flood-borne. He explained how he controls those problem weeds with timely mowing and grazing with sheep.

Then he showed me the hillside pastures and the legumes that were growing in profusion in spite of the land's not being limed for many years. Something neither of us fully understood was at work. One farmer facing another while standing in workshoe-high lush pasture is the epitome of shared satisfaction. We know how much goodness comes from good pastures and the animals that graze it.

Those steep hillside pastures were skillfully mowed with a sickle bar mower. A good and careful farmer uses a sickle bar to clip pasture fields and along fence lines because that way he can reach seven feet in beneath overhanging branches and keep encroaching trees and briars in check.

We went up Ford Lane, which runs parallel to Cane Run, to the fields where the sheep were grazing at the time and where the Belgians—the team he uses to farm—were on pasture. Along the way I noticed the good fences that Wendell maintains; five strands of taut wire attached to straight and solid posts. We have been told that "good fences make good neighbors." Wendell is a good neighbor. On this part of the farm is the tobacco barn where the Fords stored their tobacco. Not coming from tobacco country, I found the smell of the inside of the long-unused stripping room unfamiliar and new. The tools were still hanging on the walls where they were placed after last being used. All the while, Wendell shared stories of happenings that occurred on the farm and in the community over the years.

That evening Wendell brought the cows in to milk, and, as his poem says, "A cow / To milk's a good excuse / To bring you home from places / You do not want to be."[9]

It is evident that Wendell and Tanya's farm is their home. It is where their roots are and a place for nurturing things, a place filled with love and abundance, of constant wonder, a place for family and times filled with stories and joy.

Notes

1. Wendell Berry, *The Unsettling of America* (San Francisco: Sierra Club Books, 1977), 4.

2. Ibid., 7–8.

3. Ibid., 11.

4. Ibid., 45; emphasis added.

5. Claude Jérôme, *Les Anabaptistes Mennonites d'Alsace: Destin d'une minorité*, trans. Kevin J. Ruth, *Saisons d'Alsace* 76 (1981): 36–51.

6. Ibid.

7. Vladimir G. Simkhovitch, "Hay and History," in *Toward the Understanding of Jesus: And Two Additional Historical Studies* (New York: Macmillan, 1937), 161.

8. Berry, *The Unsettling of America*, 14.

9. Wendell Berry, *A Timbered Choir* (New York: Counterpoint, 1998), 140.

John Leax

Memory and Hope in the World of Port William

MEMORY AND its lively influence have always been central concerns in Wendell Berry's work. As early as "The Long-Legged House" he wrote, "The approach of a man's life out of the past is history, and the approach of time out of the future is mystery. Their meeting is the present, and it is consciousness, the only time life is alive. The endless wonder of this meeting is what causes the mind, in its inward liberty of a frozen morning, to turn back and question and remember."[1] In this early essay Berry's emphasis is on the present. "It is impossible," he wrote, "to imagine 'how it will be,' and to linger over the task is to prepare a disappointment."[2] In his more recent fiction, however, Berry has developed a more complex sense of memory that reaches forward into the future.

The Catholic writer Henri Nouwen has suggested that

> memory never copies the past, it brings the past into the potentially healing present. It breathes new life into a bygone reality and replaces it with a new context. . . . Remembering in this way allows us to live in the present with our whole history, with an awareness of the possibilities we might otherwise not think to look for.

Memory, therefore, has much to do with the future. Without memory there is no expectation. Those who have no memory have little to expect. Memory anchors us in the past and then makes us present here and now, and opens us to a new future.[3]

Although Berry's refusal to "imagine 'how it will be'" will remain a constant, and he will be particularly leery of the implications of "expectations," his exploration of memory in *Jayber Crow* and *Hannah Coulter* will lead him to conceive of it as a creative force functioning not only in the present but as a source of hope.

Hannah, summing up her remembering in *Hannah Coulter,* echoes both Nouwen and the early Berry: "When you remember the past, you are not remembering it as it was. You are remembering it as it is. It is a vision or a dream, present with you in the present, alive with you in the only time you are alive."[4] Jayber in *Jayber Crow* goes even further, seeing memory as the very life of the community:

> Back there at the beginning, as I see now, my life was all time and almost no memory. . . .
>
> And now nearing the end, I see that my life is almost entirely memory and very little time. Toward the end of my life at Squires Landing I began to understand that whenever death happened, it happened to me. That is knowledge that takes a long time to wear in. Finally it wears in. Finally I realized and fully accepted that one day I would belong entirely to memory, and it would not be my memory that I belonged to.[5]

Although this passage feels rather dark, it opens, as Jayber's narrative progresses, to an understanding of memory's connection to hope, and Jayber concludes, "This is a book about Heaven. I know it now. It floats among us like a cloud and is the realest thing we know and the least to be captured, the least to be possessed by anybody for himself."[6]

Berry himself is reluctant to speak of Heaven in his nonfiction, but he is able to give these words to Jayber because the fictive Port William is a "Bible-based culture" in which people remember Bible stories and are "prompted in their actions by Biblical ideas."[7] This culture does not find its expression in any single novel, story, or character. It is worked out in the complexly interlocking stories told over time from multiple perspectives. It exists in a flawed community where sin is real. To encounter Port William is to encounter murder, infidelity, waywardness, sloth, and greed. It is also to encounter love, mercy, faithfulness, forgiveness, and redemption. It is a community that is changing, constantly coming into being as it is remembered and narrated. Both the remembering and the narrative of the remembering are necessary, as a consideration of *Remembering* and *A World Lost* will show.

In the opening scene of *Remembering* Andy wakens from a nightmare in a hotel room in San Francisco: "A man could go so far from home, he thinks, that his own name would become unspeakable to him, unanswerable by anyone, so far that if he dared speak it, it would escape him utterly, a bird out an open window, leaving him untongued in some boundless amplitude of mere absence."[8] For Andy the distance from home is literal as well as metaphorical. The loss of the name is threatening, for it would be the loss of all the connections he is known by. Berry describes him, in his waking, as still going away on the far side of a boundary he crossed when he came up the ramp at the airport and saw the young woman whose name and description he carried in a letter in his pocket. . . . She saw him and smiled, anxiety leaving her face. She was from the college where, in two hours, he was to speak.

"Pardon me. Are you Andrew Catlett?"

He looked at her as if to be surprised to be so accosted, and stepped past.

"No mam."[9]

In his refusal to admit who he is, Andy both acknowledges that he is no longer himself—the man known to his community—and that he is not the one "becoming himself" out of his previous history and life story. Just as Andy has been dismembered in the accidental loss of his hand, he is on the verge of a total dis-membering of his character and identity. Carl D. Esbjornson identifies the pun in the title and the role of memory crucial to the redemption that is the novel's concern: "re-membering is the necessary means of spiritual healing." It is the way Andy remembers that will re-member him and restore him to his place in the fellowship of his community.[10] Though Esbjornson does not state it explicitly here, he clearly implies the re-membering of Andy's return to the company of the Port William membership.

Alone in his hotel room Andy is outside all the relationships that have defined him. The only connection he has is his memory, and his memory is out of control, taking him and the reader back over the events of the preceding day. It takes him first to his quarrel with Flora and then to the agricultural conference in which, instead of delivering his prepared speech, he recounts the stories of the community he has cared for. In doing so he does great damage to himself. Because he speaks in anger, his speaking is a betrayal:

"I say damn your systems and your numbers and your ideas. I speak for Dorie Catlett and Marce Catlett. I speak for . . ."

And as he named them, the dead and the living, they departed from him, leaving him empty, wet with sweat.[11]

The irony of the passage is that Andy must name his community, not to change anyone in the room, but to change himself. For only by losing his life, by giving up this remembering that is private, angry, and manipulative, can he enter into genuine memory that is communal and be re-membered.

The memory of a brief incident that comes to Andy defines his condition. One afternoon, at the end of a workday, he says to Nathan Coulter, "I don't know how to thank you. I don't know how I can ever repay you" (39). Andy's whining statement both insults the community by reducing it to keeping accounts and reveals that he understands his place in it as earned, something he deserves. Nathan's response refuses both. He grins, gives Andy's forearm a slight tug and answers simply, "Help us" (39). In doing so he reminds Andy that he must give up his illusion of independent competence and recognize that he holds his place in the community by grace. What the community requires of him is himself, not a quantity of labor. Merely remembering, however, is not enough to move Andy toward restoration. He leaves the hotel room and begins a walk that will take him through the city and eventually to the long pier that curves out into the bay at Aquatic Park.

At the beginning of this walk, he imagines another life for himself, a life of elegant detachment and culture. But as he imagines this life he interrupts himself: "He reminds himself of himself" (46). The sentence is wonderfully ambiguous. It identifies both who he is at the moment—a sorry fool—and who he has been and remains by the grace of others though no longer by his own acquiescence.

In the next scene he is accosted by a panhandler. Trying to determine a sufficient response, Andy questions the wisdom of digging out his wallet, for holding his wallet in his one good hand, he will be disarmed. To respond charitably, he must risk everything. Responding from the character that had been shaped in him by his long membership in the Port William community rather than from the anger that has dis-membered him, he takes the risk. He opens his wallet and gives extravagantly. The panhandler replies and speaks the truth Andy will come to understand in the course of his crosstown walk, "Oh, wow! Far out! Thanks Tex. You a man of a better time" (47). Andy's extravagant gesture is the movement into grace that readmits him to the community that departed from him with his angry naming at the agricultural conference. The panhandler's "better time" refers not only to a nostalgic, lost era of generosity but to a time coming into being as a result of Andy's present action.

When he reaches the edge of the continent, as far geographically and emotionally from Kentucky as he can go, Andy recalls raising chickens with his grandmother after his grandfather's death. One evening, putting eggs under a setting hen, Andy expresses a desire to join himself to the old ways of doing things forever. His grandmother "looks down at him, and smiles, and then suddenly pulls his head against her. 'Oh, my boy, how far away will you be sometime, remembering this?'"(57). Turning back from the bay, Andy sees the risen sun.

> He is held, though he does not hold. He is caught up again in the old pattern of entrances: of minds into minds, minds into place, places into

minds. The pattern limits and complicates him, singling him out in his own flesh. Out of the multiple possible lives that have surrounded and beckoned to him like a crowd around a star, he returns to himself, a mere meteorite, scorched, small, and fallen. He has met again his one life and one death, and he takes them back (57–58).

The remainder of the novel will recount Andy's journey into memory that will no longer separate him from himself and his place but will, like the biblical narratives remembered by the nation of Israel, reconnect him to his place, his people, and a vision, enabling him to live into an unknowable future.

Andy's memory is fruitful, able to shape his return and his future, because it is not merely a personal memory; it is a memory participating in a communal memory that contains him quite apart from his actions. It is always there. His task is to choose it. Memory, however, can fail. It can be lost. Andy comes up against its failure when he seeks to understand the life and murder of Uncle Andrew, his namesake, in *A World Lost*.

Berry foregrounds the ambiguities of memory and its limitations by changing the narrative perspective from the third person of *Remembering* to Andy's first-person narration in *A World Lost*. In doing so he gives up narrative authority and subjects his story to the fragmented and broken memories of his characters. A child at the time of Uncle Andrew's death, Andy finds his memory circumscribed by the limitations of what he was able to know about his uncle. Early in his narration Andy faces his difficulty:

> Perhaps it was from thinking about him after his death, discovering how much I remembered and how little I knew, that I learned that all human stories in this world contain many lost or unwritten or unreadable or unwritable pages and that the truth about us, though it must exist, though it must lie all around us everyday, is mostly hidden from us, like birds' nests in the woods.[12]

In attempting his narration Andy will encounter the lost, the unwritten, the unreadable, and the unwritable. Some knowledge was unavailable to Andy simply because he was a child and was oblivious to the meaning of events. Some knowledge was deliberately hidden from him for his protection. Some knowledge was hidden from the community by Uncle Andrew himself. Some knowledge was hidden from him because the adults around him could not speak, even to themselves, of what they knew. The end result is that when, as an adult, Andy begins to seek an understanding of his uncle's life, he must interrogate the community to discover what has been hidden, and he must, from what he discovers, construct a past livable in the present.

He, of course, fails, and this failure, I believe, is a crucial part of the novel.

Andy's investigation of his fifty-year-old memories is inconclusive. "All those years," he says, "stand between me and the actual event as irremediably as the end of the world."[13] More than the years, however, stands between Andy and a useable memory. What is missing is the absence of a story told and possessed by the community available for him to enter. He can never know Uncle Andrew as others may have known him, nor include him in his own life as he might wish. A world has been lost. Nevertheless, Uncle Andrew is not entirely unknown. Although Andy fails to establish fact, he does reach back to Uncle Andrew, extending compassion to the limit of imagination, and this is his success: "In drawing him toward me again after so long a time, I seem to have summoned, not into view or into thought, but just within the outmost reach of love, Uncle Andrew in the plenitude of his being—the man he would have been for my sake, and for love of us all, had he been capable. In recalling him as I knew him in mortal time, I have felt his presence as a living soul."[14]

Memory for Andy is functioning much as it did for Saint Augustine. Alan Jacobs points out that "Augustine in his *Confessions* repeatedly wonders at the faculty of memory precisely because it allows us to revisit events of our lives and discern the trajectory that they describe."[15] Though Andy knows his interrogation of the community and his constructed account of what might have happened the day Uncle Andrew died cannot have the life-giving vitality of a story handed down by constant telling and retelling, his effort is efficacious. For by his act of memory he discerns and creates a story that gives shape to the discrete, unplotted events of Uncle Andrew's life. Here, there is imagination at work, but Andy's construction within the fictive world of Port William is not false. It is, rather, life-giving. As it is articulated, the story begins to live in the present and reach into the future. Though one world is lost, a new and chosen one is coming into being.

This process of memory restructuring the past and opening to hope dominates the narrations of Jayber Crow and Hannah Coulter in the novels bearing their names. For them, as for Andy and Augustine, memory is not passive. It is what "enables [them] to think of [their] lives in meaningfully narrative terms."[16] It is also what allows them to look forward, not with expectations, but with hope, for the sense of perceived structure continues beyond the present moment. Its coherence derives from being included in something larger than personal stories and their forward reach. Its coherence is what allows Nathan to affirm at his moments of greatest testing, "I'm going to live right on."[17] The trajectory, though unknown, is hopeful and reaches into the future.

Faith in this trajectory is most clearly seen in Hannah's telling her life— significantly—to Andy. While Andy is part of the Port William membership by birth, Hannah is not. She enters the membership by marriage and by the suffering she shares with the Feltners when Virgil is sent overseas. As she tells it, "I stayed on in a life that would have been mine and Virgil's but now was only mine. I lived the daily life of Port William that he no longer lived but only read about in our letters. . . . I was making myself at home."[18] For Hannah to be at home two things must occur. First, Port William must have room for her; it must be a changeable place. Second, Hannah must choose Port William; she must find it sufficient not to her wants but to her needs. In making herself at home she learns that Port William, changeable as it is, is an immortal place, one that is "always here and now, and going on forever."[19] It is immortal because its citizens—represented by men like Jack Beecham and Jayber Crow—are men with long memories. Jayber notes, "I am an old man now. . . . I have in mind word-of-mouth memories more than a hundred years old. It is only twenty hundred years since the birth of Christ. Fifteen or twenty memories such as mine would reach all the way back to the halo-light in the manger of Bethlehem."[20] Many of these memories are of loss: "One by one, we lose our loved ones, our friends, our powers of work and pleasure, our landmarks, the days of our allotted time."[21]

Hannah also knows this from the very beginning of her entry into the membership. When Virgil disappears during the Battle of the Bulge, her knowledge of loss becomes almost unbearable. She identifies this moment as the point where she consciously enters into the understanding of her life as a story. It is a story like everyone's, a story of absence, death, and grief. The likeness of her story to other stories, however, cannot sustain her. What is necessary is the recognition of the interconnectedness of the stories. The kindness of the Feltners opens her to understanding that to be in love with Virgil is to be in love with what he belonged to and that love is the force that carried her.[22] It carries her by including her. Being part of the membership means that "if nobody can ever be quite nothing to you in Port William, then everybody finally has got to be something to you."[23] Being something to everybody and knowing that everybody is something to her allows Hannah to step out of the closet of her grief because she can see that the trajectory of her story has no necessary end in grief. She is free in her story to meet what will come. It will be mystery, something neither rigidly determined by her past nor totally unshaped by it.

The mystery that comes to her is Nathan Coulter, a new marriage, a larger family, and an opening of the room of love. Though joy comes with the opening, so too does sorrow. Hannah understands this: "You can't give yourself over to love for somebody without giving yourself over to suffering. . . . It is this body of our suffering that Christ was born into, to suffer it Himself and to fill it with light, so that beyond the suffering we can imagine Easter morning and the peace of God on little earthly homelands such as Port William and the farming villages of Okinawa."[24]

Like Jayber, Hannah speaks of Heaven. Like Jayber, she speaks of it in a traditional future sense—she will be buried beside Nathan to wait with him for the resurrection—but, like Jayber, she also speaks of it as something present. "My mind," she says,

> has started to become, it is close to being, the room of love where the absent are present, the dead are alive, time is eternal, and all creatures prosperous. The room of love is the love that holds us all, and it is not ours. . . . It is Heaven's. Or it is Heaven, and we are only in it by willingness. By whose love, Andy Catlett, do we love this world and ourselves and one another? Do you think we invented it ourselves? I ask with confidence, for I know you know we didn't.[25]

We trust Hannah's confidence, for we know, as well as she does, that Andy has had his own visions of Heaven. At the end of *Remembering* Andy travels in his dream to a hilltop overlooking Port William, and he sees below him the living and the dead, "men and women he remembers, and men and women remembered in memories he remembers, and they do not look as he ever saw or imagined them . . . they have the luminous vividness of new grass after fire. And yet they are mature as ripe fruit. And yet they are flowers."[26] He is prevented from going to them. Instead he must return to the living as they are, as he is, being made by their choosing in the present, "the only time life is alive."[27]

Andy's vision of the eternal Port William—Hannah's room of love—is most fully articulated in the concluding paragraph of *A World Lost:* "My true home is not just this place but is also that company of immortals with whom I have lived here day by day. I live in their love, and I know something of the cost. Sometimes in the darkness of my own shadow I know that I could not see at all were it not for this old injury of love and grief, this little flickering lamp that I have watched beside for all these years."[28]

The Bible-based culture of Port William is a culture lighted by the flickering light of hope. Hope is not optimism, for optimism is easy and hope is difficult. To imagine Port William an ideal world or an agrarian paradise to be somehow established in suburban America is to misunderstand it entirely. It is to skip the suffering that every character in Port William endures. Lauren F. Winner makes this error in her review of *Hannah Coulter* when she opines, "We wonder, in short, how someone who doesn't farm land in Kentucky that his family has owned forever can go about living Berry's robust and exciting vision of community."[29] She compounds this misunderstanding in her conclusion when she reads Virgie's return as a false note of "encouragement, optimism, and good cheer."[30]

Virgie's return cannot be rightly seen as optimistic. Though Hannah is glad for it, she has learned the pain of expectations. She knows that the function of memory is not to copy the past; it is, as Henri Nouwen suggested, to enliven the present with a full awareness of possibilities both promising and disappointing. Hannah is no fool. All three of her children have left the community. Not one is coming back. "For a while," she says, "especially if you have children, you shape your life according to expectations. That is arguably pretty foolish, for expectation can be a bucket of smoke. . . . After your expectations have gone their way and your future is getting along the best it can as an honest blank, you shape your life according to what is."[31] Hannah understands that Virgie is ill-prepared for his return. He has neither the knowledge necessary to accept the responsibility of a farm nor the discipline necessary to meet the work. Broken emotionally, lost to drugs, and probably in poor health, he has been away for a long time. His return is not the return of the prodigal son to the fatted calf and a fresh portion of his inheritance. His return is to be a hand to Danny Branch, the son of Burley's waywardness.

As important to the hope of the novel as Virgie's weakness is the weakness of the Port William membership itself. Hannah is an old woman. Andy is in his sixties, and the Branches, though they are all together, are more isolated from the larger culture than any of Berry's other characters. Its line of fifteen or twenty memories as long as Jayber's back to "the halo-light in the manger of Bethlehem" is reduced to Virgie's retelling the story of Burley and Big Ellis and the disconnected steering wheel. Although this invocation of the communal memory cannot reasonably be construed as optimism, it can and should be seen as evidence of the hope that sustains the culture of Port William.

Notes

1. Wendell Berry, *The Long-Legged House* (New York: Harcourt, Brace, 1969), 143.
2. Ibid., 168.
3. Henri Nouwen, *Turn My Mourning into Dancing* (Nashville: W Publishing Group, 2001), 59–60.
4. Wendell Berry, *Hannah Coulter* (Washington, DC: Shoemaker and Hoard, 2004), 148.
5. Wendell Berry, *Jayber Crow* (Washington, DC: Counterpoint, 2000), 24.
6. Ibid., 351.
7. Lionel Basney and John Leax, "A Conversation with Wendell Berry," *Image* 26 (2000): 51.

8. Wendell Berry, *Remembering* (San Francisco: North Point, 1988), 5.

9. Ibid., 5–6.

10. Carl D. Esbjornson, "*Remembering* and Home Defense," in *Wendell Berry*, ed. Paul Merchant (Lewiston, ID: Confluence Press, 1991), 157.

11. Berry, *Remembering*, 25, hereafter cited in text.

12. Wendell Berry, *A World Lost* (Washington, DC: Counterpoint, 1996), 61–62.

13. Ibid., 126.

14. Ibid., 149–50.

15. Alan Jacobs, "What Narrative Theology Forgot," *First Things* 135 (August/September, 2003), 26.

16. Ibid., 28.

17. Berry, *Hannah Coulter*, 141, 161.

18. Ibid., 42.

19. Ibid., 43.

20. Berry, *Jayber Crow*, 352–53.

21. Ibid., 353.

22. Berry, *Hannah Coulter*, 51.

23. Ibid., 63.

24. Ibid., 171.

25. Ibid., 158–59.

26. Berry, *Remembering*, 124.

27. Berry, *The Long-Legged House*, 143.

28. Berry, *World Lost*, 151.

29. Lauren F. Winner, "Inhabiting Love," review of *Hannah Coulter* by Wendell Berry, *Image* 45 (2005): 120.

30. Ibid.

31. Berry, *Hannah Coulter*, 130–31.

Eric Trethewey

Politics, Nature, and Value in Wendell Berry's "Art of the Commonplace"

WHAT IS the relationship between the natural world and the human? To this ancient theologico-philosophical question one might link another: What are the social and political implications at the present time of competing conceptions of this relationship?

One such conception rests upon a pervasive—in most cases unexamined—faith, based on habitual assumption, that whatever human beings may have in common with other earthly organisms, the differences between the human and natural realms ought to be regarded as paramount in reflections about either. To this way of thinking, the noted nineteenth-century biologist Ernst Haeckel gave the name *anthropism*—in Haeckel's words, "that powerful and worldwide group of erroneous opinions which opposes the human organism to the whole of the rest of nature, and represents it to be the preordained end of organic creation, an entity essentially distinct from it, a godlike being."[1]

Those features unique to human culture—language, art, ethical imperatives, concern with justice and law—come to be seen in the *anthropistic* view as creating a nonreciprocal, sometimes antithetical relationship between humankind and the natural world. There is, for example, the intermittent hostility to nature and the natural discernible throughout the Judeo-Christian tradition that has become militant within much of contemporary evangelical fundamentalism, insisting as it does on a crudely conceived supernaturalism that effects a radical split between the human and whatever else, in Yeats's phrase, "is begotten, born, and dies."[2] Or, to take another—perhaps only apparently unrelated—example, a good deal of modernist aesthetics, in reaction to the valorization of nature in many romantic texts, displays as the dominant motive the ambition to obviate both the natural, and whatever is merely natural in the human, by means of an appeal to the primacy of form over content, pure idea or metaphysics over the contingent and problematical ordering of experiential data. T. E. Hulme's dismissal of romanticism as so much "spilt religion" offers one amusing rhetorical reduction to the simplistic of what is complex and serious in this matter. Or, to adduce one final illustration of the consequences of assuming a quantum divide between nature and the human world, one might argue that such an assumption makes possible an easy rationalization—even at the intellectual and spiritual cost of blindness to hard scientific evidence—of the technological brutalization of the earth in the interests of short-term economic gain.[3] The tendency to focus exclusively on the differences between nature and human culture, with an unexamined anthropocentric bias, occludes a vision of their underlying kinship and leads to the cultural phenomena mentioned in my examples.[4] It is a tendency that seems to me to have enormous political import at the present time: what is at stake, it is becoming increasingly clear, is nothing less than the spiritual identity of human beings and the future of life on the planet.

There is another significant conception of the relation between the natural world and the human realm available, if not so widespread or influential, within our culture. At least since the time of Wordsworth's 1802 preface to *Lyrical Ballads* there has been in the English-speaking world a literary tradition of regarding genuine experience of nature as a palliative to specific social and intellectual disorders brought about by an emerging industrial economy. Alfred North Whitehead made the point long ago when he argued that "the nature poetry of the romantic revival was a protest on behalf of the organic view of nature, and also a protest against the exclusion of value from the essence of matter of fact. . . . The romantic reaction," Whitehead concluded, "was a protest on behalf of value."[5] Indeed, this romantic reaction to the "machinery" of reason initiated a long tradition of opposition to the mechanical, value-free paradigm of existence presented by the emergent scientific world-view and fostered by a rapidly expanding industrialism.

A number of contemporary American poets, Wendell Berry chief among them, participate in this tradition, finding in nature not only the locus and subject matter of poems but also a philosophical grounding and a mode of figuration for the cultural value, the ethos, they articulate. Berry is of particular interest not only because of the integrative tenor of his imagination but also because of the determination with which he has attempted to embrace a way of life, that of a farmer, corresponding to his imaginative imperatives. His thoughts about nature do not merely grow from contemplation but are shaped and informed by a long commitment to working the land. Berry's poems, novels, and essays embody the principle that "there is no 'world of imagination' as distinct from or opposed to the 'real world.'"[6] In his view, "the great general work of criticism to which we are all called" demands a mutual correction of imagination by experience and experience by imagination in a social and intellectual context that has not entirely subverted their organic relationship to one another. That work of criticism, as Berry has pursued it over the years, has moved steadily along a series of reconciliations that refuse to privilege imagination over experience, form over content, fact over value, or, to return to the conceptual opposition with which I began, culture over nature.

Take, for instance, his poem "The Silence":

Though the air is full of singing
my head is loud
with the labor of words.
Though the season is rich
with fruit, my tongue
hungers for the sweet of speech.
    Though the beech is golden
I cannot stand beside it
mute, but must say
    "It is golden," while the leaves
stir and fall with a sound
that is not a name.
    It is in the silence
that my hope is, and my aim.
A song whose lines
    I cannot make or sing
sounds men's silence
like a root. Let me say
    And not mourn: the world
lives in the death of speech
and sings there.[7]

The fundamental opposition the poem sets up is a version of that old antinomy, nature and human culture. The chief characteristic of culture present in the poem is language, paired throughout with aspects of the natural world that stand by themselves outside words and remain resistant to them: the music of birds and insects, the rich taste of ripened fruit, the spectacle and tones of autumn—none of which can be satisfactorily named, though the speaker of the poem cannot resist the need to try. The theme is familiar enough, central as it is to the discourse of our time. But the resolution to the speaker's dilemma may seem peculiar to some, given the prevailing intellectual currents of the past several decades. For the poem moves toward an acceptance of language's ultimate silence—not in despair but with the wise passiveness of prayer that allows for hope—because the speaker realizes and can accept that humans, by their nature, already embody a fruitful song, that of regeneration, which, though they "cannot make or sing" it, "sounds man's silence / like a root." The failure of speech, "men's silence," like human beings themselves, is grounded in the ultimately mysterious organic fecundity of creation, some deep-down reproductive freshness, life force, or what you will. Since language is at bottom a product of this mysterious fecundity, it is both secondary to the whole of which it is a part and at the same time organically shaped by the "lines" of that whole—though it cannot make or sing them. Because of this organic principle, because the world is what it is, the ultimate inadequacy of language is mandated from the beginning. But so too, by the same token, is its partial, approximate effectuality. Words, however imperfectly, no less than leaves, serve the purposes for which they have come into being.

If this is so, what contemporary circumstance would cause us to overlook or ignore that partial success in favor of focusing almost exclusively on the ways in which language fails us? Eugene Goodheart, in his lucid and persuasively argued book *The Skeptic Disposition in Contemporary Criticism,* offers the explanation that "the sense of man and his products as radically indeterminate comes from the evacuation of nature from the historical process."[8] In order to arrive at an adequate criticism, Goodheart argues, it is necessary to see how both our experience and the language that articulates it are rooted in nature—a view that implies some form of organicism. In "The Silence" Wendell Berry is speaking from such a view when he writes, "It is in the silence"—that is, the world that lives outside of words—"that my hope is, and my aim." His hope is in the regenerative, organic processes of creation; his aim is to serve wisely as instrument and agent, as "steward," of those processes. The classical *topos* embodied in Saint Paul's "The letter killeth, but the spirit giveth life" is revisited and amplified here in Berry's "The world / lives in the death of speech / and sings there."[9]

Earlier I spoke of an underlying kinship between the human world and the natural that is likely to be occluded by a tendency to dwell on their differences. One is not likely to find a more appropriate image of human and natural fellowship than in Berry's poem "The Old Elm Tree by the River":

> Shrugging in the flight of its leaves,
> it is dying. Death is slowly
> standing up in its trunk and branches

like a camouflaged hunter. In the night
I am awakened by one of its branches
crashing down, heavy as a wall, and then
lie sleepless, the world changed.
That is a life I know the country by.
Mine is a life I know the country by.
Willing to live and die, we stand here,
timely and at home, neighborly as two men.
Our place is changing in us as we stand,
and we hold up the weight that will bring us down.
In us the land enacts its history.
When we stood it was beneath us, and was
the strength by which we held to it
and stood, the daylight over it
a mighty blessing we cannot bear for long.[10]

The note of identity the poem begins and ends on is the mortal condition shared by man and tree. The speaker is reminded of his own mortality by the withering and decay of the elm. W. H. Auden, in another context, provides the term *sacramental analogies* for the conception at the heart of Berry's poem. "The poet," says Auden, "has to preserve and express by art what primitive peoples knew instinctively, namely, that for man, nature is a realm of sacramental analogies."[11] In addition to their mutual mortality, which each is "willing" to accept, the speaker and elm have also in common the land where both have stood, the land that "was / the strength by which we held to it / and stood." Implicit in this phrasing is the idea that the land's power to sustain is not separable from "the strength by which we held to it." A hint of Wendell Berry's land ethic is sounded in these lines, the idea developed at length in his essays of a reciprocity or balance between humankind and nature that is violated on a massive scale by application of the principle of economic efficiency, which amounts to a profligate waste of natural resources and a defilement of the earth. It is not surprising that a poet who sees a fundamental identity of kind between himself and an elm tree, who speaks of them with literal intent as being "neighborly as two men," should look upon the willful degradation of the environment as a degradation of the self. "In us," as we are reminded by the poem, "the land enacts its history." Not merely "through us," or "by means of us," but "in us."

Ever since giving up a promising academic career and returning to his native Kentucky to farm, Wendell Berry has been creating in his writing an image of the farmer as a model and touchstone for authentic human existence, living as he does in intimate contact with the ground of life itself. His poem "The Farmer, Speaking of Monuments" exemplifies some of the ways that model has served him:

> Always, on their generation's breaking wave,
> men think to be immortal in the world,
> as though to leap from water and stand
> in air were simple for a man. But the farmer
> knows no work or act of his can keep him
> here. He remains in what he serves
> by vanishing in it, becoming what he never was.
> He will not be immortal in words.
> All his sentences serve an art of the commonplace,
> to open the body of a woman or a field
> to take him in. His words all turn
> to leaves, answering the sun with mute
> quick reflections. Leaving their seed, his hands
> have had a million graves, from which wonders
> rose, bearing him no likeness. At summer's
> height he is surrounded by green, his
> doing, standing for him, awake and orderly.
> In autumn, all his monuments fall.[12]

Even when Berry's poems are not directly about nature, nature is a presence in them as the ground of his imaginative as of his actual world. In this particular poem the farmer is presented as one fully attuned to natural process, so much so that he harbors no illusions about fame or personal "immortality" conferred by monuments or embodied in words: "the farmer / knows no work or act of his can keep him / here. He remains in what he serves / by vanishing in it, becoming what he never was." The archaic terms of the farmer's relation to nature demand that he experience daily his dependence on it and recognize the degree of his participation in it as a natural, mortal being. This day-by-day, season-by-season experience undermines illusions of permanence and fosters a willing acceptance of death as a natural part of life. Because death, the mother of imperfection as well as of beauty, is inescapable, a biological and ecological necessity, Berry has argued, "its acceptance becomes a spiritual obligation, the only means of making life whole."[13] The repetitive, cyclical character of farm life discourages the notion that any human attainment is likely to be for all time, and this throws the farmer back on the acceptance of process, natural and agricultural, as the proper mode of human existence. As Berry has written in his essay "Discipline and Hope," "correct discipline brings us into alignment with natural process, which has no explicit or deliberate concern for the future. . . . A good farmer plants, not because of the abstractions of demand or market or his financial condition, but because it is planting time and the ground is ready—that is, he plants in response to his discipline and his place."[14]

One further characteristic of the farmer as Berry presents him in this poem is his use of language: "All his sentences serve an art of the commonplace, / to open the body of a woman or a field / to take him in." Or, as he says in "Discipline and Hope," "a man planting a crop is like a man making love to his wife."[15] The language of the farmer is primarily practical and is understood by him to be so, an understanding that those not obliged to toil daily on the land, or otherwise in harmony with natural process, may never come to. And this is true of values as well as of the speech in which they find their formulation. Language about value is practical language. "What we have forgotten is the origin of morality in fact and circumstance; we have forgotten that the nature of morality is essentially practical." The overriding value to Berry of the farmer as figure for human authenticity is that farmers—because of the archaic terms of their relation to nature and natural process—are likely to remember what others have forgotten. "A farmer's relation to his land," says Berry, "is the basic and central connection in the relation of humanity to the creation; the agricultural relation *stands for* the larger relation."[16]

A central corollary of the foregoing metonymy is that what is true of the farmer's relationship to his land also applies to the poet's relationship to his subjects and the tools of his discipline. Berry's insistence on the importance of process, the inseparability of means and ends, in the practice of farming is echoed in his attitude toward process in poetry when he refers admiringly in *A Continuous Harmony* to R. H. Blyth's view that "poetry is not the words written in a book, but the mode of activity in the mind of the poet."[17] Because farming, as Berry conceives it, is nonspecialized, based on a holistic relationship to the land; poetry, by the same token, should engage with the real world as it has been experienced over millennia. In the light of literary modernism and postmodernism, Berry's ideas might be seen, depending on one's point of view, as either reactionary or radical. They are probably neither. Rather, they self-consciously participate in a great, still living (though in questionable health) literary and cultural tradition that he as poet, essayist, and novelist has committed himself to reinterpreting, enlivening, and conserving. In his essay "The Specialization of Poetry," he takes a number of his better-known contemporary poets to task for the partialness of their engagement with modern experience. "The job now," as he sees it, "is to get back to that perennial and substantial world in which we really do live, in which the foundations of our life will be visible to us, and in which we can accept our responsibilities again within the conditions of necessity and mystery. In that world all wakeful and responsible people, dead, living, and unborn are contemporaries. And that is the only contemporaneity worth having."[18] For Berry, as we have seen, there is short-term practicality and long-term practicality, the latter of which goes also by the name of "tradition": "If, as I believe, one of the functions of tradition is to convey a sense of our perennial nature and of the necessities and values that are the foundations of our life, then it follows that, without a live tradition, we are necessarily the prey of fashion: we have no choice but to emulate in the arts the 'practical men' of commerce and industry whose mode of life is distraction of spirit and whose livelihood is the outdating of fads."[19]

It may well be that Wendell Berry's determined embrace of what many might consider *tout court* a conservative ideology and what others might see as a confirmation of the enduring values of the liberal imagination would go some way toward explaining the fact of his exclusion—in favor of considerably less accomplished but more visibly recognized poets—from such highly visible poetry anthologies as *The Norton Anthology of Modern and Contemporary Poetry, The Penguin Anthology of Contemporary Poetry,* and *Contemporary American Poetry,* edited by A. J. Poulin and Michael Waters. Then again his exclusion might be due less to literary politics than to literary politicking or, rather, the absence thereof on Berry's part. Repeatedly in his essays he has decried the influence of specialization, professionalization, and careerism in American life, including the academic and literary arenas. Careerism has always been an aspect of the literary world, but it is arguable that with the proliferation of MFA creative-writing programs, its sway has increased beyond what was known before the teaching of poetry writing became a profession. "A poet could not write a poem in order to earn a place in literary history," Berry writes. "His place in literary history is another subject, and as such a distraction. He writes because he has a poem to write [as a farmer has a field to plough and plant], he knows how, the work pleases him, and he has forgotten all else."[20] What once might have passed for a commonsensical, noncontroversial statement of fact at the present time begins to sound more and more like nostalgia for a vanished world. In any event, when and if Berry's poems come to be included in future editions of the aforementioned anthologies, it will be, in all likelihood, for the right reasons.

What then, to return to my title, have the three poems by Wendell Berry I have discussed to do with politics? Or, more precisely, what have the refusal to privilege imagination over experience, the insistence on human-natural fellowship, and the proffering of the farmer as a model and touchstone of human existence to do with politics? Berry has argued in various essays his belief that American society is in a state of general cultural disorder, a disorder so pervasive that no political program is capable of remedying it, since politics as practiced at present is itself symptomatic of the condition requiring a cure. "The political condition of the country," he has written, "is one in which the means or the discipline necessary for the achievement of ends have been devalued or corrupted or abandoned all together."[21] Dissolution of the idea of discipline—by which he means a body of traditional knowledge and practice relating to particular spheres of endeavor—in all walks of life has created an ethos tending inevitably to ecological and social disaster. In Berry's estimation, the only probable cure for the condition of cultural disorder is a fundamental change in our ways of thinking—and doing. As he says in "Discipline and Hope":

> The change I am talking about appeals to me precisely because it need not wait upon "other people." Anyone who wants to do so can begin it in himself and in his household as soon as he is ready—by becoming answerable to at least some of his own needs, by acquiring skills and tools, by learning what his real needs are, by refusing the glamorous and the frivolous. When a person learns to *act* on his own best hopes he enfranchises and validates them as no government or policy ever will. And by his action the possibility that other people will do the same is made a likelihood.[22]

At bottom, however, these appeals and strategies toward change would depend upon the fostering of a new ethos. "The key to such a change of mind," he argues, "is the realization that the first and final order of creation is not such an order as men can impose upon it, but an order in the creation itself by which the various parts and processes sustain each other and which is only to some extent understandable."[23]

Though a number of Wendell Berry's writings are obviously political—and sometimes polemical—in that they disparage some governmental programs and recommend others, the more fundamental way in which his work is political comes from his commitment, as evidenced in the examples of his own actions and the precepts of his books, to the project of articulating an alternative: an ethos charged with the vital capacity to nurture consciousness to awareness of the need for an ecologically responsible mode of being in the world. Fundamental to that ethos is a revitalized perception of our relationship to the natural world, according to which we would strive to live in harmony with it rather than simply impose ourselves on it, heedless of what more and more promises to be the inevitable consequence of such an imposition. "Because a community is, by definition, placed," Berry concludes an essay on the value of community, "its success cannot be divided from the success of its place, its natural setting and surroundings: its soils, forests, grasslands, plants and animals, water, light, and air. The two economies, the natural and the human, support each other; each is the other's hope of a durable and livable life."[24]

Notes

1. Ernst Heinrich Haeckel. *The Riddle of the Universe at the Close of the Nineteenth Century,* trans. Joseph McCabe (New York: Harper, 1900), 11. Although it may seem eccentric to some to link Berry with a writer so outspokenly hostile to historical Christianity, I think I am justified by the appropriateness of Haeckel's term to describe what both Haeckel and Berry see as a false relationship posited between humans and the natural world. Furthermore, Berry's strictures on fundamentalist religious thinking echo Haeckel's. Perhaps most important, both writers demystify morality by naturalizing it as, among other things, a survival mechanism: "Moral value, as should be obvious," writes Berry in his essay "Discipline and Hope," "is not separable from other values. An adequate morality would be ecologically sound; it would be ecologically pleasing. But the point I want to stress here is that it would be *practical.* Morality is long-term practicality." See Wendell Berry, *Recollected Essays, 1965–1980* (San Francisco: North Point, 1981), 217. Haeckel's fundamental philosophical principle is the rejection of philosophical dualism; Berry's commitment to this idea seems equally strong. In "Christianity and the Survival of Creation," Berry writes: "I have been talking, of course, about a dualism that manifests itself in several ways: as a cleavage, a radical discontinuity between Creator and creature, spirit and matter, religion and nature, religion and economy, worship and work, and so on. This dualism, I think, is the most destructive disease that afflicts us. In its best-known, its most dangerous, and perhaps its fundamental version, it is the dualism of body and soul." See Wendell Berry, *Sex, Economy, Freedom and Community* (New York: Pantheon, 1992), 105.

2. "It is hardly too much to say," writes Berry in his essay "Christianity and the Survival of the Creation," "that most Christian organizations are as happily indifferent to the ecological, cultural, and religious implications of industrial economics as are most industrial organizations. The certified Christian is as likely as anyone else to join the military-industrial conspiracy to murder Creation." See *Sex, Economy, Freedom and Community,* 94.

3. As Berry points out with considerable élan in "Discipline and Hope," one of the chief rhetorical strategies of such rationalizing is a specious argument to efficiency: "As we use the word, efficiency means no such thing, or it means short term or temporary efficiency; which is a contradiction in terms. It means cheapness at any price. It means hurrying to nowhere. It means the profligate waste of humanity and of nature. It means the greatest profits to the greatest liar. What we have called efficiency has produced among us, and to our incalculable cost, such unprecedented monuments of destructiveness and waste as the strip-mining industry, the Pentagon, the

federal bureaucracy, and the family car" (Berry, *Recollected Essays,* 158). The tendency of the American pro-business lobby and its clients to distort or ignore scientific evidence is legion.

4. Berry addresses this issue directly in "Getting Along With Nature" in *Home Economics* (San Francisco: North Point, 1987): "The defenders of nature and wilderness —like their enemies the defenders of the industrial economy—sometimes sound as if the natural and the human were two separate estates, radically different and radically divided. . . . But there is danger in this opposition, and it can be best dealt with by realizing that these pure and separate categories are pure ideas and do not otherwise exist" (6).

5. Alfred North Whitehead, *Science and the Modern World* (New York: Macmillan, 1926), 138. In various instances Berry has made invidious comments about romanticism: "Later poets [i.e., after Pope] were inclined to see nature and humankind as radically divided and were no longer much interested in the issue of a *practical* harmony between the land and its human inhabitants. The romantic poets, who subscribed to the modern doctrine of the preeminence of the human mind, tended to look upon nature not as anything they might ever have practical dealings with, but as a reservoir of symbols." Wendell Berry, "A Practical Harmony," in *What Are People For?* (San Francisco: North Point, 1990), 105. Although I am clearly in sympathy with Berry's values, I am more than skeptical of his version of literary history which seems to be indebted to currently fashionable promodernist, antiromantic viewpoints in the air when he was a graduate student.

6. In this, Berry is faithful to William Carlos Williams's adjuration "No ideas but in things," as he is to its intellectual antecedent, John Locke's "Nothing in the intellect that is not first in the senses."

7. Wendell Berry, *The Country of Marriage,* in *The Collected Poems of Wendell Berry, 1957–1982* (San Francisco: North Point, 1984), 156–57.

8. Eugene Goodheart, *The Skeptic Disposition in Contemporary Criticism* (Princeton: Princeton University Press, 1984), 62.

9. In his essay "The Loss of the University" Berry revisits this perception: "The silence in which words return to their objects, touch them and come to rest is not the silence of the plugged ear. It is the world's silence, such as occurs after the first hard freeze of autumn, when the weeks-long singing of crickets is suddenly stopped, and when, by a blessedly recurring accident, all machine noises have stopped for a moment too. It is a silence that must be prepared for and waited for; it requires a silence of one's own" (*Home Economics,* 80–81).

10. Berry, *The Country of Marriage,* in *Collected Poems,* 145.

11. Berry extends this idea by pointing specifically to the analogy between poetic form and the forms of other things: "By its formal integrity a poem reminds us of other works, creatures, and structures of the world. The form of a good poem is, in a way perhaps not altogether explainable or demonstrable, an analogue of the forms of other things. By its form it alludes to other forms, evokes them, resonates with them, and so becomes a part of the system of analogies or harmonies by which we live. Thus

the poet affirms and collaborates in the formality of Creation. This I think is a matter of supreme, and mostly unacknowledged, importance." See "The Responsibility of the Poet," in Wendell Berry, *What Are People For?* (San Francisco: North Point, 1990), 89.

12. Berry, *Farming: A Handbook,* in *Collected Poems,* 139.

13. Berry, *Recollected Essays,* 199.

14. Ibid., 195.

15. Ibid., 213

16. Ibid., 217, 213.

17. Wendell Berry, *A Continuous Harmony* (1970; Washington, DC: Shoemaker and Hoard, 2004), 12.

18. Wendell Berry, "The Specialization of Poetry," in *Standing by Words* (San Francisco: North Point, 1983), 13.

19. Ibid., 14.

20. Berry, *Recollected Essays,* 195.

21. Ibid., 157.

22. Ibid., 182–83.

23. Ibid., 172.

24. Berry, *Home Economics,* 192.

John Lane

Berry Britannica

I HAVE BEFORE ME the picture of our larder and the four handsome (empty) bottles of bourbon that are standing upon its deep slate shelves. They are labeled Labrot & Graham, Woodford Reserve, and were gifts from our dear friends Tanya and Wendell Berry on the occasion of their visits to our home. Earlier there had been a bottle of Jack Daniel's and before that something else, but what it was we have forgotten.

I first met Wendell in 1980—to be exact, on Palm Sunday of that year. A friend had shown me a little publication from the Myrin Institute, *The Agricultural Crisis: A Crisis of Culture,*[1] which I'd read with an astonished delight. It told me that its author was a farmer living in Port Royal who taught at the University of Kentucky. He had written three novels, four books of poetry, and several collections of essays in addition to *The Unsettling of America,* the book, I learned, from which the Myrin pamphlet had been extracted. This was valuable but not enough. There was a fever of restless expectation to find out more. Utterly unforeseen, the chance to do so soon came my way.

It was a trip to the West Coast of America that provided me with an opportunity to call on the Berrys on my way back home. Yet when I wrote to him, I had the gravest doubts if my letter would ever find its destination; Kentucky is large, Port Royal, according to my atlas, nonexistent. An inspired call to the university had already drawn a blank—yes, the secretary drawled in her unfamiliar accent, yes, Mr. Berry had taught there but he was one of those ecological types who did not have a telephone. I began to experience real doubts about the propriety of the proposed visit. Then things began to fall in place; I received a reply inviting me to call so long as I did not use a tape-recorder. A week or two later the book my bookseller had found it impossible to trace arrived, the book I wanted to read more than anything other—*The Unsettling of America: Culture and Agriculture*—and I read it on the flight to San Francisco, all 223 pages of it.

Within a few chapters I knew that I was reading a modest masterpiece. I had stumbled across an author saying things that had to be said, and saying them with a natural genius as pure and whole as Thoreau's or, to sharpen the resemblance, H. J. Massingham's. The last time I had felt this excitement was on reading *Small Is Beautiful* in 1973 by the then unknown economist E. F. Schumacher. Berry's work could be compared to that book.

I was met by Tanya Berry at the airport. It was late on a Friday night at the wet end of March. Yet the long journey along the featureless freeway, the silent, empty, country roads, provided as perfect an introduction to what I soon would experience as I could have wished. For as the car's headlights picked out, one by one, the landmarks of their world, his parents' home, his brother's farm, I began to appreciate at first hand one of *Unsettling*'s themes: the theme of settlement, of place, of roots, the enactment of connections. "O love," he writes in one of the poems I had not then read, "O love, / Open. Show me / my country. Take me home."

I met Wendell in the morning. He was taller than I had expected, almost gangly, with inimitable strides; the gestures few, the body vigorous, the old clothes no different from those worn by our farming neighbors at home in North Devon. His face was memorable, long, and rather narrow. It was the face of an intensely practical man yet intellectually serious and refined—and amused. Laughter, I found, played a large part in their family life, laughter punctuated every seriousness.

Wendell drove us, his son, Den, and me, along the road in front of their house bordering the broad Kentucky River. We were on our way to his brother's farm, a beautiful, white wooden house amongst wintry trees. Once in the yard, father and son worked as one, quietly calling the two Belgian mares, Peggy and Nell, from their grazing to the shafts, harnessing them, buckling the harnesses, driving them into the field amongst the cows. Den drove the wagon, Wendell cut the sisal, spreading the tightly packed bales of hay in a wide arc.

Having returned, we sat in the kitchen conversing about many things. Throughout the day we continued to talk about country life and our favorite reading. Had I read Andrew Marvell's *Upon Appelton House*? he asked. Did I know Kathleen Raine's *Blake and Tradition,* which he had been reading that winter? He was concerned, he said, about her enthusiasm for Neoplatonism and the Western esoteric tradition, which devalued the importance of matter. Was C. S. Lewis still read in Britain? Was I familiar with the novels of Edward Abbey or the work of John McPhee? And so it went on.

You may be wondering how I have remembered the details of a conversation held over a quarter of a century ago; the answer is that I haven't. At the time of the visit I made a few notes, and these I wrote up into an article that was published in the journal *Resurgence* later that year.[2] Although I have no wish to make any special claims for the importance of that piece, it was just about the first introduction to Wendell's work to be published in the United Kingdom.[3]

Over the years since that visit Tanya and Wendell have been our guests, and from our home we have had, as it were, a grandstand view of their program of visits in this country. We have learned about his poetry readings in London, his speech at the Soil Association's annual conference in Newcastle, his meeting with Prince Charles, or the Berrys' visit to Schumacher College at Dartington. It is of these that I intend to write, and if my emphasis is on Wendell, it is of them both that I am thinking. Wendell without Tanya would be like William Blake without his Catherine—a duet impossible to imagine otherwise. And it does not end there. Both Tanya and Wendell have been supported by a small group of English friends—Kathleen Raine, Satish Kumar, and Brian Keeble in particular—without whom Wendell would be even less known in this country.

Brian Keeble and the Golgonooza Press

Brian Keeble met Wendell in November 1986. The occasion was the first Temenos Conference at Dartington Hall (which I proposed and helped Kathleen Raine to organize), where Wendell delivered the lecture "Preserving Wilderness," published the following year in *The Landscape of Harmony* by the Five Seasons Press.[4]

Brian was from 1974 to 2004 the sole editor, designer, and publisher of Golgonooza Press, which has produced books by the Traditionalists—A. K. Coomaraswamy, Titus Burckhardt, and Philip Sherrard—and several collections of verse by Kathleen Raine, including her *Collected Poems*. Wendell has taken much encouragement from all these writers. Golgonooza has also published the only hardback volume of Wendell's work in the UK, *Standing on Earth: Selected Essays*. It did not sell well but has a long introduction by Brian Keeble and a foreword by the then director of the Friends of the Earth, Jonathon Porritt.[5]

According to Brian Keeble (who remains one of the Berrys' closest friends in England), Porritt gave a copy of this book to Prince Charles as a Christmas present in the year of its publication, 1991.

I don't know when the prince became aware of aspects of the agroecological philosophy as it is described by Sir Albert Howard (1873–1947) in his *An Agricultural Testament* (1940) and Lady Eve Balfour (1898–1990) in her no-less-influential *The Living Soil*. It was the latter book that inspired the leading UK organization devoted to the promotion of organic agriculture as an alternative to intensive farming methods, the Soil Association.

But whatever the date, the prince shares with Wendell the conviction that the industrialization of agriculture has had unfortunate and seriously damaging results on the environment, on animals, on food, and on the entire culture. In fact, Charles is famous, if not renowned, for his endorsement of organic farming as the way forward for agriculture in this country. In 1996 he delivered the Lady Eve Balfour Memorial Lecture on the association's fiftieth anniversary and has been its royal patron since 1999. The prince himself runs a thousand-acre organic farm, the Duchy Home Farm, which lies close to his house, Highgrove, near Tetbury in Gloucestershire.

There is little doubt that Wendell has been an inspiration for him. I remember the occasion when Wendell first traveled to Highgrove from our house for discussions with the prince but have forgotten the date. And as far as I know that was the first but not the last time they met together.

Kathleen Raine and the Temenos Academy

The poet and Blake and Yeats scholar Kathleen Raine (1908–2003), the founder and inspirer of the Temenos Academy, was another friend and admirer of Wendell's and did all she could to promote his work. The affection and respect they held for one another was considerable.

Kathleen and Wendell met at a Lindisfarne Association gathering in Colorado some time in the late 1970s. On one occasion Kathleen visited the Berrys' home, Lane's Landing, and their visits to London were always accompanied by a party at Kathleen's house in Paulton's Square in Chelsea, her club, or Thetis Blacker's flat.

In 1980, in association with Philip Sherrard, Keith Critchlow, and Brian Keeble, she cofounded the journal *Temenos*. In 2003 its thirteen book-sized volumes were superseded by the *Temenos Academy Review*, which continued to publish contributions by Wendell. Issues 4, 6, 8, 11, and 13 of *Temenos* and issues 1, 2, 3, 6, and 7 of the *Temenos Academy Review* contain either prose or poetry by him.

Wendell gave readings for Temenos in the autumns of 1991, 1998, 2000, and 2005; in 2000 he also delivered a lecture, "Going to Work," which was published as a Temenos Academy publication, *A Sacred Trust: Ecology and Spiritual Vision*, in 2002.

On a bigger scale, the original Temenos Conference concerned "to reaffirm the function of the arts as the mirror of the human spirit" was held at Dartington Hall from 13 to 16 November 1986. The first of its kind, it attracted participants from Australia, India, Spain, Argentina, France, Ireland, Canada, and the United States. Apart from Wendell, Kathleen Raine, and myself, its speakers included Philip Sherrard, Brian Keeble, Keith Critchlow, Dr. Seyyed Hossein Nasr, Joscelyn Godwin, Martin Lings, Christopher Bamford, and Satish Kumar.

Satish Kumar

Satish, a close friend and near neighbor of my wife's and mine, has also played an important role in bringing Wendell's work and vision to the attention of an international public. As the founder and then chairman of the Schumacher Society, Satish invited Wendell (and Gary Snyder) to speak at one of its annual lectures. Wendell's lecture "Land, Community and People" was delivered in Bristol on 23 October 1982.

In addition, Satish has printed a number of Wendell's essays in the leading bimonthly, spiritual, and ecological journal, *Resurgence,* of which since 1973 he has been editor. In the March/April 1990 issue appeared "The Futility of Global Thinking"; in the September/October 1990 issue, "Taking Nature's Measure"; in the May/June 1991 issue, "The Pleasure of Eating"; and in the January/February 1992 issue, "Principles of Ecology." *Resurgence's* circulation may be relatively small—around 15,000 an issue—but it has probably introduced more people to Wendell's writings than any other organ in the UK.

The third means by which Satish Kumar has been instrumental in enlarging Wendell's influence has been through his role as program director of the Schumacher College, an international center for ecological studies established by the Dartington Hall Trust on its estate in South Devon in 1991. Here Wendell has tutored two courses.

Schumacher College

Wendell's courses were held in 1992 and 2000. The first and longest—it lasted for five weeks (from 24 August to 24 September 1992)—had more than twenty students. Its theme, "Nature as Teacher: The Lineage of Writings Which Link Culture and Agriculture," touched on the importance of traditional farming practices for a sustainable modern agriculture. Readings were from Shakespeare, Sir Albert Howard, and Wes Jackson. The second and much shorter course—one week only—was held in October 2000 and was shared with Vandana Shiva and Helena Norberg Hodge, who was then living on the Dartington Hall estate. Its theme was "Community, Sustainability and Globalisation."

Peter Adams, one of the four American participants in the five-week course, has written a fine description of his experience. I quote it in full:

Dear John,
    I've been pondering your request for several days now about Wendell Berry's Schumacher course of thirteen years ago and it is hard to describe in a few words the effect the class had on me. To begin with, we were at Schumacher. That, in itself, worked its magic on both the class and Wendell, allowing all of us to open up to the full potential of each day. And having

Tanya there, as well, added another ingredient to the marvelous soup being prepared and tasted.

The path my life has taken since 1992 is very much connected with being able to listen to Wendell's formal classroom lectures ("sermons in stones") and, as important, interact with him in a way that can only happen at Schumacher. The living arrangements put flesh onto the spoken words.

My most clear and fond recollection is meeting with Wendell, not at the morning lecture space, but in the library in the afternoons just before dinner. There, four to six of us would sit, sip a little scotch, and discuss anything of importance that came up. We were all peers. Wendell sat as one with us; listened and engaged, not as teacher, but as a fellow human, interested in the stories of the day. Our circular discussions were very informative.

And, hearing Wendell read *A Jonquil for Mary Penn* has to be one of the most moving readings I have ever heard. He is a master storyteller. His heartfelt knowledge and wisdom was given in such a way that I left encouraged and empowered to look to the earth as teacher and to find out and speak those stories I had that might help my family, my neighbors, my friends and my community come to a more loving embrace with what surrounds us.

It was because of my having such an enriching five weeks with Wendell that I came back to Schumacher again and again to try and repeat the experience, seven times in all.

Warmly, Peter

North Devon

Since I am writing about Wendell's relationship to Great Britain I should comment on his visits to the region he knows better than any other in this country: North Devon.

One of the reasons my wife and I enjoy the Berrys' visits is that Tanya and Wendell aren't just city-based intellectuals who find refreshment in short visits to the countryside but country people with country values and an understanding of country life. Wendell is also a cultivated reader, one who has absorbed the "Englishness" of English literature and its visual art. So when we go for walks, say to the Scorhill stone circle on Dartmoor, or on Exmoor, or visit a rare-breeds farm or some of North Devon's ancient parish churches—Honeychurch, Samford Courtney, Kings Nympton, or maybe the cathedral in Exeter—or stroll by the river Torridge below our house, a great deal can be and is left unsaid; Wendell and Tanya don't need to be told about the work of R. D. Blackmore, Henry Williamson, Ted Hughes, and Coleridge, or even Samuel Palmer, who have left their imprints on the landscape of North Devon. Nor do they need to be told about the poetry of Edward Thomas, John Clare, and Wordsworth, whose vision informs our understanding of the rural culture in this country, nor about the patterns of farming and the cycle of the year—these are in their blood.

The second reason we enjoy their presence is their zest for life, their sense of fun—even Wendell's golden bourbon in the evening; meals are interspersed not only with good conversation but with lighthearted humor and laughter. Indeed, when I remember the Berrys, I am reminded of Samuel Palmer's famous description of William Blake: "He was a man without a mask," he wrote to Blake's biographer, Alexander Gilchrist in 1855, "his aim single, his path straight-forwards, and his wants few; so he was free, noble, and happy. His voice and manner were quiet, yet all awake with intellect. Above the tricks of littleness, or the least taint of affectation, with a natural dignity which few would have dared to affront, he was gentle and affectionate."

Conclusion

It has to be stressed that Wendell's influence in this country is really limited (as is that of John Muir, Barry Lopez, Edward Abbey, Annie Dillard—any American "nature writer" except Thoreau, really). There are those who admire his work—for example, Richard Mabey and Robert Macfarlane, who wrote an interesting series of articles in the *Guardian* newspaper about writers and landscapes—but nonetheless Wendell's books are otherwise very little known. Our farming neighbors will not have heard of him nor, for that matter, will the majority of the farmers in the UK. An organic farmer near here tells me that at the most there might be two men of the soil in North Devon who might be acquainted with his work.

Nonetheless, Patrick Holden, director of the Soil Association, is very positive about Wendell's importance. He has described him as "one of the most remarkable human beings on the planet at the moment" and tells me that the majority of the association's long-standing members—and there are 25,000 in all—regard him as one of the great figures of our time. For them he is the one with the stature to ensure that the association's present work remains anchored in its original philosophy. "Wendell," he tells me, "is important because although he is not alone in calling for change in the world, he is one of the few whose ideas can touch us at the deepest level of our being; one of the few who are telling us that change must come from the depths of our relationship with nature and ourselves. He rises above the earthly and the worldly problems towards an unprecedented spiritual plane."

Another of this country's leading environmental writers and activists, Jonathon Porritt, agrees. "Wendell Berry," he tells me, "has been one of the most influential sources of inspiration for me over the last thirty years or so. I think his writing (and underlying philosophy) goes to the heart of today's interlocking crises, which are not so much political or economic as spiritual and ontological. But even to give voice to such a representation of Wendell's work is to offer a partial explanation as to why he has been so much less influential here in the UK than he should have been. I think that our take on 'the environment' in the UK is often mind-numbingly rational and mechanistic, and tends to shy away from anything that seeks to dig down just a little deeper."

Another area where Wendell's writing is ignored is the popular press, where you will never read his name. Nonetheless, no less a figure than Andrew Marr, a hugely respected journalist and political correspondent, sang his praises in an unprecedented tribute published in the Sunday *Observer* of 21 May 1995.[6] "It is a disconcerting thing," he wrote, "a shaking thing, to find I share a private passion with the Prince of Wales. But there it is. The passion is for a man, a writer, a tobacco farmer, a poet and an essayist from Henry County, Kentucky, whom history may remember as the single most important and influential political thinker alive today. It is unlikely that you have heard of Wendell Berry. Fame is fickle and prediction mostly daft; but it is likely that your descendants, assuming they are literate, interested people, will know his name."

After the death of Kathleen Raine, a service of thanksgiving was held on 4 December 2003, in the Queen's Chapel in St. James's Palace. Apart from some beautiful music (including *Shanti-Kathleen,* composed by John Tavener) there were two speakers: a heartfelt eulogy by the Prince of Wales, patron of the Temenos Academy, and a no-less-moving tribute by Wendell Berry.

He may not be a household name in the UK, but there are very, very few Americans who have been lauded by such as Andrew Marr—and the future King of Britain.

Notes

1. Proceedings of the Myrin Institute, no. 33.

2. "A Man of Decorum," published in *Resurgence* 81 (July/August 1981).

3. Wendell's first book of poems, *The Broken Ground,* had been published in England in 1966, but most people had missed this.

4. This small but handsome book also contains Wendell's essay "Does Community Have a Value?" and an introduction by the poet and scholar Michael Hamburger, who has been a consistent champion of Wendell's writings.

5. From 1984 to 1990 Porritt was director of the Friends of the Earth, the UK's most influential national environmental campaigning organization. Under his leadership its number of supporters rose from 12,700 to 226,300. Since 1986 he has been program director for the Forum for the Future and is also chairman of the Prime Minister's Sustainable Development Commission.

6. Andrew Marr was editor of the *Independent* newspaper and the BBC's political editor from 2000 to 2005.

Allan Carlson

Wendell Berry and the Twentieth-Century Agrarian "Series"

AS AN ANALYST OF the agrarian crisis afflicting twentieth-century America, Wendell Berry comes after a "series" of writers. He chose the word *series* himself, preferring it over *succession*. He explained that he was unsure "to what extent these people have worked consciously under the influence of predecessors." Berry elaborated: "I suspect that the succession, in both poetry and agriculture, may lie in the familial and communal handing down of the agrarian common culture, rather than in any succession of teachers and students in the literary culture or in the schools."[1] A list of these loosely connected agrarian authors might include Dean Liberty Hyde Bailey of Cornell University, editor Henry Wallace of Iowa, rural sociologist Carle Zimmerman of Harvard University, economists Ralph Borsodi and Troy J. Cauley, poets Allen Tate, John Crowe Ransom, and Donald Davidson, novelists Louis Bromfield, Robert Penn Warren, and Andrew Lytle, historians Frank Owsley and Herbert Agar, biographer and editor Russell Lord, and the Iowa Catholic priest and rural activist Luigi Ligutti.[2]

Among these names, though, there are several in that "series" whom Wendell Berry has acknowledged as forerunners and teachers, toward whom he stands to a meaningful degree in a certain "succession." This short list includes Bailey and Bromfield: "Both of those people have mattered to me," Berry relates.[3] It also includes Tate, Ransom, Warren, Lytle, Davidson, Owsley, and the balance of the Twelve Southerners who published the volume *I'll Take My Stand: The South and the Agrarian Tradition* in 1930. This book's "effect on me has been large," Berry reports.[4]

Wendell Berry's relationship to the twentieth-century agrarians also helps illuminate reasons for his passionate opposition to America's wars, not only to the conflict in Vietnam and the war on terror but also and more remarkably to World War II. Berry's indictment of the "good war" actually forms a major theme in his fiction. On the other temporal side of this conflict, many of his agrarian predecessors also opposed American entry into that war, and for similar reasons. This essay considers, first, the particular influence of Bailey, Bromfield, and the Twelve Southerners, and, second, the agrarian position on war.

Liberty Hyde Bailey

In the essay, "A Practical Harmony" (1988) Berry pays homage to Liberty Hyde Bailey, who seventy-four years earlier had retired from his post as dean of the New York State College of Agriculture at Cornell University. He points specifically to Dean Bailey's "little book with the remarkable title *The Holy Earth,*" published in 1915:

> Most of our difficulty with the earth lies in the effort to do what perhaps ought not to be done. . . . A good part of agriculture is to learn how to adapt one's work to nature. . . . To live in right relation with his natural conditions is one of the first lessons that a wise farmer or any other wise man learns.

Berry also turns to Bailey's earlier, and longer, philosophical treatise, *The Outlook to Nature* (1905), which described nature as the "norm" of existence: "If nature is the norm," Bailey wrote, "then the necessity for correcting and amending the abuses of civilization becomes boldly apparent by very contrast." And he added, "The return to nature affords the very means of acquiring the incentive and energy for ambitious and constructive work of a high order."[5]

Dean Bailey was not opposed to "the necessary pursuits of the human economy," Berry says, but rather sought to bring these pursuits into harmony with nature. An early architect of the farm extension service (which usually draws Berry's critical wrath), Bailey wins praise for holding to a view of things "that, however threatened in his time and since, goes back to the roots of our experience as human beings." As products of the natural world, Berry says, we hold "an inescapable obligation to be nature's students and stewards and to live in harmony with her." Berry proceeds to attach this theme to the classical tradition of Virgil's *Georgics* and to the Old Testament lesson of Job.[6]

These references underscore the broad influence of Liberty Hyde Bailey on the twentieth-century agrarian project.[7] Born on a western Michigan apple farm in 1858, Bailey earned a degree at Michigan Agriculture College in East Lansing and went on to graduate study at Harvard under the famed botanist Isa Gray. He returned to East Lansing in 1885 as the school's first professor of horticulture. Bailey set out to transform the field: "Horticulture the art is old;

horticulture the science is new."[8] He produced a remarkable series of books, including his four-volume *Cyclopedia of American Horticulture,* his four-volume *Cyclopedia of American Agriculture,* the five-volume *Annals of Horticulture,* and *The Plant Life of North America.*

In 1888 Bailey took the chair of the Department of Practical and Experimental Horticulture at Cornell University. He created experiment stations for horticultural research and a model program of extension agents, who would carry research results directly from the university to New York's farmers. He wrote monthly nature-study leaflets for children, distributed through the state's grade-school teachers. He founded two journals, *Country Life in America* (1901) and the *Cornell Countryman* (1903). He created and became dean of Cornell's College of Agriculture in 1904. The school grew tenfold during his decade-long tenure. On his retirement, he was America's foremost plant scientist and among its best-known university professors.

Relative to Berry, though, Bailey's more important influences were as agrarian poet, activist, and metaphysician. The sage of Cornell understood that agriculture is far more than an economic endeavor. Properly pursued, farming is an expression of the mind and the spirit. Bailey saw poetry as "prophecy," a means of grasping aspirations that are "elemental and universal."[9] He wrote hundreds of agrarian poems, some of which were gathered into *Wind and Weather* and other collections. Bailey was also the primary architect of the Country Life Movement. He called for building a vital rural civilization in America, "a radical revivifying and redirection of all rural institutions" toward "the evolving of a new social economy."[10] In August 1908 President Theodore Roosevelt chose Bailey to be the chairman of a new National Commission on Country Life. The commission's report (1909) called for the "rebuilding of a new agriculture and a new rural life." Practical results included the Smith-Lever Extension Act of 1914, designed to carry modern farming techniques and homemaking skills to the countryside, and "the uplift" of rural youth through the 4-H movement.[11] He personally compiled and privately published the curriculum vitae of 2,746 Americans whose work was committed "to the betterment and advancement of rural life," called *RUS* (the *Rural Uplook Service*).[12] And he was a key organizer of the First National Country Life Conference, held 1919 in Baltimore.

More important, Bailey crafted an agrarian metaphysics, an explanation of human purpose and relation to the universe, that has attracted Berry's attention. It rested on a novel reconciliation of evolutionary science and religious faith.

Bailey's first attempt to build this philosophy was in *The Outlook to Nature.* He sought "to idealize the commonplace." His prose was frequently poetic, at times Whitmanesque: "I would preach the sky. . . . City persons have no sky, but only fragments of a leaky roof. . . . Our farm boy has the advantage: he leads something like a natural life. . . . I preach the mountains, and everything that is taller than a man."[13] In his celebration of nature, Bailey insisted that there is no real conflict between true religious faith and the evolutionary theory of Charles Darwin. He held that "the means and methods of Creation" are not parts of the biblical revelation. Darwin's theory, in turn, offers no explanation of purpose: "Strictly speaking, evolution does not attempt to explain Creation, but only the progress of Creation. Whatever its form, it begins where Genesis does—'In the beginning, God.'"[14]

In truth, though, Bailey stood far outside Christian orthodoxy. The "evolution philosophies," he said, "demand that we be willing to free ourselves from every bondage of doctrine and dogma, from tradition and superstitions, from 'authority' and prejudgments." This approach "asks us to lay aside prejudice and small dogmatisms." Bailey thought that the Christian faith had *over*emphasized the supernatural element in church and *under*emphasized it in nature. "Evolution implies that God is not outside nature, but in nature, that he is an indwelling spirit in nature as truly as in man," he concluded.[15]

Bailey's *The Holy Earth* expanded on these themes, transforming them into a fairly radical political and economic program. He drafted this tract in the equatorial heat of summer 1914, while on board a ship heading for New Zealand. In vivid prose Bailey affirmed "the mothership of the earth" and "the essential relation that we bear to it as living parts in the vast creation." For him, the earth was essentially good. His take on evolution stressed not struggle but procreation and cooperation: "The dependence of one being on another, success in leaving progeny—how accurate and how far seeing was Darwin!" Evolution was "the philosophy of the oneness in nature and the unity in living things." The "living creation" was "biocentric": "We have a genetic relation with all living things and our aristocracy is the aristocracy of nature." He called for the preservation of wilderness, free of human manipulation. "It is well to know that these spaces exist, that there are places of escape."[16]

In this natural world, urban life became parasitic. City people proved unable to reproduce themselves, relying instead on the fertility of country folk. Where the farmer "freely aids everyone or anyone to engage in his occupation," those removed from the soil to cities "may display selfishness." Indeed, "to a large extent, manufacturers are selfish." Urban life meant "the occupancy of a few dreary rooms and deathly closets in the depths of great cities."[17]

Bailey declared that "all children are born to the natural sky and to the wind and the earth," rights that are "naturally theirs." Using almost apocalyptic language, he called for a new agrarian order:

In that day we shall take down the wonderful towers and cliffs in the cities, in which people work and live, shelf on shelf, but in which they have no home. The great city expansion in the end will be horizontal rather than perpendicular. . . . We shall learn how to distribute the satisfactions in life rather than merely to assemble them.[18]

In order to give "the people access to the holy earth," Bailey called for "a new way of partitioning the surface," a "communism that is dissociated from propaganda and programs." He declared that *everyone* "should have the right and the privilege to a personal use of some part of the earth." He would redistribute through life trusts agricultural land to all wanting to farm.

Agriculture should also be lifted out of the commercial mind-set. "The measuring of farming in terms of yields and incomes introduces a dangerous standard," Bailey concluded. He defined the true good life as "to farm well; to produce it oneself; to be independent of trade . . . in the furnishing of the table." He especially deplored the modern farmer who "now raises a few prime products to sell, and then he buys his foods in the market under label and tag; and he knows not who produced the materials, and he soon comes not to care."[19]

This state of affairs frequents Wendell Berry's fiction and essays as well. In the novel *Jayber Crow,* for example, Berry points with despair to the farm wives, who formerly came to town with produce to sell and went home with money, but who now came to some more distant town "with only money and went home with only groceries."[20] Explained another way: "Commercial farming must never be separated from subsistence farming. . . . The farm family should live from the farm."[21]

While sharing this perspective on the "modern farmer," Berry does differ from Liberty Hyde Bailey in important ways. The latter held great faith in science and technology, seeing them as allies in rebuilding his new rural civilization. Berry distrusts both. Bailey was a great advocate for the work of the agricultural Extension Service, and he praised the "remarkable effectiveness" of the United States Department of Agriculture (and in truth, most USDA agents from the 1920s and '30s were students of and acolytes for Liberty Hyde Bailey, also yearning to build a great rural civilization).[22] Berry knows the post-1945 "Extension" as given over to the new farming philosophy of "get big or get out."

Still, Berry shares key views with Bailey. Both have been iconoclastic toward organized Christianity. Berry agrees with Bailey that the dualism of orthodox Christian eschatology—setting this world off against the next—has been the source of agricultural and environmental crises. As Berry writes, "If Christianity is contained within churches, which are the only holy places, then Christians are free to desecrate the rest of Creation." By focusing on the salvation of souls, Christianity has become a "specialist" creed involved "directly in the murder of Creation."[23] Both writers have looked to the preservation of wilderness as holy places. And Berry shares with Bailey the temptation to more radical solutions. The Kentuckian yearns for a new economic order, one focused on "reproduction" rather than production, one seeking a "balance between saving and spending."[24] Like Bailey, Berry emphasizes that in farming alone abundance destroys its producers. He calls for building a new "Great Economy," one derived from the Kingdom of God, where there would be no specialization, where all aspects of life would fit together. This implies that farming would need to be lifted out of the competitive economy.[25] And Berry states that "we have, within limits that are obvious and reasonable, the *right* to be small farmers," much as Bailey had earlier declared.[26]

Louis Bromfield

In his essay "Think Little" Berry refers to the Ohio-born novelist Louis Bromfield, who "liked to point out that the people of France survived crisis after crisis because they were a nation of gardeners, who in times of want turned with great skill to their own small plots of ground."[27] More broadly, Berry shares both Bromfield's indictment of industrial civilization and his vision of agrarian renewal, including the necessity of personal example.

As a freshman studying agriculture at Cornell in 1914, the outgoing Lewis Brumfield (he would later change the spelling of both his names) had at least one conversation with the legendary Liberty Hyde Bailey.[28] Bromfield left school early the next year to help out on his family farm. The farm, however, soon faced foreclosure, leaving Bromfield angry and bitter. His subsequent fiction would highlight the conflict between a decent but doomed agrarian culture and the corrupt and dehumanized industrial city.

Bromfield enlisted in the U.S. Ambulance Corps in 1917 and served on the western front in France. The French government awarded him the Croix de Guerre. After the war, he settled in Manhattan and became an editor and journalist. His first novels, *The Green Bay Tree* (1924) and *Possession* (1925), were critically and financially successful. His third novel, *Early Autumn* (1926), won a Pulitzer Prize. Bromfield left for an "extended vacation" in France. He leased a *presbytère* in Senlis, sixty miles north of Paris, and he became a fixture among the expatriate American writers and poets living in France. Bromfield devoted much of his nonliterary time to the cultivation of a large garden. Gaining the friendship of his village neighbors, he received to his great delight an honorary membership in the Workingmen-Gardeners Association of France. The French ministry of agriculture also awarded him a medal for introducing American corn and Hubbard squash to the region.[29]

It was in this setting that Bromfield wrote his great agrarian novel, *The Farm* (1933). Weary of the European literary scene, he turned here to the saga of the settling of the American Midwest and to his own family history as an example of the rise and fall of an agrarian civilization. He traced the story of the Farm from the breaking of sod on the frontier by "the Colonel" to the creation of "a great agricultural democracy" to the fall into "a new autocracy of businessmen and industry."[30]

The Farm itself reached its apogee in the late nineteenth century under the ownership of Maria and Old Jamie. In loving and intimate detail, Bromfield described the order and bounty and fertility of their place:

> Beyond the borders of the flower garden lay the vegetable-gardens with their rows of sweet corn, carrots, beets, and crisp celery and the neat little hills where muskmelons and cantaloupes grew far separated from the spot where their incestuous cousins, the cucumbers, grew. And at the edges, sprawling luxuriantly against the picket fence, grew the enormous rambling vines of the Hubbard squash with their big rocky fruits ripening.

Bromfield explored the half-acre strawberry patch that "was always weedless," where Maria "allowed her grandchildren to go out in the morning and select their own dishes of strawberries, fresh with the dew still on them." The vast garden was the heart of the Farm, "for Maria would have considered it a disgrace to have bought food of any kind." Bromfield added:

> It had been part of the Colonel's dream that his farm should be a world of its own, independent and complete, and his daughter carried on his tradition. The Farm supported a great household that was always varying in size, and in winter the vegetables came from the fruit-house or from the glass jars neatly ticketed and placed in rows on shelves in the big cellar.[31]

Sundays were "a day of festival given over to plenty," featuring "old Jamie's prayers to the Deity of plenty" and Maria, "a kind of priestess who stood apart with . . . pleasure and satisfaction at the sight of her offspring eating the things she had prepared."[32]

The balance of the book focused on the decay of this world: the triumph of "machines" over craft and individuality; the long, losing fight of the farmers against the banks and the railroads; the huge costs and risks carried by farmers for, at best, minimal gain; the land returning to the savage state; the lack of heirs interested in farming; "a whole epoch of American life . . . passing." The novelist reported that "in the end the peddler had won" out over the farmer. Even old Jamie wound up in town, and he spent his last years trying to understand what had happened to his way of life. He changed "from a liberal . . . into a radical because it seemed to him that life in America had become insufferable"; he turned to "the methods of the Anarchist and the Wobblies"[33] in a desperate bid to recover the true American democracy.

Over the balance of the 1930s, however, Bromfield convinced himself that it might be possible to restore the agrarian way through personal action. Unlike *The Farm,* his subsequent novels *The Rains Came* (1937) and *Wild Is the River* (1941) looked with optimism toward starting fresh and building a new agricultural community, "a wide green valley, all ours for the taking."[34] With war descending on Europe, Bromfield brought his family back to America, to Ohio. Not far from his old family homestead, he purchased seven hundred acres of land, naming the place Malabar Farm. He resolved to build a new "community," a large farm that would not displace families, a self-sufficient village that would use scientific methods to avoid the fate of the Farm.

Bromfield's book *Pleasant Valley* (1945) described the early years of this experiment. Openly labeled "romantic," the volume still stands as a satisfying agrarian tract. Bromfield called the book "a personal testament" written "by a man who believes that agriculture is the keystone of our economic structure" and that the prosperity and "even the future freedom of this nation" rests on the soil. He proclaimed the agrarian dream: "What I wanted was a piece of land which I could love passionately, which I could spend the rest of my life in cultivating, cherishing, and improving, which I might leave together, perhaps, with my own feeling for it, to my children who might in time leave it to their children."[35] Bromfield described the stages by which he and his partner Max Drake built Malabar Farm, including a "Big House" designed in the "purest Jefferson Greek revival" style. Like Bailey's *Holy Earth, Pleasant Valley* called for the redistribution of land so that over half the U.S. population might reside on self-sufficient farm plots. The "monstrous, ugly cities"—"as perverse and murderous as Jack the Ripper"—could only produce unrest, insecurity, delinquency, and vice. These "abominations" would be dismantled. He praised the French worker-gardener model of life for its "economic independence," which created security and stability. He lamented the breakdown of family-sized farming in America, which he attributed to "the farmer's dependence upon things which he purchased rather than producing these same things off his own land."[36]

In his later "farm books," however, Bromfield abandoned this vision of the self-sufficient farm reborn. Now dismissing his dream for Malabar Farm as "a nostalgia born of memories of my grandfather's farm," he embraced instead the "new agriculture" focused on large-scale, specialized production, the intensive use of machines, and a commitment to scientific and technological advance.[37]

Still, we find in *The Farm* and in *Pleasant Valley* prototypes for both

Wendell Berry's fiction and nonfiction. The two authors share an analysis of the decline of family-scale agriculture, a common interpretation of history, a reverence for nature, a disdain of organized religion, and a faith in the self-sufficient homestead. And both Bromfield and Berry returned from literary sojourns to create farms, to root their own work in authentic soil.

The Twelve Southerners

Wendell Berry holds a more vexing relationship with the Vanderbilt agrarians who wrote *I'll Take My Stand*. On the one hand, he distances himself from the appeal by the poet Allen Tate to "a great culture of European pattern," replying: "I do not share Mr. Tate's assumption that 'a great culture of European pattern' was either desirable or possible in America." Yet he agrees with Tate that the existence of African chattel slavery in the Old South had served as a fatal "barrier" between white people "and the soil."[38]

Berry also objects to the "condescension" and the "false mythology" of "regionalism." This literary model, "which specializes in the quaint and the eccentric and the picturesque," behaves like an exploitative industry. "The evils" of this approach, Berry insists, are "abundantly exemplified by the cult of 'the South.'" He rejects the "spurious piety" of certain southern appeals to Religion, History, Place, and Responsibility. Initially, Berry acknowledged that "the agrarianism of the Southern Agrarians was . . . a beginning that promised something in the way of a cure." But he added that "the withdrawal of the most gifted of those people into the Northern colleges and universities invalidated their thinking." When they left the South, "their agrarianism was doomed to remain theoretical."[39]

More recently Berry has backed off from this judgment on the Twelve Southerners, calling it "ungrateful and inaccurate,"[40] and later "a piece of smartassery."[41] He reports that he first heard of the book during his sophomore year at the University of Kentucky. A composition instructor, Robert D. Jacobs, labeled something that Berry had written as "agrarian" and referred the student to *I'll Take My Stand*. He bought the book "and read at least part of it about three years later, in 1956." He labels their effect on him to have been "large," and their book to be "in some ways a wonder. . . . My debt to it has increased."[42] In another essay, he proclaims that "the cause for which the Twelve Southerners spoke . . . was not a lost but a threatened cause: the cause of human civilization."[43]

Indeed, Berry goes on to quote extensively from the "Statement of Principles" in *I'll Take My Stand,* the common platform of the twelve. The words chosen include:

The regular act of applied science is to introduce into labor a labor-saving device or a machine. . . . The philosophy of applied science is generally quite sure that the saving of labor is a pure gain, and that the more of it the better. This is to assume that labor is an evil, that only the end of labor or the material product is good. On this assumption labor becomes mercenary and servile. . . . The act of labor as one of the happy functions of human life has been in effect abandoned.

The extract concludes: "The constitution of the natural man probably does not permit him to shorten his labor-time and enlarge his consuming-time indefinitely. He has to pay the penalty in satiety and aimlessness."[44]

Other themes from "A Statement of Principles" also echo in Berry's work. The Twelve Southerners referred to the "economic evils" that "follow in the wake of the machines." They argued that both art and religion depend "on a right attitude to nature"; that the "God of nature" in an industrial milieu "is merely an amiable expression, a superfluity." The statement declared that hospitality, sympathy, romantic love, and family life "also suffer under the curse of an . . . industrial civilization." The new machines did not liberate workers; they evicted them. The rise of modern advertising represented "the great effort of a false economy of life to approve itself." The Southerners declared that "the responsibility of men is for their own welfare and that of their neighbors; *not* for the hypothetical welfare of some fabulous creature called society." They lamented that the "modern man has lost his sense of vocation." They called for "an agrarian society in which agriculture is the leading vocation, whether for wealth, for pleasure, or for prestige," serving as the model that other professions would emulate. Turning to action, the Twelve concluded: "If a community, or a section, . . . or an age, is groaning under industrialism, and well aware that it is an evil dispensation, it must find the way to throw it off."[45]

In another essay, "Still Standing" (1999), Berry again quotes extensively from the Twelve's "Statement of Principles," reporting that "I have read it many times," that it is "the supreme declaration of the book," and that "it has held up startlingly well." He continues: "I know of no criticism of industrial assumptions that can equal it in clarity, economy, and eloquence." Berry praises the Twelve Southerners for their insistence, "virtually alone at the time," on "the importance of the local." He notes here that a prominent member of the Twelve, Donald Davidson, "was to the last a segregationist." Berry absolves the "Statement of Principle" from the racist-by-association charge, noting that the same argument could be leveled against the Declaration of Independence, the Constitution, and even the Gospels. Moreover, in 1930, "the most successful agrarian communities in the United States were probably those of the Midwest, which did not depend on the labor of any subject or oppressed race." Indeed, Berry points out that no racial "'liberal' of any consequence" ever spoke in defense of black American farmers. Rather, the "reduction of the farm population (black and white) has been a joint project of industrial liberals and industrial conservatives." Concluding, he points (in the late 1990s) to "hundreds of organizations, large and small" that are working to resurrect the agrarian dream. "Several of The Twelve Southerners, were they alive today, would agree, and would be pleased."[46]

The Agrarians and Modern War

As the decades pass, Wendell Berry becomes ever more closely identified with antiwar movements in America, from opposition to the Vietnam conflict in the 1960s and '70s to critiques of American-led invasions of Afghanistan in 2001 and Iraq in 2003.[47] The war most often discussed in his fiction, though, is World War II. Indeed, the *negative* impact of this war—popularly called "the good war"—emerges as a major theme of his work. In this stance, he again shares in the example and opinions of his agrarian predecessors, who also saw global war destroying what they held most dear.

Early twentieth-century agrarians commonly lamented or condemned their century's world wars.[48] Liberty Hyde Bailey denounced World War I as a "trade war," "a war of commercial frenzy." He warned that "military power heads toward destructiveness."[49] Louis Bromfield pointed to politicians who had forced "the American people into a wild career of imperialism."[50] As World War II loomed, Donald Davidson, informal leader of the Twelve Southerners, stated that the "decentralist" agrarian program could make no headway if American energies were instead focused on preparation for war. He added, "I should have thought agrarians and decentralists would oppose our entry into the conflict when such entry, no matter what results might be achieved in Europe, would probably be ruinous to their hopes for a healthy reconstruction in America."[51] Other agrarian authors agreed. Baker Brownell warned, "Keep out of European war, or give up hope of rural rehabilitation."[52] Luigi Ligutti argued that if the true American way should be preserved, "we must continue the works for social and economic reconstruction within our beloved land and we must not go out in battle array to save periodically our democracy."[53]

These same themes have resonated in Berry's work. In *Jayber Crow*, the narrator describes the prewar, farm-centered village of Port William—the locale for all Berry's fiction—as whole and complete: "The commercial places in town were still . . . doing business. The people of the town still belonged to it economically."[54] A parallel work, *Hannah Coulter*, dwells in detail on the Christmas dinner held at the Feltner home in December 1941. It becomes a kind of last communion for the still intact rural community gathered there, a great self-sufficient feast:

> On the table at last, after our long preparations, were our ham, our turkey and dressing, and our scalloped oysters under their brown crust. There was a cut glass bowl of cranberry sauce. There were mashed potatoes and gravy, green beans and butter beans, corn pudding and hot rolls.

But, as the war looms, it grows clear that this world "could not last."[55]

Instead, Hannah's first husband Virgil, "a good, decent, gentle, beloved young man with the blood keen in his veins," goes to war, where he disappears "into a storm of hate and flying metal and fire," the "outer darkness." In Port William, the war becomes "a bodily presence. It was in all of us and nobody said a word." As it takes away all the young men and boys, "a new silence," "a strange silence" settles over those left behind.[56]

Berry's judgment on World War II is harsh: there were no morally superior combatants, just "ignorant boys, killing one another." Hannah Coulter dislikes it when "the dead [are] made to agree with whatever some powerful living person wants to say," and she ponders whether the lost Virgil is a hero: "Is the life and freedom of the living a satisfactory payment to the dead in war for the dying?"[57] Berry implies that the answer is no. Similarly, Jayber Crow sees the "good war" as just another conflict inflicted by the great powers and forces on the "invisible, nameless, powerless little places" in the world. World War II "would be a test of the power of machines against people and places; whatever its causes and justifications, it would make the world worse." He continues: "The dark human monstrous thing comes and tramples the little towns and never even knows their names."[58]

Over several powerful and disturbing pages of *Hannah Coulter*, Berry describes the Battle of Okinawa. After summoning the image of Christ risen on Easter, he equates "the *little earthly homelands* such as Port William" with "the farming villages of Okinawa." He recasts the battle as one "of *both* armies making war against a place and its people," describing the deaths of 150,000 villagers "as the fighting drove them out of their homes and they wandered with children and their old people into the fields of fire."[59]

Through his characters Berry also shows the consequence of the war to be the end of Port William and of the agrarian possibility. Jayber Crow describes the people moving away and the machines coming in.[60] The war brings a "great sorrow and a great fear" into the village; "the world was changing." Hannah Coulter sees "the good farm economy" weaken and wither. The "wayward" passing of farmland across the generations starts with "the end of World War II." After 1945 the "picture puzzle" that had been Port William becomes less complete; "the lost pieces were not replaced." The "membership" that had defined the Port William community fades.[61] "The old ways were ending," the dance of community stands "broken, dismembered in the Land of Universal Suspicion."[62]

This analysis leads Berry to his view of perpetual war: "The War and the Economy were seeming more and more to be independent operators. . . . Also it seemed that the War and the Economy were more and more closely related. They were the Siamese twins of our age."[63] In a terrible vision, Hannah Coulter sees all little places, all the *true* homelands, threatened by "a human storm of explosions and quakes and fires, a man-made natural disaster gathering itself up over a long time out of ignorance and hatred, greed and pride, selfishness and a silly love of power." This force could pass like "a wind-driven fire over the quiet land and people. . . . It could happen anywhere," including Port William.[64] Berry's poem on the first Gulf War can also been read as his judgment on the "good war":

> For we have given up
> Our sight to those in power
> And to machines, and now
> Are blind to all the world.
> This is a nation where
> No lovely thing can last.
> We trample, gouge, and blast;
> The people leave the land
> The land flows to the sea.
> The men and women die,
> The fine old houses fall.
> The fine old trees come down.[65]

Many of Berry's predecessors would have agreed.

Writing in 2002, Wendell Berry remarks that "we agrarians are involved in a hard, long, momentous contest, in which we are so far, and by a considerable margin, the losers." He continues:

> I believe that this contest between industrialism and agrarianism now defines the most fundamental human difference, for it divides not just two nearly opposite concepts of agriculture and land use, but also two nearly opposite ways of understanding ourselves, our fellow creatures, and our world.[66]

In this contest, Berry should not be seen as a lone warrior. Instead, he should be understood as an eloquent voice building on a century-long agrarian conversation, and as the heir to giants such as Bailey, Bromfield, Ligutti, and the best of the Twelve Southerners.

Notes

1. Wendell Berry, "A Practical Harmony," in *What Are People For?* (San Francisco: North Point, 1990), 105.

2. This larger story is told in Allan Carlson, *The New Agrarian Mind: The Movement toward Decentralist Thought in Twentieth-Century America* (New Brunswick, NJ: Transaction, 2000).

3. Private letter, Wendell Berry to Allan Carlson, Nov. 17, 1994.

4. Wendell Berry, "The Regional Motive," in *A Continuous Harmony: Essays Cultural and Agricultural* (San Diego: Harcourt, 1972), 66.

5. Berry, *What Are People For?*, 103.

6. Ibid., 104.

7. The two principal biographies of Bailey are Phillip Dorf, *Liberty Hyde Bailey: An Informal Biography* (Ithaca: Cornell University Press, 1956) and Andrew Denny Rodgers III, *Liberty Hyde Bailey: A Story of American Plant Science* (1949; New York: Hafner Publishing, 1965 [facsimile of the 1949 edition]).

8. Quoted in Dorf, *Liberty Hyde Bailey,* 59.

9. Liberty Hyde Bailey, *The Outlook to Nature* (New York: Macmillan, 1905), 32.

10. Liberty Hyde Bailey, *The State and the Farmer* (New York: Macmillan, 1908), 111–13.

11. U.S. Congress, *Report of the Country Life Commission,* 60th Cong., 2nd sess., 1909, S. Doc. 705.

12. Liberty Hyde Bailey, *RUS: Rural Uplook Service. A Preliminary Attempt to Register the Rural Leadership in the United States and Canada* (Ithaca: Privately published, 1918), 3–5.

13. Bailey, *Outlook to Nature,* 54–56.

14. Ibid., 277–78.

15. Ibid., 286, 291–93.

16. Liberty Hyde Bailey, *The Holy Earth* (1915; Ithaca: New York State College of Agriculture and Life Sciences, 1980), 10, 23, 59, 100.

17. Ibid., 27, 30–31, 44.

18. Ibid., 44.

19. Ibid., 31–34, 38, 50, 63.

20. Wendell Berry, *Jayber Crow* (Washington, DC: Counterpoint, 2000), 275.

21. Wendell Berry, *Home Economics* (San Francisco: Counterpoint, 1987), 124–25.

22. Bailey, *Holy Earth,* 94.

23. Wendell Berry, *Sex, Economy, Freedom and Community* (New York: Pantheon, 1992/1993), 114.

24. Wendell Berry, *The Unsettling of America: Culture and Agriculture* (New York: Avon, 1977), 81–85, 217.

25. Berry, *Home Economics,* 56, 176; and Berry, *The Unsettling of America,* 42.

26. Berry, *Home Economics,* 174; emphasis in original.

27. Berry, *A Continuous Harmony,* 83.

28. Ivan Scott, "Bromfield: The Forgotten Author," unpublished manuscript, 1–24.

29. Louis Bromfield, *Pleasant Valley* (New York: Harper and Brothers, 1944), 8.

30. Louis Bromfield, *The Farm* (New York: Harper and Brothers, 1933), 310.

31. Ibid., 87–88.

32. Ibid., 93.

33. Ibid., 68–69, 257, 270, 331, 338–41.

34. Louis Bromfield, *Wild Is the River* (New York: Harper and Brothers, 1941), 323–24.

35. Bromfield, *Pleasant Valley,* 8.

36. Ibid., 51, 57–60, 232–33, 247, 300.

37. See Louis Bromfield, *Malabar Farm* (New York: Harper and Brothers, 1948); and Louis Bromfield, *Out of the Earth* (New York: Harper and Brothers, 1950).

38. Wendell Berry, *The Hidden Wound* (San Francisco: North Point, 1989), 79.

39. Berry, *A Continuous Harmony,* 63–66.

40. Ibid., footnote on 66–67.

41. Wendell Berry, "Imagination in Place," in *Place in American Fiction: Excursions and Explorations,* ed. H. L. Weatherby and George Core (Columbia: University of Missouri Press, 2004), 75.

42. Ibid., 74–75.

43. Wendell Berry, "Discipline and Hope," in *A Continuous Harmony,* 120.

44. Quotation in Berry, *A Continuous Harmony,* 120–21; from Twelve Southerners, *I'll Take My Stand: The South and the Agrarian Tradition* (1930; Baton Rouge: Louisiana State University Press, 1962), xl–xlii.

45. Twelve Southerners, *I'll Take My Stand,* xxxvii–xlviii.

46. In Wendell Berry, *Citizenship Papers* (Washington, DC: Shoemaker and Hoard, 2003), 153–63.

47. Regarding Berry's stance on "the war on terror," see Wendell Berry, "A Citizen's Response to 'The National Security Strategy of the United States of America,'" *Orion* (2003); at http://www.oriononline.org/pages/om/03-20m/Berry.html (4/10/05).

48. A prominent exception was Herbert Agar, coeditor of *Who Owns America?* (1936) and author of the agrarian tract *Land of the Free* (1935). See Carlson, *New Agrarian Mind,* 142–45.

49. Bailey, *Holy Earth,* 17, 79.

50. Bromfield, *Farm,* 179. It is true, though, that Bromfield was intensely anti-German. See *Pleasant Valley,* 8.

51. "Decentralization: The Outlook for 1941. A Symposium of Opinion," *Free America* 5 (Jan. 1941): 11–12.

52. Ibid., 10.

53. Letter, L. G. Ligutti to Senator Clyde Herring, Jan. 13, 1941; Box D-2; Luigi G. Ligutti Papers, University Archives, Marquette University, Milwaukee, WI.

54. Berry, *Jayber Crow*, 4.

55. Wendell Berry, *Hannah Coulter* (Washington, DC: Shoemaker and Hoard, 2004), 38.

56. Berry, *Hannah Coulter*, 31, 36, 168; Berry, *Jayber Crow*, 145.

57. Berry, *Hannah Coulter*, 5, 56.

58. Berry, *Jayber Crow*, 139, 142.

59. Berry, *Hannah Coulter*, 167–72; emphasis added.

60. Berry, *Jayber Crow*, 275.

61. Berry, *Hannah Coulter*, 41, 94, 121, 135, 179.

62. Wendell Berry, *Remembering* (San Francisco: North Point, 1988), 56, 95.

63. Berry, *Jayber Crow*, 273.

64. Berry, *Hannah Coulter*, 172.

65. Wendell Berry, *A Timbered Choir: The Sabbath Poems, 1979–1997* (Washington, DC: Counterpoint, 1998), 125.

66. Berry, *Citizenship Papers*, 143–44.

"I would say that maybe we can discriminate between poets who have fed on a certain kind of destructiveness for their creative glow . . . as against those who have composted themselves and turned part of themselves back in on themselves to become richer and stronger, like Wendell Berry, whose poetry lacks glamour but is really full of nutrients."—Gary Snyder, "The East West Interview," in *The Real Work: Interviews & Talks, 1964–1979*
Photograph by Guy Mendes, courtesy of Ann Tower Gallery

Bill McKibben

A Citizen of the Real World

IN THE WEEKS and months that followed the attacks of September 11, "God Bless America" became the unofficial national anthem. Soon every ball game paused in the seventh inning so some overblown tenor could belt out the bathetic words that Kate Smith had first made popular—the demand that the Almighty favor "our home sweet home." The lyrics comforted and complemented, fitting perfectly with the national conviction that we had been singled out for attack because of our goodness, our love of freedom. They were at first a balm, but soon became cheap grace.

And if there's anything Wendell Berry has never had much use for, it's cheap grace. Writing a year after the attacks, in a response to the newly announced National Security Strategy of the Bush administration, he chose as an epigraph the chorus to the second verse of another, far greater song, Katherine Lee Bates's "America the Beautiful." Indeed, he chose what I think are some of the most loving, stern, and perceptive words ever written about our country:

> America, America
> God mend thine every flaw
> Confirm thy soul in self-control
> Thy liberty in law

For a real patriot, the implied lament in those lines, the recognition of our particular national weakness, is piercing. And Wendell Berry is perhaps our greatest patriot.

That essay was not in fact Berry's first in the wake of the attacks. In the ashes and dust of the World Trade Towers, President Bush offered only the unnecessary advice to hug our children and the tragicomic admonition that we should return to normal by going back to shopping. His legislative program was war on Iraq and tax cuts for rich people. Berry, by contrast, wrote almost immediately a long essay, "In the Presence of Fear." In it he said, à la Bates, that instead of being diverted by trembling or self-righteousness, "we citizens of the industrial countries must continue the labor of self-criticism and correction" that had begun in earnest with the demonstrations against the World Trade Organization in Seattle two years before. "We must recognize our mistakes."[1]

In fact, September 11—which for a while poleaxed most of our thinkers into silence or rote repetition of the official line—offered Berry the chance, perhaps nearing the close of his long career, to write in more explicit terms about a theme implied in all the body of his long work: citizenship. In a series of essays given timely national distribution by *Orion* magazine and collected along with earlier work in a volume titled *Citizenship Papers,* he built up a sustained and powerful argument, all the more extraordinary an accomplishment because "citizenship" is not an easy idea to approach directly, at least not anymore. It's one of those words that carry a whiff of the old-fashioned, conjuring up the orator at the bandstand on the Fourth of July. It also carries more than the hint of duty, of responsibility to something larger than oneself (a hint that probably explains why it seems slightly antique). And this is precisely the sense in which Berry used the word.

Responsibility to what? Well, responsibility to land, and responsibility to one's neighbors, and responsibility forward and backward in time, not that in Berry's view these are very much different. His poems and novels and essays have always been about the citizenship of marriage, the citizenship of neighborhood and community, the citizenship of man and animal and soil. But these late essays have stripped down the argument to its bare essentials. (Stripped down the writing, too. More and more often, Berry dispenses with anecdote, with example, and even with transition, substituting a Mosaic fondness for the Roman-numeraled commandment. I confess to a nostalgia for the roomier writing of an earlier day, and I imagine these new essays may be hard for recent converts to his writing to adjust to. But there is something strong about the bare urgency and unhedged plainspokenness of this work).

In essence, Berry holds up two worlds and asks us which is the nursery of real citizenship: on the one hand, the consumer paradise that we've built since World War II, now based on an endlessly spreading globalization, and, on the other, a world in which local communities produce more of what they need and people pass up the lowest price to support their neighbors. Hence:

> A nation can be independent, as our founders instructed us. . . . Though independence may at times require some sort of self-defense, it cannot be maintained by the defiance of other nations or by making war against them. At the very least, a nation should be able sustainably to feed, clothe, and shelter its citizens, using its own sources and by its own work. And of course that requires a nation to be, in the truest sense, patriotic: Its

citizens must love their land with a knowing, intelligent, sustaining, and productive love. They must not, for any price, destroy its beauty, its health, or its productivity.[2]

That destruction, of course, is precisely what Berry has spent his career chronicling and mourning, and attempting to persuade us to reverse. From his Kentucky base he has watched the consolidation of American agriculture ("get big or get out"), not to mention the endless hunt for cheap energy that has blasted the top off countless Appalachian mountains, making low the high places and raising up the valleys in a manner quite different from the one Isaiah had in mind. "The economy, always obsessed with its need to sell products, thinks obsessively and exclusively of the consumer. It mostly takes for granted or ignores those who do the damaging or the restorative and preserving work of agriculture and forestry. The economy pays poorly for this work, with the unsurprising result that the work is mostly done poorly."[3] Or this:

> At present, in the face of declining finite sources of fossil fuel energy, we have virtually no energy policy, either for conservation or for the development of safe and clean alternative resources. At present our energy policy is simply to use all that we have. . . . At present our agricultural policy is to use up everything that we have, while depending increasingly on imported food, energy, technology and labor.[4]

This wreckage—the abandoned rural communities, the atmosphere filled with carbon dioxide, the eroding soil, the chemically soaked and tasteless food—is seen by many, including many environmentalists, as the unfortunate by-product of a basically sound system that merely needs a little tweaking, a few more filters, to make it work. But Berry is having none of it. Environmentalists, he cautions in a sharp piece called "In Distrust of Movements,"

> should begin by giving up all hope and belief in piecemeal, one-shot solutions. . . . Even now, after centuries of reductionist propaganda, the world is still intricate and vast, as dark as it is light, a place of mystery, where we cannot do one thing without doing many things, or put two things together without putting many things together. Water quality, for example, cannot be improved without improving farming and forestry, but farming and forestry cannot be improved without improving the education of consumers—and so on.[5]

There are no shortcuts, and there are no easy outs.

If all of this sounds a tad, well, grim, that's because there's a sense in which it is. Arrayed against the jolly world of "Lowest Prices Always" and yet more tax cuts and flying in Chilean lettuce all winter long, it's not the easiest of sales to make. Berry can be awfully stern, and sometimes it's hard not to take it personally. He has a sturdy agrarian contempt for "recreation," for instance, as he leans on the plow handle to watch people "bicycling or boating or hiking and camping" and knowing that they are not for the most part capable of the necessary "husbandry and wifery of the world."[6] As a person who likes to cross-country ski more than almost anything on earth (including gardening), this makes me shuffle my feet and stare at the ground. Reading Berry is a little like reading the Gospels. He tells us over and over again not to do the things we at first blush want to do, like go for the cheap price, or build the big house. (And sometimes he is very stern indeed—he adds a postscript to a recent essay, "The Failure of War," that is a daunting challenge in the name of responsibility to the liberal orthodoxy on abortion rights.)

But reading Berry is like reading the Gospels in another way as well—there is the constant undercurrent of real joy, or at least the sense that real joy is possible precisely when one takes up one's responsibility; when one stops shirking the various citizenships to which we are called and begins actually to love and honor the land and the neighbor. This joy—alloyed of course with the suffering and toil and occasional despair that is part of any ultimately joyful reality—illuminates most of all Berry's novels. The Port William membership is just that: a membership, a citizenry. It is impossible to read those tales and not fantasize at least a little about becoming a farmer, about growing old on land that you have worked and that has worked you, about passing on that land and that citizenship to your children and your neighbors. Berry is our great poet of community, and on his tongue that word loses the sentimental airiness that lately threatens to rob it of any meaning.

The proof of this particular pudding is very much in the eating, and it is here that we must pause to note something truly remarkable. In the last twenty-five years, even as the Wal-Marts have metastasized, even as the concentrated animal feeding operations have spread their stench across the Midwest, even as the air has filled with carbon dioxide and the temperature has begun ominously to rise—even in the middle of all that, the Restoration has begun. Citizens both urban and rural have begun to reemerge. "I know from my friends and neighbors and from my own family that it is now possible for farmers to sell at a premium to local customers such products as organic vegetables, organic beef and lamb, and pasture-raised chickens," he wrote as long ago as 1996. "This is the pattern of an economic revolt that is not only possible but is happening."[7] And in the decade since, it has spread like potato beetles in my garden. The number of farmers' markets has doubled, tripled—some of them draw 25,000 customers in a day. The number of projects in community-supported agriculture, in which customers buy a share of a farmer's annual production, has increased exponentially as well. Any restaurant with a tablecloth stars the local items on its menu. Yale College has a dining hall where it offers food grown only in state and in season, and the line to eat there stretches out the door.

This, as I say, is happening in the shadow of the other, giant, lumpish economy. They are juxtaposed in many places. In Vermont, where I live, another 81 dairy farms went out of business last year, leaving us with only about 1,200 where once they were in every valley. The state secretary of agriculture says not to worry because we still produce as much milk as ever; and too many local residents vote to let Wal-Mart build in their towns, hastening the endless rush toward cheapness that has undone their neighbors.

But at least those Wal-Marts face fights everywhere they want to go—the citizenry has grown emboldened to that extent. What's more, the most populated county in Vermont last year showed an increase of 19 percent in the total number of farms. Most of these are small, geared toward selling at the farmers' markets, not able to be the sole support of a family. But in the center of the state's biggest city, Burlington, 177 acres farmed by a variety of tenants under the aegis of the Intervale Foundation now supply nearly one twelfth of the city's fresh food. People pay a little more for it not only because it tastes good but because they understand that doing so is the price of citizenship, the real marker of their professed sense of community. And with that support this agrarianism spreads—I was able to make it through all of last winter in icy Vermont on entirely local food. In fact I ate like a king.

I worry that in his stern modesty Berry is not completely aware of how important a role he has played in these developments, in this reassertion of an active citizenry. I state categorically that I know of no farmer involved in this movement who does not have a well-thumbed copy of *Home Economics* or *The Unsettling of America* or some such on her shelf. I cannot tell you how many bathrooms I have peed in while reading a framed copy of "The Mad Farmer Manifesto" hung above the toilet. Through sheer power of both rhetoric and example (and without the example the rhetoric wouldn't mean nearly as much) he has touched off this Restoration.

At Middlebury College a few years ago, students—all of them having read Berry—decided to start a college farm-garden. Within a year they'd done all the bureaucratic and all the agricultural work to bring in their first crops, which were soon appearing in the dining halls and on common-room tables. It keeps growing—by now it is one of the college's showpieces, a magnet for prospective students, a point of pride for alumni. Its first graduates are leaving —not for brokerage houses and advertising agencies and the other arms of the individualist economy, but to apprentice with CSAs, to work for the Slow Food movement, patiently to build their own small farms. Not out of a sense of drear duty, but because they've discovered they wish to be citizens of the actual gritty connected and joyful world. Each patch in the garden is named for some luminary who has inspired them; it is no accident that the Berry Patch stands near the center of it all.

Notes

1. Wendell Berry, *In the Presence of Fear* (Great Barrington, MA: Orion Society), 2.
2. Wendell Berry, "A Citizen's Response to 'The National Security Strategy of the United States of America,'" in *Citizenship Papers* (Washington, DC: Shoemaker and Hoard, 2003), 10.
3. "In Distrust of Movements," in *Citizenship Papers*, 48.
4. "The Failure of War," in *Citizenship Papers*, 28.
5. "In Distrust of Movements," in *Citizenship Papers*, 49.
6. Ibid., 47.
7. "The Whole Horse," in *Citizenship Papers*, 122–23.

P. Travis Kroeker

Sexuality and the Sacramental Imagination: It All Turns on Affection

> For sexual love is the heart of community life. Sexual love is the force that in our bodily life connects us most intimately to the Creation, to the fertility of the world, to farming and the care of animals. It brings us into the dance that holds the community together and joins it to its place.
> —Wendell Berry, *Sex, Economy, Freedom and Community*

AT THE BEGINNING OF the chapter simply titled "Bridal" in Wendell Berry's elegiac novel *Remembering,* Andy Catlett passes through the airport "Gate of Universal Suspicion" and finds himself reduced. The electronic eye is not merely an abstracting, depersonalizing gaze that admits "passengers" according to the apparent harmlessness of their personal effects. Its more sinister effect is to foster the disembodying gaze of erotic fear and fantasy that comes to replace the loving eye of the soul when the vision of trust has been lost. "Where one may be dangerous, and none is known, all must be mistrusted. All must submit to the minimization and the diaspora of total strangeness and universal suspicion."[1] Andy feels himself disembodied by the lovely women who pass all around him, "flesh suggesting itself, as they move, in sweet pressures against cloth."[2] Yearning toward them in lonely desire, apart from any kind of personal knowing, Andy's longings are literally connected to disembodied relations, the realm of purely mental fantasy:

> It seems to him that he is one among the living dead, their eyes fixed and lightless, their bodies grave, doomed to hurry forever through the abstraction of the unsensed nowhere of their mutual disregard, dead to one another. *This is happening to my soul. This is happening to the soul of all the world.* All in the crowd are masked, each withdrawn from the others and from all whereabouts. The light of their eyes, the warmth of their

countenances, the regard of their consciousness and thought, their body heat—all turned inward. . . . The good level look of their eyes lost.[3]

The transportation corridor that is the modern airport is a "noplace" that represents the dismemberment of a culture in which the dance of communal love, shared imagination, and common memory has been broken. No one may dwell there. It is a site of dishabitation, not unlike the dream (in an anonymous modern hotel room) of "darkness visible"[4] that opens the novel, in which a great causeway built across the creek valley of Andy's farm has rendered his place unrecognizable. The world of nature and agrarian dwelling has been reduced to rubble, replaced by another symbol of human intention given over to the domination and exploitation of nature for private, commodified ends—a Hobbesian "state of nature" replicated in the artifices of the Leviathan that now dwarfs the landscape around the globe with its imperial vision of technological peace. Berry's claim, in the essay and the novel, is that the commodification of the world, its ugly and tawdry disembodiment—seen above all perhaps in the rush toward "virtual reality" reducible to systems of information-processing—is rooted in the loss of sacramental sexuality as the heart of community life, a claim worthy of consideration in both its religious and moral meanings.

Wendell Berry's prophetic cultural criticism is rooted in a sacramental imagination. This is evident in all of his writing—poetry, fiction, essays—especially his short novel *Remembering* and the title essay, "Sex, Economy, Freedom and Community."[5] It may ring strange to call Berry's imagination "sacramental," since he is neither a Catholic like Flannery O'Connor (in whose writing explicitly sacramental symbolism is in prominent display) nor, indeed, very overtly "religious" at all. I expect that Berry would strongly resist any attempt to locate him religiously, or perhaps to identify him as a "religious" or "Christian" writer.[6] In these regards perhaps Berry is typically liberal Protestant—deeply suspicious of institutional Christianity, especially its claims to authority, and of the separation between the sacred and the secular (not to be confused, I hasten to add, with the separation of church and state) in everyday life.

In this essay I shall nevertheless attempt to "claim" his work for membership in the Christian community—not in an ideological, triumphalist form (whether Protestant or Catholic, liberal or conservative) but in the form that bears witness to the messianic or Christic mystery that would restore all creation to its intended ordering of love in God. The word *sacrament* comes from *sacramentum,* the Latin translation of the Greek word *mysterion.* It also has a more religious, ecclesial meaning—as Augustine put it, a visible or embodied sign of an invisible grace. That is, a sacrament participates for its meaning in the mysterious gift of God's unbounded being that ever seeks incarnation.

This is why, even for Protestant Christians—who might oppose the proliferation of formal institutional sacraments because they reinforce merely institutional authority or overly restrictive boundaries between sacred and profane, holy and secular—marriage is a sacrament, as it is a visible and therefore particular sign of the unbounded mystery of divine love for all creation. One text often read at Christian weddings is Paul's agape hymn in 1 Corinthians 13, where the language of love is language of "boundlessness": love is "boundless in bearing, boundless in believing, boundless in hoping, boundless in enduring." The Greek phrase is *ta panta,* and it means "all things," which is language that relates to God. Interestingly, then, marriage as a sacrament does not privilege the love between the happy persons who form a couple, nor does it signify institutional authority and all the "rights and privileges" legally pertaining thereto. Marriage as a sacrament underwrites neither conventional sentiments about romantic love nor conventional legal definitions about the proprieties of marriage. Marriage is rather about two people giving themselves away to one another but also to the boundlessness of God's love in the world. Love is finally not a mere feeling or sentiment; it is God's activity that can be received only in humility as the gift of affection, fulfilled only by sharing it in and for the world.

I expect that is why one never sees the Bible's words about love on Hallmark wedding cards. Even Paul's great and beautiful hymn to love undercuts conventional sentiments. Love is not about great and beautiful fantasies of heroic goodness by attractive, noble, brilliant human beings. In fact, of course, 1 Corinthians was not written as advice to marrying couples. It is about the kind of love needed to build up healthy communities that are "kindly affectioned" toward one another;[7] it is written for all human beings about all of life. The Bible makes no real distinction between the love that sustains marriages and the love that sustains any other relationships. While all relationships are distinct and particular, the qualities and disciplines of love needed to sustain them are the same. This is countercultural because our culture loves to focus exclusively on the romantic couple and their exclusive happiness, whose beauty and good sentiments will somehow carry them through. The Bible doesn't see it that way. Love is not exclusive; it is shared. Love is not a feeling, but an act of giving ourselves away unconditionally, as God does. That means love cannot finally stop with the other person to whom one gives oneself. A loving marriage is a giving of everything to the end that love seeks—the "all in all" of God's boundless loving care of the world.

That is why marriage as a sacrament is so powerful and so frightening, because it is a particular expression of finding one's life by losing it. That is why love must be patient and embody the qualities stated in 1 Corinthians 13: "love is not jealous, not boastful, not puffed up, not rude, not self-centered, not irritable or resentful." Love entails the putting away of childish things for the real work of building up love in the world. And yet the hope is boundless: nothing less than the bodily transformation of all things into the mysterious glory of God's immortal beauty.[8] That is why giving ourselves away in marriage is an occasion of joy—we celebrate it because as humans we are made for intimate communion with God and with all of life. It is also, I expect, why the Bible so often invokes the metaphor of erotic intimacy, marriage and the wedding feast, for the relationship between God and the earthly community, between the land and the people,[9] for the final fulfilling unity between the earthly and heavenly cities.[10] In John's gospel, Jesus' first miracle occurs at a wedding in Cana: he turns water into wine.

The sacrament of marriage is therefore anything but a private, exclusive act; it is always related to the larger community of which it is a part. One of the great dangers of romantic love is that it privatizes love, depriving it of essential nutrients. A flourishing marriage needs the community to sustain it and will in turn build up the community and the life of the world. After all, 1 Corinthians 13 is placed right in the middle of a long section on the body of Christ—all are parts of one body. Marriage and, for that matter, sexuality are not merely the consensual sharing of bodies in private acts. Married intimacy is not private; it nurtures and is nurtured by something larger. It includes and cares for others—not only children that might come along, but also strangers, neighbors, the poor and lowly, the lonely and sorrowing, the oppressed and suffering—all to whom it is joined in the boundlessness of divine love, God's mysterious body both visible and invisible.

This sacramental imagination, one that broadens and deepens the meaning of sexual love and its kindly affection in this manner, also informs Wendell Berry's artistic and cultural vision. Such an imagination is not in the first instance a moralizing or polemicizing or indeed a "prophetizing" vision, but one that attends to the motive pulls of affection that join us to the world in love. Quoting the words of Revelation 4:11, Berry emphasizes that God created all things (*ta panta*) for God's pleasure, and he defines pleasure as "affection in action."[11] The human vocation, says Berry, is therefore to "preserve God's pleasure in our use of things," and it is this that I believe to be the center of the sacramental imagination rooted in the divine affection that moves all things to their true and glorious end.

The Body Broken: Exile

Remembering is a novel that explores embodiment and disembodiment. Andy Catlett has lost his right hand to a farming machine, and this unhanding, his bodily loss and deformity, has become for him an all-consuming grief, an obsession with absence and mortality. This obsessive grief has cut him off from his family and his community, and indeed from himself. The novel opens inside Andy's horribly disorienting nightmare in a San Francisco hotel room far from home, after he has literally crossed the boundary of communal membership from which he has lived in emotional exile since the accident. Here no one knows him, and he must finally face himself and his own absence from himself, his fall into disorientation, away from the motivating loves that have hitherto given his life purpose within a common life: "He is absent himself, perfectly absent. Only he knows where he is, and he is no place that he knows. His flesh feels its removal from other flesh that would recognize it or respond to its touch; it is numb with exile. He is present in his body, but his body is absent." And yet Berry can also describe Andy's exilic state as that of "his own disembodied soul," a soul that in the presence of his family and community these long months since the loss of his hand has been the embodiment of grievance, resisting the embodied graces all around him. In this state he has lost his hold on the purposes, the passionate intentions of his incarnate soul, and so he is "out of control" and without "the use of his best reasons."[12]

Berry's artistic vision is radically incarnational—it brooks no dualistic split between body and soul, and this prevents it from becoming ideological. While critical of the industrial capitalist ethos that animates contemporary America, Berry does not detach himself from it in a purist agrarian, antiurban stance. Instead he explores the complex capillaries of human desire—ordered and disordered—that shape its perils and possibilities. The fictional world of Port William is his own, not another's, and Andy Catlett resembles no one more closely than Wendell Berry himself: a university-educated writer who has turned away from the conventional career path of his upwardly mobile generation, choosing to return to his native farming community in order to cultivate a lived alternative to the globalizing industrial economy; yet also active beyond that local community in the American academy and wider public culture, facing like everyone else the difficult choices of which technological-cultural innovations and opportunities to engage and which to reject—and, as any true lover of wisdom must, giving the best possible account of the difference between a good life and a bad one. It is Andy's journey toward discerning this difference, rooted in a meditative exploration of the anatomy of his remembered loves, that constitutes the dramatic movement of *Remembering*.

In these crucial regards Berry's vision is both Platonic and Christian, un-conventional though that hypothesis may seem. Neither Plato nor biblical Christianity brooks a split between body and soul that drives them apart; in-deed, for both, such an isolating dualism prepares the way for idolatries and ideologies that manipulate reality in the service of disordered human desires that destroy the erotic divine-human dance of creation. Such abstracting du-alisms foster fantasies of power that damage people and places, and that may be effectively and affectively countered only by the conscious cultivation of a loving imagination held together by an "attention" or "attunement" to the mysterious spiritual-material integrity of creation. This loving imagination is cultivated by the human soul, but never in isolation from the body—one's own or the body politic, related as these are in mysterious ways to the whole body of the whole or the "all" (*pan, ta panta*) in which we live and move and have our being as mortal, time- and place-dwelling members. Of course, we find ourselves always *already* as members of a body broken, seeking to be re-stored to harmonious cosmic relationship that has been lost, cut off, dam-aged. The question is how to find our way back, the return of the exiled to a home in which all may dwell peaceably in a beloved community. This ques-tion animates the Berry corpus, and so it gives contemporary form to the ancient Platonic-Christian quest for the restoration of truth, goodness, and beauty of the created world.

In "Sex, Economy, Freedom and Community" Berry elaborates the per-spective from which we may interpret the dramatic movement in *Remembering,* a perspective both Platonic and Christian. He begins with the public scandal of the sexual harassment claim against Clarence Thomas by Anita Hill (eerily evocative of that more famous American sexual scandal that emerged in the highest public office only a few years later), which for Berry displays the pro-cess of community disintegration: the attempt to deal publicly with some-thing that lies at the vulnerable heart of public life but for which there can be no public solution, namely sexuality (what Plato would call *eros,* and for which the Bible has no one technical term but a variety of words extending from the Hebrew "to know" to eros). The problem, as Berry sees it, is not that the "public" ought not to treat of "private" matters, for sexuality is surely not merely a private matter either. Rather, the problem lies in the breakdown of the crucial "mediating third" between public (national or state) and private (individual or personal) life, namely local, embodied community defined as "the commonwealth and common interests, commonly understood, of people living together in a place."[13] Such a community is a lived interdependence of members whose mutual trust and well-being over time in a place is nurtured by their disciplined gifts of loyalty and affection. Just this has been undermined by the purveyors and propagandists of the industrial economy, who treat all desires as private and attached to the only public goods that count—commodities and rights, that is, private possessions pursued by contractual individuals whose boundless interests and lusts are governed by the technical legal procedures of an umpire state.

How has this happened? To understand this we must consider the economy of desire, in which sexuality has been detached from shared communal disciplines of loyalty and affection, and thus allowed to become a free-floating, abstract (timeless, placeless) commodity. No longer embodied in souls joined to one another and to their communities in the bonds of affection, sexual desire is fetishized, attached to whatever object of desire meets one's private fancy and procured with the currency earned by whatever marketable skills he or she brings to the public economy, limited only by "means" and the contractual conditions that govern the globally competitive marketplace of commodities and rights. In such an economy of individual-global desire, "liberated" from the burdens of community membership and its difficult temporal and spiritual disciplines and responsibilities, individuals may "fulfill" themselves according to their own global fantasies. Ironically, however, such freedom and fetishized desire quickly lead to the degeneration of community, and hence of loyalty, affection, and trust required by and nurtured through the lived interdependence of households (*oikia*)—and so, ultimately, the degeneration of *oikonomia* and of public life itself. Private fantasy detached from embodied community results in the breakdown of a truly human imagination:

> In sex, as in other things, we have liberated fantasy but killed imagination, and so have sealed ourselves in selfishness and loneliness. Fantasy is of the solitary self, and it cannot lead us away from ourselves. It is by imagination that we cross over the differences between ourselves and other beings and thus learn compassion, forbearance, mercy, forgiveness, sympathy, and love—the virtues without which neither we nor the world can live.[14]

In *Remembering*, of course, this is precisely the experience of Andy Catlett. Unable to accept the brokenness of his body, blaming himself for the moment of carelessness that allowed the harvesting machine to take his hand, ashamed of his bodily deformity (delight of the eye) and his one-handed awkwardness in work and sex (wisdom and play/power of godlikeness), Andy turns away from his community, the joined households that constitute the alternative local economy, to the prevailing globalizing economy of industrial abstraction. Increasingly, as he comes to live within himself and his own fantasies of magical restoration (only to awaken to the ongoing, poisonously bitter reality of his own brokenness), he loses trust in the possibility of his brokenness being shared in the interdependency of communal economy. He cannot respond to the beckoning bodily invitations of his friends to rejoin, as a full partner, their common life; and because he cannot respond within the imagination of love, he feels these invitations only as judgments upon his inadequacies and failures. He has literally fallen into disunion—fallen away not only from his family and local community but from himself, from love itself. He no longer knows or trusts his own desire as it becomes detached from his covenant community, and he dwells in the isolation of fear. Berry treats this with explicit reference to the biblical drama of the fall and exile, the only cure for which (as Andy's wife, Flora, tells him) is forgiveness.[15]

Without the possibility of forgiveness—repenting of his self-isolating fallen desire for a world of his own making with himself at its unbroken golden center—he cannot find a path of return, and he cannot be restored either to himself or to his loves. The root problem here—Wendell Berry is absolutely clear about this—is not primarily a sociopolitical structure or ideology. It is a disorder in the soul. The language of prayer, the soul's communion with that convocation of voices that points the soul beyond itself toward divine mystery, begins to obtrude itself increasingly as an unbidden grace in Andy's memory in the title chapter of the novel: "*This is the history of souls. This is the earthly history of immortal souls.*" It is only as he allows himself to attend to these remembered voices, rather than the litany of complaints "like a graven image of himself,"[16] that he begins to recover what it means for his soul to be ordered in the divine image, to remember the true origin and end to which his loves and life are joined. This memory is anything but abstract, anything but a fantasy or fetishized commodity.

In order to see how this makes possible a restorative response to the body broken, we need to turn to the two illuminating accounts of the soul and sexuality: the Platonic and the biblical. The Greek word for soul, *psyche,* is closely tied to the word for "breath" and thus joins together in living imagination what many caricatures of the Platonic have fatefully divided—body and spirit, intelligence and desire, mortal and immortal. The erotic movement of the soul is variously imagined by Plato, but nowhere more vividly than in Socrates' description in the *Phaedrus* of the soul as a winged chariot pulled by two horses: on the right side the noble, beautiful lover of honor who is modest and self-restrained, guided by gentle verbal command; on the left an ugly nag with bloodshot eyes, companion to beastly indecency, shaggy around the ears, deaf as a post, barely yielding to the whip and prod combined. The charioteer looks through the erotic eye—indeed in some manner *is* that eye—and sees an embodied vision of beauty. The whole soul starts to warm up and tingle with desire. The obedient horse waits, controlled by modesty, while the other horse now no longer responds to either whip or prod but just starts jumping around, trying to get to the object of desire so as to propose the pleasures of sex. Reluctantly the other horse and the charioteer follow, and as they get closer, the charioteer is bowled over by the divine vision of Beauty, not just as an object of desire but as a pathway to transcendent mystery in which particular beauty dwells. In reverent awe he pulls back on the reins fiercely. The noble horse pulls back willingly, drenching the soul with the sweat of shame and wonder, but the other horse, after having recovered from the pain of the bit and the backward fall, starts cursing the other two for their cowardice and lack of "manhood."[17]

At the next opportunity the intemperate horse lowers its head, bites the bit, and pulls shamelessly, but again the charioteer sees the vision of Beauty and yanks back on the bit so hard that it covers the foul-speaking horse's mouth in blood. This experience is repeated, and the horse is eventually humbled, so that the whole outfit may follow the object of beauty in reverence and awe. This opens the pathway to friendship—another kind of love, *philia*—with the beautiful one, which, far from diminishing the pleasure of eros, intensifies it and nurtures it in mutuality, as the soul of the loved one begins to share the beautiful vision of the lover. All of this, Plato says, happens through the *eyes,* "which are the natural routes of love and beauty to the soul," making possible, as Socrates' concluding prayer to Pan makes clear, the cultivation of friendship in the shared possessions of the good life:

> O dear Pan and all the other gods of this place, grant that I may be beautiful inside. Let all my external possessions be in friendly harmony with what is within. May I consider the wise man rich. . . . Friends have everything in common.[18]

Clearly the eye of the soul is a very different organ of perception and discernment from the electronic eye that replicates the external operations of the optic nerve. It is an eye that is intimately tied to desire in a sexual love "understood as both fact and mystery, physical motion and spiritual motive."[19] Wendell Berry, like Plato (though he prefers to cite Shakespeare), relates sexual love to the eyes and the meeting of embodied souls through shared imagination that participates in the erotic movement of divine Beauty, animating and ordering all particular communities in their specific places. The attention of such disciplined affection brings with it redemptive power to heal what is broken, to order harmoniously what is disordered and partial. This is precisely Andy's experience in the "turning around" of his own soul when he "remembers" himself, that convocation of voices and imaginings and choices that have made him who he is and which invites him to become "answerable" again, a loving soul joined to the "all" in his particular place.

There is another account of the soul and sexual love that helps illuminate Andy's return, and that is the biblical one, beginning with the Hebrew *nephesh* (soul) in Genesis 2:7: "God formed Adam from the dust of the ground and breathed into his nostrils the breath of life and he became a living being [*nephesh*]." The soul is not something you "have" but is something you "are," and this "being" is always already a "being joined," especially to the shared breath of life that is both body and spirit. The biblical language of *nephesh* is also related to the throat or the mouth, both the intake of breath and of physical sustenance, the organ of desire and also of speech.[20] "Hungry and thirsty their *nephesh* fainted within them," says the psalmist, and this may only be satisfied by divine gift: "God satisfies the thirsty *nephesh* and fills the hungry *nephesh* with good things."[21] The soul is connected not only with creation but also procreation, the striving to be fruitfully related to the ordering of creation as the ordering of love. It is no accident that the living *nephesh* Adam may be completed only by a partner to whom he is joined, nor is it accidental that God's relation to the people is imaged in graphic sexual terms. Yet the Bible is utterly clear-sighted about the disordering of desire ever couching at this threshold of relations—the lust to dominate, possess, control, consume for oneself what is really a divine gift to be shared. So in Genesis 34 the sexual crime against Dinah, the daughter of Jacob and Leah, by the prince of Shechem is evocatively depicted: "he saw her [the eye], he seized her and lay with her and violated her. And his *nephesh* was drawn to her," but in a possessive manner that elicits violent revenge by her brothers. So also are the infidelities of the people to the covenant God described as whoring and harlotry that ruin the people and their land through undisciplined, unjust grasping that destroys spiritually and physically alike.

We see in this biblical imagination of soul and sexuality the wide web of dramatic relations entailed in this most intimate language. "The blood is the *nephesh*," says the Deuteronomist,[22] which is why Cain's brother's blood cries out to God from the ground in Genesis 4. The lifeblood (like the life breath) is not merely a chemical soup but the sacred and mysterious life force that binds brothers together in sacramental consanguinity, in relation to the divine Creator through a material-spiritual ordering of love and covenantal-communal responsibility. This too is displayed in Andy's "reminding himself of himself" and his need to seek forgiveness for having broken trust with the nuptial relations that have given him his life with its orienting motives. In fleeing from rural Port William to the coastal city in which he can indulge his anonymous fantasies about other possible lives in other countries with other women, at the very "verge and immensity of the continent's meeting with the sea," he comes face to face with the flawed heart of his foolish dream—"the little hell of himself alone." Here in this place "distance comes upon him. . . . All distance is around him, and he wants nothing that he has. All choice is around him, and he knows nothing that he wants. *I've come to another of thy limits, Lord. Is this the end? Out of the depths have I cried unto thee, O Lord*."[23]

The unbidden words of prayer that beckon Andy to return at the limit of his flight from himself—here where the land joins the limitless sea, the unbounded ocean of erotic desire—come to him in the voice of his grandmother, Dorie, who herself uttered the psalmist's words in her own limited condition of economic-spiritual desperation, words scribbled on the back of a bill of crop debt that had become one of the motives of Wheeler Catlett's life passed on to Andy's life—a motive to which Andy has become unfaithful even while paying public lip service to it (25). These words now "breathe themselves out of him in her voice and leave him empty, empty as if of his very soul" (52). Into this emptiness is poured a host of erotic memories, now not fantasies of unknown foreign women and objects of exotic beauty, but rather of his own people. His turning is marked by a memory of sexual love embodied in his grandmother, to whom he has been sent after her husband's death (at a time when "the old ways were ending") to help her and to provide her company. One of their shared activities is to raise chickens hatched in the traditional way under a hen, and young Andy loves it.

> The evening comes when they put the eggs under a setting hen in the henhouse. He is holding the marked eggs in a basket, and Dorie is taking them out one by one and putting them under the hen.
> "You know, you can just order the chickens from a factory now, and they send them to you through the mail."
> "But this is the *best* way, ain't it?" He hopes it is, for he loves it.
> "It's the cheapest. And the oldest. It's been done this way for a long time."
> "How long, do you reckon?"
> "Oh, forever."
> She puts the last egg under the hen and strokes her back as she would have stroked a baby to sleep. Out the door he can see the red sky in the west. And he loves it there in the quiet with her, doing what has been done forever.
> "I hope we always do it forever," he says.

> She looks down at him, and smiles, and then suddenly pulls his head against her. "Oh, my boy, how far away will you be sometime, remembering this?" (57)

This is a motivating memory for Andy because it has come to shape his desire in a direction and purpose that gives his life its meaning. It is an erotic memory, a memory of love and sexual begetting that involves one who has "begotten" him, not only biologically but spiritually. It is also, of course, a remembered vision of beauty and the beautiful, an insemination that gives birth much later to his loving return, here at his limit. This memory is rooted in an imagination offered him in a pattern of community choosing and membership that has claimed him in affection, that he himself has chosen to become answerable to, and that continues to hold him. Andy's father, Wheeler, who himself returned from urban exile to the farm because he wanted "to see good pastures, and the cattle coming to the spring in the evening to drink," has taught his son to see this beauty: "'Look,' he says, . . . 'If that won't move a man, what will move him? It's like a woman. It'll keep you awake at night.'" There is a spiritual awareness present in this erotic imagination that binds the visible realm to what is beyond the visible, and yet is mediated always in flesh. It calls Andy back to the community of love he has abandoned, in the memory of touch, his grandmother's and others.' "Help us," says Nathan Coulter as he looks straight at the handicapped Andy, taking hold of his right forearm and giving a little tug. "Boy? The sun's up"—the words accompanied by his grandfather's old fingers prodding his shoulder and breastbone through the covers, a gesture in which Andy also remembers standing over his own sleeping son to wake him to live in the new day (68, 69, 49).

Through these erotic memories that cry out to Andy from the depths, he is able to remember himself and come to awareness of the life history of his soul—itself a tangle of embodied, remembered relations in which he may discern again, if he pays attention in affection, the true direction of his desire and longing for wholeness. In these memories—which relate him not only to his particular past but to "the shining land, the land beyond, which many travelers have seen, but never reached. . . . the flashing waves and wings, the glory that moves all things resplendent everywhere" (59; cf. 48)—Andy meets his own life and finds that "he is held, though he does not hold. He is caught up again in the old pattern of entrances: of minds into minds, minds into places, places into minds. The pattern limits and complicates him, singling him out in his own flesh" (57–58). Andy meets his own life, eternally significant within the incarnate terms within which it is *given;* claimed by love, in body and soul, he is able to recover his purpose, to return again to live out the truth of the erotic relation with wholeness, with all that is, in all of his wounded partiality. It is here that redemption may be mysteriously, sacramentally found and received.

The Body Rejoined: Bridal

Andy, having turned in penitence away from the hopeless self-pity and self-isolation that has driven him from his community and from himself, must return in penitence to the embodied attachments of his soul's loves. He must come home, moving "in the pattern of a succession of such returns" (66), as his father the prodigal before him, as he and his wife, Flora, had done early in their marriage, to his native country that now dwells in such visible cultural decline. The fulfillment of his freedom lies not in being liberated from the burdens and sufferings of love, the bonds of affection, but in giving himself away again in trust to his loved ones. The life he has been given and the hold to which he will remain answerable is possible only by trust—"all has depended upon trust":

> And then he failed his trust and his choice, and now has chosen again, again on trust. He has made again the choice he has made before, as blindly as before. How could he have thought that it would be any different? How could he have imagined that he might ever know enough to choose? As Flora seems to have known and never doubted, as he sees, one cannot know enough to trust. To trust is simply to give oneself; the giving is the future, for which there is no evidence. And once given, the self cannot be taken back, whatever the evidence (110).

The sexual and sacramental heart of community life is the pledge of love "until death," a momentous "giving themselves away" in a joining that no law or contract could ever enjoin.[24]

In contrast to the sexuality of the global industrial economy rooted in the contractual politics of commodified possessions and litigation, the sexuality of community as Berry defines it is rooted in the trust of marriage and its *leitourgia*—the visible and social cultivation of the works of love. As both Plato and Saint Paul believed, a society that is litigiously dependent upon courts and lawyers for its justice and well-being is already in serious crisis. Paul admonishes the Corinthian community, "In fact, to have lawsuits at all with one another is already a defeat for you," precisely because it signals an absence of trust and the burgeoning pursuit of narrow self-interest.[25] Those liturgically bound in the sacraments of love may not afford to be thus litigiously "liberated" from the communal disciplines of affection and loyalty, lest they find they have become alienated selves in a shared world characterized by suspicion, competition, and violence where all human eye contact has become uncomfortable, indeed dangerously untrustworthy.[26]

It could be no surprise to Berry that Paul's letter to the Corinthians discusses sex, lawsuits, and economic matters as if they were intimately interrelated. That is precisely what a sacramental imagination should expect: "Do you not know that your body is a temple of the Holy Spirit which you have from God, and that you are not your own?"[27] Such an imagination may not be acquisitive, for it does not live in the world as if it were a storehouse of commodities to be possessed: "What do you have that you did not receive? And if you received it, why do you boast as if it were not a gift?" (4:7). The body itself is, for Paul, not private or individual property, but a gift given in the service of the divine glory that indwells it and in which each part is related to all others. This gift may therefore only be enacted in membership: for Paul, membership in the messianic body celebrated in the Eucharist, the festival of paschal self-giving (5:8). Hence in Paul's controversial instructions about marriage (7:1ff), as in his comments about *porneia* and lawsuits, his primary point is that a human being ought not to treat one's self—whether one's body or one's possessions—as if it were one's "own" or worse, one's "own thing." This is to violate the meaning of creation as the gift of God to which all creatures are joined "as if not" (*hos me*) possessing it (7:29ff). This is not to say that the material world is less meaningful than the spiritual because it is "passing away." To the contrary, Paul's point is that the material is truly itself only when it selflessly bears the mysterious movement of God within it. It is precisely for this reason that he gives so much attention to material bodily matters.

Such a sacramental imagination is not morally simplistic, as Paul's discussion of the question regarding the eating of food sacrificed to idols indicates. Contrary to many conventional moralistic discussions of "the strong" and "the weak," Paul does not resolve this issue with respect to doctrinal formulations or the superiority of moral insight. "Knowledge puffs up, but love builds up. Anyone who claims to know something does not yet have the necessary knowledge; but anyone who loves God is known by God" (8:1b–3). An appeal to knowledge as a spiritual possession is no less idolatrous, no less a violation of spiritual embodiment than are litigious claims, *porneia,* and greed. In the case of food, it is the presumption that we humans have rights (moral, economic, or political) based on possessed knowledge of the true nature of things that is problematic, whether that knowledge be sacralising or secularizing (notice the complex reversals in 1 Corinthians 8–10 that subvert the knowledge claims of both the strong and the weak). Food is a mysterious divine gift, and when it is treated either as a commodity (a "mere" possession, the product of our intellectual and technical knowledge) or as a sacral object (and ascribed a fetishistic power that mediates false godlike claims to cultural authority) it becomes a weapon of violence against the eucharistic body—real people (and, one might add, the real creation that God alone names good) for whom Christ has offered himself: "Therefore, dear friends, flee from the worship of idols. . . . The bread that we break, is it not a sharing in the body of Christ? Because there is one bread, we who are many are one body, for we all partake of the one bread" (10:14ff). The only possible way of sharing in this sacramental body is to partake of the gifts of creation with thankfulness ("for the earth is the Lord's and the fullness thereof") and in a manner that seeks not one's own advantage, but that of the other, the many others, to whom one is joined in membership. This is "to do everything for the glory of God."

How does this relate to the exile and return of Andy Catlett in Berry's *Remembering*? It is a vision of divine glory, "the glory that moves all things resplendent everywhere,"[28] that stands at the culminating point of Andy's turn, and it is a vision not of knowledge but of love to which he again gives himself completely in trust. He gives himself back to that partial mortal body "whose love has claimed him forever. He will be partial, and he will die; he will live out the truth of that. Though he does not hold, he is held."[29] He is held in the love that, Paul says, "never ends," that "does not insist on its own way . . . is not irritable or resentful," that "bears all things [*ta panta*], believes all things, hopes all things, endures all things."[30] The glory of this love is no abstraction, no pious formula. It is that which moves Andy's soul and toward which he turns again in penitential trust—both in prayer, the unceasing prayer of his soul during his journey back home, and in deed as he gives himself again in nuptial trust to Flora, the Harford Place, and the membership of Port William. It is only as he asks Flora's forgiveness that he will once again be able to meet her eyes.[31] Citing in prayer the words of the penitential Psalm 51, "Have mercy upon me, O God, after thy great goodness," Andy envisions Flora giving herself to him again in mysterious power as a bride: "a gift to him such as he did not know, such as would not be known until the death that they would promise to meet together had been met, and so perhaps never to be known in this world," and he is overwhelmed by a gratitude "as if not his own."[32]

In Berry's telling, this nuptial event upon which households are founded in self-giving trust that also makes possible the shalom of living communities is above all a sacramental act, a participation in the "sabbath peace" that is the beauty of all creation. Giving himself again in penitential trust to the immortal dance that gathers up all mortal creatures into the completeness of the divine "all in all" (*ta panta en pasin*),[33] Andy is given a vision of the movement of the eternal in time:

And now above and beyond the birds' song, Andy hears a more distant singing, whether of voices or instruments, sounds or words, he cannot tell. . . . He understands presently that he is hearing the light. . . . The light's music resounds and shines in the air and over the countryside, drawing everything into the infinite, sensed but mysterious pattern of its harmony. From every tree and leaf, grass blade, stone, bird, and beast, it is answered and again answers in return. The creatures sing back their names. . . . They sing their being. The world sings. The sky sings back. It is one song, the song of the many members of one love, the whole song sung and to be sung, resounding, in each of its moments. And it is light.[34]

This vision comes to him in darkness ("now we see in a mirror darkly"[35]) but this darkness is very different from the dark hotel room that opens the novel in which Andy dreams his hellish nightmare of his and the world's diminishment. This is the darkness of human longing for God, for the wholeness of all creation, for what cannot be humanly known or named. And in this darkness in which the human self is emptied of its own dominating intentions, Andy himself and by extension all creation may be reshaped, mysteriously and wondrously reborn. In this place, as if through the eye of Heaven itself, Andy is able to see "Port William and its countryside as he never saw or dreamed them, the signs everywhere upon them of the care of a longer love than any who have lived there have ever imagined."[36]

There is present here a vision of the resurrection of the body, the resurrected body of "all things" and therefore also of the particular body of the Port William membership, "in the peace of a sabbath profound and bright."[37] The experience of the sacramental body dwells in sacramental vision, a vision that moves beyond what it knows as "its own" in an imagination of boundless love. Only the recovery of such an imagination in the lived experience of particular persons and places will enable our culture to move beyond the destructive fantasies and superstitions of the one-night stand, whether of the industrial-agriculture or the industrial-sex variety. Wendell Berry's literary corpus educates our affections in such a vision of the miracle of life mysteriously created and re-created by divine gift. For this we give thanks.

Notes

1. Wendell Berry, *Remembering* (New York: North Point, 1988), 93.

2. Ibid., 93.

3. Ibid., 94.

4. This "darkness visible" is the hell into which Milton's Satan awakes. See *Paradise Lost* 1.63. Thanks to Jason Peters for this reference.

5. The title essay in Wendell Berry, *Sex, Economy, Freedom and Community: Eight Essays* (New York: Pantheon, 1993).

6. In *The Long-Legged House*, Berry states: "Though I know that my questions *are* religious, I dislike having to *say* that they are. But when I ask them my aim is not primarily to get to heaven. Though heaven is certainly more important than the earth if all they say about it is true, it is still morally incidental to it and dependent on it, and I can only imagine it and desire it in terms of what I know of the earth. And so my questions do not aspire beyond the earth. They aspire *toward* it and *into* it. Perhaps they aspire *through* it" (1969; Washington, DC: Shoemaker and Hoard, 2004, 200). Such is the radically incarnational character of Berry's religious imagination. See also Katherine Dalton, "Rendering Us Again in Affection: An Interview with Wendell Berry," *Chronicles* (July 2006): 31–36. "I'm a Christian in a sense I'm uneasy to talk about," Berry says. "From a sectarian point of view I'm a marginal Christian. But then I'm a marginal person, I'm a marginal writer. But I do know the Bible; I've had the sound of the King James Version in my ears and mind all my life. I was never satisfied by the Protestantism that I inherited, I think because of the dualism of soul and body, heaven and Earth, Creator and creation—a dualism so fierce at times that it counted hatred of this life and this world as a virtue. From very early that kind of piety was distasteful to me" (33).

7. Romans 12:10.

8. 1 Corinthians 15.

9. Isaiah 62:4ff.

10. Revelation 19, 21.

11. Wendell Berry, "Economy and Pleasure," in *What Are People For?* (San Francisco: North Point, 1990), 136ff; cf. 98–100.

12. Berry, *Remembering*, 21, 27, 33.

13. Berry, *Sex, Economy, Freedom and Community*, 119.

14. Ibid., 143.

15. Berry, *Remembering*, 35.

16. Ibid., 41.

17. Plato, *Phaedrus*, 253d–254e.

18. Ibid., 279c.

19. Berry, *Sex, Economy, Freedom and Community*, 135.

20. See the entry *nepes* in Hans Walter Wolff, *Anthropology of the Old Testament*, trans. M. Kohl (Philadelphia: Fortress, 1974), 10–25.

21. Psalm 107: 5, 9.

22. Deuteronomy 12:23.

23. Berry, *Remembering*, 43, 45, 51; hereafter cited in text.

24. In *Sex, Economy, Freedom and Community* (137–38) Berry articulates it as follows: "Lovers must not, like usurers, live for themselves alone. They must finally turn from their gaze at one another back toward the community. If they had only themselves to consider, lovers would not need to marry, but they must think of others

and of other things. They say their vows to the community as much as to one another, and the community gathers around them to hear and to wish them well, on their behalf and on its own. It gathers around them because it understands how necessary, how joyful, and how fearful this joining is. These lovers, pledging themselves to one another 'until death,' are giving themselves away, and they are joined by this as no law or contract could ever join them. Lovers, then, 'die' into their union with one another as a soul 'dies' into its union with God. And so here, at the very heart of community life, we find not something to sell as in the public market but this momentous giving. If the community cannot protect this giving, it can protect nothing—and our time is proving that this is so."

25. 1 Corinthians 6:7.

26. Wendell Berry, like Paul in 1 Corinthians 12 and Plato in the *Republic* (462), thinks of the healthy community in terms of the metaphor of the body; see *Sex, Economy, Freedom and Community*, 155.

27. 1 Corinthians 6:19, hereafter cited in text.

28. Berry, *Remembering*, 59; cf. 48.

29. Ibid., 58.

30. 1 Corinthians 13:8, 5, 7.

31. Berry, *Remembering*, 112.

32. Ibid., 113.

33. 1 Corinthians 15:28.

34. Berry, *Remembering*, 122.

35. 1 Corinthians 13:12.

36. Berry, *Remembering*, 123.

37. Ibid., 123.

Morris A. Grubbs

A Practical
Education:
Wendell Berry
the Professor

SITTING IN a small circle of graduate students at the University of Kentucky in spring 1988, I entered into a conversation whose questions and attempts at answers are timeless. They continue to serve humanity more essentially, more pressingly, with each passing day. The course was "Readings in Agriculture"; the students were mostly in graduate programs of agriculture and English; the professor was Wendell Berry. Focusing on the links between culture and nature, we read selections by seventeenth-, eighteenth-, and nineteenth-century British poets and twentieth-century British and American agriculturalists. Reading them for pleasure and instruction—and for encouragement, as our professor insisted—we noted several recurring ideas. Central among them was nature as teacher and judge, a nature not global or abstract but local and specific, or, in Alexander Pope's words, "the genius of the place." A set of critical and practical questions emerged from our conversations with the texts and with each other: What is humanity's proper relationship to nature? What is the most appropriate scale of the relationship? What is the extent of the human right to use gifts of the natural world? What happens when humans fail to balance use with return? What is it that humans can do, and what mustn't they do? These questions became our mantra. And, although I didn't fully realize it until semester's end (for our professor mentioned his own published writing only once, when he surprised us near the end of the course by handing us each a gift copy of *The Unsettling of America*), they are the core questions that Wendell Berry's life and work attempt to answer.

Just as he is as a farmer, a neighbor, and a writer, Berry as a professor was concerned foremostly with the local and the practical issues of a problem. His grounded thinking was one of his great professorial traits. The elements of the text—words, images, settings, and the like—were crucial to interpretation, certainly. But what was paramount to him were the patterns within and connections between texts that pointed to didactic themes. What he watched for in his reading, and taught us to watch for, are the ways a text intersects with the practical and ethical life. The supreme concern in our conversations was how a piece of literature affirms principles of sustainable living, how it instructs human beings for a harmonious relationship with nature and with each other. Through this lens we read Edmund Spenser's *Mutabilitie Cantos,* John Milton's *Comus,* William Shakespeare's *As You Like It,* Alexander Pope's "Epistle to the Earl of Burlington," William Wordsworth's "Michael," and other poems. Our literary readings were coupled with selections from the work of more recent agricultural writers: F. H. King's *Farmers of Forty Centuries,* Sir Albert Howard's *The Soil and Health* and *An Agricultural Testament,* J. Russell Smith's *Tree Crops,* Wes Jackson's *New Roots for Agriculture,* and an essay by Gene Logsdon in *Meeting the Expectations of the Land.* What we realized by this rare and fruitful juxtaposition is that the modern scientific agrarian writers are trying to answer in very practical ways many of the same haunting questions that had preoccupied the earlier poets. Even our term-paper topics were to be governed by practical questions—issues of scale, pollution, fertility, nutrition, community, economy, education, the city, stewardship, and so forth. In short, it was the practical value of literature that he steered us toward. And for some of us this was a welcomed, refreshing approach to reading and interpreting texts. Leaving our schools of literary theory—and much of the jargon —at the door, we managed to see the texts in a new and clearer light. With a poet, fictionist, essayist, and fifth-generation farmer as our guide, we tapped into ancient truths previously hidden to many of us.

When I began my doctoral work two years later, I took a second course with Professor Berry, "The Pastoral." Like "Readings in Agriculture," this course explored the links between culture and nature, but this time we focused exclusively on literary texts, among them Shakespeare's *King Lear,* Andrew Marvell's *Upon Appleton House,* Thomas Hardy's *Tess of the d'Urbervilles,* and E. M. Forster's *Howard's End.* We watched closely the small cast of characters who serve as conduits between culture and nature—those who have an unusual intimacy with the natural world, gained by working closely with the earth, or by having a spiritual kinship with it, or both. The writers our professor selected, like so many other great writers, shared a deep respect for the profound mysteries at work in the relationship between human beings and nature. And yet in our readings we were encouraged by the discovery that human beings do not achieve harmony simply by turning toward nature or by seeking to be "natural"; they achieve it through a combination of cultivating a meaningful relationship with nature *and* exercising the virtues of loving companionship, compassion, and self-restraint.

These virtues, of course, are at the very heart of Berry's own writing, especially in his fictional world of Port William. It is clear to me now, as I look back at these courses and after having read all of his books, that he arrived at his conclusions about nature and humanity by living in his community, working on his farm, and essaying the old questions himself. Certainly, many of the virtues he values most are perpetuated in the literary and biblical traditions, which he knows well. But his own understanding of the complexity of humanity and of the vitality of these virtues is predominantly practical. He is as authentic as any writer and any teacher could ever hope to be. His frame of reference is his membership in his home community; his line of thinking moves in one direction—from the particular to the general, from the local to the universal. In the hands of some writers and teachers, this dogged emphasis on the local might be labeled "regionalism" or "local color," terms sometimes used dismissively. But, like the work of so many of the world's great writers, Berry's is at once grounded and transcendent. Perhaps this is one reason he was so effective as a teacher: he taught us to read like such a writer, one authentically and passionately bound to the local world, one deeply invested in its practical life, and one fully appreciating this local fidelity in the broad spectrum of humanity.

Even his decision to return to the classroom at the University of Kentucky was in service to the practical arts. He had left the university in 1977 after having taught creative writing since 1964. On his return in 1987, his new agreement was to teach the graduate-level agricultural and pastoral literature courses and "Composition for Teachers," a course for English-education majors focusing on the technical competencies of nonfiction writing, mainly exposition, persuasion, and argument. His roots as an English teacher were in both expository writing and imaginative writing. He had begun his teaching career in 1957 as a freshman writing instructor at Georgetown College in Kentucky, and two years later served as a creative writing instructor at Stanford University in California. Between 1962 and 1964 he had served as director of freshman composition at the University College of New York University in the Bronx. During his last span of service as a professor at the University of Kentucky (1987–1993), he returned to his "composition" roots with his preference for teaching nonfiction writing. It was clear by then, too, that he preferred teaching students who would likely find work in practical service to others in small communities, such as schoolteachers and traditional agriculturalists.

In Professor Berry's classroom, "practical" translated into "useful," "direct," and "clear," but it never meant "easy." Berry was an exacting teacher. Precision pencil in hand, he would meticulously edit our submitted prose with an eye toward pruning overgrown sentences, cutting needless words, and improving readability. We felt his exacting nature most acutely when he graded and returned our quizzes. In "Readings in Agriculture," he would ask us to write a one-sentence answer to a question on an assigned reading or an idea in the previous class discussion (later, in "The Pastoral," he allowed a three-sentence answer). Directing us to be straightforward, clear, and, of course, correct in substance and language use, he would give us approximately twenty minutes to compose our response. The first quiz was a disaster for most of the class, including me, mainly because we were not accustomed to writing, much less thinking, so directly and precisely. His quizzes demanded archerlike strength and accuracy, and we had to get in shape and practice. Focusing our minds to make every sentence and every word matter, we tried our best to rise to our teacher's challenge. Some of our sentences even came close to the mark. Of all of the skills I practiced as a graduate student, this skill of achieving directness and accuracy—this astonishingly practical but difficult skill—is the single most valuable one to me as a writer and a teacher.

The summer after completing my first class with Professor Berry, I decided to try to go home again, despite Thomas Wolfe's famous edict. In fall 1988, I continued my graduate work at Western Kentucky University in Bowling Green, about an hour from where I grew up on a small farm near Burkesville, Kentucky. I devoured as many of Professor Berry's books as I could get into my hands. *The Long-Legged House, A Place on Earth, A Continuous Harmony, The Memory of Old Jack, Collected Poems, Standing by Words*—all of these stand out as milestones in my life. I completed my master's degree with a thesis titled "Traditional Farming as Metaphor: Wendell Berry's Cyclic Vision." While I explored the omnipresence of the wheel of life in the poetry and nonfiction, my impetus was to read Professor Berry's work through the lens of what I had learned in his class about the weblike connections between culture and nature. It also was a way for me to test further the skills of practical reading and writing I had learned from the author himself. My education was working. Placing my sentences in the company of Berry's was and still is humbling—a great means of continuing my education.

I count myself among the truly fortunate to have encountered Professor Berry, especially since I enrolled in his first class by chance and without knowing anything about him or his books. Today, I teach his work every chance I get; I find in it a mind passionately and sensibly engaged with our culture's and the world's most pressing problems, and a voice steadfast and reassuring.

My students need to hear such a voice, one weighted by worry but lifted, at crucial times, by humor.

If only my students could hear his laugh, so hearty and genuine, which I occasionally heard echoing through the halls of the University of Kentucky's English department, they too would feel the old promise of reassurance and endurance. I am certain of it.

Norman Wirzba

An Economy of Gratitude

> The world
> is a holy vision, had we clarity
> to see it—a clarity that men
> depend on men to make.
> —Wendell Berry, "The Mad Farmer Manifesto: The First Amendment"

> Lov is the true Means by which the World is Enjoyed. Our Lov to others,
> and Others Lov to us. We ought therfore above all Things to get acquainted
> with the Nature of Lov. For Lov is the Root and Foundation of Nature: Lov
> is the Soul of Life, and Crown of Rewards. If we cannot be satisfied in the
> Nature of Lov we can never be satisfied at all.
> —Thomas Traherne, *Centuries of Meditations II*, 62

IT DOES NOT take long for readers of Wendell Berry's work to find themselves in a personal conundrum. First, there is usually the admission that his
diagnosis of our cultural ills is in many respects correct and that his critique
of the industrial mind and its economy is lucid and persuasive. For many,
Berry is so compelling precisely because he draws our attention to what (on
closer investigation) is obvious and decent but has been forgotten or over-
looked: that we live through the kindnesses and sacrifices of others; that our
embodiment necessarily and beneficially ties us to agricultural/ecological
cycles; that an economy based on unrestricted competition finally ends in war
and mutual destruction; that health is a feature of the wholeness of our mem-
berships in social and biological communities of life and death; that we are
the beneficiaries of traditions of memory, insight, and wisdom; and that eating is finally a sacramental act. Berry has clearly tapped into a widespread
sentiment that our culture is deeply flawed because of its denial and destruction of the many good sources of life. We need a better way, a way that pre-
serves, promotes, and celebrates the gift of life.

But as readers consider what this better way might entail and how they might concretely realize it in their lives, they become much less likely to accept and implement Berry's practical recommendations: develop habits of accurate memory, patient attention, careful examination, and reverence; practice fidelity to community and place; shop locally; learn the arts of homemaking and home care; do good work that is durable and beautiful and that honors the sources and recipients of the work; become responsible for other living human beings; and learn the art of the minimum. Berry is clear that none of these recommendations requires that we become farmers—we can adopt agrarian responsibilities without moving "back to the land." Even so, many balk at the prospect of realigning their practical lives according to agrarian priorities and ways.

This, then, is our conundrum: How can we accept the agrarian diagnosis as a comprehensive and compelling critique of our culture but reject the prescribed agrarian treatment? We cannot explain the incongruity between thought and action by arguing that Berry's recommendations do not adequately or directly address the problems he so clearly describes. Fidelity to place and community, including the complex rearrangement of priorities and practices this fidelity requires, is simply the proper response to the fragmentation, isolation, ennui, and ignorance that are the roots of our destructiveness. The development of an affectionate or sympathetic mind, a mind that is committed to the preservation and nurturing of the good (no matter how small), is clearly the urgent priority for a culture dominated by cost-benefit analysis, profitability, and economic utility. Why, then, our resistance to ways we "know" to be better for us?

Part of an answer to this very complex question depends on our seeing how the American political climate has shifted from what Michael Sandel calls a classical "republican" to a modern "liberal" philosophical point of view. According to republican political theory, being part of a democracy entails citizen participation in self-rule and collective deliberation about the common good. "It requires a knowledge of public affairs and also a sense of belonging, a concern for the whole, a moral bond with the community whose fate is at stake." Liberal political philosophy, on the other hand, which has gained the ascendancy in the last fifty years or so (and is well represented in both American political parties), maintains that governments should be neutral with respect to the good of life. Government "should provide a framework of rights that respects persons as free and independent selves, capable of choosing their own values and ends."[1] On this view, no one can tell us how to live and what goals to choose because we are autonomous beings, unencumbered by the needs or claims of others.

This recent political and cultural development is so striking because it represents a radical departure from earlier traditions that founded civic life on training in moral virtue. A good society must inculcate in its members a sense for the supreme collective good in life, and then provide the practical conditions for its attainment. Personal freedom, in this context, is worked out with constant reference to common need and the common good. We, on the other hand, live in a consumer culture in which all claimed "goods" are on a shelf competing for market share. As consumers we are in charge of what will count as a good for us. Our individual right to choose our own ends in life (the primary role of governments is now to secure such autonomy) trumps any claim to a common good. Indeed, many of us, doubting the possibility of widespread agreement on what the supreme good is, would have considerable trouble envisioning how a public discussion on the common good might even begin.

One of Berry's definitive contributions is to have shown us that the dream of an unencumbered autonomous life is false and delusional. We are not self-determining gods whose livelihoods require no regard for ecological or social circumstance. As embodied creatures who eat, drink, and breathe, we are necessarily and beneficially connected to natural habitats, myriads of (large and microscopically small) organisms, and the evolutionary processes that sustain us all: because we live in and through flesh we undoubtedly also live in soil. As social beings who converse, plan, argue, and celebrate, we clearly depend on others to nurture us into adulthood and to equip us with tools of language and understanding and with gifts of friendship and purpose. If we truly are moral beings, then we are beholden to and accountable for these biological and cultural contexts that give us life. Quite rightly, therefore, Berry concludes: "There is, in practice, no such thing as autonomy. Practically, there is only a distinction between responsible and irresponsible dependence."[2] We are all implicated in the living of one another and could not possibly survive or thrive alone.

This fact of our mutual implication and need for one another can be a source of joy. But it can also be perceived as an unwelcome burden because it raises in a profound manner the need for self-restraint, or, as Berry puts it in *Life Is a Miracle,* submission to the demands of propriety. All life is costly and precious because it is secured on the basis of cycles of life and death: in order for an organism to eat and grow, others must die. Human beings, however, are unique in this web of life because we can discern whether our eating and growing are extravagant and wasteful or unnecessarily destructive. We can contemplate, based on careful consideration and regard for our life-giving neighborhoods, whether the patterns of our living can be justified as contributing to a *common* good. In this possibility we see our nobility. In its refusal we witness our mutual ruin.

The signs of ruin, though always having been visible to the sensitive and astute, have now become too numerous to hide or ignore. We see this in eroded topsoil, degraded watersheds, extinct species, abandoned rural communities, and anxious and abused workers. Clearly, we have not sufficiently exercised our moral responsibility to consider, understand, and then order our living in ways that would contribute to the health and vitality of us all, or that would encourage the celebration of the many gifts we enjoy and can be to one another. We have not restrained our desires so as to be in sympathetic alignment with the limits and possibilities of our natural and cultural homes. We have not resisted greed and pride. We have not paused long enough from our self-serving ways to show gratitude, and then see in our gratitude the basis of and inspiration for a more responsible, convivial life together. Our lack of restraint and our want of joy suggest a failure of humanity.

The problem, of course, is that we all chafe at the prospect of personal restraint. Though we may at times acknowledge our status as finite, dependent, and mortal beings, we easily succumb to pretensions of infinity, independence, and immortality. What we need, then, are ways that will lead us into the discipline of restraint and, in so doing, help us recover what is vital about our humanity—namely, our necessary and beneficial entanglement in the vast web of life we call creation. As creatures we need to be able to identify limits and interdependencies, take up forms of living that respect and nurture our social and biological homes, and develop perceptual habits that encourage us to see our multiple interdependencies not as a burden but as a joy. At issue is the prospect of a culture that affirms, promotes, and celebrates what is truly our most supreme and common good: the health and vitality of all life together. Can we envision and then realize communities where we spontaneously dance and sing, or take pleasure in small profitless things, or find the time for Sabbath rest and wonder?

For this effort we can do no better than to cultivate an economy of gratitude. Before proceeding to a description of the defining marks of such an economy—affection, attention, delight, kindness, praise, conviviality, and repentance—and the appropriate steps that will lead us to its realization, we need to be more aware of how our current economy works against gratitude. We must note not only the relative absence of genuine thanksgiving in our society but the systemic, widespread ingratitude that economic "success" necessitates. Without an accurate assessment of where we now are, we will have difficulty arriving at where we want to go.

The causes of our ingratitude are multiple and have been described from a variety of angles. One of these has been to note that in a consumerist culture the focus and identity of individuals rest primarily on what they can purchase. "Personal style" and institutional "branding" are features of commodities acquired and then displayed, images packaged and presented, to others. As popular culture now shows, we increasingly turn to commodities to help us navigate among the key issues of public debate—what we do and the ordering of our priorities are increasingly features of what we can afford and what companies (most clearly in the form of corporate sponsorships) make available to us as "viable options."

Given that meaning and personal identity are made so dependent on what we possess, the potential for ingratitude grows on many levels. First, there is the growing resentment among the underclass that their lives do not count very much because they do not have the purchasing power to put them on a competitive stylistic footing with the wealthy. If a "successful" identity is a feature of what we own, then poverty severely impairs our ability to be equal participants in communities and institutions. Sensing their inequality, their relative unworth in the eyes of their wealthy counterparts, the "nickled and dimed" among us become resentful and ungrateful for their lot. The wealthy, however, are not much better off. Perhaps sensing the growing resentment among the underclass, they cannot really enjoy their wealth for fear that it is at risk, and so must devote ample resources to protect their possessions.

Ingratitude, however, is not primarily a problem of poverty itself. In fact, it is well known that in preconsumerist, predominantly rural cultures, the poor show many more signs of gratitude than the wealthy in our culture do today. We know this because of their readiness to show delight and their capacity to be more generous with themselves and their possessions. Their generosity is, in fact, directly related to the recognition that they subsist through the gifts of the earth and one another. It is, therefore, more accurate to say that ingratitude is less a feature of poverty than it is a feature of the specifically consumerist trend to form identity and measure self-worth in terms of what we own.

What this means is that, whether we are rich or poor, the extent to which we buy into the consumerist mentality will determine the rate and the severity of our ingratitude. Given that consumerism dominates the economies of the developed world (we are now told by our national leaders that the best thing we can do for our economies is to shop), we should not be surprised to find that most of us, verbal pretensions notwithstanding, exhibit in our practical living profound ingratitude. Whether out of a deep-rooted personal insecurity or the competitive drive to be better than the next person, few of us feel that we can rest in the drive to have more. Feeling the vulnerability of our worth if we do not purchase yet one more commodity, and sensing the cheapness of many acquired "goods," we stay on the consumerism treadmill, unable to get off. We are thus easy prey for advertisers and creditors who aim to keep us unhappy and ungrateful by telling us that what we currently possess is not good enough, particularly when compared to the flash of the new and improved product. After all, why should we be deeply grateful for objects that have so little intrinsic or abiding value?

While it is important that we not lose sight of the power of consumerism in promoting ingratitude among us, there is a more fundamental feature of our current economic life that contributes directly to our malaise. Though not discussed nearly enough in public debate, one of the merits of Berry's agrarian critique of culture is to have shown us that in our economic lives we operate in an immense, thick cloud of ignorance and blindness. Consumerism, of course, encourages this trend because the relationships between consumers and the world are so attenuated—we connect with others (products, producers, the sources of production) not on the level of sustained, practical, or personal investment but through the ease and ephemerality of the credit-card swipe. Never before have so many people lived in ignorance about the requirements and costs of biological and social life. The extent of our ignorance and naïveté are directly relevant to the prospect of developing an economy of gratitude. Put simply, we cannot be grateful for what we do not know intimately.

In the essay "The Whole Horse" Berry describes our culture and economy as patterned on "the one-night stand." What he means is that in an industrial economy, relationships of significance or meaning have been severed even as the pursuit of pleasure or satisfaction intensifies. For instance, in a one-night stand buyers and sellers do not really know one another before the event. They enter into it more or less anonymously and then commit to stay away from one another, and *deny all consequences,* after the transaction is complete. In a similar manner, consumers and producers have almost no understanding of one another. If they come together at all, they do so in a highly tangential way, mediated by several hands, each claiming a part of the transaction cost. Consumers do not know because they are anonymously exchanging favors in the dark: they do not see, share in, or care about the contexts in which the purchased good was made. They have little appreciation for the complete costs to communities and habitats that are associated with production, because products (especially in global markets) are made far away from the point of consumption. For instance, when food travels an average of 1,300 miles from factory-farm gate to dinner plate, consumers really have no idea if farmworkers, animals, soils, watersheds, rural communities, factory workers, truckers, and grocery-store employees were handled or compensated in a humane, healthy, and just manner. As consumers all we really know is that to-day's price is higher (or lower) than yesterday's. Our consumption of the food, facilitated by the ease of a financial transaction, occurs in a cloud of ignorance and anonymity. Today's food economy takes place in a dark hotel room.

Our ignorance, besides leading to considerable economic injustice and ecological destruction, feeds directly into our ingratitude, what Berry calls our "persistent want of satisfaction." Because we do not have meaningful histories with producers and products, histories built upon relationships of understanding, sympathy, affection, and long-term commitment, we do not cherish the things we buy or see in them any deep value or beauty. Producers, in turn, having little direct contact with the consumers who purchase what they make or provide (and thus being unable to see how their work improves or impairs consumers' lives, to say nothing about the health of the places of production), have much less reason to invest themselves in their work, to treat the elements and processes of work with affection and care. The result, oftentimes, is shoddy work or work done for no honorable purpose. "The global economy institutionalizes a global ignorance, in which producers and consumers cannot know or care about one another, and in which the histories of all products will be lost. In such a circumstance, the degradation of products and places, producers and consumers, is inevitable."[3] In a context such as this there is little room for gratitude or appreciation for the costly and precious nature of life.

If we were not in such a fog of ignorance, what would we see? For starters we would have to come to grips with the fact that for too long humans have thrived at the expense of their biological and social communities. As Berry rightly maintains, human economies, for the most part, have succeeded by "invading and pillaging" the sources of life and by twisting the very patterns of order and stability to our advantage. We have rarely been attentive to or deeply loved—and thus have not responsibly settled—the places we have been, treating them instead as resources that are to be used up for our benefit. As our penchant to pit the elements of creation against one another in competitive struggle clearly shows, we have not acted enough on the eternal truth that in the order of creation, what Berry calls the "Great Economy," "each part stands for the whole and is joined to it; the whole is present in the part and is its health."[4] Each member of creation, in other words, is indispensable for the health of the whole. Our capacity to exploit and degrade is so systemic and deep that we should all give in to despair were it not for the few examples in our history of communities that have lived responsibly and charitably upon the earth and with one another.

It would be a mistake, however, to keep our vision focused only or primarily on our destructive ways. No doubt, we need to be honest about our past by not hiding what we have done. We need to face our terrible potential to inflict pain. But there is so much more to see: most important, a vision of the world as holy. Thomas Traherne, a seventeenth-century poet whom Berry admires, put it this way:

> You never Enjoy the World aright, till you so lov the Beauty of Enjoying it, that you are Covetous and Earnest to Persuade others to Enjoy it. And so perfectly hate the Abominable Corruption of Men in Despising it, that you had rather suffer the flames of Hell then willingly be guilty of their Error. There is so much Blindness, Ingratitud, and Damned folly in it. The World is a Mirror of infinit Beauty, yet no Man sees it. It is a Temple of Majesty yet no Man regards it. It is a Region of Light and Peace, did not Men Disquiet it. It is the Paradice of God.[5]

Traherne, much like Berry, is convinced that we are blind to this world as the "paradice of God." In our practical living we clearly show that we are not much impressed or informed by the multitude of gifts—water, soil, sunshine, photosynthesis, flowers, earthworms, bees, honey, parental self-sacrifice, friendship, hospitality, and the gifts of song and dance—that make life possible and a joy. We prefer the hyperbolic flash, speed, and explosiveness of virtual worlds of our own making (and unmaking). What we need to appreciate, however, is that our blindness is not simply physical. In the poem "Walking" Traherne says:

> To *walk* abroad is, not with Eys,
> But Thoughts, the Fields to see and prize;
> Els may the silent Feet,
> Like logs of Wood,
> Mov up and down, and see no Good,
> Nor Joy nor Glory meet . . .
> To *walk* is by a Thought to go;
> To mov in Spirit to and fro;
> To mind the Good we see;
> To taste the Sweet;
> Observing all the things we meet
> How choice and rich they be.[6]

What Berry and Traherne fear is that we have lost, or are in the process of losing, the capacity to see the good in things. Our vision is shallow because it is impatient, rushed, or simply clouded by self-interest. With our minds we do not prize the joy and glory that are perpetually before us, nor do we sufficiently taste the sweetness of this life. If we could see to this deep level, what we would find, Traherne maintains, is unending, inexhaustible love as "the

Root and Foundation of Nature." We would experience the world and all its inexplicable gifts as holy. Rushing through life in automobiles and sitting through it in climate-controlled buildings, we are incapable of mindfulness, the basic ability to attend to the gifts of nurture that everywhere surround us.

It is important to stress how the structure of our practical living forms an impediment to this profound vision and experience. Suburban, computer, automobile life, characterized as it is by anonymity and separation from the world outside, does not foster well enough the neighborhood sense of belonging and commitment that would lead us into a deep encounter or sustained engagement with one another. We do not walk. We do not have the practical proximity or intimacy with the sources of biological and social well-being to appreciate them *as gifts*. We live, for the most part, with the illusion that what we need and what we desire can be procured at the store, through our own effort, and by the strength and cunning of our hands.

To appreciate the world as a gift marks a profound transformation in consciousness and a reorientation in the ways we live, for we now no longer welcome others as potential possessions or things with which to do whatever we want. The world is never reducible to things to be taken. Here it is instructive to remember that Berry chose as the opening epigraph for *The Unsettling of America* the words from Michel de Montaigne: "Who so hath his minde on taking, hath it no more on what he hath taken." The clearest indicator that another, no matter how small or seemingly insignificant, has registered with me as a gift is that it is treasured and cherished. Gifts cannot be taken for granted if we see in them the generosity or sacrifice of another. The expression of gratitude is thus at the same time the acknowledgment and the affirmation of our interdependence, the recognition that for our livelihood we depend upon and receive benefit from the love that is the root of community and nature, and is the basis of new possibility and the foundation of our hope. It is no wonder, then, that Berry has sought to retrieve the arts of the husbandry and wifery of the world, as well as the affection and patient attention they entail, as our future and most urgent task.

We should recall, however, that to attain to a vision of life as holy and as a gift, we need the help of one another to clarify it. In his recent novel, *Hannah Coulter,* as in most all his writing, Berry describes how it is through the affectionate giving of ourselves to a place that the vision of it as holy becomes possible. Nathan and Hannah Coulter, newly married, purchase an abandoned farm that shows all the signs of neglect. What draws them to this place, however, is the promise of possibility and the goodness of grace that is within every natural place. It is their love and dedication over the length of years, combined with the practical support and wisdom of family, neighbors, and friends, that bring them to the realization that their farm is all they need. They have no desire to go to some other place because in their affectionate embrace of this land, and the sustained hard work this embrace entails, a glimpse of heaven dawns upon them. As Hannah puts it, "There is no 'better place' than this, not in *this* world. And it is by the place we've got, and our love for it and our keeping of it, that this world is joined to Heaven."[7] To think that some other place will always be better is to have abandoned the potential latent in the place in which one is. It is to refuse—and to bear witness to previous refusals of—responsibility and care.

It is unlikely that we will develop Berry's "holy vision" alone or by ourselves. We depend on others to sharpen our clarity to see holiness, because personal vision is too limited or does not see expansively enough. We need the length of generations and the depth of numerous points of view to appreciate the full register of our folly and to note the varied potential for celebration and joy latent within every life. We need the insight of traditions, the memory of communal wisdom—what Berry refers to as "the handing down"—to enlarge our minds and widen our sympathies so that we can learn to appreciate the vast complex patterns of mutual involvement and help that we are to one another. Only then will the true wealth of the world, what John Ruskin referred to as life's fecundity and mystery, become more apparent to us.

In the practical, mundane, sustained commitment to place and community the marks of gratitude mentioned earlier come into clearer focus. *Attention* is vital because so much of the time we engage others not for who or what they are but for how we wish them to be. Engagement becomes indistinguishable from imposition. Our vision, in other words, perpetually runs the risk of fanciful distortion and so needs the discipline of correction made possible by honest, detailed attention to the particularities and the potential of any given place or person. We need, quite simply, for others to tell us when we see falsely. This takes resolve and communal support and wisdom.

> One must stay to experience and study and understand the consequences —must understand them by living with them, and then correct them, if necessary, by longer living and more work. It won't do to correct mistakes made in one place by moving to another place, as has been the common fashion in America, or by adding on another place, as is the fashion in any sort of "growth economy."[8]

As we develop our attention to place and community, our desire for what we *want* can come into more faithful and sympathetic alignment with who and where we in fact *are,* if for no other reason than that we now appreciate the places and communities in which we live as our life-giving root and home.

Resolve, at its best, is maintained by *affection*. It is easy to confuse affection with romantic bliss and ease, particularly in a consumerist culture. Affection, however, grows over time and is the effect of sustained commitment and involvement. As we work with others, and as we endeavor to get to know them, we learn to appreciate them in their depth and integrity and with a better appreciation for their potential and need. We see them for the unique creatures they are and begin to approach the complexity, beauty, and mystery of every created thing and person. The loveliness of who they are starts to dawn on us, calling forth within us a response of love and celebration. This is a learning process that is throughout accompanied by the need for *repentance* as we discover and confront in ourselves the arrogant and anxious desire to control others and to deny their potential to be. Repentance is vital in the life of gratitude because it is the gateway to the full acknowledgment of our interdependence with others, the recognition that together we form a membership in which need and satisfaction can meet because we have given up the tenacious drive to maintain ourselves at the expense of others. When we repent, we acknowledge before others that we have been wrong and are now prepared to embark on a better path informed less by our wants and more by another's need. Through confession and repentance we become detached from ourselves and thus freed to experience, cherish, and nurture the gifts we are to one another.

To experience creation as a gift quite naturally leads to our mutual *delight*. One of the primary obstacles to delight lies in our unwillingness to give up control. As moderns and sophisticates we like to think we can have the world on our own terms. As skeptics and cynics we handle one another at arm's length, never getting too close or involved, for fear that our interdependence might overwhelm and subjugate us, might even lead to our annihilation. And so we build protective walls, believing we will thus escape life unscathed and in charge. What we fail to appreciate is that this is a path that leads to loneliness and sadness because we are now deprived of the richness and splendor that creation itself is. To experience delight is to be amazed by the sheer wonder and excellence of what lies before us, and to underline the many kindnesses that surround us on multiple sides. It is to be overwhelmed by the sense that we are a blessing to one another the moment we devote ourselves to one another's care.

If we could imagine, let alone fully implement, a community of care, we would find that our relationships with one another would be governed by conviviality rather than suspicion, by praise rather than blame. In a community of care people are turned toward one another. They have given up the false, perpetually deferred dream that happiness lies somewhere else with other people. In this community people would learn to trust that the love that brought creation into being—a costly love that is daily made concrete in the gifts of birth, growth, healing, and strength in the face of suffering and pain—is sufficient for their daily living. Indeed, the ways of love form the paradigm by which to judge and correct our priorities and plans. The celebration of goodness and our thanksgiving for the bounty of gifts would be this community's foremost concern.

Can a community of care and gratitude become a reality, or must it be relegated to a fictional world? In Berry's novels and short stories it is painfully clear that in the last several decades we have made choices as a society that make an economy of gratitude seem like little more than a dream. Although it may be the case that communities of care and delight were possible in the heyday of Port William (remembering, however, that they were never easy or without their serious faults and pains), to us, living in the fast-paced and precarious world of global markets, they seem an impossibility. Global economics, premised as it is on ephemeral purchasing and human mobility, demands the sacrifice of depth of relationship that would enable us to encounter one another and the world as gifts. And so we need to ask: Do we have any reasons or resources to move us in the direction of gratitude?

Clearly we do, particularly if we consider the growing dissatisfaction of consumers who are sensing the blindness, foolishness, destructiveness, and loneliness of our ungrateful ways. The death-wielding consequences of our culture's current priorities suggest that we simply must change course. It is safe to say that, despite our high "standard of living," never before have people felt so unhappy, so cut off from one another, and so without hope (if we did have hope, would we so compromise the sources of life on which our grandchildren will depend?). It is not unreasonable to suppose that our dissatisfaction and disenchantment with our culture's dominant priorities and ways can form the preliminary inspiration for the pursuit of an economy of gratitude. But dissatisfaction can only be a beginning. As we dedicate ourselves to one another, and thus experience daily and directly the diverse array of gifts that contribute to our living, gratitude will take its rightful place as the fundamental disposition that guides and forms our ways. Indeed, in small pockets here and there, the work of cultural transformation that is borne and carried by gratitude is beginning or is well under way.

We witness it in the growing support for local economies and currencies. At work here we see the bringing together of producers and consumers so that at a bare minimum we at least get to know one another again. In this knowledge we gain an appreciation for one another's needs, struggles, joys, challenges, strengths, and happiness. Equipped with this knowledge we are then in a much better position to shop, work, and act responsibly—that is, to give and be given—so that the gifts we can be to one another are respected and nurtured. Directly seeing the kindness and sacrifice of others, we are much more likely to be kind and generous in return. The intimacy of our relationships and the exactitude of our vision are crucial because if we are to do good work, work that honors one another, we need to commit to live with the effects of our actions over the long term. Although this commitment will not always be easy or convenient, it will be maintained by the joy and delight that comes from engaging creation and one another *as gifts*.

The witness of gardeners is here instructive. Living in such close, practical proximity with the gifts of the earth that nourish us and beautify our lives, and sensing directly their inability to control or predict a garden's many gifts—they are continually being surprised by joy—gardeners are known to be generous in return. They find it easier to give away their produce and flowers because they directly see how they are the beneficiaries of gifts beyond their comprehension or merit. They model an economy of gratitude and care because they smell in their nostrils, taste in their mouths, behold with their eyes, and feel with their hands the sheer grace and blessings of life.

We also become witnesses to gratitude in the lure and satisfaction of what Albert Borgmann has called "focal practices."[9] Focal practices are habits and events that bring people together in regular, sustained ways so that they can achieve an understanding of and participation in a common good. The goal of a focal practice is for people to have encounters in which to feel once again the eloquence and the loveliness of reality, to appreciate what we might also describe as its capacity to surprise us with its wonder and mystery, its inexhaustible resourcefulness. Prime examples of focal practices would include the family meal, music festivals, and community sports leagues. What makes these festivals and leagues so important is that they bring people into the presence of one another, lifting them out of their often narrowly focused routines, so that they can enjoy and cultivate what they have in common and what they cannot live well without: the development and celebration of talent; the joy of work done together for a common goal and without the pressures of profitability; the appreciation of personal and social differences as sources of strength rather than occasions for conflict; and the building of a shared history as the basis for communal wisdom and hope.

In a fast food, drive-through world in which many people eat alone and on the run, the family meal is a traditional and (therefore) revolutionary practice. What is at stake in it is the coming together of people over one of our most pleasurable activities: eating. In the preparation of a meal, and then its tasting and nourishment, we have the opportunity to think carefully and practically about the gifts of food, family, and friendship. We can become attentive to where our food comes from, under what conditions it is produced, and whether it is conducive to our overall health. We also take the time to listen to and consider the needs and opportunities, the struggles and the joys, of the people we eat with because we have now created a concrete place for them to be heard and regularly engaged. Around the table we create the conditions for conviviality and praise. We make the time to find creation delectable. And we participate in the hospitality that creation itself is, as we invite others to our homes to share those gifts of food and friendship that have already been a blessing to us. In the sharing of the meal we give concrete expression to our gratitude. We catch a taste of heaven.

We are not without hope. As we together commit ourselves to one another—intentionally join ourselves "with all the living," as Ecclesiastes 9:4 puts it—we will come to see how we are also gifts to one another.[10] Living in the conscious presence of gift upon gift, we will gradually become aware that the only proper or fitting response is for us to turn our own lives into gifts to be given to others. Out of our newly formed grateful hearts, and with the help of our biological and social communities, we will slowly but surely be moved to practices and commitments that have at their core fidelity, care, and celebration.

Notes

1. Michael Sandel, *Democracy's Discontent: America in Search of a Public Philosophy* (Cambridge, MA: Harvard University Press, 1996), 4–5.

2. Wendell Berry, *The Unsettling of America: Culture and Agriculture* (San Francisco: Sierra Club Books, 1977), 111.

3. Wendell Berry, "The Whole Horse," in *The Art of the Commonplace: The Agrarian Essays of Wendell Berry,* ed. Norman Wirzba (Washington, DC: Counterpoint, 2002), 244.

4. Wendell Berry, "Two Economies," in *The Art of the Commonplace,* 234.

5. Thomas Traherne, "Centuries of Meditations," in *Poems, Centuries, and Three Thanksgivings,* ed. Anne Ridler (Oxford: Oxford University Press, 1966), 1, 31, 178.

6. Ibid., 123.

7. Wendell Berry, *Hannah Coulter: A Novel* (Washington, DC: Shoemaker and Hoard, 2004), 83.

8. Wendell Berry, "People, Land, and Community," in *The Art of the Commonplace,* 187.

9. Albert Borgmann, *Crossing the Postmodern Divide* (Chicago: University of Chicago Press, 1992).

10. New Revised Standard Version.

Wes Jackson

Letters from a Humble Radical

IT IS HARD FOR ME to think about Wendell Berry without also thinking about Tanya, his wife, and with no effort my mind runs to their children, Mary and Den, and to Chuck and Billie, Mary's and Den's spouses, and then to their children and then to Wendell's brother, John, and his wife, Carol, and Wendell's now deceased father and mother and Tanya's parents and then my children and their spouses and their children and then the characters in Wendell's novels and the friends we share in common and phone conversations, two, three times a week.

For several months now I have tried to write about Wendell, and I end up with a stream of consciousness—somewhat like the above one-sentence paragraph, with no room for a period or question mark—confused, dazzled, leaning on my left elbow, chewing on my left thumbnail and making it jagged, hoping for an outline to pop into my mind so that I can say something that captures what Wendell and Tanya and their family and friends and Wendell's writings and conversations have meant to me and my family and The Land Institute and agrarians everywhere and our entire country and much of the world.

And now there is the second one-sentence paragraph, this one of a seemingly plaintive nature.

So, be warned: it is nearly impossible to write or talk about Wendell without writing or talking about me and The Land Institute. This is precisely because so much of what I think and who I have become is due to the influence of Wendell's life and thoughts. That said, the conventional disclaimer still holds: what flaws you might see in The Land Institute or me are not his. I have tried to discover what is wrong with Wendell both in his life and thought, and, as far as what matters, I find no fault with this man.

Wendell and I have never come at one another in anger. Our disagreements almost invariably lead to more conversation to determine the underlying assumptions of the other.

Our correspondence and conversation began with a letter from him dated

November 11, 1980. It opens with a compliment on my recent book *New Roots for Agriculture.* But rather than wait for me to let the praise soak in, Wendell pleads in the next paragraph for reconsideration about parts in the last chapter. He argues that I should reconsider the role of draft farm animals in the utopian future I had outlined.

He concludes his letter with the following paragraph:

> As one who has farmed with both tractors and teams, I would insist (to you; I would be more cautious, at present, in a public statement) that with the use of a tractor certain vital excitements, pleasures, and sensitivities are lost. How much numb metal can we put between ourselves and our land and still know where we are and what we are doing? Working with a tractor is damned dulling and boring. It is like making love in boxing gloves.

I answered his letter. I took his critique seriously. The next connection was his voice over the phone one evening: "This is Wendell Berry." I responded, "Oh, my gosh," then turned and announced to the whole family, "It's Wendell Berry." My admiration for his writings, especially *The Unsettling of America,* had already placed him at the top of my list for modern writers. With *The Unsettling* I had found an ally. Long before I finished reading that very great book, I felt less lonely.

Wendell placed the call to say that he wanted to do a story on The Land Institute for Rodale's *New Farm.* He came. I picked him up at the Salina airport. We toured the premises, looked at the various projects, talked of our families, of our origins: I had grown up in the Kansas River valley; his home looks over the Kentucky River valley. It was as though we had the brands of our rivers and states on our backs. We talked of designs in our minds about our places.

It wasn't long before I made a trip to Kentucky to see the home and farm of Wendell and Tanya. Since then the lives of the two families and both communities have melded—marriages, grandchildren, schooling, college, in-laws, his parents, my parents, his siblings, my siblings, and so on. We learn of his neighbors. He learns of our staff. We rejoice with one another, lament with one another, keep track of the health and comings and goings of our families and friends.

What a gain this friendship was for me and for the Land Institute and its supporters. Here was a man saying what I felt but never brought to full cognition and was inarticulate about when I tried. He expanded my education as he introduced me to my intellectual ancestors, people I never knew but ancestors who had informed the agrarian culture, the cultural handing down of the likes of Liberty Hyde Bailey and Sir Albert Howard. I had known of Liberty

Hyde Bailey through his manual of cultivated plants but not Bailey the cultural agrarian, and not Albert Howard at all. We both had read *Tree Crops* by J. Russell Smith, another agrarian.

But here was this Kentucky farmer educated in the humanities who had gone home. Trained in the sciences, I had gone home too. The fact that we had come from different disciplines was of no consequence. We came together in what we both liked—land and farming. Wendell's side trip away from his origins into the professional world of literature must have helped him adjust his lens and see his place for what it was. My side trip into genetics was sponsored in no small part by our Kansas River valley farm, where heredity had been my earliest interest. Family and neighbor likenesses and gestures, as well as livestock traits, made genetics an easy discipline for me and also the closest I could get to the culture of agriculture in academic life. But I couldn't get close enough. At some level I knew that what I loved about farm life was flying away faster than I could approach it through my academic interests and responsibilities.

I came home and found my life's work. But I was a late arrival. Several years before, Wendell had come home, and once home he found his subject. Here I must pause, so as not to be misunderstood. Wendell used his subject in a way different from most artists. Rather than regard his homeland, his people, his community, as a mere reservoir for his art, he assumed the responsibility to defend that land, defend those neighbors, defend that community, and by doing so defend rural culture everywhere with his art. It is this eloquent defense that has heartened all of us who had some inkling of the need for connectedness to what really counts. He has taught us its necessity and possibility. And while few of us even yet can be optimistic, Wendell has given us enough to be hopeful. His novels accomplish this alone. His essays accomplish this alone. His poetry certainly speaks to all of that and more. I can say without hesitation or qualification that Wendell Berry may be the most practical person I know, precisely because he made his art capture the roundness of a rooted, grounded life beyond acres and calories, foundations and roofs, crops and livestock.

It wasn't long before Wendell introduced me to some of his friends, his fellow agrarians—Maury Telleen, publisher and editor of the *Draft Horse Journal,* Maury the man Wendell dedicated *The Unsettling* to, and then Gene Logsdon. Among those three there was a trinity, unholy in the conventional understanding but whole, in fact the whole I needed. In July of 1983 he introduced me to David and Elsie Kline and their Amish family in Ohio. These were real allies. The conversation among all five of us continues by letter and by phone.

As one who started out in plant taxonomy, I assumed I could classify Wendell's own letters easily. Well, not so fast. It was like separating strands in a fabric and classifying them by color, texture, strength, and length. Even so, here are a few themes:

- He's busy, frantic about getting his work done, getting ready for a trip, trying to clear his desk so he can get outside.
- He's frustrated with too much rain, wet fields, or no rain, a dry cistern, "sitting around dirty."
- He's criticizing my writing (this is his only persistent criticism of me).
- He's frustrated with intellectuals given to abstractions with no particularities. This shows up time and again.
- He's irritated with global thinkers.
- He's irritated with the industrial economy and the industrial mind.

But this list doesn't capture the content, not by a long shot. A better illustration of the range can be drawn from his own writing. After the first letter of November 11, 1980, about the virtues of draft animals versus tractors, other letter exchanges followed on the same subject. More than two months later (January 17, 1981), we were still discussing the draft-animal economy:

> We have to assume that, in an efficient workhorse-energy economy, the horses would be eaten. The last I heard, the slaughter price for horses was about $.50 per pound.
>
> So if you raised a colt, broke him, and worked him to the age of 15, and he weighed 1,500 lbs, and you then sold him for meat, he would bring $750. That is, he would have earned an average of $50 per year during his lifetime just by being a horse. To a self-employed, self-sufficient small farmer, then, this horse's work would come extremely cheap. In money terms. But this horse has produced energy in his work, in his manure and urine, and in his flesh—which should put the net value of his energy pretty high.
>
> I couldn't eat a friend, myself. But I could eat a horse I didn't know a damn sight quicker than I could eat a tractor.

He saw the possibilities in the love of what he described above. Five months earlier he was describing the practical necessity of small-scale farming. On April 20, 1981, came a letter with this paragraph with echoes of *The Unsettling*, in which the defenders of the practical necessity of small-scale farming are so few:

> Who is going to defend [the small farm]? If its justification were only cultural or political, then one might cynically give it up. But I am convinced that it is necessary to the survival of agriculture too, that, in general, the best husbanded, most productive farms are small. I believe I

have looked carefully at as many farms as anybody, and I'm convinced that the physical, practical evidence is overwhelmingly in favor of small-scale, balanced structure, and diversity—along with the necessary cultural supports.

I am feeling weary and contrary this morning, but plenty contrary.

What follows represents an expression of the ideal Wendell has relentlessly featured: people, land, and community as one, engaged in our oldest work. No mere nostalgia here; rather, the art and the practical necessity are one. Here is a world that is so compelling to so many of us that it showed the possibility of being widespread again:

> August 22, 1981
>
> I was standing at the corner of Ed Poe's little cattle shed the day before yesterday (Ed is the neighbor who was mowing grass when we talked to him). All cornering in there within easy range of a cheap camera were a small pasture, a one-acre tobacco patch, a one-acre field of soybeans (for hay), and a patch of potatoes (for eating), patches of woodland on two sides and not far away. And men of four households at work in the shed, putting up a harvest of about 400 bales of excellent bean and millet hay from about two acres of very "marginal" ground. Pleasant work, good economy, truth, and beauty. One big tractor would ruin it all.

What was going against those men of four households was a combination of economics made possible by low-priced nonrenewable energy. It was perhaps this paragraph that caused me to consider the possibility of a general rule: high energy destroys information, in this case the information of both the cultural and biological varieties. Here was the human scale, the "small is beautiful" reality described by E. F. Schumacher in the 1970s. Here was the "culture" of agriculture. The cultural information in the workers and the biological information stored in the genes of the crop diversity are apparent.

At times Wendell seems to enjoy his conflicts with technology as well as certain nuisance species:

> September 4, 1981
>
> You noted, I reckon, my wife's happy remedy for my lack of discipline on the telephone. It is sad but true that I cannot, or will not, talk a short time with you or Gene Logsdon or Maury Telleen. You reckon some foundation would give me a grant to talk on the phone? The irony of it is that I hate telephones. Also automobiles, tractors, airplanes, TV, power plants, the Pentagon, nodding thistles, Johnson grass, and cockleburs. That is a neat, well-tended list.
>
> When you geneticists produce a rootless Johnson grass, and a burrless cocklebur, and a prickleless thistle, I will quit hating them.

At other times it's the father and the son at a colt sale, the generational handing down, and in the last sentence the irresistible poet:

October 5, 1981
Went up to Goshen, Ind., with Den to the fall Colt Sale on the 1st. Bought a nice chestnut filly. Have a pair of old grade mares, broke well and bred, and a good grade stud colt for sale—in case you run into anybody who is looking.
I'm hurrying too much, doing too much, head humming like a hive.

A month later comes a letter. It is clear he wants a team and that his head is still "humming like a hive":

November 4, 1981
I believe I'm going to turn right around and invest the money in a yearling full sister to this weanling filly Den and I bought at Goshen. I feel a little reckless in that, since my instinct is to "save." But I'm trying too, though not optimistically, to be realistic. Saving money, in this economy, is closer to crap-shooting than husbandry, and I prefer to gamble in my own game—to put as solid a foundation as I can under the possibility that exists here for my family. Of course, it would make no sense if I weren't aching for the yearling filly.

In the same letter he mentions a conference we both attended in California, where several high-powered intellectuals were present. Wendell was my defender in a minor shoot-out I had with one of the participants:

That people disagree about thoughts may still leave them in the category of people who deal only in thoughts—a category dangerous both to those in it and those out of it. What I notice and regret more and more—because, for one thing, I feel isolated and threatened by it—is the lack of people who have worked a long time at any worldly task, who therefore know the dignity and the recalcitrance of material reality. I thought this was what moved you to take out after —— the other Sunday, for his talk about "the idiocy of country life." Adverse judgments certainly have to be made, but there is a height they must not be made from by mere humans. That is why I thought you were right. There is of course plenty of idiocy in country life, because there is plenty in human life. But let —— wait to call it idiocy until he has been up against it for twenty-five years, and has understood his own inescapable kinship with it.

Wendell's value as a critic and editor has been indispensable to me. Here are parts of two letters a week apart dealing with two different essays. In both cases the sting was at once acute and necessary:

July 9, 1983

Dear Wes,

Here's your essay with the addition of a lot of imprudent red ink. I'm sure this is not a definitive job of criticism. I've proposed a lot of little editorial changes, have conversed with you some, and have resisted your opposite tendencies to say in some places less than you have thought and in other places considerably more. In dealing with the first tendency, I'm at a disadvantage, for it involves trying to clarify concepts that I may not understand. I'm probably more trustworthy in dealing with the second, for even the scientifically ignorant can see when a writer is rambling.

You are naturally becoming more and more aware of the intricacy of the problems. And that naturally means that you are going to have to become tougher and tougher in defining a subject and staying with it. Sometimes in your effort to anticipate all possibilities you grow almost as heroic as the Pentagon. But only God can think of everything.

July 16, 1983

My dear Wes, my dear friend and teacher, I'm bound to tell you, with great reluctance and entire respect, that I think this is bad work. It is full of ideas and insights that I recognize as brilliant and that have already been of the greatest usefulness to me, but I recognize them here only because I have heard you tell about them better than you have written about them here.

The problem is merely compositional. Nothing is fully or particularly or patiently developed. Some very large and problematical concepts you wave by with only a perfunctory assertion. And you don't make the connections, the transitions. Sometimes in lieu of a transition you offer only a label or heading. Sometimes you just ran the head of one concept into the tail of another. Reading, one is constantly wondering how you got to where you are from where you just were. (I'm talking about the writing now; more often than not, I know what you mean, but not from this writing.)

Twenty-three years later he hasn't given up on the possibility that I can get better. In the year of this writing, he is seventy-three and I am seventy-one, and not so long ago came comments just as sharp as many of those delivered earlier. So Wendell's patience is another virtue.

As is his humor. His letter of September 4, 1981, is a self-deprecating, clear example of what he meant when he once said, "If you can't laugh, you're not serious enough." What follows is an example of another form of humor from a letter dated January 7, 1984:

As a name for The Land Institute mud volleyball team, I first thought of the Rhizomes—suggestive of determination, tenacity, and the ability to move in soft ground.

But rhizomes are not what you would call overbearing, their performance is hardly spectacular, and the name suggests few rhymes for the cheerleaders. There is nothing snobbier than a blank verse cheer.

So I suggest the Johnson Grass, which has all the before mentioned traits and, of course, more. Johnson grass is the epitome of vegetable aggression. The very name chills the blood. The performance drives all hope from the human heart. And think of the rhymes!

We can also add prescience to the list of his virtues. Although most of us know that *The Unsettling of America* was meant to be corrective, not prophetic, there have been instances in which Wendell, though not in a prophetic mode, seems aware of a coming wind. It is as though his nose is up and he is sniffing it when it's a mere breeze. To illustrate this I have selected the following three paragraphs smack against one another in a letter of October 23, 1984:

> I'm watching it drizzle, waiting for the cow to calve, waiting to get back to work outdoors.
>
> Mary Catherine Bateson says: "More and more, it has seemed to me that the idea of an individual, the idea that there is someone to be known, separate from the relationships, is simply an error" (*With a Daughter's Eye*, 117).
>
> There is a sense in which that Maximilian sunflower you showed me had failed to be a Maximilian sunflower by living outside its definition—its definition and its proper community being one and the same.

That sunflower plant of which he spoke had achieved its "potential" because we had eliminated all competing plants. It therefore grew extra large and broke over. He was speaking, ten years before it became a hot topic, about the reality of context dependency.

On the necessity of forgiveness:

> January 5, 1991
>
> After we talked I put down some notes about forgiveness: to give offense (intentionally) is to attempt a taking of power. To take offense is to grant that power. To forgive is to see that the offender, in fact, does not have the power he or she is attempting to take; to see that you do not desire to have power over the offender (that is, that you do not desire even justice); and, therefore, to be able to imagine (sympathize with) the offender.
>
> To accept forgiveness is to see that you do not desire to set the terms on which you will receive sympathy.

To forgive or to be forgiven is to go free of offense. It is to live again a life undiminished by offense and by the anger or humiliation of shame that accompany offense.

All personal entities are conducted on the assumption that the combat is proceeding toward adjudication and justice. But no adequate case can be made, and there is no adequate court. Between parents and children, brothers and sisters, husbands and wives, justice has never been done in this world. (And we must hope that forgiveness in this world will relieve the necessity of justice in the next.) If the desire for justice cannot be given up, the quarrel cannot be ended.

A man who writes so elegantly about forgiveness can surely forgive my breach of trust in citing the following letter. (I read the letter to Tanya over the phone. She said "Oh, that was a long time ago and the word got out around here and so everybody knows about it anyway.")

September 12, 1992

We've been here [England] three weeks now. After much driving and walking, I'm getting a pretty good sense of this landscape—as also, inevitably, an ever fuller sense of myself as a stranger here. Much as I admire and love it, I can't at all belong to it.

Last Tuesday, I went to talk with Prince Charles (Jonathon Porritt arranged for me to be invited, I think.) I talked with him for an hour at Highgrove House, near Tetbury. It was a much easier meeting than I expected, for he is intelligent, considerate, and talks and listens well. He is an ally, is deeply concerned about what is happening to rural life and to civilization. He is establishing organic methods on his own farm at Highgrove, and was curious to know what is going on in the U.S. I told him a little about my own farming, much about your work, much about the Amish, etc. I'll tell you about the visit in more detail later. Make as little as you can of this visit, please, or keep quiet about it altogether. I don't want to seem to exploit the contact.

Also much is afoot here in Dartington. So far, the farmland has been farmed conventionally—in fact, it was a pioneer in what we now call conventional farming. But now they want,—and badly need—to head it the other way. Yesterday, I walked and talked for 2½ hours with the estate steward, Charles Taylor. We were looking at a tract of 120–130 acres that they plan to divide off as an independent, small, diversified farm, using the native South Devon cattle, etc. Charles Taylor is a very intelligent young man, has farm experience, great love for the countryside, and competent knowledge of natural history; he is a good companion. He likes the idea of farming the place with horses, but is worried about appearing "quaint." I alerted him to your visit. When you come he'll need a visit with you and will want to hear in detail about the sunshine farm.

We're well and enjoying ourselves. We send our love.

Wendell once wrote me that "to write is to discover." I suppose he meant that as we write and are forced to reflect on what we have written, we are expected to see if it holds together. Writing is a "work-a-day task": we either "discover" the coherence of the argument or it fails. Wendell can do this before breakfast—all in the interest of seeking clarity, which happened to turn into his putting out another book, in this case *Life Is a Miracle:*

> August 16, 2000
>
> Let me see if I can work at your letter of August 8 by way of definitions of some terms.
>
> One definition of "empirical" in my *American Heritage Dictionary* is "Verifiable or provable by means of observation or experiment." That is the definition I have been using because I have had the impression that it is the one in general use. The true empiricist, as I understand it, limits his or her thinking to the provably factual, or to theories leading to proofs of factuality.
>
> Your dictionary's definition of "superstition" is correct, of course. But my thinking about our problem has led me to phrase the definition in another way: superstition is disprovable belief; but also (and this is the meaning in the subtitle of my book) it is belief in the sufficiency, or the soon-to-be sufficiency, of what is provable. And I'm assuming that authentic religious faith occurs beyond or outside the issue of provability.
>
> My accusation against empirical processes is simply that they do not and cannot give a description of reality that is true enough or complete enough. My description of reality, because of my experience, has to include, for examples, faith and love and beauty, which I think cannot be experimentally verified, as some kinds of goodness also cannot be.
>
> Empirical knowledge has to do with the things of time. It cannot touch the things of eternity. If, as people of faith have always believed, time is contingent upon eternity and utterly different from it (eternity is not a long time; it is not "infinity"), then empirical knowledge is limited knowledge and is at least no less limited than knowledge of any other kind. A fact may have a standing in time that is entirely different from its standing in eternity.
>
> For the mythologies of religion, the scientific empiricists have tried to substitute what I see as a mythology or ideology (or sometimes a superstition) of factuality. —— seems to believe that factuality eliminates, or ought to eliminate, ideology. This, I think, is impossible, because factuality, as a doctrine, insisting on its exclusive adequacy to truth or reality, is itself an ideology.

This is a momentous issue, for if we see reality as consisting only of the things of time, the humanly provable, then we have no argument for preserving the things of time. Human intelligence, whether genetically determined or "free," is supreme. If the human intelligence collectively decides that life is an accident and so depreciates and destroys it, then that is only another fact among facts, and, to a mind self-limited to factuality, this ought to be acceptable.

As for your affirmation of our ability to know more now than in the past, I will say that the mind, as I understand it, is by definition a plenum. It is always, from the beginning until now, as full as it can be of various kinds of knowledge: facts, dreams, theories, imaginings, visions, plans, skills, memories, desires, etc. The quality of these contents, I think, is not a matter of their provability, but rather of their formal integrity or cultural completeness.

If we know more now, how is it that we are not the "inventors" of anything like the moral law (what C. S. Lewis called "the Tao") and in fact have been moronically slow and clumsy in giving any more dimension at all to our present situation?

Well, that's about as far as I can take it before breakfast. Later for "Special Effects."

If that is the work of a man yet to have his breakfast, then it's no wonder Wendell is always trying to do too much. This sort of paragraph shows up time and again:

December 9, 2000

I was away from home 70 or so days this year, and that much absence has been too nearly a disaster. Everything here has suffered. It may take a year for me to restore this place and my life to tolerable order. I finally got the last load of firewood to the house yesterday, and that should have been done in October. I haven't hauled a single load of manure out of the barns, and that should have been done mostly in the spring and the rest in October. And so it is with everything. A big part of the trouble, of course, is that I'm not as much account as I used to be.

Sometimes we can catch Wendell attempting a unified field theory, which Einstein failed at, perhaps because, unlike Wendell, he was a scientist, given to a reductive approach to the world. Wendell, the humanities person, is toned up for integration. Here he is obviously commenting on a piece he sent me:

March 3, 2002

This piece seems to carry me some distance farther toward my hope of finally putting science, art, politics, agriculture, etc. all on the same ground or foothold.

I think this has a structure, but its structure is not exactly linear. For that reason, I've felt right so far in putting it in separate blocks, rather than the usual paragraphs. It's a series of inspirations strung along a line of thought more than a consecutive development from one premise.

To my discomfort, it is far better than my Georgetown speech. Do you think that speech is anywhere near good enough?

Note in the first paragraph—as in the letter of August 16, 2000—his desire to integrate. That shows the reality we are accustomed to in his writings. But note that what he is describing in the second paragraph cannot be integrated to his satisfaction in a narrative where one sentence follows another toward some acceptable coherence. So he has organized his piece in blocks—we see this in some of the later essays—and thereby he honors the coherent narrative. He honors the art of writing. (It is instructive to look back on his July 9 and 16, 1983, letters as guidelines for narrative writing.) Note finally in the third paragraph the characteristic humility—Wendell wondering if he has been good enough at his art. But here comes an interesting and not surprising reality. He says he thinks it better than a speech, implying his willingness to acknowledge that useful nuggets can sometimes be more important than integrated coherence. This could be submitted as evidence that practicality on important issues has priority over art.

What follows here, from the same year, is the result of several conversations involving the domestic and the wild. I had argued that sustainability would rest on a three-legged stool. One leg was conservation of the wild biodiversity. Another leg was restoration, and the third leg was an agriculture or forestry or fishery built such that conservation was a consequence of production. Some ecologists have argued that to save the biodiversity we need to intensify the industrial processes for food production "where it is already screwed up." Here is a good summary of Wendell's take:

May 30, 2002

The job we have now is to oppose the proposition that natural diversity and the integrity of the natural world can be preserved (1) by making a strict division between the natural world and the human world and (2) by radically reducing the cultural, economic, and domestic-genetic diversity of the human world.

Evidence of the currency and prestige of this proposition is in Borlaug's article (that I sent to you) in which he dismisses with contempt the importance of "man-made biodiversity," and in Wilson's *The Future of Life*, in which he advocates intensive industrial agriculture, including genetic engineering and "tree farming . . . conducted like the agribusiness it is"—this activity to be confined to half the world: "Half the world for humanity, half for the rest of life. . . ."

To answer this, your two questions in your Schumacher lecture make a good enough starting place: What is the agricultural system that can replace the system dependent on fossil fuels? And what can replace the toxic agricultural chemicals?

And maybe you can make no better structure for your argument than by proceeding in rational order to the further obvious questions:

Can we preserve nature intact in half the world by utterly degrading it in the other half?

Can we preserve nature intact anywhere by radically oversimplifying our economic relation to it, dismissing nature's integrity as an economic standard, and ignoring its processes—in effect, replacing it with the standards and processes of industrialism?

Can we afford to abandon forever the possibility of a living harmony between humanity and nature, economy and ecology? It is just to say "forever" here, because if we destroy all the land-using or land-based cultures, we may be unable to develop them again—not, at least, with the present population in the foreseeable future.

Wilson would counter this by saying that such a harmony never existed: "Eden was a slaughterhouse." But you don't need to be trapped by this. You're not arguing from "nostalgia" or proposing to give up anything learned by modern science. You're talking about a future harmony over the whole world to be worked toward by informed people.

What kind of humanity does it take to preserve the diversity and integrity of nature? Can complexity of any kind be preserved by a humanity reduced and oversimplified by the requirements of industrial science and economics?

Because the thinking of Wilson and Borlaug would simply abandon the human half of the world to the rule of the agribusiness and industrial corporations, you must ask what sort of stewardship or caretaking we might realistically expect from the corporations? What has been their record in food production, forestry, mining, and other forms of land use? What, in short, is the difference between being saved by the food, timber, and mineral corporations and being destroyed by them?

What are the political implications of reserving half the world for nature and delivering the other half to the corporate economy? What governmental, police, and military powers and measures will be required for that? There is no possibility here of separating science from politics and industry. This, in fact, looks like a deliberate relinquishment of science (and every other discipline) to politics and industry. You'll recognize this as the issue I tried without noticeable success to raise with Doug Tompkins and John Davis.

Finally, what is to keep the corporations, once they have demolished the natural integrity and diversity of the human half of the world, by the prescribed industrial methods of land use, from going directly on to apply the same methods to the natural half? (I'm adapting my language only by courtesy to the absurd notion that nature can be whole in half the world.)

So, as I see it, the long-building opposition between agrarian conservationists and puritan conservationists is now becoming public. That's too bad. In many ways it will be destructive. But I see no alternative to standing up and defending the side we're now forced to take.

I had argued, following the Canadian ecologist the late J. Stan Rowe, that the proper way to look at our problems and to solve them is to take an outside-in view of the earth rather than the more commonsense view of inside-out. Stan Rowe had started with the ecosphere (not biosphere, a term which should be eliminated) with the embedded ecosystems, which includes the embedded organisms and so on downward in this hierarchy of structure to organs, tissues, cells, molecules, and atoms. In this hierarchy the ecosystem has standing and, as I see it, following the UC–Berkeley ecologist Arnold Schulz, is the necessary conceptual tool for the management of our resources. With the ecosystem concept we can draw the boundary anywhere. I was arguing that it is only within the ecosystem that true creativity happened. It is here that new life forms evolve as the consequence of adaptation to local reality.

Here is part of Wendell's response following discussion on this subject. Once again he has a most useful and practical take on the issue.

October 26, 2002

I no longer remember my letter to you of August 31. But in the sentence you quote I am not by any means sure that I was wrong.

How distinct is an ecosystem? Do ecosystems overlap? Or can a smaller ecosystem exist within a larger one? My unscientific assumption is that the answer to both questions is yes. I'm assuming that a completely independent ecosystem is as impossible as a completely independent organism.

Furthermore, what do we mean by local? Does a locality gain or lose its identity because of its size? Is the Gulf of Alaska or San Francisco Bay more or less a place than the Pacific Ocean? It seems certain to me that places, at least, can overlap, and that a smaller place can be contained within a larger one.

But whether local adaptation means adaptation to place or ecosystem, it seems to me that it has to happen as the fundamental condition of survival. If the arctic tern flies an annual round trip of 22,000 miles, that does not mean that it is not locally adapted. It means that it has successfully adapted either to the many small places or the one big place it flies over. If it had not so adapted, it would not survive the trip. It has to be capable of navigating, finding nourishment, maintaining body temperature, etc., wherever it is.

Most of us humans, by contrast, couldn't cross our home states without an almost unaccountable array of "outside" helps and subsidies. We have not adapted, and we can stay alive, let alone travel, at present only by the means that have assured our failure to adapt.

Whatever I may have been talking about in my August 31 letter, my thoughts have been running more and more to the necessity of local adaptation. A lot of lines cross there. I was fairly sure until I got your letter today that the evolutionists looked on local adaptation as the fundamental requirement for survival: a roadrunner couldn't survive in a swamp, etc. J. Russell Smith, Albert Howard, and you have insisted on the importance of local adaptation in agriculture. And it seems clear to me that authentic human cultures arise from the effort to adapt economies to place. Without the outside helps and subsidies, you would have to have different cultures in the Sonora Desert and the lower Kentucky River valley because you would have to have different economies.

So I was arguing yesterday at a meeting in Frankfort that the great weakness of industrial agriculture, including biotechnology, is in its governing principle of uniformity—whereas the inescapable governing principle of agriculture is local adaptation ("fit the farming to the farm"), which is absolutely contrary to uniformity.

The internal processes of evolution or adaptation—the "shifting gene frequencies"—I will have to leave to you because, as you know, of ignorance. I am very glad to do so, trusting you not to be wrong. And now that I have placed upon you that horrifying burden, I see that I must hope you will hold me ever under suspicion.

We have had conversations from time to time about the stir generated over the decision on the part of the Kansas Board of Education to allow the Creation story in Kansas public schools. Here is Wendell's take:

March 12, 2003

The creationist–evolution quarrel is interesting only as a quarrel. It is based on a sort of confusion of categories. Both sides seem to insist that Genesis or Creation is a competing "theory." It's not. It explains some things, but not others. Evolution is a theory, and it too explains some things but not others. Both are useful. Both are limited. Both leave us ignorant, fallible, and dangerous. It would be best if organized science and organized religion and organized politics got away from the school and let the curriculum be decided by the parents and the teachers. The proposition that education of science or religion on young minds will be seriously impaired by evolution or by Genesis is preposterous. Whatever side one is on, it seems clear that more can be learned from a smart teacher who is "wrong" than from a dummy who is "right."

The next day came a letter on the same subject to show that once he gets a problem on his mind, he doesn't let it go until he comes either to a standoff or a resolution:

March 13, 2003

A further mistake—continuing my thoughts of yesterday—is to isolate creation and evolution from their stories. The Creation is only the beginning of the Genesis story. It is followed by a thoroughly fierce and unflattering history that shows humans (chosen and unchosen) to be ignorant, fallible, and dangerous. That is the conclusion or the judgment that is handed down in Genesis and right through the Bible. Humans can be righteous and admirable, but often they are not. Often they are disappointment to God and dangerous to one another and to the rest of creation.

Evolution is part of the story of modern science, which certainly shows humans to be ignorant, fallible, and dangerous. But that is not the most popular conclusion about that story. The popular conclusion, supported by some prominent scientists and other big-top intellectuals, is that evolution relieves us of the old burden, or eventually will relieve us, of ignorance, fallibility, and danger. Humans are smart animals who, by their cleverness and cunning, are getting smarter all the time and will soon learn "the secret of the universe."

There is, of course, much more to be said about who Wendell Berry is and what he has meant to all of us. Knowing this, I am still comfortable in saying that Wendell Berry is a radical. The Latin root is *radix*. A radical is grounded. That's Wendell, forever asking "What are the assumptions?" Maybe that is because he comes out of a family of lawyers who are given to asking such questions as "Where is the evidence?" From Wendell's quotations mentioned here one can see that much of his life is devoted to dealing with first principles.

But there is more. Wendell Berry is also a humble man. Because this can be misunderstood, I refer to D. H. Lawrence's notion of humility. I read somewhere that Lawrence thought modern industrialized humans were "doggy," meaning they were given to wagging their tails at the conveniences of modern society. Wendell will ask, "Why is this piece of technology necessary?" "What is the cost to our earth's resources?" "What is it going to do to our humanity?" These are radical questions and they are all derived from a spirited humility. Wendell Berry and D. H. Lawrence would be on the same handwritten page in this consideration.

I should add that Wendell's quick wit, not just in letters but in almost every conversation, is a source of delight. Once on the phone I was commenting on certain highly productive scientists, people who had published five or six hundred papers, thirty or forty books, and who get by on three or four hours of sleep and live to be ninety-five. Wendell's immediate response was, "Well, Wes, they've got to live to be ninety-five if they are to get enough sleep."

He's given me several memorable quotations over the years. One of my favorites, and one I often use, came as I was describing an exchange I had with an agricultural economist at one of our nation's land-grant universities. The professor had characterized himself as a "hardheaded realist." This time Wended responded with, "Well, a hardheaded realist is usually someone who uses a lot less information than what is available." I wrote that one down as he continued without pause to counter the economist's argument.

And so this is Wendell in correspondence and conversation, consistently radical, back to first principles, humble but not doggy. As a writer and a thinker and a farmer whose passion is agriculture, he is a hander-down of traditional knowledge, which in turn helps him create new knowledge out of the old.

I have been asked how it is that one man steeped in the humanities—poet, essayist, novelist—and the other trained in science can interact so comfortably with each other. I think it is because we don't think of ourselves as in our disciplines. Our point of convergence is the land, agriculture, the work both of us like, and the common experience of life on a farm from our youth. That's the hub. Lots of spokes come off that hub. That is what makes Wendell accessible to anyone inclined to questioning how we are going to live on this earth.

Eric T. Freyfogle

Wendell Berry and the Limits of Populism

A CENTRAL THEME IN the writings of Wendell Berry—maybe the most important one—is his concern about relationships and about the practical and moral urgency of mending them. The world that Berry observes is not made up of parts in isolation: of individual people, distinct tracts of land, and natural resources. It is composed of connected elements, and the connections are as significant as the elements themselves. We have neglected these many connections, Berry tells us, in varied powerful ways. We see the world in fragmented terms, valuing its parts in isolation and ignoring or underestimating the bonds. This fragmentation in perceptions and values extends beyond the physical realm to the intellectual and the moral; here, too, we are prone to see and value pieces and to discount the necessary ties.

Berry's embrace of an integrated worldview situates him where he can roundly criticize much of contemporary society. It is little wonder that his writings range so widely, from soil erosion to abortion to free trade to the curricula of universities. Fragmentation bears ill fruit, Berry observes, in all of these settings and more. The solution to weak or torn relationships is to recognize their value and then somehow mend them, by respecting ecological processes, for instance; by becoming good neighbors and community members; and by connecting secular and sacred, the present generation with past and future ones.

The social problems that Berry diagnoses, however, are not likely to disappear merely through efforts by individuals, one by one. More than that is needed, particularly in the political realm, to build relationships that Berry views as vital. The welfare of the parts often depends upon the welfare of the integrated whole. The health of that whole, in turn, can depend upon corrective action undertaken at the level of the whole, by people acting together. Individual reform—in values, perceptions, even daily conduct—can take us only so far. Indeed, to lay stress simply on change at the individual level is to risk reducing complex economic and social problems to matters merely of private morality. It can divert attention from our insistent needs for structural change. It can sap strength from the kinds of organized political efforts that make wide-ranging change possible.

To note this limitation on Berry's thought is hardly to criticize it, except to say (as we can say of all writers) that he has given us part of the solution but not all of it. We need to take Berry's moral vision and connect it with more forceful efforts to promote structural changes of a kind out of reach to individuals acting alone. Yet here too we need to do more than just unite the parts—Berry's prophecy with, say, the organizing and lobbying efforts of environmental groups. A union of moral criticism and political organizing needs to give rise to something larger than these parts—to some sort of organized cultural push for the resettlement of the continent; to a new understanding of the human place in the community of life; ultimately to new structures of daily life that help people as individuals and families live the kinds of moral, satisfying lives that Berry so warmly presents.

Relationships

Berry is a married man in many ways, and he wants other men, women, and children to marry as well. He is bound to his wife and to his children and grandchildren. He is also bound to his land, to his community, and to the generations that lie dead up on the hill. Although he uses livestock and kills them in time, the human–animal bond on his side reflects respect and honor. We live with animals, Berry says, as much today as in the past. These many paths of interconnection extend to memories, loyalties, affections, and cultural traditions. To live well in a place, Berry relates, is to become part of this community of life, entering into its memories, reworking them, and then passing them along. This type of cultural interdependence is just as vital as the cycle of natural fertility, which begins (in the case of terrestrial life) with the soil, moves through plants and animals, and returns to the earth by death and decay, making way for new life. It forms overall a great wheel, Berry tells us, linking present, past, and future life. For all life to flourish, the many cycles and links must remain intact.

Berry's commitment to relationships shows up in nearly all of his cultural criticism. His concerns about abortion, for instance, mostly have to do with the ways abortion illustrates and accepts weaknesses in marital bonds and in attitudes toward childbearing. Berry worries about feminism for the same reason: not because it honors women but because it threatens to value the human part in isolation from the roles that women fulfill. Higher education incurs criticism because it treats students as isolated creatures, not situated beings. It trains them to become cogs in an economic system that treats labor and nature as commodities or inputs while ignoring the duties of belonging to place. To study science apart from philosophy, literature, or history is to deny the many bonds that link human experiences and knowledge into an integrated, evolving whole. To distinguish book learning from practical experience—and both from the wisdom of elders—is to presume a division if not a hierarchy that promotes blindness and error. Work and leisure should flow together, Berry tells us, and so should the secular and religious. Wholeness arises when labor overlaps with prayer.

Berry illustrates these connections in a recent brief essay, "Contempt for Small Places," in which he expresses hope that people some day will see the links between the Gulf of Mexico's "dead zone" and strip-mining in Kentucky. In this instance, water provides the tie:

> The health of the oceans depends on the health of rivers; the health of rivers depends on the health of small streams; the health of small streams depends on the health of their watersheds. The health of the water is exactly the same as the health of the land; the health of small places is exactly the same as the health of large places. As we know, disease is hard to confine. Because natural law is in force everywhere, infections move.[1]

A more developed expression of the theme is present in Berry's masterful short story "The Boundary," in which an elderly, tottering Mat Feltner inspects the wire fence that surrounds his farm to see that it remains taut enough to contain livestock. At first glance the story appears to exalt the sturdy fence, much as does Robert Frost's poem "Mending Wall." Yet, even more than Frost, Berry pushes readers to question fences and to see the dangers of them. Mat's fence contains his cattle but little more than that, physically and in Mat's mind. The fence permits life to flow over and through it. Wild animals pass the boundary with ease. As owner, Mat is linked to his neighbors in ways that benefit both. And, as his memory takes hold, Mat reveals how connected he is to past generations, to his extended family, to the community itself, to future land tenants, and most vividly to his elderly, worried wife, waiting in the house on the hill. Mat's thoughts on his farm's productivity are not detached from his thinking about its beauty; his utilitarian calculations of market profit are not cut off from the aesthetic and spiritual harvests. Mat accepts responsibility for his individual actions yet entertains no illusion that he can go it alone. Particularly on ecologically challenging land, good farming necessarily builds upon local experience-based wisdom that takes generations to arise. A handing down is thus needed, from generation to generation, good owner to good owner. As for the behavioral misfits that afflict all families and places, good ties are essential here as well. Thus, the survival of an Uncle Peach (in "Thicker than Liquor") depends on the willingness of good neighbors like Wheeler Catlett to recognize family duties and step into them.

Perhaps inevitably Berry is drawn to circular images when he talks about life. Endings become new beginnings, or they need to, if life is to flourish. And so we recognize fragmentation in its many forms as the bane of fertility and health. Glad and Clara Pettit promote fragmentation (in "It Wasn't Me") when they deny their bonds to Clara's father, Old Jack Beecham, and to the farm tradition of which he was a part. For the Pettits, the Beecham farm is a capital asset properly valued for its annual crop yield—which is to say valued apart from its roles in surrounding natural and human landscapes. It is left to the lawyer Wheeler Catlett and good community leaders like him to strive to keep bonds intact—in the instance of Jack Beecham's farm, to promote an orderly handing down from Jack to the Penns and, should the Penns prove worthy, to the good tenders next in line. Jack's scribbled instructions about his last wishes for the farm (selling to Elton Penn at below market value) are construed by Wheeler in the context of Jack's life and of his agrarian culture; they are interpreted, that is, in a way that honors the connections among Jack's words, his life, his good tenants, and the needs of the land. The small-minded Pettits deny the context, detaching the written words from people and place and interpreting them in legal isolation.

Standing Apart

One hardly needs to dip into Berry's writing to recognize his detachment from much of modern culture. The contrast is especially stark when we compare his work with areas of modernity in which fragmentation has proceeded farthest: the aspects of industry, the market, and education. Industry and the market view nature as warehouses of discrete commodities to extract, process, buy, and sell. Parts are judged in isolation, not in integration. We can see the mentality at work in the economic treatment of the individual tree. As it grows and interacts with its surroundings, year by year, it adds no value to national income as economists calculate it. Value arises only when the tree is cut and hauled away. Then the value is assessed in market terms—that is, in terms that ignore its place of origin. Meanwhile, the loss of the living tree is economically irrelevant, as are the ecological effects of harvesting it. Contrasting this attitude is the perspective of the caring landowner, who values the growing tree and appraises it as part of a forest or woodlot, as well as alone. The caring owner knows, too, the losses that come when the tree is removed.

What is true of the tree is true of nature's other components. A flow of water that a person diverts and uses for irrigation has value only when it is diverted. (In the western United States, a prior-appropriation water right only arises if and when a person does divert the water.) Water has no market value when left in place to sustain the river. Nor does the river as a whole, given that it cannot be bought or sold. Tracts of farmland valued for yield are assigned prices with little or no regard for location or surroundings. Human labor is treated much the same, mostly valued at the going commodity rate.

As for the academy, intellectual fragmentation is greater than outsiders usually realize. Work that one department values, given its peculiar culture, another department might reject as nearly worthless. Although critics have long lamented the separation of science and literature, the fragmentation continues, within fields of study as well as between them. In the case of farmland, industrial scientists are happy to manipulate nature at will, down to the smallest genetic unit, paying little regard to the effects of farming on ecological processes, landscape beauty, and wildlife populations—natural elements that researchers elsewhere in the academy value highly. While scholars in one corner probe the limits on human knowledge, scholars in another charge ahead as if knowledge were complete. While one group considers the extension of moral value to other life forms, another group remains confident that humans alone possess worth. While one group, committed to mathematical models, touts the ability of the market to move nature's parts to their highest uses, another group, actually studying the land, catalogs the many ways that market processes bring degradation. More and more, research entails by definition the collection and analysis of factual data in ever-more-specialized niches. Meanwhile, few people think seriously about the whole of things, landscapes included. What is good land use, for instance? And what kind of culture is needed to promote it? The questions go unasked because they fit within no specialty. Academic fields charge ahead with proposals to reshape the land without any comprehensive way to evaluate the results. Is it any wonder that the works of Berry himself are pushed to the academic fringe? Is it a surprise that few academics can imagine finding useful truth in fiction or poetry?

Fragmentation in American culture is particularly evident in social and political thought, in which step by step we have "liberated" individuals from social shackles, which is to say, exalted people as autonomous individuals while minimizing the centrality of loyalties, duties, and interdependencies. Countertrends do exist, to be sure—the billboards encouraging men to become good fathers, and families to take in foster children. But even here we might ask whether the parent–child relationship has independent or collective value or whether it is mostly a means to a personal end. America is the

paradigmatic land of liberalism (to use the term in its classic meaning of exalting the individual and the individual's right to pursue self-selected goals).
Though often labeled "conservatism" by the political right, the economic libertarianism of Wall Street advocates stands squarely in America's tradition of
liberal autonomy. So does the social liberalism of what is termed the Far Left.
Time and again, we reduce social disputes to competing claims of individual
rights—the right to have an abortion, to own guns, to drain wetlands—as if
the defended activities did not implicate neighbors, family members, and the
community as a whole. For the economic libertarian as well as the ardent
Left-liberal, relationships are mostly voluntary and transient, lasting only so
long as an individual wants them to last. At the extreme (or perhaps now the
"cutting edge") we have the ardent liberals known as contractarians, who deny
nearly all responsibilities save those agreed to voluntarily and who assert that
one can even freely break contracts if one is willing to pay for the resulting
monetary harms.

Berry's dissent from this kind of fragmentation appears vividly when we
turn to food and to other basics of life. Berry seeks to connect eaters to food
producers and to specific food sources on the land. The free market, in contrast, pushes in the opposite direction, reducing food transactions to matters
of price and cash flow. Berry encourages consumers to engage morally with
the methods used to produce their goods (the pollution, land degradation,
social displacement, child labor) and with the fates of their postconsumption
wastes (the leaking landfills and disrupted fertility cycles). Again, he stands
apart from the dominant market view, in which goods appear on store shelves
shorn of histories and thus of moral complications. The same shallow cash
nexus weakly connects the consumer to the modern waste hauler and landfill
operator. In Berry's view (borrowed from agrarians of the past), barter rises
above the cash sale in supporting a sound relationship between bargaining
parties. Best of all are links between friends and neighbors involving exchanges
of labor that are left unrecorded. Not cash and bargain, but love itself, forges
the strongest bond.

Theories of Progress

Implicit in much of Berry's work are claims that we can move ahead as a
people, or at least recover lost ground, by improving our many relationships.
To the extent Berry offers a theory of progress, this is likely it. To understand
this component of his thought—and get clear on what he might overlook—we
can compare Berry's views with three competing perspectives on human nature and progress.

Jacksonian democracy. Growing up in rural Kentucky, Berry naturally embraced elements of the ideology known as Jacksonian democracy: a commitment to individual initiative, free enterprise, minimal government, and a safety net provided by family, friends, or parish rather than society. Like other lovers of liberty, Berry recoils from vestiges of feudalism and binding hierarchy (slavery most of all). In various writings he embraces not just free labor but something akin to a labor theory of value, particularly for skilled craftsmen. Antebellum Democrats held high the ideal of the independent farmer or small businessman, beholden to no baron or bank. Berry still honors the ideal.

Where Berry stands apart from this still lively strand of American thought is in his rejection of the Jacksonian's theory of progress. Jacksonians assumed that a release of entrepreneurial energy would somehow lead automatically to improvements in the public good. The most popular explanation employed Adam Smith's invisible hand: as individuals aggressively pursue their self-interest, the theory posits, the market magically transforms their selfishness into public virtue. Few Jacksonians may have read Smith or understood his logic, but the spirit of liberty was alive on the land.[2] Somehow, liberty and progress would travel hand in hand.

Berry largely rejects this belief that the market can transform private vice into public good. We see his stance clearly in his fiction, in which good farmers such as Mat Feltner, Nathan Coulter, and Elton Penn think constantly about the community and the future as well as themselves. These leaders stand apart from characters such as Troy Chatham in *Jayber Crow,* who is quick to borrow, expand, and add equipment in a headlong pursuit of wealth. When the deceased Jack Beecham's farm is up for auction, we have no illusion that the best new owner is the one who can pay the most. When Troy Chatham sells the Keith family's "Nest Egg," his foolishness is evident.

Berry's rejection of Adam Smith, though, leaves a serious void in his own economic libertarianism. If the market is not strong enough to turn selfishness into public progress, then what force is? Without Smith's invisible hand, how might liberty lead to healthy lands?

Marxism. Nearly as strong are the parallels in Berry's work with the fundamentals of Karl Marx's thought, particularly Marx's critique of capitalism and "bourgeois" property and his emphasis on the cultural implications of the modes of economic production. Here again we find overlap on key elements but a disagreement on the driving force of progress. Berry shares Marx's criticisms of industrialism but not his ideas about change.[3]

Marx as economic historian presented an extended critique of industrial capitalism and a prediction that, in time, class conflict would lead workers (the proletariat) to displace capitalists. The result would be a peaceful, class-less society in which wants were met and conflict ended. Marx spoke only vaguely about his ultimate vision of harmony; what interested him instead were the ills of the industrial order and the initial steps of the journey to a new age. Marx railed against the cash nexus and "the icy water of egotistical calculation,"[4] which degraded loyalties and interpersonal bonds. Industrialization sapped the craftsman of all sense of pride, he complained, and transformed even professionals into paid wage laborers. As for private property, Marx supported it when used by the owner. What he attacked was property in the form of capital: property from which an owner extracted value by controlling the labor of others. It was the factory owner and the farm landlord who drew Marx's wrath, not the independent farmer or shop owner. Marx's popular appeal rested on his embrace of the labor theory of value—a theory that he wrested from economic liberals and transformed from a defense of private property (as it was under John Locke) into a weapon to attack capitalist accumulation. Workers should own their tools, Marx announced; only if they did could they retain their pride. Bourgeois capitalism turned people into machines and would eventually, he (wrongly) predicted, drive all wages down to subsistence levels with profits going entirely to capitalist owners. In time, though, workers would awaken to their plight, Marx explained. The ensuing conflict would displace capitalism and take society to a higher cultural level.

Berry's thought is usefully put side by side with Marxist criticism because the body of thought known as southern agrarianism or conservatism supplies the most direct, homegrown analogy, in terms of a wide-ranging criticism of industrial capitalism, to European Marxism. (The point has been developed by the historian Eugene Genovese, once a Marxist and now, like Berry, a proponent of ideas selectively drawn from the South's conservative heritage.)[5] Like Marx, Berry stresses the central importance to society of the means used to produce basic commodities. A mode of production based on small farms and independent craftsmen, Berry suggests, leads to a moral order quite different from the one that results when production comes from industrial farms, factories, and global enterprises. Echoing Marx (and, even more, Proudhon) Berry calls for mutualist, cooperative enterprises that displace ruthless competition. Berry, of course, does not use the language of class, yet his comments about community bear a distinct resemblance. All people who dwell in a place belong to the resident community, whether they know it or not, Berry contends. We hear an echo of Marx's "false consciousness" in comments (by the fictional Burley Coulter and others) about the inability of many community members to awaken to their true membership.[6] And we see faintly, too, a vision of a small-town classless society, in which social hierarchy disappears, solidarity prevails, and people equate their personal welfare with the welfare of the whole.

Even more than in the case of Jacksonian democracy, though, we need to avoid pushing this comparison too far. Far more than the materialist Marx, Berry sees power in ideas and holds out the possibility of moral progress. Berry pleads with readers to consider a change of heart in a manner Marx would have rejected. Indeed, Berry's individualism distinctly distances him from Marx, who scoffed at liberalism and saw little prospect that individuals could change on their own. More pertinent is the lack of overlap on Marx's theory of historical change. A strong believer in the determining force of history, Marx predicted that class conflict would inevitably arise and usher in a new era; just as capitalists as a class had displaced the feudal landowners, moving society from feudalism to the industrial age, so too workers would awaken to their solidarity and push aside and ultimately eliminate the capitalist rulers. Progress came through class conflict, which was largely inevitable (though usefully aided, Marx noted, by far-seeing intellectuals).

Civic republicanism. A third point of contrast for Berry's thought, particularly useful on the issue of progressive change, is offered by civic republicanism, a body of thought in the Anglo-American world that gained strength in eighteenth-century Britain, heavily influenced the colonies during the Revolution, and survived in diminishing form thereafter. Republicanism remains alive in various strands of communitarian thought and in older, largely displaced forms of political conservatism.

Civic republicans (Thomas Jefferson among them) worried about the corrupting influence of the market and the aggressive pursuit of self-interest. They worried also about the loss of independence that came when one person became subject to the economic or social control of another. Good governance could emerge, they believed, only if talented citizens gained economic independence, rose above self interest, and then engaged with one another in the important work of collective self-rule. Virtue was the key to it all, and governments were best designed when they promoted virtue. Private interest and the public good often diverged. The selfish ego threatened civic stability, particularly when private interests manipulated government to their advantage.

In this third body of thought we again see similarities and differences with Berry's views. Like the civic republicans, Berry perceives a clash between the common good and the aggressive pursuit of self-interest. He agrees, too, that leadership requires virtue and that virtue is endangered, particularly by money. Good governance, in turn, is a communal aspiration, and people who provide good leadership deserve praise for their service. The highest calling, for Berry as for civic republicans, is for a person to rise up to become a community's exemplar, leading by individual virtue as well as by community-minded acts.

Civic republicanism is particularly useful in clarifying Berry's relative inattention to any theory of progressive change. Where (as noted) Jacksonian democrats placed faith in the market and Karl Marx deferred to the force of history and class conflict, civic republicans have looked to virtuous leaders to craft policies to promote the common good. They have endorsed structures of government that draw in qualified leaders, diffuse power, and diminish the chance that selfishness can corrode public welfare. Ultimately, progress here rests on concerted action—on what America's revolutionaries termed their "self-rule" (a revealing label, given our tendency now to equate self-rule with individual liberty). Republican progress came when good people set aside their personal economic interests and labored collectively to promote the common good.

The Responsible Individual

On balance, Berry leaves us with the suggestion that social progress will come, if at all, when people become more aware of their relationships and then labor to improve them. Progress, that is, requires people to improve themselves by becoming better members of families, communities, and home landscapes. The market's invisible hand will not bring about improvement, particularly to the land, Berry implies. Nor can we await some inexorable force of history to bring healing. People need to act, one by one, by becoming more moral. Berry expresses this message mostly by implication, yet he is nonetheless clear. He criticizes social "movements" and does not want to be part of one. Just as telling, his dozens of books contain scarcely any recognition that the decades-long labors of environmental groups have brought any good. (His few favorable references are mostly to local, Kentucky-based activities.) Indeed, in essay after essay we hear hardly a word about organizing, joining groups, or getting together with fellow citizens to push for political change. Berry promotes the idea of community-supported agriculture and organized sustainable farming and forestry initiatives. But his rare mention of such local efforts highlights his relative silence on the subject overall.

We see this limit clearly in Berry's masterful novel *Jayber Crow,* in which Jayber struggles to respond to the ills of modernity, particularly the arrival of the market mentality and industrial farming to small-town Kentucky. Berry as novelist is true to his fictional setting when he has Jayber and his fellow good citizens stand back and do nothing while industrial capitalism drags down their town. His best option, Jayber senses, is to respond individually as a good Christian and love his neighbors, all of them. It is moral advice so far as it goes—and extraordinarily hard to embrace, as Berry vividly displays. Yet we can hardly be so naive as to think that Crow's Christian love will halt the industrial juggernaut. In time, Port William's lands will pass into the hands of farmers willing to push them hard to make money. When one aggressive farmer falls, another will take his place. Berry, to be sure, is not Jayber, nor is Jayber put forth as a model citizen, yet the reticence we see in Jayber runs through much of Berry's writing.

We can say that Jayber acts irresponsibly in his reaction to industrial agriculture, and perhaps he does, if he thinks his love will somehow soon improve the land. We could complain, too, that Jayber is more interested in assuaging his conscience than in promoting the common good—though we need to go easy here because the moral life is itself a worthy and difficult end. The important point, though, is we find little evidence, in this novel or elsewhere, of any call for concerted action by citizens acting as such—for self-rule of the kind that America's founders sought when they broke ties with Britain. We can admire the virtuous, sensitive individuals like Jayber Crow while at the same time complain, loudly, that little is being done to halt the rural decline. Here and there, Berry emphasizes key ways in which structural change is needed: governments ought to protect small towns from invasion by the market as well as by foreign troops, he tells us. Something must be done about the power of global free trade, and about the vast illegitimate constitutional powers that corporations possess. Public agricultural policies are also miscast, he stresses, and agencies that hold strip-miners accountable for their harms too often defer to their wishes. Even in the case of private property, which Berry supports, he sees need for fundamental legal change, halting uses of property that entail obvious degradation. But how are these structural changes to take place, if good people remain silent? How are they to come about if no movement pushes for them? And is it really true, as Berry sometimes implies, that collective action is largely useless or untimely unless we first simplify and purify our lives as individuals, disconnecting ourselves insofar as possible from the industrial juggernaut?

Ultimately, what we see in Berry's work—and he presents it as finely as any author—are images of the responsible individual, the farmer or barber or tradesman who stands tall on his land or doorstep, lives as virtuously as possible, cares for neighbors, respects other life, and lends support to the surrounding community. They are good and indispensable images, valuable so far as they can take us. But they do not take us as far as we need to go. And by dropping us off where they do, they leave us vulnerable. By exalting the responsible individual and calling for individual reform, Berry implies that (1) individuals are mostly to blame for our ills; (2) individuals can change their ways if they would only do so (albeit the labor might prove hard); and (3) overall reform can come one convert at a time. There are problems, though, with these claims, and their inadequacies pose dangers.

The Populist Persuasion

In his work Berry openly borrows from the writings of earlier agrarians, particularly the authors of the manifesto *I'll Take My Stand* (1930). Less clear to many readers are the similarities between Berry's work and the stances of farm- and labor-based reform efforts in American history. In his call for wide-ranging popular change, beginning at the bottom, Berry's advocacy resembles messages of the Patrons of Husbandry (the Grange), the Farmers' Alliances, the Knights of Labor, and other nineteenth-century efforts that led to the Populist Movement of the 1890s. These reform groups saw themselves pitted in conflict with the new industrial order. They were guided by memories of earlier days, when farmers and craftsmen had greater control over their plights. In the view of Gilded Age reformers, the era pitted people against the vested interests. Proposals for economic reform were blended with calls for social and moral change—including, in the case of Farmers' Alliances, vast improvements in the public status of women.

For the most part these postbellum reform efforts produced little, except in the regulation of grain elevators and railroad rates. With the rise and (in 1897) rapid fall of the Populist party, reform efforts shifted gears—or, more aptly, one reform template gave way to another. The Populists' inclusive, wide-ranging calls for moral reform and economic and cultural change gave way to more narrowly focused efforts to achieve limited results, often economic ones. In the realm of labor, for instance, the inclusive vision of the Knights of Labor yielded to the AFL and its smaller craft unions, which sought to achieve economic gains for their skilled members, not to change society. Farm-related reform efforts divided into numerous groups, again with narrower, targeted aims, leading in time to the rise of the group that worked aggressively not for all farmers but only for the large, industrial few—the American Farm Bureau Federation. In effect, the Populist impulse provided the background for the varied reform efforts that composed the early twentieth-century Progressive Movement.

Efforts by many of these new Progressive reformers did in time bear fruit. And they did so because leaders learned from Populist failings. Moral outrage, leaders realized, was not enough to bring about change, even when directed against specifically described ills. Organization was required, leading to political and economic power. "It became clear" to the new reformers, historian Maury Klein recounts in *The Flowering of the Third America*, "that power could be obtained only through organization, and that those who organized effectively did far better than those who did not. The tighter the organization, the narrower its aims, and the greater the resources at its command, the more likely it was to achieve its aims."[7] Individualism remained an icon and object of folklore, but success at law and in the market required more-orchestrated efforts. Craft unions gained ground when they accepted the existence of industrial capitalism and negotiated on bread-and-butter basics. Advocates of various reform efforts learned the same lesson: organize, keep focused, and push hard. Independent individuals were pawns of the system.

The Progressive experience also yielded other lessons. Voters, it seemed, were inclined to constrain economic enterprises (given the nation's love of economic liberty) only when the evidence of public harm was fairly obvious. In addition, the public's attention span on reform issues was typically short, which meant reformers had only a brief window of opportunity to achieve gains. To endure, real change had to become part of the bureaucratic and organizational structures of society; otherwise, gains could fade away. Even then, corporations were displaying a disturbing ability to mute calls for change by modifying their activities slightly and presenting an appearance of reform. And, once the public's attention faded, corporations stepped in to take over regulatory agencies, weakening reform efforts and even bending regulations to their advantage.

Berry's writing presents instructive parallels with the efforts of early Populist reformers, especially the Grange and Knights of Labor. The parallels are hardly exact, but they are apt in that Berry exhibits many of the cultural traits of these reform movements—holdovers, many of them, from the antebellum era before industrialization gained the upper hand. Like the Populists, Berry ranges widely in his complaints (though to be sure he displays no tendency to latch on to nostrums like free coinage of silver). He frames issues in moral terms, often reducing them to the individual level. His hope is to appeal to citizens from all walks of life. And he dreams of a new order. His vision of success comes mostly from the past, and it is a vision distinctly familiar—the independent farmer or craftsman who plies his trade with little interference from industrial outsiders. This was the dream of many Populists, and agrarians today might dream of it still. The Populists rose and fell because their moral dreams lacked any means of accomplishment. Their problem was not so much looking backward for goals; it was that they failed to find effective ways to achieve the goals. New moneyed powers were roaming the land. The Populists had no countervailing force to deploy in response.

Cussed Individualism

Many of today's environmental goals—most of them, probably—are ones that require concerted action. The individual acting alone can accomplish little. Garrett Hardin highlighted one source of this predicament, which he termed the tragedy of the commons. Hardin's tragedy arose when users of a natural commons were able to increase their uses at will, exceeding the land's carrying capacity and causing degradation. What difference did it make if one person refrained from overusing the commons when someone else would do so? Matched with this ill is the tragedy of fragmentation—probably the greater tragedy in the United States today.[8] This tragedy arises when a landscape is fragmented into small pieces and no person or entity retains enough power to promote goals that require landscape-scale planning. Urban sprawl provides one example of this tragedy. The decline of connected wildlife habitats and of sensibly used rivers are others. If we want to point fingers, in terms of causes, we can take note of the institution of private property, at law and (more significantly) in American culture, which accords individual landowners the power to degrade lands if they choose—neighbors be damned. The effect of private property is to vest so much power in individual owners that the community as such cannot coordinate activities at larger scales. Land abusers benefit from governments that govern least. Then there is the competitive market, which pressures participants to cut costs and, in the case of products from land, encourages or even compels landowners to work lands too hard. When the low-cost market leaders abuse their lands, pushing external harms on neighbors, on future generations, and on other life forms, other market participants can be compelled to follow suit or else lose out.

The point here—and it needs emphasizing—is that individuals are subject to forces beyond their control. They live and work within systems that they did not make or choose. Their choices are constrained, particularly as laborers and producers. In addition, the economics of sound living are often skewed against moral behavior when the individual acts alone. Illustrative here is the individual who rides a bicycle to avoid polluting the air. The cost in inconvenience is borne by the individual alone; the air-quality benefits are enjoyed by everyone. The situation presents a mismatch in the allocation of costs and benefits. The game, thus, is heavily stacked against moral living. Were the rules of the game different, moral living could become far easier. ˙

Like many critics, Berry implies that personal behavior is a matter of choice and that lifestyle choices reveal values; different personal values would yield different choices. The reasoning has merit, to be sure, and yet it shortchanges a critical point. We can see what is missing by returning to Hardin's tragedy of the commons, which he illustrated with the case of the hypothetical livestock grazer who continues adding animals to the commons even though overgrazing results. A grazer might well do this and at the same time support strict collective limits on overgrazing. The grazer who acts alone, that is, might degrade the commons; the same grazer, getting together with others to develop rules for using the commons, could readily vote to protect the land's health. The stances might appear inconsistent, but they are not. In both cases, the grazer promotes his interest. The difference is that the grazer in one setting acts as isolated individual and in another as citizen or cogovernor. As an individual the grazer can do little to protect the commons; as a member of a governing board she can do far more. This distinction is sometimes termed the citizen–consumer dichotomy, and it can be vast. People can vote to ban activities in which they would freely engage if allowed to do so. Again, the positions seem inconsistent but they are not. The roles are different, the economics are different, and so, often, are the outcomes.

The danger of Berry's approach, focused on individual morality, is that it largely blames the individual for problems that are far bigger than the individual. It increases the level of guilt in a way that can detract attention from the larger failures of collective responsibility.[9] It can also portray individuals in an unduly harsh light—as being less responsible than they might be. A frequent, critical response to polls showing wide support for environmental protection is the argument that people display their true, more selfish values when they spend their money. It is an argument that contains a serious flaw, as elementary economics reveals. A person who drives a gas-guzzler could logically support mandatory gas-mileage laws. So which response, then, reveals a person's true values: the individual choice made in isolation or the decision made as citizen, when the power exists to change the system? Berry's inclination, like that of many others, is to judge individuals by choices made in isolation. But in the frequent case of actions where costs and benefits are greatly misaligned (as they are in the instance of the gas-guzzler), this tendency is unfair. It is troubling, too, because it implicitly exaggerates what individuals acting alone can accomplish, thereby weakening much-needed calls for collective action.

Like other agrarians, Berry extends an influential strand of American individualism and a commitment to liberty that are, in fact, inconsistent with the kinds of public policies needed to bring about structural change—in the market, in private property and land use, and in our interactions with nature generally. He displays a typically American commitment to small government, local autonomy, private property, and the preservation of liberties, values that taken together clash with sensible, regional-scale land planning. A common complaint against Berry and others is that they are nostalgic in wanting to restore a lost order. But the flaw here, again, is not chiefly in the aims they seek but rather in the means they propose to achieve them. Calls for individual moral reform are just not going to get us there, or anywhere close. Indeed, to call for individual change is largely to endorse the ideology of Wall Street libertarians who tout the market as the most efficient, even most democratic, of institutions. The market, it is said, gives individuals what they want as individuals. If Berry is right and people merely have bad wants, then the free market itself is not to blame. People can change their wants, and the market will then serve their new wants. Viewed this way—though Berry would balk at the perspective—agrarian ideals become just another lifestyle choice, like organic produce or hybrid cars. The market can satisfy these choices, right along with the choices of people who want greasy fast food, consumptive SUVs, and rural McMansions. This is reasoning that the most antienvironmental libertarian could support: leave the economic system alone, tell government to stay away, and advise consumers simply to make different market choices. It is a prescription, mostly, for inaction.

The Path Ahead

To see these limits on individual power, the gap between citizens and consumers, and the many needs for collective action is to highlight where Wendell Berry's thought might usefully give way to the ideas of others—to work of observers who have thought more particularly about ecological economics, collective governance, private property, and the biology of conservation. Berry's strength is moral challenge, and he is a master of it. To the extent individuals can make progress acting alone, they should listen to Berry and act. But to the extent that progress requires working together, we need to augment Berry's work with more effective means of social change. We need to draw in some version of civic republicanism that accentuates collective self-rule and promotes structures of public decision-making that nurture the common good. We cannot, as Berry proposes, respond to global problems only by thinking and acting at the local level—at the level, as he puts it, "of our competence."[10]

The temptation, perhaps, is to say that we merely need to take Berry's moral prophecy and mix it with the kinds of practical organizing that today's environmental groups undertake. The combination, we might hope, could yield plentiful fruit. But we need to appreciate here what an awkward match this would be, particularly given trends in the conservation cause itself. The conservation movement exhibited a moral edge decades ago when it had bad actors to blame and it could attack them with a vengeance—the polluters, poisoners, and irresponsible dam-builders. But those were the old days, when culprits were few and well-known. The situation today is more complex. The ills that afflict land arise from widespread sources. The opposition is stronger, and moral language appears suspect. Most conservation groups have run for cover. Dollars increasingly flow to land trusts that do little to ruffle feathers or cast aspersions. The way to improve land use, one now hears, is to buy land or pay bad-acting landowners to change their ways, not to criticize their bad actions. If the market itself is an ongoing cause of ecological destruction, no one seems willing to say so. And if, for instance, the destruction of critical wildlife habitat is a communal harm, few people are standing up to press charges against offenders. In truth, the conservation movement has become tame. Its fragmented elements mostly pursue narrowly defined aims, often under vague, unobjectionable slogans ("connecting people to wildlife" or "conserving land for people"). Hardly anyone on the environmental side wants to talk about private property, liberty, or any other high cultural element. In an effort to ward off the unfounded charge of extremism, they have become lambs. The moral edge is off; goals are modest; and cultural criticism is largely gone.[11]

It is important to lay this reality on the table because it explains why Wendell Berry enjoys little influence with today's conservation organizations. Berry's strident moralism could hardly stand more distant from the tepid and technical rhetoric that conservation groups employ. Indeed, if the rise in land trusts is much indication, few conservation groups have anything critical to say of anyone. They accept and work within the system, buying a piece of land or conservation easement here and there while prodding environmental agencies actually to implement their statutes as written. The right wing's vision of private property has taken the stage, with little competition. Increasingly the talk is about promoting "ecosystem services" by paying landowners to use their lands more gently; the underlying assumption, apparently shared by nearly all, is that landowners have and should have the legal right to destroy what they own. The challenge to selfish individualism is largely gone; few structures of society face any real threat.

The conservation movement, in sum, would need to change its ways significantly if it were to welcome Wendell Berry as guiding intellect and moralist. It would need to embrace the kind of harsh edge that Berry supplies, a willingness to challenge complacency and old ways of seeing and valuing land. Berry has called loudly and wisely for efforts to promote the health of the entire community of life. He has embedded the individual into natural and social systems in ways that challenge American liberalism and the many fragmentations of modern life. The conservation movement could not adopt these stances without challenging modern life with far more vigor: speaking truth to power; confronting entrenched authority; and questioning assumptions that Americans hold dear. Beyond that, the many conservation groups would need to do something they are obviously loath to consider: to work together, far better than they ever have, orchestrating their messages, collectively engaging in cultural debates, taking stances on issues like individual liberty and private property, and otherwise coordinating calls for change.

As for Berry himself, a merger of his criticism with collective action might well worry him just as much. His chief goals—for land health, for new ideas of private ownership, for limits on corporate power, and for measures that protect small towns from global capitalism—would all require legal measures that challenge his deep-seated individualism. They would require social movements. And they would cast doubt on the merits of the quiet leaders whom Berry most admires—the Mat Feltners and Wheeler Catletts, who display exceptional moral fiber yet remain disengaged from public power. Like their followers, Berry's fictional leaders remain outsiders. They cope with change but do not shape it.

Berry's moral prophecy supplies a much-needed corrective for the fragmentation of American society. We need Berry more than ever, and his criticism rings true. At the same time, we need to attach this criticism to a realistic understanding of structural change and how it might come about. Power speaks, and small towns and individual people are easily crushed. Berry the writer remains too wedded to Jacksonian democracy and dated images of the independent entrepreneur to give advice on the best means of confronting global capitalism. Just as surely, though, we are cast adrift without his prophecy or something very much like it. Berry holds a mirror to our faces. We would be foolish to look away.

Notes

1. Wendell Berry, "Contempt for Small Places," in *The Way of Ignorance* (Washington, DC: Shoemaker and Hoard, 2005), 7.

2. A particularly perceptive meditation on Adam Smith and his inattention to nature is offered in the title essay of Donald Worster's *The Wealth of Nature: Environmental History and the Ecological Imagination* (New York: Oxford University Press, 1993), 203–19.

3. Marxism, it should be clear, stands quite far from the version of communism embodied in the former Soviet Union (which was in essence a form of national socialism having little to do with the writings of Marx). In several writings, Berry makes clear that his critique of industrial capitalism applies with essentially the same force to the brutal industrialism of state-run economic systems. See, e.g., "The Total Economy," in *Citizenship Papers* (Washington, DC: Shoemaker and Hoard, 2003).

4. Karl Marx and Friedrich Engels, *The Communist Manifesto,* ed. Eric Hobsbawm (London: Verso, 1998), 37.

5. Genovese's writings on the subject include *The Southern Tradition: The Achievements and Limitations of an American Conservatism* (Cambridge, MA: Harvard University Press, 1994).

6. For instance, Burley's important comment in "The Wild Birds": "The way we are, we are members of each other. All of us. Everything. The difference ain't in who is a member and who is not, but in who knows it and who don't." Wendell Berry, *The Wild Birds: Six Stories of the Port William Membership* (San Francisco: North Point, 1986), 136–37.

7. Maury Klein, *The Flowering of the Third America: The Making of an Organizational Society, 1850–1920* (Chicago: Ivan R. Dee, 1993), 104.

8. I explore the tragedy in *The Land We Share: Private Property and the Common Good* (Washington: Island Press, 2003), 157–78.

9. The point is made in Robert N. Bellah et al., *Habits of the Heart: Individualism and Commitment in American Life,* rev. ed. (Berkeley: University of California Press, 1996), xxiii.

10. Wendell Berry, "Word and Flesh," in *What Are People For?* (San Francisco: North Point, 1990), 200.

11. I develop the criticism in this paragraph at length in *Why Conservation Is Failing and How It Can Regain Ground* (New Haven: Yale University Press, 2006).

David Crowe

Hemingway's Nick
and Wendell Berry's Art

IT SHOULD PROBABLY come as no surprise that Wendell Berry sees his fiction "in conversation" with rather than emulating the work of such writers as Ernest Hemingway and Norman Maclean.[1] After all, Berry is emphatically his own man. And he is in the best sense our American Jeremiah, a prophet who decries the extent to which we have fallen away from a sacred duty—to cultivate God's creation respectfully and modestly, to build community, finally to rest in the immortality of love.[2] Berry's jeremiad has called into conversation, and into question, varying social and economic practices and theories, not to mention literary styles and authorial worldviews. So when Berry writes in "Style and Grace" that he admires Hemingway's short story "Big Two-Hearted River" (1925) yet regrets Hemingway's controlling and reductive literary style, we begin to deduce Berry's own literary calling. Berry lays claim to a vision that is not similarly reductive, but more accurately and fully expressive of his world's merits and demerits and human struggles. He implies as much as he compares Hemingway's work with Maclean's in *A River Runs Through It* (1988). Here, Berry says, is a "far more moving" story than Hemingway's and one that, because it conveys the importance of companionship across generations, represents nature as a gift, and demonstrates the "power of culture," is open to grace.[3] "Grace" in its religious sense is the unmerited gift of God's loving and redeeming attention. Yet here grace also seems to be a condition of understanding: knowledge of the terms and obligations of this gift, the loving and caring response that people ought to make to the world and one another if they know what people are for.

Berry's remarks in "Style and Grace" raise a series of questions whose answers might clarify the nature and mission of his own literary art. The first of these questions concerns Berry's qualified appreciation for Hemingway's famous "soldier's homecoming" story, "Big Two-Hearted River." Berry's reading of "Big Two-Hearted River" is appreciative, but is it a fair, full, or generous reading? Should we be convinced that Hemingway's art is in some way "reductive" and that Berry's own work avoids reduction? A second question concerns Berry's choices of writers whose work he implies invites comparison to his own: What do the poles of Hemingway's "literary purity" and Maclean's "modest, solitary, somewhat secretive" art tell us about Berry's work? Finally, answering this question might help us to read properly Berry's own story of a soldier's anxious homecoming and quest for restoration, "Making It Home." If this story is understood as a conscious response to "Big Two-Hearted River," as I think it should be, then what does Berry have to show us about his calling as a writer of fiction, and teach us about our methods for dealing with trauma and nearness to death? What can he teach us about the preciousness of people's homes, the liabilities of wartime regimentation, and the difficulties of a veteran's resuming work and loving familial relations?

I see Berry's remarks in "Style and Grace" as both accurate and problematic, but the remarks are to me more interesting for what they imply about Berry's own literary values. In celebrating Maclean's modest and even secretive work (I take "secretive" to mean avoiding overt confessions of belief or expressions of piety), Berry is marking out his own literary terrain. This modest terrain seems to involve at least the following: (1) openness to mysteries rather than doctrines, especially mysteries about ultimate questions of existence and meaning; (2) a transparent prose style that calls attention to people's ethical decisions rather than to the author's aesthetic or ideological commitments; (3) the representation of unassuming and hardworking families and communities as the model for social organization; and (4) representations of the land both as real substance deserving our stewardship and as analogue to those things, physical and metaphysical, for which we are responsible. These aspects of the Berry terrain are all on display in "Making It Home," a story in which a returning soldier less bright and experienced than Nick Adams nevertheless possesses resources for his situation that Nick lacks for his. Berry implies that Nick need not lack these resources, that his fictive situation reflects very real authorial stubbornness and misapprehension.

What sort of reading of "Big Two-Hearted River" has Berry made? Here we need to consider what Berry means by Hemingway's literary purity and tendency to write reductively. Berry is quite clear about what he admires in the story.

> I have read the story many times, always with affection and gratitude, noticing and naming its virtues, and always seeing clearly in imagination the landscape and all the events of Nick Adams's restorative fishing trip. It is this clarity with which Hemingway speaks his story into the reader's imagination that is his great and characterizing virtue. . . . There is a moving courage in this plainness, freeing details, refusing clutter.[4]

Clearly, Berry shares these priorities—courage, plainness, freeing details, refusing clutter—in his own work. Berry's complaint is with Nick's remarks near the end of the story about refusing to fish in the swamp. Nick calls such fishing "tragic," which it clearly is not. Berry understands that such fishing might become "mysterious or bewildering," but rejects the word *tragic* and proposes the more accurate word *melancholy.* (Neither works for me; I would propose *frustrating.*) "If [Hemingway] means the word [*tragic*] seriously," Berry writes, "then he is talking about a tragedy that he knows about but the reader does not."[5]

Berry is perfectly correct that the word *tragic* is out of scale with Nick's fishing experience. It is not difficult for readers of *In Our Time,* however, to understand if not endorse Nick's use of the overblown word. "Big Two-Hearted River" was written to be read within the context of Nick's fragmentary bildungsroman in *In Our Time,* a book patterned after such story-novellas as James Joyce's *Dubliners* (1914) and Sherwood Anderson's *Winesburg, Ohio* (1919).[6] By the time we read the concluding story of Hemingway's first serious, and most experimentally modernist, book, we know that Nick has grown up living in and loving the Michigan woods, followed his restless heart to war, and received a wound to his spine that might have paralyzed him and certainly affects his movement; he has married and is expecting a child, and finds himself back in the United States and able to visit Michigan. It is then that Nick undertakes his solitary and, as Berry notes, "restorative" fishing trip. During this trip, Nick enjoys creating an orderly camp, managing his own meals and other business without interference, and fishing in ways that gratify him and do not cause him anxiety. When Nick thinks of fishing in the swamp as tragic, he may be indicating that in his current emotional state any sharp frustration would be intolerable, that it is his post-traumatic stress that is tragic. Or he may be sharing a mostly private memory with Hemingway himself of another widened, swampy stretch of river—the Piave River in northern Italy—where Hemingway nearly lost his life to an exploding trench mortar shell in July of 1918, very definitely a near-tragic moment.

In either case, Nick would be enacting a Freudian theory of which the modernist Hemingway was very familiar. Freud argues that repressed impulses, such as an intolerably frightening memory, must come forward into consciousness in allusive forms, such as jokes, allusions, and omissions.[7] Another allusive form would be the non sequitur, such as Nick's sloppy, perhaps self-aggrandizing use of the word *tragic.* I follow Malcolm Cowley, Philip Young, Carlos Baker, and many other Hemingway scholars in viewing Nick in "Big Two-Hearted River" as psychologically troubled. I also agree that Nick's wartime wounding is a cause of this psychological distress, a repressed memory that vexes Nick's mind and complicates his relationships.[8] Reading "Big Two-Hearted River" in the context of *In Our Time,* however, I also view Nick's marriage, his becoming a father, and his anxiety about experiencing these straitened freedoms while commencing a career as a writer as complicating his mental state. This reason becomes clear when a relieved Nick, arriving at his fishing spot, "felt he had left everything behind, the need for thinking, the need to write, other needs."[9] These unnamed "other needs" must involve Nick's initiation into the cycles of life and death and fundamental adult responsibilities through his wife's pregnancy. The title of the story tells us so: What is big and two-hearted? A pregnant woman.

So I don't share Berry's view of Nick as an exaggerated and inauthentic figure of tragedy, though if I were to read Nick this way I would share Berry's distaste for such a sloppy-thinking and self-oriented young man. More accurately, I think, Berry has detected that Nick Adams is an unusually alienated character, cut off from his own history and community and in this sense a kind of nonperson: "So far as we can learn from the story itself, the man comes from nowhere, knows and is known by nobody, and is going nowhere—nowhere, at least, that he cannot see in full daylight."[10] This judgment, which will give rise to important traits in Art Rowanberry in his story, depends upon our reading Nick without either literary or biographical context, which of course we may do. We may also, on the other hand, read Nick as a roughly autobiographical character whose growth we have tracked in *In Our Time* from his preteen years in "Indian Camp." This boy grown to manhood is much like Hemingway himself: child of a pious, domineering mother and mild physician father, native of Chicago whose heart really lives in the northwestern Michigan lake country, wounded veteran of World War I, and in the early 1920s a newly married man whose wife is, to his regret, pregnant.

Nick's adolescent reticence about important matters—in "Cross-Country Snow" he refuses to share his thoughts with a friend and grudgingly assents to having the baby in the States—point to the central and overwhelming frustration in Nick's life as he prepares for his trip to the country. He is giving up what he loves—is it skiing with buddies or writing as an expatriate?—in order to return his pregnant wife to the States. (Hemingway and Hadley had returned to Canada for their first child's delivery; presumably this is Nick's and Helen's decision as well.) Although Berry might ignore other Hemingway stories in which Nick appears, he does recognize a strange isolation in Nick, a fundamental disconnect from his family and lover. Nick does indeed lack a mature personhood, the kind that meets new responsibilities with grace and that prizes human connection especially with those we love. Berry takes seriously the biblical injunction to love our neighbors; Nick seems to fail in this duty even in regard to the person Søren Kierkegaard calls the "first neighbor," his wife.[11]

Yet Nick presents a personhood that even Berry might approve. After all, throughout his prewar years Nick, like Hemingway, has chosen the beauty, mystery, and filial community of the Michigan lake country over the conformist ambitions and pieties of Oak Park; he has chosen the honesty and craftsmanship of clear, elegant writing over careers merely remunerative; in traveling to the Big Two-Hearted he accepts the consolations of an intact and nourishing place, and attempts some clear thinking about the terms of his existence and his responsibilities. This is choosing as Berry would have us choose; living as Berry would have us live. However, Nick is also sharply different from Hemingway in unattractive ways. He has apparently avoided a postwar confrontation with his family and their values (which Hemingway could not do, once receiving a letter from his mother that called him "lazy, loafing and pleasure seeking" and calling him to perform his "duties to God and his Son Jesus Christ"[12]). He has adopted an itinerant expatriate lifestyle—Hemingway notably portraying Nick's skiing in the Alps rather than performing Hemingway's own long workdays in a rue du Cardinal Lemoine garret or Montparnasse cafés. And he has retreated to the river country to escape the "home economics" of a pregnant wife, and, we are told, the need for thinking, the need to write, other needs. In these ways, Nick is boyish, unformed, lacking a calling, and reluctant to assume responsibility for his wife and child. He is a member of no real community and depends on no real friends or family. For Berry, such boyishness is a failure of personhood. Berry senses an inappropriate artifice in this Nick Adams, an artifice that serves a literary style that "imposes its terms upon its subject." "It is a fine story, on its terms," Berry writes in "Style and Grace," "but its terms are straitly limited." What are these terms? Ones that are reductive of "both humanity and nature." According to Berry, Nick refuses, as does his author, to plumb the mysteries of "history and bewilderment."[13]

Perhaps so. As we see in examining "Making It Home," such a distressed young man as Nick can seek other consolations than solitude, memory, recreation, and emotional self-evaluation.[14] I share Berry's strongly implied sense that Hemingway lived and wrote in troubled relation to such crucial helps as the family, the childhood home, wise members of the community, and spiritual sources of meaning. Hemingway's characters often seem alienated, often by their own choice, from consoling and healing powers. Think of Frederic Henry in *A Farewell to Arms,* who by the novel's end has no lover, no child, no country, no army, no faith, no diversions, no friends, no home, no family to speak of, no work. "Poor things," Leslie A. Fiedler writes of Frederic and Catherine. "All they wanted was innocent orgasm after orgasm on an island of peace in a world at war, lovemaking without end in a scarcely real country to which neither owed life or allegiance."[15] This is cruel satire but somehow expressive of the "literary purity" that concerns Berry as well. Hemingway plans for an ambivalent ending to "Big Two-Hearted River" and tragic outcome to *A Farewell to Arms,* but to accomplish either outcome must strip his characters of the sources of meaning—including family, neighbors, "real country" (in both the national and natural sense), and faith—through which they might avoid tragedy.

Berry might rightly chide Hemingway for failing to present us with an autobiographical character who understands total war and threatening military-industrial modernity as emerging evils, who dwells upon his own distress while neglecting the family and community for which he is fundamentally responsible and where others live in responsibility for him as well. But surely Berry goes too far when he writes, "Like the similarly reductive technical and professional specializations of our time, this style [of Hemingway's] minimizes to avoid mystery. It deals with what it does not understand by leaving it out."[16] This is a stunning and I think ultimately unfair accusation, to claim that Hemingway somehow refuses to confront mysteries, that his literary style is complicit with the balkanized, deadened, uncritical consciousness that serves corporate interests. Granted, Hemingway's commitment to a rigid ideology of inevitable loss was the downfall of his career. Hemingway at his best wrote with a courageous openness to renewal, hope, and grace.[17] This is an openness Berry sees nowhere in Hemingway's work, but does see in Maclean's *A River Runs Through It,* in which the tragic death of the gifted and willful brother, Paul, is balanced with Norman's and their father's sense of Paul's beauty and capacity for love. Maclean, for Berry, believes in the "connective power of culture" while Hemingway does not. True enough. Hemingway confronted mysteries aplenty, but his nascent Catholicism and republican solidarity in the 1920s and '30s seem to have been powerless to provide him with an image of an intact culture founded in spiritual communion, mutual *caritas,* and stewardship of one's own place. Hemingway's faith apparently could not quiet his fears about his fragile talent, his purposes in life, his anxious connections with his wives and children, and possibly the meaning of his death. Nowhere do we see a Hemingway hero build a home, honor his promises before God to love and cherish his wife, cultivate his corner of the natural and artistic worlds, and worship a creator who, after all, made the rushing streams of the Italian Alps, the dusty mountains of Spain, the chestnut trees along the Seine, and the firm trout in the Big Two-Hearted. A fictive world absent these representations of the basic human duties of work, worship, and stewardship is perhaps reductive in imagining a full range of what Kierkegaard calls joyful duties, if not complicit with the very real draining of our awareness of mystery from our now consumerist consciousness.[18]

> And by now the transformation of the ancient story is nearly complete. Our society, on the whole, has forgotten or repudiated the theme of return.[19]

As if to reimagine Hemingway's reductive postwar river tale, Berry in "Making It Home" tells the tale of another near-mortally-wounded veteran of a world war, uncertain about his return to the cherished country of his youth and suffering the blunted affect of battle fatigue. Berry has modeled his story after Hemingway's in other ways as well, including at least its two-day, two-part structure; its interior monologue relieved by intricately described local color; the attention to hunger and hunger assuaged, to anxiety and anxiety calmed; even its references to fishing. Berry follows Hemingway in exploring the state of mind of a young man who loves living things, their cycles of birth and growth and death, and the places they occupy—but who has witnessed the wanton destruction of human and other life in a war that thinking people know is muddied with industrial-financial motives. As John Dos Passos suspected, Nick's war may have been less about making the world safe for democracy than making the loans of J. Pierpont Morgan to European powers safe for repayment.[20] Art Rowanberry's war, for Berry, initiated a military-industrial partnership that has done great damage to the American household economy and environment. Hemingway and Berry both, then, explore the response that a sensitive young man might have to trauma, disillusionment, and nihilistic destruction. Yet the literary waters Berry fishes are different and perhaps deeper. If Nick Adams explores submerged feelings—the size and difficulty of the catch is the objective correlative—then Art Rowanberry struggles to recover a more fully conscious volitional attitude toward home. Here the journey is the proper correlative, with walking-as-thinking leading to the chosen telos of home. The complexity of Berry's reimagining is implied by the story's resonant title: Art needs to renew a sense of both "making" and "home." "Making" will be the antidote to wartime killing and destroying. "Home" will be defined, or at least represented, as a multigenerational community founded on love and meaningful work. "Making it home" means, of course, to arrive at a place where one rests and works; but it also means creating, building, and tending a physical place and a vital metaphysical concept.

For Berry to bring Art home, either physically or emotionally, is no great narrative task. Art has no wish to go anywhere else. Far more difficult for Berry, yet skillfully accomplished, is bringing home the logical ties between wartime regimentation, bureaucratic amorality, and wanton destruction in 1945, with a nominally peaceful American economy since. I say "nominally" because, as Berry has convincingly shown, a war has been waged upon American communities and farms during those sixty-odd years, the enemy an axis of multinational oligarchs, exploiters, and benefactors of the so-called free market. To bring Art home to a consciousness of the process would be obviously anachronistic. But for Berry to help us, his readers, to understand a love of making and a hatred of waste, a love for home and a hatred of the ineluctably strange, a love for meaningful work and a hatred of inauthentic or aimless pleasures—this would be laying the foundation for a credible society. Art Rowanberry needs to become what Berry calls "a peaceable man," for if he does, and resumes his task of tending the earth—"which we all have in common," writes Berry, and which is "our deepest bond"—then we ensure the future of the human race.[21]

Art's story is posed as a kind of spiritual tale or parable in four acts, the progression of acts assisting us in this fundamental understanding. First, Art dwells upon issues of independent, self-reliant personhood, much as Nick Adams does in the Michigan woods. Art has had his fill of military regimentation, and as he begins walking home he savors his solitude. "Arthur Rowanberry has come a long way, trusting somebody else to know where he was, and now he knew where he was himself." Here regimentation is implicated in loss of control and loss of direction. These for Berry are issues of personhood: moral choosing and knowledge of one's place are crucial. The instinct for these things is alive in Art: "He walked . . . like a man who had been taught to march, and he wore a uniform. But whatever was military in his walk was an overlay, like the uniform, for he had been a man long before he had been a soldier, and a farmer long before he had been a man." Yet Art has experienced a great threat to his personhood, a threat far more insidious than the shell fragment that nearly takes his life. He has taken pleasure in what he shouldn't, a "reduction" as he puts it, in his responsibility as he "did what he was told." But on this walk home he begins to realize the threat: "That laying around half a day, waiting for somebody else to think—that was something I had to *learn*."[22]

The famous wartime memoirist and scholar Paul Fussell had to learn the same passivity through regimentation when he was inducted into the American army in 1943. He describes a similar effect of the experience: "We were lined up, insulted, shouted at, numbered, and hustled into a barracks building by contemptuous sergeants." Although Fussell and his companions were destined to become officers, "here, we were serfs, or even lower than that: we felt the dog tags issued to us accurately named. . . . We knew that we'd been cruelly duped [in believing that as officers-in-training they would be treated as gentlemen] and our ever emerging from our current social status seemed quite impossible."[23] Fussell's preoccupation with social and intellectual status, remained, it seems, lifelong (though he is amusingly self-aware about this attitude). He suffered under demeaning regimentation primarily because his intellect was improperly valued, as his reading in Mencken in those days taught him: "All government, in its essence, is a conspiracy against the superior man: its one permanent object is to oppress him and cripple him. . . . One of its primary functions is to regiment men by force, to make them as much alike as possible . . . , to search out and combat originality among them."[24] Berry would agree with the portrait of the coercive nature of regimentation here, and with the forced conformity, but would surely quarrel with its perceived effect. The problem is not that one's originality is quashed, let alone one's superiority, but that one's responsibility for moral-ethical decision is diminished and perhaps voided during one's enlistment period. Art Rowanberry has learned moral-ethical passivity so that he will follow orders obediently. This, Berry implicitly warns us, is likely prelude to joining up with "mass man," the peacetime form of unfelt regimentation in which a person does and thinks what the others do and think because the others do and think it.[25]

Personhood, for Berry, requires a rejection of mass experience. "Making It Home" opens with, and employs throughout, imagery of the massive and strange reduced to a knowable human scale. The opening sentence begins this imagery: "He had crossed the wide ocean and many a river. Now not another river lay between him and home but only a few creeks that he knew by name."[26] The last of these creeks Art knows by name will be the Sand Ripple, which drains the western edge of the Rowanberry farm and leads Art home. Images of the roads Art walks upon function similarly, as paved highways become "lesser roads" and finally "still narrower" pairs of graveled wheel tracks.[27] Set against such homely familiarity and reassuringly diminishing scale is a view of the world Art has confronted during and since the war, a view of an impersonal, frightening, and immense universe. "But now, having gone and returned from so far, he knew that he was walking on the whole round world. He felt the great, empty distance that the world was turning in, far from the sun and the moon and the stars." This cosmic awareness seems to cut two ways for Art. On the one hand, this is an image of the great cosmic "nothing" of space, associated through imagery with Art's near-death experience and with his obvious anxiety regarding the meaning of this life. On the other hand, awareness of the immense universe supplies Art with a new point of view that we might call earth-centered and ecological: "Here," Art thinks, apparently meaning here on the earth, "is where we do what we are going to do—the only chance we got. And if somebody was to be looking down from up there, it would all look a lot littler to him than it does to us."[28] The fragility and small-ness of the earth is an important insight for one who has participated in the greatest assault of men and machines upon that earth in history—World War II. Art is beginning to internalize, if not consciously understand, his respon-sibility for this small, fragile earth—a responsibility he will enact upon his even smaller, knowable place on it, the Rowanberry farm.

The greatest wrong Art has experienced while under the control of the regimental bureaucracy seems to be that no matter the virtue of the war against National Socialism, he has been trained in the ugly and arguably amoral act of wanton destruction of lives and homes and farms. This training and these acts may have been necessary during the Allied campaign in Europe, but are wretchedly profane during peacetime. Art recoils from these memo-ries, and rightly so. In 1945 another ethic of casual and wanton destruction is about to begin. Since World War II, Berry writes in *What Are People For?*, "governing agricultural doctrines" have enforced a productivity "based on the ruin both of the producers and of the source of production." Through mis-judgment or greedy manipulation, agribusiness interests are at war with the American land and its people. The family farm and functioning farm com-munities are being destroyed so that corporate interests can shape the econo-my to their ends. And government funds that might have been directed to conservation or other enduring values are directed toward the short-term cri-sis of war.[29] And so, "absent farmers," writes Berry, "have had to be replaced by machinery, petroleum, chemicals, credit, and other expensive goods and services from the agribusiness economy of what used to be called farming."[30] More than Nick Adams, then, Art Rowanberry is alive if not alert to the de-struction that he has participated in. He has of course no inkling of the im-pending fate of the American family farm, but he knows that the Allied as-saults in which he took part were at least partly assaults on people like his own, hardworking folk connected to the land and tending their families and their farms and their towns. "Them fellers over there," Art says to his friend on the battlefront, a friend who hates the Germans and wishes to kill every one, "are doing about the same work we are, 'pears like to me."[31]

It is unclear from the terms of the story whether Berry takes a pacifist stance even toward the so-called Good War. It is quite clear that Berry de-plores deeply the deadened consciousness required to wage war against not only an enemy but against women, children, homes, and farms. This critique of mass violence is more than a historical-sociological matter for Berry, as he publishes "Making It Home" during the first Gulf War and, more important,

views wartime assaults as paradigms for destructive group behavior under-
written, endorsed, and enforced by large and distant bureaucratic organizations. For Art, this organization is the "government," made up, he realizes, of
men who do not fight and are not harmed or subject to harm. "The government was made up of people who thought about fighting, not of those who
did it. The men sitting behind the desks—they spent other men to buy ground,
and then they ruined the ground they had and more men to get the ground
beyond" (226). Men sitting behind desks ruining the land for ambiguous
though finally possessive, territorial purposes: perhaps Berry requires the
plodding interior speech on Art's part so that he, Berry, can display such general utterances, calculated by their author to apply both to Art's wartime experience and perhaps to modern agribusiness practices. Art's speech calls into
question not only acts of governments at war but grasping bureaucratic assaults on precious things generally.

In the story's "second act," Art grows beyond Nick's and his own sense of
individualistic revulsion. Now begins a drama in which Art, unlike Nick, will
be reintegrated with his family and will resume his calling as a farmer. The
threat to this reintegration and resumption has been Art's growing sense of
nihilism while in combat. The subtext of Art's eventless and almost tension-
free walk home (there seems to be little animating tension in this story, no
real corollary to Nick's distress) thus involves a quasi-theological contrast between the "nothing" of profane acts and the "something" of life and work in
stewardship of neighbor and place. Through careful and repeated use of the
word *nothing*, Berry establishes a meaning not far from the important use
Karl Barth made of the word. For Barth, nothing (*das Nichtige*) is all that is
not-God and all that is not God's will, including evil. This evil cannot be tamed
or intellectually justified (for example, as needed in a particular theodicy to
make experientially available its opposite, goodness) but exists in absolute
opposition to creation: it is de-creation, death. In a description of Art's wartime experience just prior to his near death, Berry uses the word *nothing* four
times and the word *whole*, nothing's opposite, three times:

> The fighting went on, the great tearing apart. People and everything else
> were torn into pieces. Everything was only pieces put together that were
> ready to fly apart, and *nothing* was *whole*. You got to where you could not
> look at a man without knowing how little it would take to kill him. For a
> man was *nothing* but just a little morsel of soft flesh and brittle bone in-
> side of some clothes. . . . There was *nothing* you could look at that was
> *whole*—man or beast or house or tree—that had the right to stay *whole*
> very long. There was *nothing* above the ground that was *whole* but you

had the measure of it and could separate its pieces and bring it down. You moved always in a landscape of death, wreckage, cinders, and snow (224; my emphases).

Immediately following this meditation on wholeness and nothingness, Art recalls his wounding, made all the more horrific when the same shell disintegrates his buddy: "McBride just disappeared" (224). Art immediately undergoes the change that he must reverse in this story. "From a man in the light on the outside of the world, he was transformed in the twinkling of an eye into a man in the dark on the inside of himself, in pain, and he thought that he was dead" (225). The profane inversion of Paul's promise to the Corinthians that through faith they would be "transformed . . . in the twinkling of an eye" (1 Corinthians 15:52–53) is intentional and telling. Paul prophesies a change at the last trumpet in which believers will be raised into new life and into communion with divine will. In shocking contrast, Art has seen and felt the implacable effect of death: nothingness, *nihil*. Before his wounding, he had been forced to treat bodies as though they were nothing, stepping over and beyond bodies as though they were "only a low mound of something in the way," but now death is personal. Art awakens in the hospital and is a different person, "newborn from his death . . . tender and a little afraid" (224–25). Perhaps Art is more than a little afraid, as he is tormented by the waking dream "in which every creature and every thing sat, like that boy McBride, in the dead center of the possibility of its disappearance" (228).

The paradoxical existence of "nothing" has been made so frighteningly real to Art that, in order to live and love and work, he has to regain confidence in the good things that God commands into existence. Art's task seems quite different from Nick's. While Nick must manage extremely raw anxiety and avoid a panic that may be set off by any strong disappointment—thus removing Nick from any pleasure involving risk—Art requires a more conscious, intellectual adjustment to his existential situation. He requires reentry from the airless space of "nothing" to his own earth, his own land, his own farm, his own family, his own work.

The emblem of Art's moral progress in this second act seems to be his "choice" of a lonely rural church for his night's rest, but Art has made no conscious choice of this sacred space. Rather, his feet "carried him on to the church" when Art "told them" to walk (229). Here Berry hints that Art in his current anxiety places no value upon the church and all it represents—community in common faith and spiritual nourishment at least, in this instance. Significantly, the church is empty, and the hunger Art knows he ought to feel is also absent. This is a gently profane representation of spiritual communion, if not a parody. Art eats a chocolate bar, but does so mechanically. This meal is a gentle reminder of wartime habits (the hurried munching of empty calories for sustenance) rather than a sacrament. Far less gentle is the reminder of another wartime habit, Art's fearful waking throughout the night to listen for threats. These are profoundly nonsacred and noncommunal feelings that Art must overcome.

Art wakes still feeling far less than whole. It is the springtime morning that begins to revive him, helping Art to think about his seasonal responsibilities, which he will enact with his family. A kind of creation drama begins. First there is light, and Art realizes that he can see. A world that the day before had seemed as large as the unfathomable cosmos today seems (only) "wide as the whole country and deep as the sky." Art is no longer threatened by the absurdity of "nothing," but living in "a kind of story" in which he is an intended character. "As he more and more saw where he was, it seemed to him more and more that he was walking in his memory or that he had entered, awake, a dream that he had been dreaming for a long time." His hunger returns like a "landmark," like a "tree that put its roots in the ground and spread its branches against the sky" (230). Rooted and yet set in relief against the infinite sky, Art regains his personhood and place, both physical and metaphysical.

But perhaps not his joy. This further turning point in "act three" will be restored by a series of Art's personal acts with biblical resonances. Having now hinted at Art's progress through self-awareness and then awareness of the sacral qualities of quiet, rest, and hunger (both physical and spiritual hunger), Berry must, if he can, illustrate the healing powers of home and its messages of love.

He can: first, Art notices the "marks of the flood that had recently covered the valley floor." Like the fire that burned the town of Seney in "Big Two-Hearted River," this flood's destructiveness is a correlative to wartime destruction, a quiet reminder of what the young veteran has experienced. However, Berry's choice of a flood allows him further biblical echoes: specifically, reminders of the post-Flood covenant God makes with God's people—a promise that Art requires as he hopes to regain confidence in the goodness and durability of his natural world. Next, Art bathes in preparation for his homecoming. Berry's language leads us to the transcendent importance of this baptismal bathing: "And then warmth came to him. It came from inside himself and from the sun outside; he felt suddenly radiant in every vein and fiber of this body." In this radiance, Art is like the risen Christ in Hebrews 1:3, like Moses after witnessing God, like Daniel in the lions' den, and like many others who experience the immediate presence or incarnation of God. "[Art] was clean and warm and rested and hungry. He was well" (232).

Twice in the next two pages, Art remarks that there was nothing now around him that he didn't know. Twice he remarks that he is no longer a stranger, an observation that takes on added significance with a second, more sacral reference to Paul's first letter to the Corinthians: "I am not a stranger, but *I am changed*" (232, my emphasis). Art really is changed, rather than changed back. He begins to dwell upon the meaning of his experience at war, realizing for the first time that he has known "a mighty power of death and fire. An anger beyond the power of any man." This personification of the mighty power is interesting. Perhaps Art is drawing upon his knowledge of Revelation 13, with its portrait of the mighty beast allowed to mock God and control God's creation. In any case, the new warmth and radiance Art feels carry him onward to his home and far away from this mighty power.

In "act four," the actual homecoming, Berry poses his denouement in imagery that is far more complex than it first seems. The situation echoes the parable of the prodigal son in some respects, though of course Art has spent neither his money nor his integrity prodigally. Nevertheless, the hardworking brother who stays home is present and working hard; the father's joy in seeing his son return is heartfelt. "Well now!" the father says twice, an epithet that taken another way punctuates Art's own judgment that he is "well now." The contrast with Nick's experience is sharp here. Berry knows it is, placing three common fishing rods by the bank of the creek, their lines in the water awaiting the worms that Art's nephew is collecting from the newly plowed furrow—fishing for sport and pleasure versus fishing for familial companionship and food. This fishing imagery is embellished by the young nephew's work digging worms. Berry has written vigorously about the need for both the young and the old, neither normally counted in the American workforce, to have meaningful work. He argues that, in "viable household and local economies," children and older people "would have work to do by which they would be useful to themselves and to others." He continues, "The ecological damage of centralization and waste is thus inextricably involved with human damage. For we have . . . classrooms full of children who lack the experience and discipline of fundamental human tasks, and various institutions full of still capable old people who are useless and lonely."[32] But not on the Rowanberry farm. Here the father and older son are "*bent* to their work, their hands riding easy on the handles of the plows." The little boy, Roy Lee, "bent" (the repetition of this word reinforcing the parallel work) "and picked something up from the freshly turned earth and dropped it into the can."[33]

And finally, as an important leitmotif in the story is rounded out, Art will be truly fed. The father calls for food, grown no doubt on the farm and prepared by Art's mother (curiously present only by verbal reference). Then, echoing the famous line from the parable of the prodigal son in Luke 15:24 ("For this my son was dead, and is alive again; he was lost and is found"), the father says, "For we have our own that was gone and has come again."[34] The biblical cadence is appropriate given the transformation Art has undergone—from a dead man marching at the command of bureaucratic others, to a responsible and responsive member of a self-reliant farming family.

This transformation Hemingway denies to Nick—thus the reductiveness that Berry sees in "Big Two-Hearted River." What are we to conclude about Berry's judgment upon Hemingway's art? I am reluctant to join Berry in requiring "right consciousness" from Hemingway, though my faith claims are nearer Berry's than Hemingway's—so far as I can tell about either man's commitments and quandaries. I am inclined to let each be a powerful literary craftsman in his own right, Hemingway perhaps offering questions about balancing the endlessly unstable choice between duty and desire; Berry with greater certainty offering prophetic images of waste and destruction and the quasi-occult forces that wish to control us—and the possibility of right thinking with regard to community and creation.

Notes

1. Wendell Berry, "Style and Grace," in *What Are People For?* (New York: North Point, 1990), 64.

2. See Sacvan Bercovitch, *The American Jeremiad* (Madison: University of Wisconsin Press, 1980). The jeremiad is a rhetorical offering in which a biblical ideal is contrasted with real human acts—precisely, so far as I can tell, Berry's project. So is the American form of the jeremiad, which holds out hope for reform even if no specific solutions are offered.

3. Berry, "Style and Grace," 66.

4. Ibid., 64.

5. Ibid., 65.

6. James Joyce, *Dubliners* (New York: Penguin, 1992); Sherwood Anderson, *Winesburg, Ohio* (New York: Oxford University Press, 1997).

7. Sigmund Freud, *Five Lectures in Psychoanalysis* (New York: Norton, 1989), 28. Obviously, this concept will appear in many of Freud's writings.

8. This argument about the causes of Nick's distress was, to my mind, put to rest by Matthew C. Stewart in "Ernest Hemingway and World War I: Combating Recent Psychobiographical Reassessments, Restoring the War," *Papers on Language and Literature* 36, no. 2 (spring 2000): 198–218. Stewart says it's the war and perhaps oth-

er causes. These other causes need to be carefully established through readings of the other Nick Adams stories in *In Our Time*—a project that needs doing.

9. Ernest Hemingway, *In Our Time* (New York: Scribner, 2003), 134.

10. Berry, "Style and Grace," 65.

11. Søren Kierkegaard, *Works of Love* (Princeton: Princeton University Press, 1998), 141.

12. Michael Reynolds, *The Young Hemingway* (New York: Basil Blackwell, 1986), 137–38.

13. Berry, "Style and Grace," 65–66.

14. I include "memory" here deliberately. It is curious that Berry calls Nick "a solitary man in an *unmemoried time*" ("Style and Grace," 65, emphasis mine). "Unmemoried"? Nick specifically dwells on memories of Hopkins and his arguments about making coffee, his moneymaking, and his gift-giving. It's true, however, that few other memories intrude during the story.

15. Leslie Fiedler, *Love and Death in the American Novel* (New York: Stein and Day, 1966), 317.

16. Berry, "Style and Grace," 66.

17. In my dissertation (1992) I argue that *A Farewell to Arms* (1929) is the last of Hemingway's genuinely "open" novels, open in a Bakhtinian sense, nearer to Dostoyevsky's work than Tolstoy's—although even that novel shows the signs of Hemingway's growing commitment to a frozen-over ideology of inevitable tragedy.

18. Kierkegaard, *Works of Love,* 159.

19. Berry, *What Are People For?*, 162.

20. John Dos Passos, *1919* (New York: Mariner Books, 2000), 80.

21. Wendell Berry, "Some Thoughts on Citizenship and Conscience," in *The Long-Legged House* (1969; Washington, DC: Shoemaker and Hoard, 2004), 85. See also "A Letter to Daniel Kemmis," in *The Way of Ignorance and Other Essays* (Washington, DC: Shoemaker and Hoard, 2005), 147, in which Berry describes for his friend, a former Montana legislator and mayor of Missoula, the hypocrisy of war: "We make war, we are told, for the love of peace. We subvert our Bill of Rights and impose our will abroad for the sake of freedom and the rule of law. We honor greed and waste with the name of economy. We allow ever greater wealth and power to accumulate in the hands of a privileged few only to provide jobs for working people and charity to the poor. And we sanctify all this as Christian, though the Gospels support none of it by so much as a line or a word."

22. Wendell Berry, "Making It Home," in *Fidelity: Five Stories* (New York: Pantheon, 1992), 227.

23. Paul Fussell, *Doing Battle: The Making of a Skeptic* (Boston: Back Bay Books, 1998), 75.

24. Ibid., 73.

25. Josef Kentenich, *Marianische Erziehung: Pädagogische Tagungen 1932–1934,* quoted, translated, and paraphrased in M. Doria Schlickmann, "The Mass Man and

the Free Personality in the Pedagogical Thinking and Practice of Josef Kentenich" (paper presented as part of the Colloquium on Violence and Religion, Koblenz-Schoenstatt, Germany, 6–10 July 2005), www.cla.purdue.edu/academic/engl/confer ences/covar/Program/doria.pdf, 1.

26. Berry, "Making It Home," 221.

27. Ibid., 233.

28. Ibid., 222.

29. See Wendell Berry, "A Statement Against the War in Vietnam," in *The Long-Legged House,* 71.

30. Berry, *What Are People For?*

31. Berry, "Making It Home," 224, hereafter cited in text.

32. Berry, *What Are People For?*, 128.

33. Berry, "Making It Home," 234.

34. Ibid., 236.

Hayden Carruth

At His Desk as
on His Land

PERHAPS THE BEST contribution I can make to this symposium would be an account of how this long, close, important friendship between Wendell and Hayden began.

Go back to New York in the 1950s. Wendell was a young man from rural Kentucky who felt uncertain about what he should do and how and where he should do it. But he knew he was interested in poetry, and he had the great good sense to become friends with Denise Levertov. What a marvelous thing to happen to a young poet. I was older than Wendell, a little further along in the adventure of becoming a poet, and Denise and I were already friends. She made sure both Wendell and I knew each other's work, and shortly afterward, when she became the interim literary editor of the *Nation,* she assigned one of my early books, I think *North Winter,* published by Carroll Coleman in Iowa, to Wendell for review. Wendell and I fell into correspondence at that time, and we are still exchanging letters regularly.

Do not be misled, my friends, by my blithe way with dates and places. I am doing this from memory. In my old age my memory has become a nuisance, not to say a joke. Hence my "data" are approximate, but I don't think anyone will be seriously misinformed by what I am doing.

In our letters Wendell and I soon found that we were in agreement on many things. Not everything. In matters philosophical Wendell was, like Denise, more inclined toward intuited, not to say mystical, understanding than my nonbeliever's love of reason can accommodate. And in politics and social thought my anarchic tendencies seemed irresponsible and maybe childish to Wendell. But we easily set these differences to one side. Instead of whanging away at them whenever they arise, as so many of our friends do, we don't mention them. It's easy. We recommend this course to everyone.

Our large area of agreement was in our attitude toward nature. We both loved to live and work close to the plants and animals and lights and sounds of the natural environment. We have done so all our lives, and we are knowledgeable. I know that if I mention seeing a northern shrike in my woods,

Wendell will understand what I am talking about. This means a great deal in our age of persistent idiocy and misdirection in the public exchange of ideas; it means an immense deal. Wendell and I are confident of each other, and that is the main supporting element of all friendship.

In the spring of 1970 my suffering from the ubiquitous allergens of Vermont became so acute that I decided to visit friends in New Mexico. Perhaps life there would be easier for me. Impetuously I piled my suitcase, briefcase, typewriter, and shoes into my old F250 pickup, stopped at the market for a carton of Camel filters, and headed out. The next day I was somewhere in eastern Ohio not far from Port Royal, Kentucky, where Wendell lives. Impetuosity was the order of the day, apparently, because I immediately turned south and crossed the big river somewhere near Cincinnati.

With my road map open on the seat beside me, I wended westward on secondary roads until I found myself at the bottom of a long hill where a sign pointed upward to Port Royal. I drove on slowly. Something was coming down the hill toward me on the edge of the road. Soon I saw it was a man leading a horse or mule with a halter and with his other hand holding onto a medium-sized boy. I stopped and cranked down my window. "Are you Wendell Berry?" I hollered.

"Yes," he hollered back.

I waved and shouted, "I'm Hayden Carruth."

"The hell you are!" he replied.

I got out and we shook hands. And except in pictures on book jackets, that was the first time Wendell and Hayden had seen each other. It was an unexpected and happy occasion.

I drove on up the hill to town, where I turned around and drove to Wendell's place, following the directions he had given me. It was, and is, a small farm on a steep hill that leads down to the bank of the Kentucky River from one of the ridges that characterize that part of the country. A splendid white clapboard house in the back, a big garden in front, a reddish barn on the side. When I drove into the driveway, Wendell was already there, having walked home across his north pasture. He introduced me to the boy, whose name was Den, though I did not catch what Den was short for. In New York it would have been short for Denise.

Soon Tanya, Wendell's wife, came out and welcomed me.

I stayed for a couple of days, I think, and Wendell showed me his woods and fields, especially the parts I could recognize from his poems. I recall particularly a poem titled "Meditation" and the little nook of his woods where Wendell had written it. Both the poem and the nook struck me forcibly. We cruised his fences, examined the garden, walked by the river, inspected the cow, the horse, the hens, and so forth, but mostly we talked and told stories, great subtle whoppers that embarrassed the trees and made the fields lie flat. Without doubt Wendell is the best storyteller I know.

What a visit it was. I do not exaggerate at all when I say, from the vantage of old age, that those few days with Tanya and Wendell were by far the most important event of their kind in my whole life.

After a couple of days I moved on to New Mexico, where I spent two or three months driving around, looking at the land, observing the people. Eventually I decided that clearly I belonged in Vermont, and I drove home. Over the years since then Wendell and I have visited each other whenever opportunities arose, we have read each other's manuscripts and offered suggestions, we have written hundreds of letters back and forth, we have enjoyed many phone calls. I have hammered continually at him to reduce his heavy schedule of traveling, lecturing, attending conferences, and the like—all the burdens he has undertaken in his personal but highly public campaign for economic, agricultural, and social sanity in our country. He has agreed with me that this work is too demanding and takes too much time and energy away from his writing, but at the same time he has found himself too bound by conscience to give up the obligations he took on years and years ago. Even so, he has completed much important writing in recent years—poetry, fiction, memoirs, critical and theoretical essays. Wendell has always worked harder than anyone else I know, at his desk as on his land.

Inevitably when we wish to express gratitude for the presence of important people in our collective and individual lives, we run the risk of sentimentality and foolishness. Allow me to say simply that to me the past fifty years in America without Wendell—the poet, the critic, the great proponent of humane reason and natural propriety, the staunch but courteous iconoclast, and in all his modes and motives—would be and are unimaginable.

Jeremy Beer

Wendell Berry and the Traditionalist Critique of Meritocracy

WENDELL BERRY has insisted, vehemently and consistently, that he speaks for no school, no movement, no man but himself.[1] But while Berry speaks for no one but Berry, he would be the last to deny that he writes—and lives—from within particular and overlapping traditions, which he is quick to enumerate and acknowledge. As Kimberly Smith has noted, he takes seriously not only the traditions in which he has found himself embedded but also the very concept of "tradition," a term he almost always uses in an approbative sense.[2] To think of him as an "American traditionalist" checks the tendency to place his work comfortably under the heading of more misleading labels, including "progressive." It clarifies his position in our intellectual history and helps to broaden our understanding of what he has hoped to accomplish. In this respect, we might attend especially to his perceptive critique of meritocracy—a critique, as we shall see, that forms an important part of what we might call the traditionalist tradition.

What does it mean to be a traditionalist? And what's the problem with meritocracy anyway? Isn't it the most just way of achieving a tolerable social order?

Numerous coherent and defensible definitions of traditionalism have been offered, but the term is typically employed negatively as a worldview characterized by a non- or even antirationalist outlook in unshakeable thrall to the past. The traditionalist is supposed to be a superstitiously pious creature incapable of bringing critical reason to bear on his fears, beliefs, and actions. To him, what is not traditional is taboo. He represents the human race in its childhood, and he is supposed to have been all but eradicated from the

Western world, whose history consists precisely in the rationalization—and therefore detraditionalization or desacralization—of the cosmos.

But there is another way of regarding traditionalism, which is to see it as a social-political philosophy that strives to create or maintain those conditions and structures in which tradition is a pervasive ordering and authoritative force in the lives of individuals and their communities. The traditionalist, in this view, regards inhabitance within a community enlivened by a matrix of vital and living traditions as essential to human flourishing. This is a traditionalism that emerges from the other side of reason. It consists in the critical appropriation and appreciation of traditional practices and mores by a reason that has come to realize its own limits. It recognizes, as Wendell Berry has argued, that one of the purposes of culture is to guide us in acting well even though our knowledge is incomplete, as well as to *tell* us that our knowledge is incomplete—a perfectly rational proposition.[3]

Traditionalism, we ought to emphasize, is distinguishable from conservatism, even "traditionalist conservatism," in that American conservatives, especially in the postwar era, have largely ignored certain issues about which authentic traditionalists might have been expected to have much to say—technology, for example. Most thinkers aligned with the conservative intellectual movement have had little to say about technology except, perhaps, to lament that the speed of its development, vertiginous as it has been, has not been fast enough, owing to government restrictions on industry. But even so-called traditionalist conservatives' complaints about the ways in which the cultural dynamism fueled by new technologies disrupts the fabric of community life have rarely risen to the level of theoretical criticism. Heidegger, Romano Guardini, Friedrich Jünger, Ivan Illich, Albert Borgmann, and Neil Postman all produced theoretical critiques of technology in the decades spanning the middle-to-late decades of the twentieth century,[4] critiques that one might have expected to be acceptable to if not welcomed by the American Right. But none of these men was a self-described conservative. Indeed, if one discounts the early work of the southern agrarians and their successor Richard Weaver (whose work on the subject pretty much ceased after the publication of *Ideas Have Consequences*), the absence of a single major, sustained critique of contemporary technological society in the postwar conservative literature must be considered extraordinary.

One reason traditionalist conservatives did not produce in the last sixty years a fundamental criticism of the technological whirl that was seemingly tearing apart the world they sought to defend was their commitment to a "free-market" economy. It might be argued that this commitment was not intellectual but tactical, that traditionalist conservatives' alliance with libertarian and classical-liberal anticommunists trumped all other considerations in the Cold War world. But I do not think that the writings of many traditionalist conservatives ultimately support such an interpretation. Although traditionalist conservatives occasionally voiced concerns about capitalism, in the end they sought only to modify its worst excesses. To many, while Ludwig von Mises seemed an ideologue, Friedrich Hayek was perfectly acceptable; indeed several leading traditionalist conservatives, including Richard Weaver and Eric Voegelin, maintained strong friendships with Hayek and held his work in high regard.

Furthermore, the favorite economist of the traditionalist conservatives was Wilhelm Röpke, a Swiss economist who subscribed to the fundamentals of the Austrian-school economics promoted by Mises, Hayek, and their colleagues. Röpke taught that the state must not interfere with the market's price mechanism. He argued that once government sets the ground rules it must clear out of the way, and that free trade must be strongly protected. At the same time, he expressed a fear that capitalism inherently depleted the moral, social, and cultural capital on which it depended. He therefore called for the state to support the family and other intermediary associations that provided this capital—without interfering with market mechanisms, of course. Röpke's economics, the traditionalist conservatives seemed to agree, was the best practical alternative to state socialism and laissez-faire capitalism. Needless to say, this agreement hardly signaled a rejection of market liberalism.[5]

Thus, even to the least liberal of the postwar conservatives, the capitalist order was not only a fait accompli but also about the best economics one could hope for in this fallen world, a world not only fallen but also threatened by communist aggression. Often they suspected the harshest critics of capitalism of espousing "utopianism," one of the most frequent charges of postwar rightists and one intended to preclude further debate. And so, even in the realm of theory, the traditionalist conservatives chose not to take up the cudgels of prewar conservative radicals and populists against the aggrandizement of corporations (see, e.g., Allen Tate's essay in *Who Owns America?*),[6] and they chose not to consider seriously the decentralized and small-scale economic proposals of postwar radicals and Greens (e.g., they kept their distance from E. F. Schumacher and other serious economic decentralists).[7] The failure to produce a theoretical critique of industrial economics is yet another indication of the fundamental antitraditionalism of the postwar American Right.

Finally, one might have expected that twentieth-century conservatives would have integrated into their cultural analyses the insights and concerns of the ecological movement. Conservationism would seem to be at home—

indeed would seem only to be at home—in the broader context of a truly conservative worldview. Skepticism toward the ideology of progress is a surprisingly consistent feature of the American nature-writing and conservationist literature, from Aldo Leopold to Sigurd Olson to Edward Abbey.[8] But as with technology, postwar American conservatives were content, in their intellectual work if not their personal lives, either to lament ineffectually the pollution of rivers, the ruination of the land, and the extinction of species or—less nobly and against the evidence of the senses—to accuse environmentalists of concocting crises and spreading fear. Thus was the natural alliance between conservationists and conservatives deftly avoided.

As an ideologically unaligned thinker, Wendell Berry has been able to avoid this split-mindedness. He has defended both nature and human culture as complementary parts of a holistic concern with the conditions of human flourishing, or what he often calls simply "health." In so doing, he has not only defended a particular and traditional way of life, but he has also argued that to live well is to live at least in part by the guidance of, and always in conversation with, the traditions one inherits.

It is not uncommon for Berry to argue from tradition, or to approve of someone or something by noting his or its concordance with long-standing communal practices and beliefs. He praises the Kentucky writer Harry Caudill for understanding and venerating "the traditions of justice." Edward Abbey he happily identifies as "a traditionalist—as he has said himself, expecting, perhaps, not to be believed." He identifies "the classical and biblical traditions" as the preeminent source of authority in enjoining us to act responsibly as stewards of nature. And of Wes Jackson's Land Institute Berry writes that if it "is innovative, it is so partly in response to a long tradition and an old hope. It is not merely another episode in our time's random pursuit of novelty."[9]

Berry holds in high regard "the traditions of religious and political thought that influenced the shaping of our society and the founding of our government."[10] Elsewhere, he claims to derive a list of recommendations for the pursuit of localist economics "from Western political and religious traditions"—not, that is, from an abstract ideological blueprint or pure philosophical inquiry. He rejects the use of the language of a public commons because it is not part of "our history and tradition," and for the same reason he accepts and believes in "the right of private property." He faults many contemporary intellectuals for seeing in "American history" and the "Western cultural tradition" only an "inheritance of greed and destruction."[11] And he argues that the hope of conservationists lies ultimately in the Western tradition. Here he is worth quoting at length:

> If we want to use the world with care, we cannot exempt ourselves from
> our cultural inheritance, our tradition. This is a delicate subject at pres-
> ent because our cultural tradition happens to be Western, and there is
> now a fashion of disfavor toward the Western tradition. But most of us
> are in the Western tradition somewhat as we are in the world: we are in
> it because we were born in it. We can't get out of it because it made us
> what we are; we are, to some extent, what it is. And perhaps we would
> not like to get out of it if that meant giving up, as we would have to do,
> our language and its literature, our hereditary belief that all people mat-
> ter individually, our heritage of democracy, liberty, civic responsibility,
> stewardship, and so on. This tradition obviously involves errors and mis-
> takes, damages and tragedies. But that only means that the tradition too
> must be used with care. It is properly subject to critical intelligence and
> is just as properly subject to helps and influences from other traditions.
> But criticize and qualify as we may, we cannot get along without it, for we
> have no other way to learn care; and in fact care is a subject about which
> our tradition has much to teach.[12]

Clearly, it is not difficult to marshal an abundance of textual support for the
notion that Berry writes and works and lives and thinks as a traditionalist.
Look in particular at one of the most important manifestations of his traditionalist outlook: his brief against meritocracy and its resonances with similar
arguments made during the last two and a half centuries by other thinkers
with at least one foot in the traditionalist tradition.

America's self-styled traditionalist conservatives have owed and conceded
considerably more to liberalism than they or their interpreters sometimes
suppose. But from a traditionalist standpoint, this has not vitiated completely
their thought, which undeniably has included important traditionalist elements. One of those elements—and perhaps the one that is not only most
relevant today, but most shockingly un-American—concerns their critique of
meritocracy.

Now meritocracy—the distribution of social awards according to an objective measure of aptitude and/or achievement, that is, "merit"—might serve
as a tolerably just and healthy ideal on which to order society, were it not for
genes. But because genes matter—or, to be more precise, because individual
differences in the attainment of success, prestige, status, wealth, are ineluctably and closely tied to natural differences among individuals—meritocracy, as
a coherent justification for the ordering of society, is, strictly speaking, a lie.
Such, it seems, is the conclusion that one must inevitably draw from the social
science research that culminated in the publication, a decade ago, of *The Bell
Curve.*[13] It is not the conclusion drawn by *The Bell Curve*'s authors, Richard

Herrnstein and Charles Murray, but it is defensible, perhaps even unavoidable. This fundamental insight has, in fact, served to buttress the arguments of traditionalist thinkers ever since the meritocratic ideal began to challenge strongly the privileges of class, birth, and rank in the eighteenth century. And, oddly enough, Wendell Berry, the Jeffersonian democrat, because he shares in this traditionalist tradition, has in fact helped to revitalize it, putting the pretenses and shams and inhumanity of meritocracy front and center without resorting to elitism. But this is to get ahead of ourselves. Let's first take a sidelong look at *The Bell Curve* and try to understand why it poses such a terrible challenge for the meritocratic ideal.

With the publication of *The Bell Curve*, Herrnstein and Murray sought to show through a monumental synthesis of research in the fields of behavior genetics, intelligence, personality, criminology, and education that a natural aristocracy of talent had come to fruition in the United States. Natural advantages, not environmental ones, account for individual differences in achievement, status, educational attainment, income, criminality, and other variables associated with social stratification. Moreover, the most reasonable conclusion to be drawn from the research is that this stratification results from (rather than causes) these differences. In America, talent triumphs. If justice is to be found where each is given his due, in the ancient formulation, what could be more just?

Two problems arise. Liberal individualism, which might be regarded as the ideology of meritocracy, had always posited that the rule of the talented or the skilled would be most in accord with justice, but for that very reason it also propagated the myth that hard work—*will, effort,* and *not* nature—was responsible for one's level of skill or talent, and hence ought to be the basis of individual achievement. As Christopher Lasch noted in *The Culture of Narcissism,* "America's reputation as a land of opportunity rested on its claim that the destruction of hereditary obstacles to advancement had created conditions in which social mobility depended on individual initiative alone."[14]

For justice to be served, then, it was important to eliminate, or at least to equalize, social or environmental barriers to the development of talent. To stunt artificially the development and flourishing of talent would not be just, and everyone ought to have an equal opportunity to achieve success. But, it was assumed, once this removal of barriers was accomplished, individual initiative would more than anything account for differences among people. It might be necessary to tear (some) children from their families and redistribute wealth to an extent heretofore unimagined, but in theory justice, eventually, could be served.

The Bell Curve's authors brought together evidence that effectively dis-

pelled this myth. In fact, by the late twentieth century, social and environmental impediments to achievement in America *had* been removed to an
unprecedented degree. But all this had done was reveal the ruthless extent to
which nature contributed to human differences. In flattening and homogeniz-
ing culture, the twin engines of liberal individualism and social engineering
had not so much created the conditions under which will or effort mattered as
they had made nature matter more than ever. The entire concept of "will" or
"initiative," in fact, now slipped into the background; James Q. Wilson and
Herrnstein doubted whether the concept of "free will," at any rate, had any
validity at all.[15]

What, then, of justice? Herrnstein and Murray were not too worried by
this obvious question, but here it is: if nature, which no one merits, is to account for the distribution of wealth and prestige and power, how is that distribution just? Individual initiative as the agent of justice makes some sense,
since it is a moral concept; if the only thing standing between a man and the
American dream is laziness, that seems fair enough. But genes? One ends up
with them through no merit of one's own. How then can one lay claim to what
they make possible? The liberal individualist society's claim as being *uniquely*
just is exposed as fraudulent by the sort of research reported and synthesized
by Herrnstein and Murray.

For many, it has not taken long for the solution to this dilemma to become clear. And ironically that solution was provided by advances in the very
area—human genetics—that had first exposed the problem: nature, like culture or environment before it, would have to give way, would have to become
malleable. This is a simple requirement of justice in a society governed by the
meritocratic ideal. For if meritocracy is to be just—or, again, at least more just
than any imaginable alternative—it cannot simply reward individuals ran-
domly, which is essentially what it does when it rewards them according to
their largely genetically controlled differences in capabilities. They must lay
moral claim to its rewards, and that can be done only if each individual has an
equal opportunity to succeed. Since that opportunity is manifestly unequal
because of differing genetic capacities, we must aim toward the equalization
of those capacities. For only in that way can our society lay claim to being
just.[16]

Note that this is simply the old eugenics argument in a different key. The
eugenicists of old—and even, indirectly, Herrnstein and Murray—argued that
eliminating the genetically unfit was an act of justice. The same is being said
here, with the elimination taking place by different means. Large-scale, thoroughgoing, state-mandated genetic engineering or "therapy" will be required

if the liberal society is to be a just one. As Kass commission member Peter Lawler has predicted, despite the assurances of some that "the new eugenic regime would be the very opposite of tyranny, because individuals would be perfectly free to make biotechnological choices for themselves and their children," such a sanguine view does not account for the requirements of meritocratic justice. The reality is that "personal choice would not be allowed to burden others with unnecessary risks. . . . The state, in pursuit of risk management or eradication, would therefore intrude more and more into the most intimate details of people's lives."[17]

Now there are several alternatives to this argument. One is to argue that Herrnstein and Murray, and all those social scientists who agree with the basic core of their analysis, are simply wrong. In accounting for individual differences, nature doesn't matter nearly as much as they say—in fact, very little—and it can be overcome through further and more drastic environmental modifications. But, on the basis of all available evidence, there is no reason to think that, this side of heaven, there is any perfect environment that if offered to all humans would completely obscure their innate differences (although, of course, sufficiently bad environments can do this). I do not even think that most of those who take issue with the basic reading of the research offered by Herrnstein and Murray know that they are arguing this. But they are, and it is as implausible as it is disingenuous.

Another alternative is to recognize the essential validity of the behavior-genetics evidence but reject trying to equalize conditions at the beginning through genetic engineering and instead focus on equality at the end, through massive redistribution, artificial competitive boosts to the less naturally gifted, and so forth. This is the approach of the welfare state, and as some critics of *The Bell Curve* were quick to point out, it seems actually to be strengthened by Herrnstein and Murray's work as a prudent and humane attempt to compensate the genetically disadvantaged, at least partially, for their bad luck.[18] Yet, to put it gently, the modern welfare state has not proved to be without its difficulties, among which are its invasion and undermining of family life, the massive managerial bureaucracy required to sustain it, and the denial of local and communal liberties.

Finally, there is a more radical approach, and that is to argue that the idea of meritocracy is itself mistaken. Those in this camp argue that in order to lay claim to justice, a meritocracy must ultimately become a tyranny, either mandating genetic engineering and other eugenic "solutions" to the problem of individual differences, or severely curtailing liberties through a large centralized bureaucratic apparatus, or both. The better approach, from this perspective, is to abandon the destructive meritocratic ideal in favor of one that might be called traditionalist.

Warnings and prophecies against the follies of meritocracy have been present in the literature of traditionalist writers since the eighteenth century. These criticisms were usually employed to defend—self-interestedly, perhaps—the relatively static class structure of the ancien régime, but they still contained genuine insight.

Consider Justus Moser's "No Promotion According to Merit" (1770).[19] Moser, who from approximately 1764 to 1794 was the highest government official in the Westphalia bishopric of Osnabrück, wrote this essay in response to reformers' efforts to create a civil service in which positions would be open to all according to merit, not birth or rank. He marshals several arguments against this proposed change. First, he claims that the only honorable thing to do in the face of a system that distributes offices and honors solely on the basis of merit is to withdraw oneself from consideration, since if one were rewarded, one's less honored friends would be humiliated, while if one were passed over, one would be ashamed and disgraced. "Believe me," writes Moser, "so long as we remain human, it is better that from time to time fortune and favor distribute the prizes, than that human wisdom award them to each according to his merit."

Moser also questions whether a true meritocracy is even workable, for surely those passed over in promotion by those younger than they, for instance, would merely resign in embarrassment or anger. On the other hand, if men are promoted because of factors other than merit, "everybody will be free to flatter himself that merit is not the measure of the world; nobody can regard himself as calumniated; self-love acquiesces, and we think that time and fortune will bring up our turn, too."

As long as humans have their "present nature and passions," concludes Moser, by which he means chiefly pride and self-love, a system of doling out awards and honors according to merit alone can produce only confusion and resentment. As things stand now, on the other hand, "people can think to their comfort: fortune and not merit has elevated these. . . . But if everything went according to merit, this so necessary comfort would completely disappear, and the cobbler who . . . can flatter himself that he would be doing something entirely different from mending the Lady Mayor's slippers if merit were respected in this world could not possibly be happy."

While meritocracy has proved to be acceptable to many more than Moser predicted, his cogent and concise brief against such a system has proved prescient in its prediction that such a system would generate social resentment.

Similar warnings were issued by others. In England and America, the traditionalist case against meritocracy descends clearly from Edmund Burke's *Reflections on the Revolution in France* and provides Burke with his finest credentials as a traditionalist thinker.

In ignoring natural human differences, the French revolutionaries, Burke warned, were propagating a "monstrous fiction, which, by inspiring false ideas and vain expectations into men destined to travel in the obscure walk of laborious life, serves only to aggravate and imbitter that real inequality, which it never can remove; and which the order of civil life establishes as much for the benefit of those whom it must leave in an humble state, as those whom it is able to exalt to a condition more splendid, but not more happy."[20]

There is much to meditate on here. First, it is clear that there is nothing in the behavior-geneticists' work that would have surprised Burke. There is "real inequality" among men that can "never" be erased; to pretend that it can is to inspire false hopes, which when dashed will no doubt lead to bitterness and resentment. For Burke, the old class structure served to mask somewhat the ineluctability of natural individual differences; it humbled some and exalted others, but by making deliberately obscure the mechanism by which this separation of men occurred, it allowed the man of low social status to blame his estate not on himself or his God but on the randomness of birth.

A century and a half later, Wilhelm Röpke insisted on the same point. It "deserves to be stressed," he wrote in *A Humane Economy,*

> that if equality of opportunity is to be achieved by socializing education, envy and resentment will only be exacerbated. If everybody has the same chances of advancement, those left behind will lose the face-saving and acceptable excuse of social injustice and lowly birth. The weakness of mind or character of the overwhelming majority of average or below-average people will be harshly revealed as the reason for failure, and it would be a poor observer of the human soul who thought that this revelation would not prove poisonous. No more murderous attack on the sum total of human happiness can be imagined than this kind of equality of opportunity, for, given the aristocratic distribution of the higher gifts of mind and character among a few only, such equality will benefit a small minority and make the majority all the unhappier.[21]

This seems no less harsh now than it must have when it was written, but Röpke was no Spencerian social Darwinist who delighted in the social survival of the fittest. As a decentralist and ardent supporter of small-scale or "peasant" agriculture, Röpke holds much in common with Wendell Berry. But on individual differences and their primary source Röpke was a realist, and this particular insight into human nature helps form the core of the traditionalist position.

Berry, in fact, is in possession of the same insight. In *Life Is a Miracle,* he assails the meritocratic lie propagated by our schools. In words reminiscent of Burke's and Röpke's, he writes:

> Young people are told, "You can be anything you want to be." Every stu-
> dent is given to understand that he or she is being prepared for "leader-
> ship." All of this is a lie. . . . You can't be everything you want to be;
> nobody can. Everybody can't be a leader; not everybody even wants to
> be. And these lies are not innocent. They lead to disappointment. They
> lead good young people to think that if they have an ordinary job, if they
> work with their hands, if they are farmers or housewives or mechanics or
> carpenters, they are no good.[22]

In his essay on Peruvian farming included in *The Gift of Good Land,* Berry approaches the problem from an opposite direction. Having observed for several days the methods used by highland farmers to wrest an existence from a comparatively difficult and unforgiving land, he is struck by the way in which the culture of traditional, rooted peoples helps to overcome and soften natural variation in human abilities. His friend and guide Steve "talked of the difficulty of finding out about methods and reasons from these farmers," which they seemed strangely unable to articulate.

> They do as they have done, as their ancestors did before them. The meth-
> ods and reasons are assuredly complex—this is an agriculture of extraor-
> dinary craftsmanship and ecological intelligence—but they were worked
> out over a long time, long ago; learned so well, one might say, that they
> are forgotten. It seems to me that this is probably the only kind of culture
> that works: thought sufficiently complex, but submerged or embodied in
> traditional acts. It is at least as unconscious as it is conscious—and so is
> available to all levels of intelligence. Two people, one highly intelligent,
> the other unintelligent, will work fields on the same slope, and both will
> farm well, keeping the ways that keep the land. You can look at a whole
> mountainside covered with these little farms and not see anything egre-
> giously wasteful or stupid. Not so with us. With us, it grows harder and
> harder even for intelligent people to behave intelligently, and the unintel-
> ligent are condemned to a stupidity probably unknown in traditional
> cultures.[23]

Berry recognizes that a primary function of a healthy culture is to make important knowledge widely available by "submerging" and "embodying" it in "traditional acts." He has made the Chestertonian observation that tradition is democratic, humane—fair. Conversely, to uproot, dislocate, or otherwise severely disturb a traditional people and its culture is to injure most those with the fewest intellectual resources and to condemn them to survive more or less on their own. This, of course, is precisely the aim of a meritocracy. Its justifying ideology, liberal individualism, seeks to remove the multiform barriers posed by traditional institutions and affections to the mobility of the intelligent.

Burke's famous defense of prejudice rested on a similar basis. "We are afraid to put men to live and trade each on his own private stock of reason," he wrote in *Reflections,* "because we suspect that this stock in each man is small, and that the individuals would be better to avail themselves of the general bank and capital of nations, and of ages." At its best, prejudice is the means by which the humble, especially, may be engaged in "a steady course of wisdom and virtue." Prejudice "does not leave the man hesitating in the moment of decision, sceptical, puzzled, and unresolved. Prejudice renders a man's virtue his habit."[24]

As we have seen, the seemingly unassailable ideal of "equality of opportunity" demanded by the meritocratic ideal has also drawn scorn from traditionalist thinkers. In large part, this is because they have understood that in order for talent to triumph, it must be mobile. Thus, the better the meritocracy, the more mobility—both geographic and social—is required, until talent is able to flow freely to where it can command the highest price (i.e., the most prestige, the highest status, the most money, the most power, and so on). A perfect market for talent is the dream and goal of liberal individualism: nothing must stand in the way of the rise of talent to primacy—not the state, not intermediate institutions, not religion, not tradition, not families.

The historiography offered by F. A. Hayek in his classic *The Road to Serfdom* is representative of the rosy meritocratic view of the unleashing of talent or, as Hayek terms it, "human ingenuity." "Wherever the barriers to the free exercise of human ingenuity were removed," claims Hayek,

> man became rapidly able to satisfy ever-widening ranges of desire. And while the rising standard soon led to the discovery of very dark spots in society, spots which men were no longer willing to tolerate, there was probably no class that did not substantially benefit from the general advance. . . . By the beginning of the twentieth century the workingman in the Western world had reached a degree of material comfort, security, and personal independence which a hundred years before had seemed scarcely possible.[25]

But it is precisely from the perspective of the workingman that this lyrical, Whiggish view of the progress of liberal individualism has been challenged by traditionalists. Christopher Lasch's indictment of meritocracy, best articulated in his final work, *The Revolt of the Elites and the Betrayal of Democracy* (1995), is especially insightful.

One consequence of meritocracy, Lasch argues at the beginning of this book, is that the elites in such a system become "dangerously isolated" from their neighbors. Because meritocracy requires that populations—or at least elites—be exceptionally mobile, loyalty to community, region, and nation become severely attenuated. Indeed, "advancement in business and the professions, these days, requires a willingness to follow the siren call of opportunity wherever it leads. Those who stay at home forfeit the chance of upward mobility."[26]

It is no surprise, then, that the "new aristocracy of brains," more mobile than ever and indeed committed to a "migratory way of life" as "the price of getting ahead," has little use for Middle America, which is thought to be "technologically backward, politically reactionary, repressive in its sexual morality, middlebrow in its tastes, smug and complacent, dull and dowdy." America's meritocratic elites, Lasch claims, "are at home only in transit, en route to a high-level conference, to the grand opening of a new franchise, to an international film festival, or to an undiscovered resort. Theirs is essentially a tourist's view of the world—not a perspective likely to encourage a passionate devotion to democracy" (6).

As a populist, Lasch, unlike Moser and Burke and the rest of the conservative traditionalists, has no use for the argument that ordinary citizens cannot be trusted to govern themselves or "to grasp complex issues and to make critical judgments" (10). To him, it is this view that has led to the cult of the expert and indeed to the advent of the new elites, who in a meritocratic society cannot and should not be expected to live and work among the rabble, much less to include them among those who have a say in governance and the ordering of social life.

The fact that our meritocracy rewards most those who are at home in the world of "abstractions and images" has further isolated our new elites from the rest of us by their insulation from manual labor. "The thinking classes are fatally removed from the physical side of life," and indeed only under such circumstances could such academic theories as "the social construction of reality" gain any purchase on the mind, concludes Lasch (20).

There are other serious disadvantages to rule by the "best and brightest." Unlike the older, premeritocratic elite, with its codes of chivalry and concern for honor and family, the new elite, thinking that it owes its power to intelligence alone, has "little sense of ancestral gratitude or of an obligation to live up to responsibilities inherited from the past." It "thinks of itself as a self-made elite owing its privileges exclusively to its own efforts" (39).

> Meritocratic elites find it difficult to imagine a community, even a community of the intellect, that reaches into both the past and the future and

is constituted by an awareness of intergenerational obligation. . . . Populated by transients, they lack the continuity that derives from a sense of place and from standards of conduct self-consciously cultivated and handed down from generation to generation (39–40).

Indeed, Lasch's argument is that the ingratitude, historical ignorance, and provincialism of Ortega's mass man can be applied more properly to the elites in our new meritocracy than to our common men and women. Meritocracy in fact drives the process of the declension from the generalist man of letters to the specialist (one of Ortega's complaints) and is therefore a "parody of democracy," which envisoned a general diffusion of cultural knowledge and the "means of civilization" (in R. H. Tawney's words). Thus, social mobility, far from being the sine qua non of democracy, actually "helps to solidify [elites'] influence by supporting the illusion that it rests solely on merit." It also helps to increase the chances that elites will act in communally irresponsible ways, since they are encouraged to think that they owe their rise to nothing but their own efforts and talents (41).

The paradox, then, for Lasch, is that meritocracy is supposed to be a democratic way of doling out social rewards because meritocracy is open to all regardless of birth, but the results are anything but democratic in that they lead to greater social stratification: "segregation of social classes; contempt for manual labor; collapse of the common schools; loss of a common culture." In the end, Lasch concludes, meritocracy, or "an aristocracy of talent," must be judged undesirable: "The talented retain many of the vices of aristocracy without its virtues" (44).

How, then, can we disentangle the ideal of democracy—quite compatible with the American version of traditionalism—with that of meritocracy? Lasch's answer—and also Berry's—is to pursue a decentralized, producer- (rather than consumer-) centered social order as the best way of diffusing intelligence and competence through all classes. The only stable basis of social equality, in the view of Lasch, Berry, and like-minded thinkers, rests in the hope of democratizing intelligence and virtue rather than stripping away barriers to social mobility. This goal requires that tradition play a vital social role as a source of intelligence and wisdom.

Lasch notes that the public-school system has been envisioned by meritocrats as an engine of social mobility, redistributing opportunity according to talent. But social mobility and the ideal of a "classless society" are entirely at odds. In making this argument, Lasch relies largely on Berry, whom he quotes at length, especially his discussion of Justin Smith Morrill in *The Unsettling of America*. Lasch concludes that

> Berry's interrogation of Morrill defines the most important choice a democratic society has to make: whether to raise the general level of competence, energy, and devotion—"virtue," as it was called in an older political tradition—or merely to promote a broader recruitment of elites. Our society has clearly chosen the second course. It has identified opportunity with upward mobility and made upward mobility the overriding goal of social policy (78–79).

That is, it has chosen meritocracy. Both liberals and conservatives, Lasch reminds his readers, see "careers open to talent as the be-all and end-all of democracy when in fact careerism tends to undermine democracy by divorcing knowledge from practical experience, devaluing the kind of knowledge that is gained from experience, and generating social conditions in which ordinary people are not expected to know anything at all" (79).

As Berry puts it in *Life Is a Miracle,* "the context of professionalism is not a place or a community but a career, and this explains the phenomenon of 'social mobility' and all the evils that proceed from it."[27] Like Lasch (who wrote that "it is a mistake to base the defense of democracy on the sentimental fiction that people are all alike. In fact, people are not alike in their capacities. . . . Sameness is not equality"),[28] Berry notes that in order for social mobility to be marketed as essential to personal "liberation," it must deny the existence of "authentic differences and distinctions."[29] If such were recognized, the implication would be that upward mobility would serve fundamentally as a way of justifying an exploitative, "original-discovery" mentality that served the needs of industrial economies but not those of actual communities. Thus does Berry arraign the antitraditional dynamism of meritocracy as fundamentally opposed to the "living integrity of creatures, places, communities, cultures, and human souls."[30]

The requirements of the ideology of meritocracy are opposed to those of stable and healthy communities, the highest priority of the traditionalist. Meritocracy precludes or acts as a retardant on the development of those complex disciplines, practices, and habits that are not the fruit of abstract, rationalistic cognition but depend rather on sustained membership in a particular community.

Furthermore, the ever-improving American meritocracy, despite the claims it makes for itself, in fact seems to have no special claim to justice. Unlike traditionalism, it does not rest upon a foundation of psychological realism that recognizes and accepts both individual differences and the rootedness of some ineradicable portion of those differences in nature.

It is hardly original to notice that despite their incessant employment of a rhetoric celebrating "diversity," political liberals in our meritocratic culture take little pleasure in the recognition of anything but superficial, quite literally skin-deep differences. Nor, for that matter, do most political conservatives, who regard differences in intelligence and its rewards as (perhaps) unfortunate but necessary—though a good number look forward to their eradication through genetic therapy—and who otherwise work as assiduously as the liberals toward the universal and homogeneous state. In this respect, both our liberals and our conservatives accept meritocracy.

Traditionalists, in contrast, can afford to delight in human variation because, unlike our liberals, they see it as largely unavoidable and because, unlike our conservatives, they forbear to defend an exploitative system of social status and reward built around the putative but necessarily indefensible "justice" of its existence. As both our liberals and conservatives look increasingly to genetic manipulation and a "posthuman future" as the "solution" to the problem of justice in the American meritocracy, the insights of the humane and realistic traditionalist tradition and its finest contemporary exponent, Wendell Berry, have become unmistakably and radically necessary.

Notes

1. In any number of places, but see, e.g., Wendell Berry, "In Distrust of Movements," in *Citizenship Papers* (Washington, DC: Shoemaker and Hoard, 2003).

2. See Kimberly Smith, *Wendell Berry and the Agrarian Tradition: A Common Grace* (Lawrence: University Press of Kansas, 2003), 6–8, 76–77, 87ff.

3. Wendell Berry, *Life Is a Miracle* (Washington, DC: Counterpoint, 2000), 11.

4. See, e.g., Martin Heidegger, *The Question Concerning Technology and Other Essays* (New York: Harper and Row, 1977), trans. by William Lovitt; Romano Guardini, *Letters from Lake Como: Explorations in Technology and the Human Race* (Grand Rapids, MI: W. B. Eerdmans, 1994), trans. Geoffrey Bromiley; Friedrich Georg Jünger, *The Failure of Technology: Perfection without Purpose* (Hinsdale, IL: H. Regnery, 1949); Ivan Illich, *Tools for Conviviality* (New York: Harper and Row, 1973); Albert Borgmann, *Technology and the Character of Contemporary Life: A Philosophical Inquiry* (Chicago: University of Chicago Press, 1984); and Neil Postman, *Technopoly: The Surrender of Culture to Technology* (New York: Knopf, 1992).

5. For an argument that Röpke is the economist of traditionalist conservatism, see Mark C. Henrie's essay "Understanding Traditionalist Conservatism," in Peter Berkowitz, ed., *Varieties of Conservatism in America* (Stanford, CA: Hoover Institution Press, 2004). The classic Röpke text on economics and culture is *A Humane Economy: The Social Framework of the Free Market,* 3rd ed. (Wilmington, DE: ISI Books, 1998). The most accessible and successful explication of Röpke's social and political thought

is provided by John Zmirak in *Wilhelm Röpke: Swiss Globalist, Local Economist* (Wilmington, DE: ISI Books, 2002).

6. *Who Owns America?* (New York: Houghton Mifflin, 1936) was both underrated and unjustly neglected. Tate's essay is titled "Notes on Liberty and Property."

7. Typified, e.g., by Schumacher's *Small Is Beautiful: Economics As If People Mattered* (New York: Harper and Row, 1973) and the works of earlier figures such as Herbert Agar and Ralph Borsodi, such as their *Land of the Free* (Boston: Houghton Mifflin, 1935) and *This Ugly Civilization* (New York: Harper and Bros., 1933), respectively.

8. See, e.g., Aldo Leopold, *A Sand County Almanac* (New York: Oxford University Press, 1949) and *For the Health of the Land* (Washington, DC: Island Press, 1999); Sigurd Olson, *Listening Point* (New York: Alfred Knopf, 1958) and *The Lonely Land* (New York: Alfred Knopf, 1961); and Edward Abbey, *Desert Solitaire: A Season in the Wilderness* (New York: Simon and Schuster, 1968) and *The Serpents of Paradise: A Reader* (New York: Henry Holt, 1995), ed. John MacRae. See also Bret Wallach, *At Odds with Progress: Americans and Conservation* (Tucson: University of Arizona Press, 1991).

9. The quotations regarding Caudill, Abbey, and Jackson are from Wendell Berry, *What Are People For?* (San Francisco: North Point, 1990), 31, 40, 107, respectively.

10. Ibid., 129.

11. Wendell Berry, *Another Turn of the Crank* (Washington, DC: Counterpoint, 1995), 21, 49, 66.

12. Ibid., 73–74.

13. Richard J. Herrnstein and Charles Murray, *The Bell Curve: Intelligence and Class Structure in American Life* (New York: Free Press, 1994).

14. Christopher Lasch, *Culture of Narcissism: American Life in an Age of Diminishing Expectations* (New York: Norton, 1978), 52.

15. James Q. Wilson and Richard J. Herrnstein, *Crime and Human Nature* (New York: Simon and Schuster, 1985).

16. Murray himself has worried about this implication in "Deeper into the Brain," *National Review*, January 24, 2000. Yet he confesses that he "find[s] it hard to get too upset" by "popular voluntary uses of gene manipulation . . . that avoid birth defects and . . . lead to improved overall physical and mental abilities."

17. Peter Augustine Lawler, *Stuck with Virtue: The American Individual and Our Biotechnological Future* (Wilmington, DE: ISI Books, 2005), 18–19.

18. See Steven Fraser, ed., *The Bell Curve Wars: Race, Intelligence, and the Future of America* (New York: Basic Books, 1995).

19. This essay was exhumed by Jerry Z. Muller in his edited collection, *Conservatism: An Anthology of Social and Political Thought from David Hume to the Present* (Princeton: Princeton University Press, 1997). All Moser quotations provided here derive from pages 74–77 in this collection.

20. Edmund Burke, *Reflections on the Revolution in France* (Oxford: Oxford University Press, 1993), 37.

21. Röpke, *A Humane Economy,* 233.

22. Berry, *Life Is a Miracle,* 58.

23. Wendell Berry, *The Gift of Good Land: Further Essays, Cultural and Agricultural* (San Francisco: North Point, 1981), 27.

24. Burke, *Reflections on the Revolution in France*, 87.

25. F. A. Hayek, *The Road to Serfdom*, 16–17.

26. Christopher Lasch, *The Revolt of the Elites and the Betrayal of Democracy* (New York: Norton, 1995), 5.

27. Berry, *Life Is a Miracle*, 130.

28. Lasch, *Revolt of the Elites*, 88.

29. Berry, *Life Is a Miracle*, 133.

30. Ibid., 76.

Sven Birkerts

Looking the Technological Gift Horse in the Mouth

ESSAY-WRITING FOR me is in large part about assembling the elements. I don't generally get an idea and then go out looking for my supporting instances. Rather, especially with pieces of a more exploratory sort, I find that the process often works in reverse. Aware of a certain pressure, a sense of upcoming inner occasion, I look to see what I'm looking at; I check in to see where the charge is to be found. And usually, given the kinds of things I think about, it's not in any one place, but dispersed, distributed. Just how this works, I don't know. But my learning to write has, in some important way, been about beginning to trust this process.

My assumption, underlying everything, is that the world is telling me things, announcing its changes, offering up stories in scattered discrete bits, much like a newspaper might, except that a newspaper delivers its account of the world filtered through a particular formal grid defined by economic, political, and other so-called consequential considerations. The world I look at may include these elements, but they are always overwhelmed by a sense of totality, by a belief that all information potentially matters. That is, that styles of clothing, jokes and cartoons, etiquette at bus stops, the innuendo of disc jockeys, new sounds and syncopations in popular music, the packaging and marketing of children's toys, and additional layers of coded instruction in automated transactions are all kinds of information and might be a meaningful part of the story of how things are for us now.

Needless to say, unless you are Jorge Luis Borges writing the fantasy of the Aleph, that mythical spot in the universe where everything is visible and knowable at once, you can't set out to present the complete picture of anything. You go for a "take," hoping it will possess enough relevance, enough connection to what others elsewhere might be picking up on the screens of *their* intuition, to make it worth presenting.

In my case, I had little more than a potential title—"Looking the Technological Gift Horse in the Mouth"—which came to me, as sometimes happens, before I knew exactly what I wanted to say, only that I wanted to create a kind of magnetic field for drawing scattered iron filings together.

Of course the process is not completely arbitrary. My title did come from *some*where. It came from a deep-seated intellectual bias, a conviction I've had for years that our reliance on ever-more-sophisticated technologies—not to mention our faith in the rightness and necessity of the technological solution—is overblown, if not misplaced, and that we would do well to check in on this assumption, to test it and keep testing it against our sense of personal and societal well-being. Simply: Has our immersion in the dream of technology really brought us closer to the "life, liberty and pursuit of happiness" we profess as our collective goal?

Once I had my title and its implied concept, I trusted that my newly alerted sensors, those little antennae of vigilance, would bring me the clues I needed. And so they did, though hardly from the places you would expect. For I was not researching the archives of MIT's *Technology Review,* say, or reading through the usual roster of technology critics. That kind of thing had become all too predictable. I needed to surprise myself. So in this case I was going through my average American days, driving my eight-year-old son to karate practice, leafing through magazines at the newsstand, daydreaming at traffic intersections. And out of this I put together a rather peculiar collection of things. Not one of them was especially likely by itself, but as they accumulated I could sense them building up a kind of combinatory energy. My trophies finally included, among other things, two separate items from an old *New Yorker,* one a cartoon, the other a small section from John Updike's review of what was then Ian McEwan's latest novel, *Atonement;* a download from the *Washington Post's* Web site of an essay on beauty; a bit of gleaned research about the father of one of my son's school friends, the text of Elizabeth Bishop's haunting poem "Crusoe in England," brought to mind when my son and I watched a glaringly unfaithful movie remake of Defoe's *Robinson Crusoe* starring Pierce Brosnan, and an essay I came upon by Wendell Berry.

Contemplating this list you may be baffled about what, if anything, these "found objects" share in common; you may also be ready to call me the worst sort of hypocrite. For what is glaringly obvious is that I have relied almost exclusively on materials discovered via computer and through my patrolling of the image-and-word stream of popular culture. How dare I question the benefits of technology when it is technology that is giving me the means and the ammunition to do so? The only way I can respond to this—sheepishly, begging for indulgence—is to say that we have come to such a place in our cultural life, attained a state of such thorough saturation, that we are forced to make use of the ancient Eastern martial principle of jujitsu, which applies the thrust of the adversary's force against itself. Taking on technology using the means of technology—a paradox perhaps, but not an out-and-out contradiction. If I were to deprive myself of this strategy, my field of relevant data would shrink considerably.

My procedure will make sense only when you see it in practice. So I begin at the beginning, with the midmorning errand of dropping my son at a play-date, in the course of which I met for the first time and chatted with the friend's father. His name—I don't think he will mind my using it—is Ted Selker, and when at one point I asked Ted what he did, he said that he worked at the Media Lab at MIT, a place where top-notch cyber-thinkers ponder applications for cutting-edge developments in the technology. We traded a few anecdotes about Nicholas Negroponte, author of *Being Digital,* who is Ted's boss and who was at one time my spirited opponent on various panels and talk shows about the impact of computing on our culture. I didn't get a chance to ask Ted what he did specifically, but I was curious enough that when I got home I typed his name into the Google search engine. Ted Selker. And what I found, embedded in the thousand-odd bits of info-clutter that spew forth in the course of any such search, was that he was one of the chief proselytizers of what are popularly known as "smart environments." The deeper idea of the smart environment, so far as I understand it, is that the world we interact with can be engineered so cunningly, circuited so completely and at such a level of specificity, that it becomes itself a kind of interface, a totality almost self-responsive to our needs and desires. Think of Bill Gates's house, which greets visitors in their rooms with a kind of wraparound hospitality, all needs and desires anticipated by sensors reading the least telltale movements.

My first bemused response after taking in this most basic identifying information was to think, "This man and I could not be more opposite—his premises are exactly counter to mine." Hoping that we would at some point get a chance to compare our views, I logged off. But even as I sat there, my screen dimming down, I knew that there was something useful for me in this notion of the smart environment.

By itself, with nothing to resonate against, this concept was relatively inert. I had only my long-standing belief that all developments in the technological sphere are part of a basic gain/loss dynamic, with so-called improvements in one area leading to possible erosions in the broader human arena.

Implementing a radical speedup in delivery (of anything), for instance, cuts away at our willingness, and ability, to tolerate delay; automating phone systems creates intolerable—and psychologically alienating—selection-trees. "If you have a touch-tone phone, please say or enter 'one' now." Surely the insertion of technologically responsive interfaces in our daily living environment could only modify further our already modified sense of agency or connection and our basic sense of placement in a world of functional objects.

The first more useful "click" did not come until a day or two later when I sat down with no special thought in my mind to look through an old unread *New Yorker*. I found myself staring at and then ripping out a cartoon, one I would probably have just smiled at—if even that—at any other time.

The cartoon shows a mother sitting on a couch with her arm draped consolingly around the shoulder of her young daughter, who is looking up at her and shedding a single large tear. "It's all right, sweetie," says the mother, "in the information age everybody feels stupid." The trigger for me was, obviously, the word *stupid*, and it triggered precisely because of its absolute opposition to the word *smart*, which was still active in my thoughts. Suddenly I had the first ghostly contour of a thought, an idea; I had gotten the confirming nod I needed. For of course the thing about cartoons, *New Yorker* cartoons especially, I would say, is that they achieve their effects—they work—exactly to the degree that they tap something in the so-called collective mind, venting our fears and anxieties, putting an agreeable twist on our common recognitions. To me the cartoon said, basically: many of us go around these days with a sense of being diminished, made to feel stupid—less intelligent and in control than before—by the information environment surrounding us. And if this information environment is not the same as the technological interface of the smart environment, it is not unrelated either.

Here were the beginnings of a thought, then, but a very general thought, and one that I did not feel ready to pursue yet. Flipping on through the same issue, however, I paused to read John Updike's review of Ian McEwan's novel —a novel set in England in 1935 incidentally—and there, following right on the heels of my cartoon insight, I read:

> *Atonement* . . . has a striking happenstance resemblance to Margaret Atwood's *The Blind Assassin*. Both revert, from the perspective of an old woman facing death near the bloated end of the twentieth century, to an era when a certain grandeur could attach to human decisions, made as they were under the shadow of a global war and in living memory of the faded virtues—loyalty and honesty and valor—that sought to soften what McEwan calls the "iron principle" of self-love. People could still dedicate a life, gamble it on one throw. Compared with today's easy

knowingness and self-protective irony, feelings then had a hearty naïve-té, a force developed amid repression and scarcity and linked to a sense of transcendent adventure.[1]

Once again, more pronounced for me because it came so quickly after the other "click," I had the inkling of a necessary connection. This one, I realize, is not so obvious as my sense of a link between smart environments and a feel-ing people may have of being stupid, of being overwhelmed by their cultural surroundings. But the stretch promised me that there was a larger dimension to the subject. What I found myself doing automatically, before giving it any more systematic or abstract thought, was asserting that there was something in common between the expressed sense of stupidity, or inadequacy, in the former example, and the longing, so clearly captured in the Updike passage, for greater dramatic resonance in human experience—more sense of, for lack of a better phrase, romantic consequentiality. Updike's insight is hardly new. It is one of the truisms of the postmodern analysis: that the fragmented self experiences a fragmented, hypersaturated world. The accompanying idea, a staple of contemporary psychological thought, is that we nevertheless live with a deeply programmed need for coherence. We are creatures who crave clear experience and strong meaning in our lives.

The general tendency of my thinking must be getting obvious by now. But before I make some more specific observations, let me offer one more associa-tive connection. This, which plays directly into the sentiment of the Updike quotation, is again drawn from the outermost—the broad-based, public mind—layer of things, that layer essentially created and catered to by the me-dia pundits, and this connection was an article I discovered while trolling the Internet for some other bit of information. Originally printed in the *Washington Post*, the piece, by Joel Garreau, titled "The Call for Beauty, Coming in Loud and Clear," offers the impossibly general, essentially unfounded argument that "beauty is back." Garreau has rounded up snippets of quotations from scholarly and cultural opinion-makers, added what in this context could pass for supporting instances. He insists on this basis that after long decades of disregard, decades of artistic exile, the deeply planted human appetite for beauty is vigorously reasserting itself. In a world become chaotic and threat-ening, more and more people are now—so he argues—in search of the pat-terned integrity, the radiance, of beauty. I scoffed at the feature-page oppor-tunism of the piece, even as I pounced on it as further evidence.

What I am steering toward, under the general rubric of "Looking the Technological Gift Horse in the Mouth," is in no sense a revolutionary new interpretation of our circumstance. It is, rather, yet another version of what I have been saying, and writing about, since this subject first began to interest me some years ago. The only real difference—one, though, that allows me to venture my thoughts again—is not in the underlying situation but in how we are positioned in terms of that situation. When I was first offering up my analysis of the basic trade-off—the gain/loss dynamic—the cyberworld was young, had not yet established absolute dominance. It was still possible to believe that people would understand what sacrifices the coming of the golden age of circuit technologies required, and that this would possibly slow, if not stall, our mad forward rush. Now, a mere decade later, we see that there was no stalling action at all—we have leapt forward with the full conviction of inevitability. Any critique I venture now will not be preemptive so much as explanatory.

There is, for me, one other difference between then and now, and that is that if we *have* taken up what I once thought of as the devil's bargain, the Faustian pact, we are not creatures utterly incapable of reactive afterthought. I mean that, yes, we have given ourselves over to the technological system without notion of retreat, but we are beginning to show some of the strains of our situation. I point to the cartoon, to Updike's openly wistful characterization of romantic faith, to what Joel Garreau calls the rediscovery of beauty. These casual findings—I'm sure I could have found hundreds—signal unease, disaffection. They suggest to me the widening gulf between how we live and how we want to live, or feel we ought to live. They intimate that all is not well in what the poet Rilke called "our interpreted world." And they make me think that a true analysis of life in the technological millennium is not just a descriptive account of the *what*—the complex tools and systems we have brought into our midst—but a psychological reflection upon how the new procedures and expectations are altering our existential relation to ourselves.

Here is what I find. Very basically, and very briefly, the changes that millennial technology has brought us include (1) the further—now quite radical—condensation of time and space that began with the arrival of high-speed transport and electricity-based modes of communication, (2) the saturation of our airspace with theoretically endless information—indeed, the historically sudden creation of an all-surrounding information space, and (3) a media-originated sense of collective simultaneity—the fact that our myriad tools of connection have planted us in the midst of what feels like a perpetual historical "now." We are increasingly bonded with our fellow citizens, at least through electronic participation part of a large protoplasmic mass.

All these developments—and of course there are many others—undermine the old-style subjective self at the very root. It gets harder and harder to tell ourselves a story in which we star believably as intended, purposeful, clearly bounded protagonists. The desire and will may be there—we do have an almost genetic call to coherence and singularity—but the new context makes it almost impossible to realize. How do you believe yourself bound to a place and time when you live in the midst of a pure potentiality of space and time? How do you sustain a consistent presence, a clarity of thought and imagination, when you are bombarded at every instant by waves of distracting stimuli, with an endless menu of possible conceptual frameworks? "It's all right, sweetie," says the mother, "in the information age everybody feels stupid." As Friedrich Nietzsche wrote, reflecting on the crisis of overload at the end of the nineteenth century: "The massive influx of impressions is so great; surprising, barbaric, and violent things press so overpoweringly . . . in the youthful soul; that it can save itself only by taking recourse in premeditated stupidity." Pondering this assertion in a *Harper's Magazine* article I'd saved, Thomas de Zengotita observed that Nietzsche "thought people at the end of the *nineteenth* century were suffocating in a vast goo of meaningless stimulation," adding: "Ever notice how, when your hand is numb, everything feels thin? Even a solid block of wood lacks depth and texture. . . . Well, numb is to the soul as thin is to a mediated world." [2] Anesthetization: the deprivation of sensation, and for us the loss of the primary sense of contact with the world and the self.

From another angle, when everything feels possible, nothing feels inevitable anymore. No thought, no action, feels like the authentic, the unquestionably right thought or action. Our polyglot culture offers no strong echoing paradigms, no vivid pictures that say: this is the way of things. Relativism rules. We may long, with Updike, for a time when "people could still dedicate a life, gamble it on one throw." For that to be possible, however, you need to feel the weight, the gravity pull of a life. You have to feel the self as essential.

Here I begin to look the technological gift horse in the mouth, though for this I need the rest of my coincidental connections. I love how in the act of writing the mind organizes itself around a question, how everything I look at becomes a possible part of an answer. Even the PG-13 rental film of *Robinson Crusoe* that my son and I watched together the other night, though to be fair, the movie was only a prompt reminding me of a poem I have always loved, Elizabeth Bishop's "Crusoe in England."

The situation of the poem is that the castaway, rescued after many long years on his island, is now home in England, looking back from the vantage of age on the core experience of his life. He reflects:

Now I live here, another island,
that doesn't seem like one, but who decides?

My blood was full of them; my brain
bred islands. But that archipelago
has petered out. I'm old.
I'm bored, too, drinking my real tea,
surrounded by uninteresting lumber.
The knife there on the shelf—
it reeked of meaning, like a crucifix.
It lived. How many years did I
beg it, implore it, not to break?
I knew each nick and scratch by heart,
the bluish blade, the broken tip,
the lines of wood-grain on the handle . . .
Now it won't look at me at all.
The living soul has dribbled away.
My eyes rest on it and pass on. [3]

What does this have to do with technology? Very little. What does this have to do with our condition? A great deal. Among many other things, "Crusoe in England" is a poem about the contexts of mattering; it is a poem about deprivation, urgency, about the investment in circumstance that is the very basis of our sense of being truly alive. It is—and this is what makes it so wrenching to read—about how that sense can slip away, how new circumstance and new angles of regard can bring about a crisis of mattering. I can't read the poem without feeling that it is, in a way, also about the passage we all make from the perceptual and emotional intensities of childhood into the more diffuse, complicated atmospheres of adulthood. All of us know what Bishop called that reek of meaning, now gone. We know that sense that the living soul of some thing or place has dribbled away. We bear this sorrow because we have other compensating awarenesses, but also because we have no real choice.

The point I am building toward is that Crusoe's situation in age and exile can be linked to our situation. Here we are, clothed in our knowing late modernity, blessed with tools of access and retrieval, awash in images and narratives that ought to stimulate and enrich, able as never before to create around ourselves environments of comfort, in ready electronic hailing distance of our nearest and dearest—and what do we feel? Do we feel enriched and joyful? Do we move through our days with a larger intensity of purpose? Do we feel the radiance of arrival? I don't think we do. No, we are, if I can generalize, inside Crusoe's cottage of ease, looking back with a pang to our memories of when there was more mattering. We want the thingness of things, the volume sensation of time, the awakened possibility of the unknown, the unexperienced.

We don't want the information—we want the sense of congruence, things fitting to their explanation, that information once seemed to bring. This has disappeared under the flow of endless data and the proliferation of contexts that this data brings into being. We don't want touch-tone relationships—we want our circuits and keypads to connect us with the people who are important to us. But something in these tools of contact—mobile phones, e-mail—infects the contact, wraps us in an environment in which the focus of deeper communication becomes ever more difficult. We look away more readily, find ourselves listening past what it is our friend might be telling us. In this way, the finer details—the textures—of place recede before the momentum of our arrivals and departures. These are contemporary clichés—I recognize this. But when they are taken all together they clarify the nature of our subtle but deep complaint. Simply, our means of living—our technologies—are with every upgrade, every speeding up, putting us more at odds with the delicate system of balances and proportions that our psychological well-being depends upon. And our preferred solution—to look to further technologies to intensify sensation, expedite communication, gather and organize information—only makes things worse, bringing in further abstractions, further removals, further dissipations of focus. We cannot solve the crisis of proliferation and saturation through further proliferation and saturation.

What can we do? Do we imagine we can send the aging Crusoe back to his island, as if a restoring of deprivation will do the trick? No, it's too late. And even if he were to return, he would no longer be able to recover his former state, his old relation to the things around him. His mind has been altered. Returning to civilization has effectively short-circuited him. Asking whether there is any getting free of the media-saturated, ersatz environment in order to reconnect with real sensation, Zengotita writes in his *Harper's* essay that "a couple of weeks out in Nature doesn't make it anymore. Even if you eschew the resonant clutter of The Tour and The Gear, you will virtualize everything you encounter, all by yourself. You won't see wolves, you'll see 'wolves.' You'll be murmuring to yourself, at some level, 'Wow, look, a real wolf, not in a cage, not on TV. I can't believe it.'" [4] Zengotita, like Walker Percy before him, has put his finger squarely on the real problem, which is that after enough exposure to the all-surrounding system, we become its agents—we internalize. It doesn't block us off—we learn to block ourselves.

The external forces are, of course, nearly absolute, assuring for one thing that we are not likely to remedy this private sense of distance by getting rid of our tools and our toys. So long as society runs on an economics of capitalist growth—the creation and marketing of ever-new technologies and shareholder insistence on good news from the quarterly profit and loss statement—

we will see only an intensification of more of the same. Whatever else we can say about our globalized electronic culture, it is immensely profitable to the corporations and individuals who preside over it.

It is at this point that I would take a cue from one of our few wise elders, Wendell Berry, a thinker attuned at many different levels to what might be called the logic of organic interdependence. Berry has made it his practice through a lifetime of writing to reflect on questions of balance and scale, and on the need for a harmonic—call it Vitruvean—relation between the values of the individual and the imperatives of the larger collective.

Back in 1971, in the very midst of the social turbulence we now call, inaccurately, the sixties, or the Watergate era, when it seemed to all of us that the culture had divided irrevocably into warring camps and, to paraphrase Dante, "the straight way was lost," Berry wrote a deeply reflective essay titled "Discipline and Hope."[5] The piece took an elevated—by which I mean vertically removed—vantage on the crisis of values brought about by our hubristic disregard for our long-standing natural and human ecologies. Berry smartly excoriated our abstracting tendencies and our push to narrow specialization.

More than thirty years later, "Discipline and Hope" remains an informed and ominous critique, but also, alas, the very sort of thing we have learned to disregard, not because we don't care about the implications but because it shows the situation to be systemic and therefore beyond the most energetic and well-meant individual initiatives. Berry is naturally very much aware of this problem. Indeed, he begins the closing section of the essay, subtitled "The Spring of Hope," by writing, "The most destructive of ideas is that extraordinary times justify extraordinary measures." In the context of 1971 this would have meant complete social revolution—nothing less would do—with the supporting rationale, in Berry's words, "let us deal with our enemies by whatever means are handiest; in view of our high aim history will justify and forgive."

But Berry cannot endorse any such response, just as he would probably not put his chips on the unlikely dismantling of the technosphere we have created around ourselves. He advises, instead, a return to personal spiritual sources, to living in accord with the ancient balances and counter to the prevailing trends. While he does not propose this so much as an effective practical solution—isolated private actions will not of themselves counter the large-scale destructive momentum—it is symbolic. It marks an embrace of the essential sanity out of which any serious moves to change will come. Berry declares the recognition that individual choice matters, and that care and attention are the only viable basis for a living culture. His conclusion, darkly comic, deeply paradoxical, invokes a kindred tradition and a fellow philosopher-sage: "Asked why the Shakers, who expected the end of the world at any moment, were nevertheless consummate craftsmen, Thomas Merton replied: 'When you expect the world to end at any moment, you know there is no need to hurry. You take your time, you do your work well.'"[6]

I close by citing Berry's essay here because his turn to the personal echoes something of the movement of my own thought in the face of overwhelming obstacles. But there is a significant difference, too. Where Berry posits the return to inner sources as a volitional response, I see it more as an unpremeditated reflex. I believe that we have, each of us, a kind of private economy, a structure within which we negotiate our sense of significance and decide how much meaning we need in our lives. When life overpowers us, bringing anxiety, stress, or depression, we either succumb to the Nietzschean stupidity, or else we act—we seek out therapy, anxiety medication. But more than that, we change things in our lives—look for new jobs, leave the city, find new partners. Simply, when the threshold of the intolerable is crossed, so long as we feel it as intolerable, *we do things.* From this I take what faith I have that the gulf between how we live and how we want to live will not necessarily just keep growing. We may, singly—but also, perhaps, collectively, in ways yet to be imagined—stop, swerve, retract, do whatever we need to do to counter the dissonance we feel, what Auden called "the intolerable neural itch." The development of technology might well be fixed on a permanently rising curve, but our response to this is by no means predictable. The neural psyche may function, as the scientists tell us, like a circuit, but I think we are discovering that with circuits come circuit breakers, shutdown reflexes that, better than anything, help us map out the limits of the human. If anything changes, it will be because we will have insisted on wholeness of feeling over speed, efficiency, and a sense of being electronically merged. In our discomfort we might search out some tiny grains of hope.

Notes

1. John Updike, "Flesh on Flesh," *New Yorker*, March 4, 2002, 82.

2. Thomas de Zengotita, "The Numbing of the American Mind: Culture as Anesthetic," *Harper's Magazine*, April 2002, 33–34.

3. Elizabeth Bishop, *The Complete Poems 1927–1979* (New York: Farrar, Straus and Giroux, 1983), 166.

4. Zengotita, "The Numbing of the American Mind," 37.

5. A portion of "Discipline and Hope" was originally offered at the University of Kentucky as the Distinguished Professor Lecture on November 17, 1971. The essay appears in Wendell Berry, *A Continuous Harmony: Essays Cultural and Agricultural* (1970; Washington, DC: Shoemaker and Hoard, 2004).

6. Ibid., 161.

Gene Logsdon

Wendell Berry:
Agrarian Artist

I WAS SITTING AT my desk in Philadelphia at the headquarters of *Farm Journal* magazine one dreary day in 1971, watching the clock wind its ponderous way toward five o'clock. At exactly 5:01, I would flee my office and, if I ran, catch the 5:12 train nine blocks away to my home in exurbia where I was pretending to be a farmer on two acres of land. Three hours to go. I was not very happy, and the martini at lunch had not helped matters, except to infuse me with that reckless kind of bravado that could make me say something in the presence of senior editors that I would regret later. My unhappiness stemmed from a deep uneasiness. As a journalist covering agricultural news, I was witnessing the end of farming as I knew and liked it. The "get big or get out" philosophy was turning the food-production system into a monstrous international factory where poor people did the work for wages guaranteed to keep them poor.

One of the "scatter girls," as they were called, came by and dumped a bunch of paper debris into my in-box. There was a memo from an editor whom I had irritated at lunch. The rest of the scatter was press releases. Day after day, week after week, year after year, an unending flutter of press releases, like mockingbirds going south in winter and north in spring, chirping breathlessly the same old repetitive songs about how some new product was sure to bring heaven on earth to farmers if they were willing to spend the money. If they spent the money, those of us sitting in urban offices could get paid enough to keep on sitting in urban offices. A person could live a whole *life* writing farm-market drivel and agribusiness boasts without ever having to be tested in the fires of real farming, without ever growing a stalk of corn, or changing the points and plugs on a tractor, or losing a corn crop to hail. I had to escape this cuckoo's nest.

But something else slid out of the in-box with the press releases. A slim paperback. Title: *Farming: A Handbook*. Oh, this ought to be good. I flipped it open. To my surprise, it was poetry. The author was somebody named Wendell

Berry from Kentucky. Poetry? Purporting to be a handbook about farming? What next?

The poems were mostly short. So I read the first one, "The Man Born to Farming." It had an unusual grace to it. Not like Frost but, well, not unlike Frost either. The same kind of heft, but where Frost's poems often seemed chipped from New Hampshire granite, Berry's eased along smooth and soulful without losing their edge, like good Kentucky bourbon. So I read another. And another. I was drawn on by a voice that I had never heard before but had heard all my life. Mr. Berry was talking to me. I was a man born to farming who had been too stupid to know it until I was almost trapped in a big city. With increasing excitement, I read maybe twenty poems more before I came to "On a Hill Late at Night." The last five lines rocked my soul.

> I am wholly willing to be here
> between the bright silent thousands of stars
> and the life of the grass pouring out of the ground.
> The hill has grown to me like a foot.
> Until I lift the earth I cannot move.

I slapped the book closed, got up, and walked down to the managing editor's (Lane Palmer's) office. I was not moving under my own power. I had just read something that struck me as extraordinary. If the experts said I was wrong, that was their problem. Get out of my way. Maybe it was the martini.

"Lane, you see this?" I waved the little volume at him from the doorway. He squinted. Shook his head.

"You read poetry?" I asked.

"Not much. Can't understand it."

"Here's some you can understand."

I handed him the book. He looked at it briefly, handed it back. He was busy.

"Lane, this guy is good. And he knows farming. I'm going to go see him and do a profile. He lives in Kentucky."

Lane was a little taken aback. I wasn't exactly asking him.

"Lane, I'm *sure* there's a story here. This guy lives on a farm, actually works a farm." (At this point I was only guessing, but anyone who wrote like this Berry guy almost had to really work on a farm.) "And he can write poetry as good as Frost's." I could get away with making grandiose statements like that because I was the only editor who had been to graduate school in American studies. There was always the fear that I might know what I was talking about in such matters.

He was still not wholly focused on what I was saying. He just wanted me to go away right then. "Write up a proposal. Be a good one to bring up at the next staff conference. See what the other editors think."

"Lane, I don't give a damn what the other editors think," I countered. "I'm going to go and interview this guy."

Lane looked up from his typewriter. I had his full attention now.

"Where did you say he lived?"

"Kentucky."

Lane looked perplexed. Iowa grew more corn and soybeans in four counties than Kentucky did in the whole state. Corn-'n-Beans was god, generating the ad revenue that the magazine lived on. Editorial policy barely admitted that Kentucky's whiskey and tobacco existed. *Farm Journal* pretended that farmers did not drink alcohol. Honest. Heavens, we couldn't even publish recipes that called for a dash of wine.

I could see Lane's mind churning. If only this Wendell Berry lived in Iowa. Or Illinois. Then he could justify the story to the publisher. Oh well, Logsdon was showing initiative. Initiative meant a lot.

"Okay. But find another story to do while you're out there."

I did go to see Mr. Berry shortly thereafter and wrote an article for the magazine about him. (Didn't find another story to do while I was out there either.) I was still going to see him thirty-three years later. Something happened between us that was more than friendship, if there can be anything more than friendship. We were cultural twins, farm boys who had grown up with similar experiences—we had both even thrown horsehairs in water tanks to see if they would turn into snakes. Unusual for farm boys, we had both received similar liberal arts educations. Also both of us had gone to boarding-schools for high school, and so shared that singular kind of suffering only boarding-school students knew. When I read the first part of his novel *Jayber Crow* in which Jayber attends boarding school, I thought surely Wendell was writing about me. Wendell had gone to Italy on a Guggenheim, then taught a while in New York City before realizing, in 1964, that he had to get back to his roots. I had received, as another of my preposterous gifts from the heights of Olympus, a four-year National Defense Education Act Fellowship to Indiana University, from which I was supposed to go on to some big-city university too. But I wouldn't do it. I wanted to be a writer, and *Farm Journal* seemed to offer a better chance than a university. Ten years after Wendell went home, I did the same, and his influence figured largely in my decision.

Wendell Berry is a writer of many parts. Once I watched him at a confrontation with Earl Butz, then secretary of agriculture, known for his quick wit and swift repartee. Wendell, with his disarming Kentucky hillbilly drawl, made the secretary look ridiculous by the end of the debate. The industrial grain farmers who had come to cheer their governmental hero of the "fencerow to fencerow" farming policy that eventually bankrupted about half of them ended up in sympathy with Wendell instead. Ignoring Mr. Butz, they kept asking Wendell question after question about what they could do to extricate themselves from the terrible problems that industrialized agribusiness had brought on them. Long after the debate was over, they talked to Wendell while Mr. Butz sat there like a little wart, looking on.

While that kind of disputation, or critical analysis, or formidable display of logic is an art, and I thrill to it as I would to anyone I think is speaking truth, it is not the kind of art that endeared me to him. Wendell Berry the essayist is a somewhat different kind of artist from Wendell Berry the poet or novelist. Poetry forces him, as it does all good poets, to be brief. Wendell can write a long and arduous book about what farming should be like if humankind would open its eyes to nature. That kind of argument needs to be argued, and in that form, but other writers can do that too. Wendell in addition can distill the truth of a whole book into one ingenious little poem like "A Standing Ground."

In his fiction, and sometimes in his poetry, Wendell becomes yet a third person, a man of gentle, subtle humor and sometimes hilarious, raucous humor. In novels, instead of trying to line up indisputable historical or logical evidence in favor of his arguments, he lets his voice speak through his fictional characters, who are mostly farmers. He has a genius for storytelling. He can infuse a droll anecdote with a knowing recognition and patient acceptance of the whole tragically pathetic human condition. He uses his unerring ear for dialect to portray that mixture of sanity and idiocy that gives humans both their saving grace and their hell-bent desire for destruction.

I was first attracted to Wendell's writing because farming was our mutual agrarian inheritance. For the first time I had found a living writer who wrote about farming not only knowing what farmers were all about but respecting them. Farmers worked hard and long to put out crops and raise animals, then waited for weather, plant and animal diseases, not to mention political diseases, to either support the work or ruin it enough to be unprofitable. That fatalism bred in them a patient, dry, droll, humble wit. Wendell has a near-perfect ear for it. He doesn't have to mimic it. It is part of him. Or, as he says it much better, "I have not lived here, or worked with my neighbors and my family or listened to the storytellers and the rememberers, in order to be a writer." He is one of his "fictional" characters. He has even put together a book, *Sayings and Doings,* honoring the language of his inheritance. For example:

> 'Pap, health officer said
> you got to get them damn
> hogs out of the house.
> It ain't healthy.'
> 'You tell that son of a bitch
> I've raised many
> a hog in this house,
> and ain't lost one yet.'

Or again:

> Had to give up grave diggin'
> Could still get them dug
> all right; but got so old
> could barely get out.

Or again, and my favorite because it cleverly reveals how timeliness is every-thing in farming:

> He lacks just two weeks
> Being a good farmer.

Another good one, which I had experienced too:

> Hey!
> You read
> that book
> You wrote?

On my first visit with Wendell, he already displayed the knack of using the droll anecdote to make a point. We were standing on the bank of the Kentucky River, which flows past his farm. I was skipping flat rocks on the surface of the water while we talked. We were discussing the "farm problem." One of the verities of American history is that in any year there is always a "farm problem" to discuss. He drawled: "The farmer today reminds me of the pioneer who was so agitated about getting across the Ohio River to claim more land for himself that he decided to swim over instead of waiting for a boat. He got maybe three-fourths of the way when he noticed the appearance of a band of hostile Indians on the other bank. He realized that his decision to cross the river had not been such a good one. But he was too tired to turn around and swim back. He had to go on."

In private life, and in his fiction, his humor comes bubbling up. He might outright cackle at something that strikes him as the inimitable wit of farmers and working-class people who know they are never going to get rich or famous and don't want to. In *Nathan Coulter,* he describes a scene in which a couple of his characters enter a poolroom:

> "Good afternoon, gentlemen," Uncle Burley said. He held his hands over the top of the stove and rubbed them together. "That wind's kind of brittle around the edges, ain't she?"
>
> "We haven't seen you for a while, Burley," Gander said. "Where you been keeping yourself?"
>
> Big Ellis giggled. "We heard you were dead, Burley."
>
> "So did I," Uncle Burley said. "But I knew it was a lie as soon as I heard it."

Or from "Pray Without Ceasing," a short story in *Fidelity:*

> "Tell you," he said, "there ain't a way in this world to know what a human creature is going to do next. I loaned a feller five hundred dollars once. He was a fine feller, too, wasn't a thing wrong with him far as I knew, I liked him. And dogged if he didn't kill himself fore it was a week."
>
> "Killed himself?" I said.
>
> "*Killed* himself," Braymer said. He meditated a moment, looking off at his memory of the fellow and wiggling two of the fingers that hung over the steering wheel. "Don't you know," he said, "not wishing him no bad luck, but I wished he'd a done it a week or two sooner."

Wendell is about as tall as a Kentucky beanpole and not much wider. Unless he is looking at his wife, Tanya, or a sprightly child, or a fine draft horse, or a farm well tended, or a great piece of writing, his face remains fixed in a mask of sad patience, giving no hint of this underlying reservoir of humor. Hard not to think of him as Abraham Lincoln reborn. When giving readings or speeches, he assumes a gravity that leads admirers to call him a prophet in the biblical sense. That makes him most uncomfortable, and he rejects the picture of himself as the Savanarola of the American farmlands. But he accepts, sometimes grudgingly, sometimes almost fearfully, the mantle of leadership that clings to him as a result of his birth. The Berrys were never a family to stand by silently in the face of injustice. Wendell's father, John, as lawyer and farmer, was a tireless defender of family farming and the tobacco program, which made family farming profitable enough to keep the rural economy alive in Kentucky. Wendell's brother, also John, and also a lawyer as well as a state senator at one time, was especially opposed to the environmental atrocities of the coal-mining industry in Kentucky, as all the Berrys were. As Wendell puts it in the introduction to one of my books, "coal mining is (so far) our most direct and deliberate act of Hell-making."

"My father was the hardest-working man I ever knew," said Wendell. "He would look over the farm early, go to the office to attend to pressing business, drive to Louisville, catch a plane to Washington, spend all day there arguing about the program, fly back to Louisville, get home after dark, and careen around the fields in his car, checking cattle and fences. He might get up and do the same thing the next day."

Wendell's father took me for a ride once to "view the land." He was driving a black Chevrolet, which he seemed to believe could go anywhere a tractor was made to go. He was doing about fifty on a dirt lane back through some of Wendell's land, intent on his conversation, not his driving. He was saying how, at first, he was a little disappointed that Wendell didn't become a lawyer, too, and carry on the battle that way, but that eventually he understood and respected Wendell's decision. "I've learned that there are things a poem can do that lawsuits can't." About that time, we hit a spot in the "road" where a gully was eating into the left tire track. The car listed into the washout, which drained off into a drop of about twenty feet down the embankment on the left side of the lane. I had my hand on the door latch on the other side, ready to dive out. But John had been over this terrain before and showed no fear. Muttering something about the possibility of getting "hung up," he floored the Chevy. Rocks and dirt flew in the general direction of the Kentucky River, and the car came careening up out of the depression. Full speed ahead. He hardly paused in his conversation. "But I don't think he did a smart thing buying that rundown old hillside farm. There was better farmland around. But he made it work. He's very independent and stubborn, and I'm glad of it." Those may not be his exact words. I was a mite bit distracted at the time.

Wendell threw himself into public service as energetically as his father had. (He also drove like his father, adding conviction to my fear that, at least when I was riding with him, the world could end at any moment.) He traveled incessantly, not only back and forth across the United States but to Europe and South America and I don't know where-all. He experienced disappointment as well as accomplishment. Once he drove a hundred miles into Canada in subzero weather to give a talk. Only four people showed up.

When tobacco smoking became a health issue, he found himself on the horns of a cruel dilemma. To support tobacco farming was looked upon as supporting cancer; but not to support tobacco farming made him look like a traitor to his own rural society, whose economy was based on tobacco. The problem was especially agonizing because not supporting tobacco farmers was not going to solve any cancer problem but simply hasten tobacco production out of the hands of small, dispersed family farmers and into the coffers of corporate, consolidated agribusiness. Nevertheless Wendell threw his energy into encouraging alternatives to tobacco that seemed to promise a similar high per-acre return.

In the process, something wonderful occurred. Both of his children, Den and Mary, and their spouses got into alternative farming ventures. "I think that's probably the best thing that could have happened to Tanya and me," Wendell said, "to see our children follow in our footsteps." Den raised squash for a seed company and potatoes and sweet potatoes for a local CSA (community-supported agriculture) market, assisted his father and uncle in their farming operations, and, on the side, did woodworking. Mary and her husband, Chuck Smith, started as dairy farmers, changed to beef cattle and vegetables for a local farmers' market, added chickens for retail marketing, and then turned the farm into a vineyard and winery. Along the way, they created a cultural center for the local arts on their farm. The former milking barn, the stanchions removed, is now an art gallery. There, in not-so-mute testimony, art and agriculture become one. Katie, one of Chuck and Mary's daughters, showing me around the gallery, seemed suddenly sad. "Yes, this is really nice," she said. "But you know, when I stand here, I think of Daddy and me milking the cows. That was nice too."

Wendell has managed to do something never before accomplished in the literary history I know. In addition to carrying on the family tradition of public service, he combines a devotion to the art of writing with a devotion to the art of farming and is a credit to himself and all of us both ways. Robert Frost might have been a greater poet, but he was a dismal farmer compared to Wendell. Wendell needs help from his whole family, especially his son, Den, to make it all work, but he can fill a book with literary gems and fill a barn with well-bred sheep both in the same year.

Wendell's farming accomplishment that I most admire is the reclamation of an eroded, "gone to bushes" hill behind his house.

His hill is a living monument to the kind of farming that could produce ample food for the world in a practical *permanent* system, even on the millions of acres of Appalachian hillside thought to be marginal or too erosive for profitable food production. It speaks of an ancient wisdom: by pastoral farming —that is, by *not* cultivating the face of the earth—humankind might get lucky and survive.

And by the mysterious way in which beauty begets more beauty, his hill sanctifies that wisdom. The Berry hill could not be cultivated without being destroyed. But allowing for a careful partnership of pastoral farming and nature, not only it could be saved, but, by extension, a continent, an earth could be saved. Wendell knows it.

"It occurs to me," he wrote in his "A Native Hill,"

> that it is no longer possible to imagine how this country looked in the beginning, before the white people drove their plows into it. It is not possible to know what was the shape of the land here in this hollow when it was first cleared. Too much of it is gone, loosened by the plows and washed away by the rain. [As I walk over my land] I am walking the route of the departure of the virgin soil of the hill. I am not looking at the same land the firstcomers saw. The original surface of the hill is as extinct as the passenger pigeon. The pristine America that the first white man saw is a lost continent, sunk like Atlantis into the seas. . . . It is as though I walk knee-deep in its absence.

Actually, the soil loss was more than knee-deep in many places. We once walked a field near his farm that was dominated by a little graveyard. *Dominated* is the right word because the cemetery plot stuck up a good four feet above the surface of the surrounding cultivated field. That was how much soil had washed away, and this field was not particularly hilly. Erosion on steeper hills could be so destructive that sometimes rocks "as big as pianos," as Wendell once described them to me, were laid bare. And where soil remained, and the field had been abandoned after years of cultivation, the land had gone to thorns, weeds, and brush on its relentless march back to pristine forest.

But where sunlight pierced the brush, Wendell noticed, bluegrass was growing. Cut the brush away to let in more sun, and more grass grew. Add a little lime if the soil needed it, and what I called the Salvation of Mankind occurred, as it could occur over much of America: white clover would begin to volunteer with the grass, or could be sown, to start again the everlasting pasture partnership of grass and legume that made sustainable permanent farming possible.

Wendell wrote in some detail in *The Unsettling of America* how he brought his hillside into productivity, and there are little glimpses of it here and there in his poetry. But it has been my privilege on occasion to watch him work or to witness the result of his work. Since cultivation was out of the question on the steep hill, and use of tractors dangerous, he would cut the brush with horses and horse-drawn mower or with scythe, and follow, as soon as it was feasible, with grazing animals. Continually each spring, he would broadcast several varieties of grass and clover seed where the sod needed strengthening.

In places being taken over by weed trees, he laboriously made clearings, saving a promising oak or walnut here and there. In some pastured areas, he planted good trees for fruits, nuts, or lumber, thinly placed so as not to shade the grass too much. I saw where he had carefully placed literally tons of rocks *by hand* into gullies in the lower reaches of the hill to stop erosion. Slowly, finally, the grass and clover took over and could be kept in dominance by careful grazing management and occasional mowings. Wendell says:

> The whole Kentucky bluegrass region can be farmed this way, taking advantage of our usually abundant rainfall, natural limestone soils, and the tendency of grasses and clovers to reseed and spread themselves. . . . Only in recent years has the corn and soybean craze gripped this land, and where it does, destructive erosion becomes the ever-present danger. The pity is that on these hills, even those not as steep as this one, grass and clover will make better growth and at less cost than corn and soybeans and therefore a better profit. For years Kentucky had a good market in Europe for our grass-fed beef and lamb. That market could be expanded if we would get over our suicidal adoration of corn.

As his hill blossomed into a pasture nearly as productive of meat, dairy products, tree fruit, and lumber as the best Illinois corn ground was capable of, it also blossomed with Wendell's written art until the two became inseparable. In 1982, in an essay titled "Poetry and Place" (in *Standing by Words*), he repeated a sentence he had written earlier in discussing the connection between his writing work and his little hill farm: "This place has become the form of my work, its discipline, in the same way the sonnet has been the form and discipline of the work of other poets: if it doesn't fit, it's not true."

But he was not satisfied with that statement. He worried it all the way through that essay and distilled it down in the final paragraphs to this:

> If we ask the forest how to farm—as Sir Albert Howard instructed, remembering, we may almost suppose, Shakepeare and Pope—it will tell us. And what it will tell us, as I think the great tradition represented by these poets also tells us, is that one's farm—like any other place on earth, like one's place in the order of Creation—is indeed a form. It's not a literary form, but *like* a literary form, and it cannot properly be ignored or its influence safely excluded by any literary form that is made within it.

Still not satisfied, in a more recent essay, "Imagination in Place," he has returned to the way farming can influence art. After discussing all the other and very complicated influences that a writer-farmer received from education, from reading, from living in other places, and so forth, he gets down to the crux of it:

> What I have learned as a farmer, I have learned also as a writer, and vice versa. I have farmed as a writer and written as a farmer . . . I am talking

about an experience that is resistant to any kind of simplification. . . . [W]hen one passes from any abstract order, whether that of the consumer economy . . . or a brochure from the Extension Service, to the daily life and work of one's own farm, one passes from a relative simplicity into a complexity that is irreducible except by disaster, and ultimately incomprehensible. . . . One meets not only the weather and the wildness of the world, but also the limitations of one's knowledge, intelligence, character and bodily strength. To do this of course is to accept the place as an influence.

My further point is that to do this, if one is a writer, is to accept the place and the farming of it as a literary influence [too]. One accepts the place . . . not just as a circumstance, but as a part of the informing ambiance of one's mind and imagination.

These observations about remaining faithful to the *truth* of a place bear squarely on the characteristic quality of Wendell's novels and on my belief that farming influences art because farming *is* an art. Reading *Hannah Coulter* opened my eyes. In this novel, Hannah Coulter narrates the story of her life, and does so at a slow pace, full of introspection, and rich in description. Normally, I prefer novels of action, not introspection. But *Hannah Coulter* captivated me. No. Better, it *soothed* me.

How? Most fiction seems obsessed with convincing the reader that sex is, or should be, just a casual affair demanding no commitment. I call it "coffee break" sex. All really cool people view sex this way, we are told. Really cool people expect characters in novels to copulate every twenty pages or so with just about anyone who strikes their fancy or just to relieve themselves of sexual tension. Otherwise, say the cool generations, who will read the book?

As cynical as I have become, I don't think that most people act that way. Sex is not a casual affair, and pretending otherwise becomes self-fulfilling prophecy for people looking for any excuse at all to justify copulation. That kind of writing is certainly the antithesis of Tolstoy's definition of art as "the transmission to others of the highest and best feelings to which men have risen."

In contrast, *Hannah Coulter* represents another kind of novel. The story begins with the courtship of Hannah and her first husband, Virgil, who is subsequently killed in World War II. For thirty-seven pages, the young farmer courts his beloved Hannah in a gentlemanly way. In a year of keeping company leading up to marriage, there is no hint that they ever "had" sex. The courting goes on in great restraint, ruled by what intelligent people really care about: a concern over whether either of them is worthy of the other, over whether, as a married couple, they will be capable of really supporting each other. At one point Virgil puts his hand on Hannah's thigh but quickly withdraws it when she seems uncomfortable. She actually is not uncomfortable, she informs the reader, just surprised. But she decides that for now she will not encourage further foreplay. He, in concerned *human* regard for her feelings, does not press the issue. As far as the reader is allowed to know, they marry before their marriage is consummated.

The result of Wendell's restraint in writing is quite the opposite of what today's "realists" might predict, at least for me. Over the years, I have read about every kind of sexual adventurism known to mankind (I think), and I can't recall any story about two people in love that is as sexy to me as Virgil's and Hannah's chastity. They are truly sexy because they act in a truly human manner, not like two animals. As a farmer, I know that two animals copulating is not sexy.

I understand then why this novel is so comforting to me. Virgil's and Hannah's way of courtship is the way I had tried to court too. That standard of conduct was held up to me in an agrarian culture as the proper code of ethics. I was expected to follow it, and, damn it anyway, I did. And so did most of the people around me. I acted like a human being because I was expected to act like one, not like a boar hog. Having been taught that way, I was drawn to girls who had been similarly taught. And those girls were drawn to me for the same reason. We were the real people. We kept the less disciplined from destroying society.

I asked Wendell what he thought. He wrote to me: "I think that Virgil's behavior is credible, but I doubt it is representative. Beyond that, my own view of *Hannah Coulter* is that it is a strongly sexual novel. She understands herself as a woman sexually powerful, but she also understands sexuality as a power that is life-making, family-making, farm-making. It is a part of a pattern, involved in everything she values. Therefore: no 'sex scenes.' They would not only violate her sense of her own dignity and modesty (which are *not* inconsistent with sexual power) but would also (from my point of view as the author) isolate sex from everything else and make a specialty of it, even an irrelevancy."

Not that Wendell soft-soaps the world he writes about. Unsavory or weak-willed characters wander in and out of his novels as regularly as they do in real life. There are brothels in his novels, and drunkards and thieves and murderers. But the honorable people are in control most of the time. Evil is punished most of the time, just as it is in real life. Inevitably, virtue reaches out and neutralizes vice. Or good simply overwhelms evil with love, as in *Jayber Crow*. If moral order does not rule in the end, society will fly apart in unhappiness and chaos.

It seems to me that Wendell is saying: art should sanctify that truth *first* and show that virtue really does pay. If art insists only on glorifying the kingdom of boar hogs, the only peace to look forward to is the peace after the Bomb.

Hannah Coulter's world is a more or less stable community where families lived generation after generation with mutual common interests. Being agrarian, these local complexes of villages and farms have to depend on one another economically and socially, and so they have to *take care of* one another whether they want to or not. I think of what a car salesman in my hometown said to me once: "I drive around the countryside watching the crops grow with as much worry as the farmers do because if the corn and beans are good, I'll sell cars, and if they aren't, I won't."

In the agrarian community that Wendell describes, when a farmer gets down on his luck and needs help, the neighbors come in and give it, even though they are all competitors in business. That is the code, and you live up to it. When farmers "industrialized," they learned from the business world that when a competitor falters, you try to buy him out. That is the root worm of the instability of the modern noncommunity, and why the world moves steadily toward chaos. Humans are abandoning real community, are abandoning the world of Hannah Coulter and Jayber Crow, not realizing that the security of a local, interdependent community is better than the security of the stock market, or Social Security, or so-called homeland security.

I pulled a copy of Wendell's *Sex, Economy, Freedom and Community* off my bookshelf, remembering something that I had read there. I turned to the essay of that title. Now, with new insight, I see that the blueprint, so to speak, of his novels is written there. The philosophy that guides his art comes down to the importance of caring communities. In discussing the issue of sex and how to handle it in art, he argues that sex can't be dealt with as a public issue because it is too secretive most of the time. Nor can it be dealt with only privately. Sex "is not and cannot be any individual's 'own business' nor is it merely the private concern of any couple. Sex, like any other necessary, precious and volatile power that is commonly held, is everybody's business."

So, how is this or any other issue to be handled?

> The indispensable form that can intervene between public and private interests is that of community. The concerns of public and private, republic and citizen, necessary as they are, are not adequate for the shaping of human life. Community alone, as principle and as fact, can raise the standards of local health (ecological, economic, social, and spiritual) without which the other two interests will destroy each other.

And what is community?

Community is a locally understood interdependence of local people, local culture, local economy and local nature. . . . A community identifies itself by an understood mutuality of interest. But it lives and acts by the common virtues of trust, good will, forbearance, self-restraint, compassion, and forgiveness. . . . [S]uch a community has the power . . . to enforce decency without litigation. It has the power, that is, to influence behavior.

Although such a community could exist anywhere, Wendell in his novels is describing it as it existed until the final stages of the Industrial Revolution and as it still exists in some places. His novels are an example of the agrarian culture that nurtured him, that influenced his art. And now his art is in turn influencing a new agrarian culture.

Of all the visits I enjoyed with Wendell, walking over his fields and woods, one day stands out. After a long walk with him and Tanya, Carol and I were sitting in their house, the four of us talking. We had just finished one of Tanya's scrumptious meals. I was looking out the back window at the hill pasture that so affected me. With that steep hill seemingly tilted up on edge, I could see the sheep grazing almost as if in a painting hanging on the wall, an advantage we flatlanders in northern Ohio don't appreciate. There was a summer tanager flitting in the grapevines right outside the window. I don't remember anymore what we were talking about, but the tanager reminded Wendell of something in somebody's book that he liked. He reached up on the bookshelf, retrieved the book, thumbed through it while the tanager serenaded us. Then he read, the pleasure of enjoying good literature on his face.

If I wrote that into a modern novel, most modern critics would say I was describing an unreal, make-believe world. Who now would take the time to relax and talk about some arcane subject from literature? But we were doing just that, and it was real time, *today,* not as if we were sitting in an English country house in Victorian times, overlooking pleasant farmland, listening to, let's say, John Ruskin. How could I make anyone on this side of television-bound and computer-tied America believe it? A lazy summer afternoon, a little sun-dappled world snuggled down on a Kentucky hillside, not even the sound of an automobile to disturb the magic, a poet reading, a tanager warbling, sheep bleating on a hillside. We were caught in a calm and quiet interlude, but nonetheless a *real* interlude, of art and agriculture holding hands.

"Along with Stegner, Wendell taught me to behave as a writer."—Barry Lopez, in a conversation with Jason Peters
Photograph by Guy Mendes, courtesy of Ann Tower Gallery

Jason Peters

Education, Heresy, and the "Deadly Disease of the World"

> Education insisted on finding a moral foundation for robbery.
> —Henry Adams

I AM GIVING the commencement address at a highly selective, which is to say highly expensive, liberal-arts college. In a surprising departure from custom, the students pay attention to the person standing in front of them, for despite all convention, and against my one good instinct, I have just said, "Congratulations on your new purchase."

In this annual little fantasy of mine the parents snicker, a few colleagues (the ones listening) smirk, and the administrators mark me for the RightThink Reeducation Seminars.

"Pending remittance of all dormitory and parking fines, the college, upon recommendation of the faculty, will confer upon you the degree BS." That's bachelor of spending. "You will be full-fledged, card-carrying members of the consumer culture, with all the rights and privileges thereunto appertaining."

Of course that's unfair. It's insufficiently cynical and also inaccurate: most undergraduates have been fully vested members of this elite club for a long time. Already accomplished bargain hunters in high school, many of them go into the educational marketplace savvy hagglers, using one financial-aid package to leverage another and turning colleges into desperate contractors bidding for jobs. Whatever money students borrow thereafter in their four-year effort to convince themselves that reading does not make a full, nor conference a ready, nor writing an exact, man adds up to a kind of debt different from the one Bertrand de Jouvenel had in mind when he said that "every self-aware person sees himself as a debtor."[1] Self-awareness, the pleasures we take in what Wendell Berry calls our "wakefulness in this world," our pilgrimage toward becoming what he calls "responsible heirs and members of human culture"[2]—little of this registers in the education mall, where the diploma retailers promise a campus so luxurious that there are e-mail kiosks between urinals, Mongolian barbecue in the cafeteria, and a sports complex with—*O altitudo!*—an elevator that lifts the fitness-minded students up to the third-floor exercise room, where stands the stair-climber, that curious invention on which one climbs and climbs but ascends to no heights. (Is it any wonder that *actual* college graduates have TVs in their cars and exercise machines in front of their TVs?) Year after year, from small colleges and large multiversities alike, graduators formerly known as educators send chomping out into the putative real world giant mouths—mutations of Emerson's giant eyeball. In accordance with institutional and governmental expectations, these mouths dutifully consume at the rate prescribed by the most rapacious economy that history has ever known.

I do not hereby join the puling malcontents who go on about how the American Mind, whatever that is, has closed; nor do I mean wholly to disparage one of the things I've devoted my life to and partly believe in, which is undergraduate education, although I often have the uncomfortable feeling that I and many others must choose either to pimp for or whore with a system neither likable nor admirable. Everywhere confronted with what Berry long ago pegged as "intellectual fashionableness pinned up on such shibboleths as . . . 'relevance' (the most reactionary and totalitarian of educational doctrines),"[3] we perambulators in the graves of academe tell ourselves that we are not managing a minor league for the job market, all the while assuring our aspirants that *of course* we can get them to the big leagues if only they'll float all that nice borrowed money our way. Self-respect can go pretty quickly when disingenuousness—I had almost said lying—is the default mode. For whatever good comes of liberal education—and I do believe much good *can* come of it—much done in its name is indefensible, is indeed destructive.

On that point Berry has been unambiguous. In contrast to the judgment of one certified expert who asserts that "everybody now agrees that college is a virtual prerequisite for success and a decent life,"[4] Berry admitted forty years ago to being "skeptical of education. It seems to me a most doubtful process," he said, "and I think the good of it is taken too much for granted. It is a matter that is overtheorized and overvalued and always approached with too much confidence."[5]

Since then his skepticism has turned into acerb criticism: what we call education is actually "career preparation" and therefore "a commodity—something *bought* in order to make money."[6] This education, this commodity, is purchased by careerists, educated at public expense, pursuing their own private ends.[7] The prevarications we use to sustain "commercial education," and so to produce these careerists, are borne by a "cultish faith in the future" and by a "hysterical rhetoric of 'change,' 'the future,' 'the frontiers of modern science' . . . and the like, as if there is nothing worth learning from the past and nothing worth preserving in the present."[8] Students on whom these sorts of lies work—and that amounts to pretty much all of them—major in "upward mobility," which major allows them to "outmode" their parents and serve, in accordance with the official script, "the government's economy and the economy's government."[9] Why should students do otherwise? Education itself does not serve communities, nor incline itself toward them, nor "consult the genius of the place" to determine what should be done locally.[10] Beholden to outside interests, education avers that children should leave home "and earn money in a provisional future that has nothing to do with place or community" and so proves itself inimical to community.[11] Worse: it is the industrial economy writ small, mining where it does not live. Of his own community, Berry said (in 1989), "We have had no schools of our own for nearly thirty years. The school system takes our young people, prepares them for 'the world of tomorrow'—which it does not expect to take place in any rural area—and gives back 'expert' (that is, extremely generalized) ideas."[12] Education, in other words, intends to exhaust the quarries that support it, writes checks against human and natural capital to which it contributes very little. Anyone with a bank account should be able to see that this is disastrous.

The good news is that education, though not cheap, is also not very difficult.[13] In fact it's a kind of movie—call it *Deracinator*—that lasts a minimum of thirteen years, seventeen for those who agree with the experts that indeed "college is a virtual prerequisite for success and a decent life."

The better news is that this deracinating education does, however, prepare students for "productive," which is to say consumptive, lives in the economy: "The corporate producers and their sycophants in the universities and the government," Berry says, "will do virtually anything (or so they have obliged us to assume) to keep people from acquiring necessities in any way except by *buying* them," which means that the one skill education must teach is check-writing. So long as a man can write a check, he need not know how to do anything. True enough, he is the "model citizen" and "sophisticate"—someone who can do nothing without money and so will do anything to get it[14]—but this sophisticate still has only one skill: check-writing.

An education reputed to be "liberal" (from the Latin *liber,* "free") liberates no one by this kind of narrowing. It creates what Berry in another context calls that variety of specialist known as a consumer, which means he is the abject dependent of producers. How can he be free if he can do nothing for himself? What is the First Amendment to him whose mouth is stuck to the tit of the "affluent society"? Men are free precisely to the extent that they are equal to their own needs. The most able are the most free.[15]

Or, as we now say, the most able *to pay* are the most free.

This is crucial to Berry's critique. He directs his criticism at the assumption, everywhere implicit, that buying is better than doing. Why? It is in indiscriminate buying, in doing less and less for ourselves, that we have brought on the ecological degradation and moral torpor that is now our common condition. We have assumed that our balm in this toxic Gilead is science—even though "science does not seem to be lighting the way; we seem rather to be leapfrogging into the dark along [a] series of scientific solutions, which become problems, which call for further solutions, which science is always eager to supply, and which it sometimes cannot supply."[16] Add to all this "that the most characteristic product of our age of scientific miracles is junk"[17] and you have some idea of Berry's sanguinity toward the denizens of the nice new gee-whiz buildings on campus.

Which is not to say that he therefore trusts the humanities, for if the sciences "mindlessly serve economics . . . the humanities defer abjectly to the sciences."[18] In an essay appropriately titled "A Conversation Out of School" Berry says that the

> sciences are sectioned like a stockyard the better to serve the corporations. The so-called humanities, which might have supplied at least a corrective or chastening remembrance of the good that humans have sometimes accomplished, have been dismembered into utter fecklessness, turning out "communicators" who have nothing to say and "educators" who have nothing to teach.[19]

These same humanists behave like "ethologists, students of the behavior of a species to which they do not belong, in whose history and fate they have no part, their aim being, not to know anything for themselves, but to 'advance knowledge.'"[20] The humanists say, "we will study, record, analyze, criticize, and appreciate. But we will not believe; we will not, in the full sense, know."[21] Fully to know—and this is also crucial—we must be willing and able to learn not only *about* but also *from* the things we study, able to understand that a poem can be taught but that it can also teach.[22] If we fail in this, we ignore and default on our cultural heritage.[23]

Among the many examples of learning *from* that appear and reappear in

Berry's essays—I think of Wordsworth's "Michael," which Berry calls "a sort of cultural watershed" for its depiction of the destruction of rural life by a centralized economy, or of *The Odyssey,* wherein we read of "the death Tiresias foresaw for Odysseus and the one Homer seems to recommend"[24]—among these examples, Spenser's depiction of nature in *The Faerie Queene* is especially relevant here. In his own attempt to define "nature," Berry has always had in the back of his mind Spenser's rendering nature as both Mother and Judge:

> she deals "Right to all . . . indifferently," for she is "the equal mother" of all "And knittest each to each, as brother unto brother." Thus, in Spenser, the natural principles of fecundity and order are pointedly linked with the principle of justice, which we may be a little surprised to see that he attributes also to nature. And yet in his insistence on an "indifferent" natural justice, resting on the "brotherhood" of *all* creatures, not just of humans, Spenser would now be said to be on sound ecological footing.[25]

He is on sound ecological footing because he recognizes that although in the next life "the Lord may forgive our wrongs against nature," in this one, "so far as we know, He does not overturn her decisions," nor does she herself "tolerate or excuse our abuses."[26] Perhaps a few generous souls grudgingly allow that knowing *about* Spenser is valuable; Berry implies that there might be less topsoil rolling down the Mississippi were we willing to learn *from* him, able to be tutored by him, attentive to "culture-borne instructions about who or what humans are and how and on what assumptions they should act."[27] We might even see that profligate purchasing, which has replaced thrift and competence, leads to abuses that Nature neither tolerates nor excuses, resilient though she has sometimes proven herself to be.

All of this is a way of saying that education, which ought to lead to health, often leads instead to disease. It encourages ecological degradation insofar as it serves the interests of, and fails to arrest, the "legalized vandalism known as 'the economy' ";[28] it fails to stop or correct the degradation because it is inattentive to the culture-borne instructions that can make us wise enough to live. For we do live—too comfortably, it would seem—with an abiding contradiction: "The air is unfit to breathe, the water is unfit to drink, the soil is washing away, the cities are violent and the countryside neglected, all because we are intelligent, enterprising, industrious, and generous."[29]

Those who would accuse Berry of hyperbole might explain how an educational system that teaches us to destroy the source we live from makes any sense at all. To those who think we live in a postagrarian world of abundance—to those from whose minivans the amber waves of grain look plentiful—he has said, "Get out of your spaceship, out of your car, off your horse, and walk over the ground" to get the necessary closer look.[30] Anticipating the objection that because of our dependencies we can't change, he has said that this is the addict's excuse and simply won't do.[31]

For all his distrust of science—it has unjustifiably "crowned and mitered itself"—Berry has never suggested it has no place in the university; for all his distaste for specialization—it shrinks rather than enlarges the mind—he acknowledges that some specialization is obviously necessary; for all his repulsion to technology—we must be willing in the allure of its field to "limit our desires"—he has never said there should be none.[32] He has argued, however, that we must always have an artist's and craftsman's "concern for the thing made," and he has insisted that the thing made in the university is a human being, that, indeed, what public universities "are *mandated* to make or to help to make is human beings in the fullest sense of those words—not just trained workers or knowledgeable citizens but responsible heirs and members of human culture."[33] This is what Berry puts in the place of the thing now made, which is the "careerist," the economy's robotic hireling, the sophisticated, check-writing Half-Man.

But "human culture" is what it is, not what we think it is or reduce it to by storing it in various academic departments. If a certain aspect of it flourishes at the expense of another, the whole ceases in some manner to flourish.

Berry had this very much on his mind when he went to work in "Poetry and Place" on the insidious lines Milton gave to Satan:

> The mind is its own place, and of itself
> Can make a Heaven of Hell, a Hell of Heaven.[34]

In fact, much of *Standing by Words* is a meditation on this essentially industrial dream of disembodied existence, and Berry's criticism of it bears directly upon what he means by "human culture." In fine, the idea of culture as a concern of mind but not also of body, of consciousness but not also of place, conduces to abuse. The "mind that elects itself a place maintains itself as such by the ruin of earthly places. One cannot divide one's mind from its earthly place, preferring the inner place to the outer, without denying the mind's care to the earthly place."[35] Berry's interest here is poetry, but his pronouncements, as he himself acknowledges, clearly apply elsewhere: "If a *culture* goes for too long without producing poets and others who concern themselves with the problems and proprieties of humanity's practical connection to nature, then the work of all poets may suffer, and so may nature, "[36] for "it is the mind, not the body, whose appetite for material things is insatiable."[37]

That all of this bears on education may be understood, if it is not already self-evident, by the obvious fact that for Berry "human culture" is not the property of schools and opera houses and the Arts and Leisure pages of the *New York Times*. It is not limited to the work of the mind but includes also the work of the body; otherwise it is "reduced" and so "divorced from work . . . and from action."[38] Culture properly understood includes agriculture; the two exist by a mutual grace. "How much excellence in 'the arts,'" Berry asks, "is to be expected from a people who are poor at carpentry, sewing, farming, gardening, and cooking? To believe that you can have a culture distinct from, or as a whole greatly better than, such work is not just illogical or wrong—it is to make peace with the shoddy, the meretricious, and the false."[39] So for Berry an old galvanized bucket collecting leaves and moisture and turning them through time to humus resembles a community that collects stories about itself and its members and turns them through time to good account, the one slowly building the basis of life—a trust of fertile soil—and the other the basis of living—the soils of fecund trust.[40] We have no chance of understanding Berry if we cannot see that "human culture," far from being the small thing that art critics think it is, includes, is founded on, the human disciplines of making and doing, of what Berry more recently has called the domestic arts of husbandry and wifery.[41] And it is certainly with something like both the liberal and domestic arts in mind, together, that Berry has weighed education in the balance and found it wanting. We commit no treachery in slightly recasting his words to clarify this: if *education* goes for too long without producing graduates who concern themselves with the problems and proprieties of humanity's practical connection to nature, then the work of all graduates may suffer, and so may nature.

Aldo Leopold, who feared that education had become an exercise in "learning to see one thing by going blind to another," noted that education also "makes no mention of obligations to land over and above those dictated by self-interest." "Time was," he said, "when education moved toward soil, not away from it." Then (in the 1940s), as now,

> the ecological fundamentals of agriculture are just as poorly known to the public as in other fields of land-use. For example, few educated people realize that the marvelous advances in technique made during recent decades are improvements in the pump, rather than the well. Acre for acre, they have barely sufficed to offset the sinking level of fertility.[42]

Berry, for his part, has sounded these same observations from the very beginning of his writing life. As early as *The Long-Legged House* (1969) he said, "No matter how sophisticated and complex and powerful our institutions, we are still exactly as dependent on the earth as the earthworms. To cease to know this, and to fail to act upon the knowledge, is to begin to die the death of a broken machine."[43] Nearly fifteen years later he said, "Our life and livelihood are the gift of the topsoil and of our willingness and ability to care for it, to grow good wheat, to make good bread; they do not derive from stockpiles of raw materials or accumulations of purchasing power."[44] His agrarian essays have consistently emphasized the importance of our being tutored by the soil,[45] and his dissent from education currently conceived takes its impetus from that very neglect of which Leopold so eloquently wrote.

What I have been saying thus far is that when Berry declared himself skeptical of education, he did so against the backdrop of farming, of bodily life and physical dependencies, of doing rather than buying. Ever alert to the dangers of "selective bookkeeping," Berry has thought about education in terms of *net gains*—by remembering that after you add up your improved pumps, you must subtract for your depleted wells.[46] It is with this sort of calculus in mind that he has criticized education and offered his alternative vision, and we will neither see the genius nor understand the urgency of that alternative vision if we refuse to acknowledge that we are as dependent on the soil as the earthworms.

The question, then, is how do we make an alternative to the careerist Half-Man? How do we craft that full human being, that "responsible heir and member of human culture"?

It would be nice if we could just send him to college—to someplace with a crest that shows a poet at his craft on the one side, and on the other side a tiller of the ground at his, and beneath them both the motto *vivere pauperius, exiguius habere* after Berry at his best: "We must achieve the character and acquire the skills to live much poorer than we do."[47] It would be a bonus if the crest and motto were featured prominently on the admissions material the recruitment office sends out, and better still if a college representative—the amply compensated president, for example—would make a habit of saying to the parents of high-school seniors, "We pledge to teach your sons and daughters to achieve the character and acquire the skills to live much poorer than they do." Perhaps the dean, that exemplar of downward mobility, could implement a curriculum founded on the Franciscan trivium of poverty, chastity, and obedience.

Save that such a college is unthinkable—every bit of it. Imagine the endowment of the institution committed to such an ideal. Imagine its donor base. Imagine the enrollments in its business and accounting classes. Imagine which academic majors could actually be offered. Behold another chapter 11.

That is to say, we cannot merely send the careerist to school. Yet the recovery of character and skill—the character to choose less and the skill to do more for oneself—is what is missing everywhere, especially in the current making of human beings. Education, ubiquitously instinct with the "values" of an extravagant economy—that is, confused by a "murderous paradox"— and at the same time idiotically committed to value-free objectivity, has nothing meaningful or useful to say about character and skill—has, indeed, no interest in real correctives to the deficits in character and skill under which its charges currently languish.[48] And yet if it is going to say anything meaningful to them, it must achieve the good sense and acquire the courage to correct those deficits.

Concerning the first of these—character—Berry's keyword has been "restraint." Having imagined education as a means to freedom from constraints of time, place, and condition, we have made a virtue of accumulating things that have nothing to recommend them except that they are purchasable. Against this frivolity Berry has consistently spoken of the restraints without which we "are not 'natural,' not 'thinking animals' or 'naked apes,' but monsters, indiscriminate and insatiable killers and destroyers."[49] These necessary restraints come not from the Future, which doesn't exist, but from our past, which does.[50] That is, they comprise a kind of knowledge that comes from our cultural heritage.

Some of that knowledge—for example, our place on the Chain of Being, our charge to live not by competition but by justice and mercy—comes from books, and we should know such books.[51] But some of that knowledge does not come from books. Our literary inheritance may teach us not to rob the land. That is a "principle that can be learned from books. But the ways of living on the land so as not to rob it," Berry says, "probably cannot be learned from books."[52] They are disciplines, at once physical and spiritual, that the young learn and assent to by instruction and witness. They are the necessary restraints available to us only from culture in its broadest sense. Or again, the *principles* of, say, trust, trustworthiness, and neighborliness that are necessary to the survival of community may be recommended in books, but the *ways* constitute "a kind of knowledge," Berry says, "inestimably valuable and probably indispensable, that comes out of common culture and that cannot be taught as part of the formal curriculum of a school." This is not to say that curricula should not respect such knowledge. "Though I don't believe that it can be taught and learned in a university, I think it should be known about and respected in a university." Where in the sciences and humanities that might happen Berry says he does not know. "It is certainly no part of banking or of economics as now taught and practiced."[53]

We have, rather, the Ben Franklin approach—"In the affairs of this world, men are saved, not by faith, but by the want of it"—which may explain why so many people communicate only through lawyers. Where restraint, trust, and neighborliness are concerned, education has proven itself not only indifferent to the knowledge, because it abhors what is value-laden, but also spiteful of the ways, because it neither knows nor practices them. We are realists; we will treat you with suspicion.

If achieving the *character* to live poorer requires restraints available to us only from that which we have learned to despise, namely, the past, which we despise because it isn't the Future, then acquiring the *skills* to live poorer likewise requires a willingness to *do* the work we've also learned to despise, having discounted it by handing it over to machines or to people who haven't purchased a bachelor's degree in spending. Such is the behavior of the Sophisticate and Model Citizen, graduated if not educated, whose one skill is check-writing and who knows that "our major economic practice is to delegate the practice to others."[54]

But he can't live poorer if, in addition to being unwilling to live poorer, he has no other skills to enable him to do so. He needs cash to make up for his incompetence as a man. So he delegates once again, if not to cash then to "credit," which comes with the added benefit of debt, which sustains better than anything the illusion of wealth. It covers a multitude of sins.

I have noted that Berry does not consider such a man free. What little freedom he has is compromised by his fragility. Just as a food economy is fragile insofar as it depends on the availability of "cheap" oil, or just as a mega-farm is fragile insofar as it depends on an annual monoculture, so a college graduate is vulnerable insofar as he depends on a single so-called skill and a checking account. Check-writing is the basket all his store-bought eggs are in, and school, everywhere trumpeting the unassailable virtues of Diversity, is to blame for this dangerous want of diversification. But the check-writer doesn't understand his vulnerability, because school, unwilling to do the honest thing and saw off the grafted limb it sits on, never told him about the vulnerability. It merely pointed to the fellow roofing a house on a hot day and, misconstruing the word *argument*, said, "now *there's* an argument for education." Check-writer has only to wait for bouncing checks and a leaking roof for his education to be complete. His life is an exercise in "risk[ing] correction by disaster."[55] We all necessarily do this, of course, but we do it less to the extent that we are able and willing to live poorer than what the official script calls for.

For as Berry notes, although "people have not progressed beyond the need to eat food and drink water and wear clothes and live in houses, most people have progressed beyond the domestic arts—the husbandry and wifery of the world—by which those needful things are produced and conserved." They have "progressed" thus because they have "been carefully taught in our education system"—and by the professional prevaricators in advertising— "that those arts are degrading and unworthy of people's talents."[56] The snobbery of those who by virtue of their purchasing power have progressed beyond the domestic arts—I have in mind, for example, those countless icons of success whose work is joyless, whose leisure is desperate, and whose yards are maintained by ChemLawn—is one thing. But Berry criticizes them for something far more damning: they do not merely pursue a "degrading affluence" and an "undisciplined abundance";[57] in taking food, water, clothing, and shelter for granted, "the modern educated mind reveals itself also to be as superstitious a mind as ever has existed in the world. What could be more superstitious than the idea that money brings forth food?"[58]

One obvious corrective to the sophisticate's primitivism is gardening. ("The high must descend to learn, not what it would choose to learn, but what is indispensable to high and low alike.")[59] A basic acquaintance with this or any domestic art can teach even a college graduate that money is not more fertile than topsoil,[60] nor warmer than a sock, nor cooler than spring water. Such arts, says Berry—such "callings and disciplines"—

> are stationed all along the way from the farm to the prepared dinner, from the forest to the dinner table, from stewardship of the land to hospitality to friends and strangers. These arts are as demanding and gratifying, as instructive and as pleasing as the so-called fine arts. To learn them, to practice them, to honor and reward them is, I believe, our profoundest calling. Our reward is that they will enrich our lives and make us glad.[61]

Berry's admiration for capable, resourceful, and self-reliant people is everywhere evident in both his work and his life. To those who do not farm— and he acknowledges that not everyone can or should be a farmer[62]—he has consistently recommended voluntary, piecemeal involvement in the processes that sustain life; he has recommended the accumulation, steady if slow, of skills: growing something somewhere, preparing meals, learning something about the food on the table, supporting local suppliers, figuring out which end of a hammer to grab—cultivating, that is to say, the domestic arts.[63] To those strange half-humans who reply that they simply don't enjoy yard work or gardening or cooking, that they don't have time in their busy movie-going, health-clubbing schedules to do any of this, Berry's answer is: reconcile yourself to your condition, which is to work.[64] Reconcile rather than put asunder work and exercise; allow for the possibility that there is joy in doing for your-self what you have hitherto given your proxies to others to do, that there is fulfillment and peace and gladness in such doing. Do *that,* or continue to la-ment ecological degradation and the price of "health" care, to point fingers at politicians and corporations, and to complain—in the muted babbling of one whose infant mouth is stuck to the plump tit of the affluent society—about how hard it is to keep the weight off.

Back of all that Berry says about education stands an ideal: truly large-minded, truly well-educated people. Such men and women have achieved a synthesis of the liberal and domestic arts; they have learned from, not merely about, Spenser; they can also (and also will) grow a potato. They understand that the less they do for themselves—the less walking and more driving, for example—the more they will be implicated in degradation of many kinds.[65]

And since driving is the most obvious example of our major economic practice, which is to delegate the work to something else, consider briefly the example of locomotion. Emerson said that civilized man has built the coach but lost the use of his feet. Uncivilized Half-Man, Emerson's lazy, overweight heir, has built the car—Berry includes it among the "unprecedented monu-ments of destructiveness and waste"[66]—and surrendered at once his own health and his neighbor's clean air. It takes a college graduate not to see this.

And there are other losses; much else has been surrendered.

Time was when work—which now is what other people or waterways or landfills do—could be understood as "vocation." But mind-centeredness,[67] the desuetude into which the domestic arts have fallen, has diminished, if not wholly obliterated, any sense of vocation.

To have a "vocation" once meant to have a "calling" to an ecclesiastical or monastic order. The Reformers enlarged this to mean the work one does in this world—not necessarily in the cloister or before the altar—to honor God, serve others, and restore the lapsed order to its essential goodness: an impor-tant contribution, I think, of the Reformation. Of course vocation has been conceptually corrupted—as when the Puritans began to see the wealth that follows from diligence in one's vocation as a sign of God's favor, or when God "calls" a man to work for Monsanto and conveniently provides hearing loss to all those nearby who might serve as independent witnesses to this call. But in the main vocation has been a serviceable category for the worthiest heirs of Luther and Calvin especially. And it is certainly a serviceable category for anyone who wishes to do and work well.

I know of no book in which Berry actually claims that the loss of the do-mestic arts is implicated in a diminished sense of vocation, but I think he would agree that the loss of well-made objects in domestic as in academic life corresponds to, and is coeval with, a diminished sense of vocation. He considers shoddy workmanship a kind of blasphemy, [68] for example, and it is clear that he sees vocation historically understood as incompatible with work as currently conceived, which on his account amounts to little more than a floating professionalism: "I feel no hesitation in saying that the standards and goals of the [academic] disciplines need to be changed," he says.

> It used to be that we thought of the disciplines as ways of being useful to ourselves, for we needed to earn a living, but also and more importantly we thought of them as ways of being useful to one another. As long as the idea of vocation was still viable among us, I don't believe it was ever understood that a person was "called" to be rich or powerful or even successful. People were taught the disciplines at home or in school for two reasons: to enable them to live and work both as self-sustaining individuals and as useful members of their communities, and to see that the disciplines themselves survived the passing of the generations. [69]

The professionalism with which we have replaced vocation cares nothing for "good work, citizenship and membership," only for "social mobility." [70] Where shoddy workmanship is de rigueur, membership shunned, mobility admired, and money and power made objects par excellence, vocation has no chance. Self-interest by definition excludes it.

But justice does not. Berry cites Ananda K. Coomaraswamy, who in an essay on

> the origin of civilization in traditional cultures . . . wrote that "the principal of justice is the same throughout . . . [it is] that each member should perform the task for which he is fitted by nature. . . ." The two ideas, justice and vocation, are inseparable. That is why Coomaraswamy spoke of industrialism as "the mammon of injustice," incompatible with civilization. It is by way of the principle and practice of vocation that sanctity and reverence enter into the human economy. It was thus possible for traditional cultures to conceive that "to work is to pray." [71]

Of course this has long been a part of the religious tradition into which Berry was born. [72] I should think that those disinclined to attend to traditional cultures or to religious traditions can at least imagine that scrubbing a floor suggests a posture more conducive to humility and peace than to arrogance and warfare. Vocation, properly understood, involves work that serves the welfare of others. It involves work that harmonizes with the other sounds around it; its scale and reach are proper, its effects redemptive rather than destructive; it says, as Jayber Crow learns to say, "Not my will, but thine, be done." [73] Those who have jobs quickly learn that a job is something from which one often needs a vacation; a vocation is a need for something other than a job. It assumes work *is* good that *does* good. Against such there is no law.

Education, which serves an economy that cares only for efficient, not for good, work, can neither value good work nor honor vocation. And so an irony of our circumstance is that art, which is distinctively human, survives not in the educational so much as in the domestic sphere: in good farming, carpentry, cooking, homemaking, gardening. Let anyone who doubts this compare a good garden or chair to most literary criticism written in the last thirty years. Education, which, as Berry says, has treated the domestic arts as if they are degrading and unworthy of people's talents, has become less artful than that which it demeans. No wonder education fails to make full human beings. It has less concern for good and honest *making* than a master breeder or a man mending his fences. Yet such making and artistry are a kind of anthropological sine qua non. They designate men and women made in the image of God—a God whose first act was to create something good. If recognition of this is lost, if the situation, says David Jones,

> is such that men can no longer regard what they do as though it possessed this quality of "art"—then indeed he is of all creatures most miserable, for he is deprived of the one and only balm available to him, as a worker. "Good man" he can still be, and heroic may be, but a complete man he cannot be. And that is the kind of deprivation which the conditions of our kind of age seem to impose upon great numbers of people, upon most people. This deprivation is, in the sphere of art, analogous to a sterilization or a castration in the physical sphere.[74]

I acknowledge that there are those who will countenance no talk of "vocation" or "work as prayer" or the *imago dei.* I make no quarrel here. I merely invite them to go in search of a language equal to the task at hand.

But let them understand plainly that Berry will countenance no talk of a gnostic renewal. There is no evidence anywhere in Berry's work that mind-centered, disembodied work—computer "work" would be an example—can save us. On the contrary, there is nothing but counterevidence.

And so I come to the last point that needs to be made. It is a point that merits sustained, book-length attention. But it cannot go unremarked merely for want of space.

I am attending a reading by Wendell Berry, after which a grizzled professor-type stands—grandstands, to be precise—and, in his tripping, inelegant manner, says, "I was wondering—and thank you, by the way, for that fine reading—just truly amazing; I find your work fascinating and and and so, ah, relevant—I've been thinking, wondering, actually, whence you learned your emphatic, your your your pro*found* anti-Manichaeanism." And so forth and so on.

In this other little fantasy of mine I see Berry leaning forward, cupping his hand behind his ear, and borrowing a line from Uncle Stanley, his half-deaf grave-digger in *A Place on Earth:*

"*Says which?*"

"Your anti-Manichaeanism. Where did you learn it?"

"*Yessir!*"

But Berry is gentlemanly in public—he handles such grandstanders well—and his grizzled interlocutor happens for once to be correct: there is a profoundly anti-Manichaean, which is to say anti-gnostic, streak in Berry's work. I am speaking of his intractable emphasis on the body. Although his footnotes don't show the proper training, and his references don't suggest familiarity with official academic itineraries, the streak is there, a mile wide, and we cannot step over it.

By Gnosticism I mean an abiding dualism, a suspicion of and contempt for matter: the belief that the stuff of creation is at best bad and at worst evil, and the prejudice, therefore, for mind over body, for knowing over doing. By Manichaeanism (which is a gnostic heresy) I mean, again, dualism: the belief that matter and spirit are separable and separate—that spirit is "achieved" apart from and in spite of matter.[75]

Berry often complains about a mind-centeredness that by now registers in an insane but for the most part undetected desire to live in the realm of pure mind—an impulse currently abetted by all forms of abstraction: power, ownership, communication, administration.[76] In religion this impulse manifests itself as a man's "aspir[ing] to heaven with his mind and his heart while destroying the earth, and his fellow men, with his hands." Indeed,

> some varieties of Christianity have held that one should despise the things of this world—which made it all but mandatory that they should be neglected as well. In that way men of conscience—or men who might reasonably have been expected to be men of conscience—have been led to abandon the world, and their own posterity, to the exploiters and ruiners. So exclusively focused on the hereafter, they have been neither here nor there.[77]

Berry says that this species of late Gnosticism—he doesn't call it that, but that is what it is: a belief, to use Harold Bloom's useful idiom, that the Creation and the Fall were one and the same event[78]—amounts to a desire for heaven at the expense of the earth and that it is therefore "a rarefied form of gluttony."[79]

Against this, and speaking emphatically as a "placed person,"[80] Berry has said from the beginning, "I can only imagine [heaven] and desire it in terms of what I know of the earth. And so my questions do not aspire beyond the earth. They aspire *toward* it and *into* it. Perhaps they aspire *through* it."[81] We can measure the extent to which this passage is profoundly anti-Manichaean, the extent to which it expresses from a hillside in Kentucky an essentially Catholic orthodoxy, if we hold it next to an intentionally anti-Manichaean passage from the Catholic theologian Fr. William F. Lynch, one of whose main concerns was to develop a Christology "under the terms of total and actual, positive and 'athletic' penetration of the finite (*exultavit ut gigas*)"—a Christology, that is, scrubbed clean of any Manichaean residue:

> A failure of interest in the infinite is certainly not our problem, but rather the fact that we attack it directly, immediately, and violently, refusing the mediation of the finite, or putting it only to brief, magical uses to contact the infinite, or rebelling against the finite, resenting it, skipping through it with violence at some isolated salient.[82]

Lynch's theological interests, like Berry's literary and practical interests, accord with the formulation of Saint Irenaeus: the infinite is seen only in the finite; "in God nothing is empty of sense."[83] Contra Manichaeanism, Berry accepts the essential goodness of Creation (or matter, if you prefer) and rejects the separation of matter and spirit, of finite and infinite, of material and immaterial. He rejects, that is to say, what the church had the good sense long ago to condemn as heresy, the eventual endorsements of Harold Bloom notwithstanding. And Berry distrusts absolutely any emphasis on mind that excludes or minimizes the body. It may be the case, he says, that what is here on Earth is not all that exists; but that does not alter what *is* here, which is where *we* are:

> Another [angel] lifts a hand
> with forefinger pointing up
> to admonish that all's not here.
> All's not. But I aspire
> downward. Flyers embrace
> the air, and I'm a man
> who needs something to hug.
> All my dawns cross the horizon
> and rise, from underfoot.
> What I stand for
> is what I stand on—

so "Below," Berry's poem that considers the difference between himself and those who live by "pure / abstraction."[84]

The similarities between Berry and Lynch—one aspiring through the earth, the other recommending the athletic penetration of it, and both noting the violence we perpetrate as we skip mindlessly through it—are striking, to say the least. But what I am pointing out here is mere orthodoxy—or, if you prefer, a doctrine of salvation according to which "absolutely no escape from this tangible world of sensory perception is allowed. Salvation from the world by any other route than through the world will be called a fraud."[85]

Those are the words of Philip Lee in *Against the Protestant Gnostics*, which we may also usefully hold up next to Berry. Gnosticism, Lee argues, underwrites the signal but regrettable features that follow upon American Protestantism, among them individualism, millennialism, and a comfortable business association with capitalism. Following Max Weber, he sees a similarity between a religion that emphasizes individual spiritual redemption and an economy that encourages individual material prosperity; both are "lonely" and "self-centered," well suited to so excessively abstract a thing as a money economy.[86] Lee calls this an essentially gnostic emphasis on the individual: the economy values individual achievement; its religion emphasizes the salvation of individual souls.[87] Berry likewise says:

> The familiar idea that a man's governing religious obligation is to 'save' himself, procure *for himself* an eternal life, is based on a concept of individualism that is both vicious and absurd. And this religious concept is the counterpart, and to a considerable extent the cause, of the vicious secular individualism that suggests that a man's governing obligation is to enrich himself in this world. . . . So when a man seeks to live on the earth only for the eternal perpetuation, or only for the economic enrichment, of a life that he has devalued and despised, he is involved not only in absurdity but in perversion—a perversion that has now become the deadly disease of the world.[88]

In comparing the gnostic tendencies of capitalism, which is the "spiritualization of economics," to the parallel gnostic tendencies in Protestantism, which is "a spiritualized, soul-saving faith," Lee says that "of course, a gnostic God could not participate at all in such mundane affairs, but the 'invisible hand' of capitalism freed the spiritualized Church of its worldly responsibilities and allowed it to concentrate entirely on the extramundane."[89]

Berry more efficiently says: "No wonder so many sermons are devoted exclusively to 'spiritual' subjects. If one is living by the tithes of history's most destructive economy, then the disembodiment of the soul becomes the chief of worldly conveniences."[90]

Such disembodiment goes hand in hand with an easy gnostic displacement in the world. Lee says that in the Old Testament men and women are bound to one another, as well as to others, by also being plighted to a particular place. Mobility and placelessness in contemporary life, by contrast, accord with the "gnostic philosophy that *place* does not matter."[91] Berry, for his part, consistently grounds marriage and community in—what else?—the ground. The marriage of Hannah and Nathan Coulter, to take a recent example from the fiction, begins as a discussion of where the marriage will be *placed*. Nathan brings Hannah to the farm he's thinking of buying and shows it to her. "It's not the Feltner place," he says. Hannah understands perfectly: "He meant it as a question. He was asking me if I would marry him."[92] Nor is the scene anomalous. Berry, everywhere concerned with concrete, knowable places with which human actions must be commensurate in scale, criticizes our "present 'leaders' —the people of wealth and power—[because they] do not know what it means to take a place seriously: to think it worthy, for its own sake, of love and study and careful work. They cannot take any place seriously because they must be ready at any moment, by the terms of power and wealth in the modern world, to destroy any place."[93]

At a certain concentration evidence, like manure, ceases to fertilize and begins instead to burn. And space requires that I do more piling than spreading here. But the similarities between Lee and Berry are hardly irrelevant. We understand Berry correctly if we understand that he has flatly rejected an ancient heresy that to my knowledge he has never been rash enough—and prais'd be rashness for it—to name.

Berry came to this orthodoxy not by study but by meditating poetry and place, by attending to soil and practicing the disciplines by which it is maintained. Such meditating, such attending, such practicing fends off a suspicion of matter, knows it commits self-slaughter if it puts asunder the matter and spirit that God has joined. A great many of us, by contrast, abstracted from the soil and disinclined toward the domestic arts, languish under a resuscitated gnosticism that our education perpetuates. Whereas we dupe ourselves into owning all the technologies of abstraction and so float ever more airily into an unbearable lightness of unbeing, Berry has walked the good earth behind a good horse named Nick, contemplated the soil, and found therein, amid the ravages of an economy and a system of education largely given over to the gnostic suspicion of the body, the genius of his religion: the resurrection of the body. The soil, he says, is always "doing something that, if we are not careful, we will call 'unearthly': It is making life out of death." It "exists as such because it is ceaselessly transforming death into life."[94] And

After death, willing or not, the body serves,
entering the earth. And so what was heaviest
and most mute is at last raised up into song.[95]

This discussion of Berry's unwillingness to brook the ancient dualism is a gold to airy thinness beat. But that such a discussion could be fully developed, and that it has consequences for education, I have no doubt. It would include —and this would also be crucial—a description of the bestialism and angel-ism that follow upon our flight from the flesh. Walker Percy spent a whole novel, *Love in the Ruins,* dramatizing the disasters of such a flight.[96] Lynch said it leads to "terrible distortions."[97] Berry himself has implied as much in saying that those who "long for the realm of pure mind—or pure machine; the difference is negligible"—when they take leave of flesh and blood "are go-ing to cause a lot of dangerous commotion on their way out."[98] But I will limit myself instead to saying that Berry's clearest exposition of this is in the pieces for which he is most traduced. And yet they remain for me definitive and signal. They bear as much upon education, and they name our common malady, as clearly as anything he has written. They represent, I think, the most important critique he has yet proffered.

I am speaking of the companion essays "Why I Am Not Going to Buy a Computer" and "Feminism, the Body, and the Machine," wherein we read about our flight from the body, our hatred of it—even as we indulge its appetites—and the consequences of this on our work and our world. "The danger most immediately to be feared in 'technological progress,'" Berry says, "is the degradation and obsolescence of the body"—that's Gnosticism. "Implicit in the technological revolution from the beginning has been a new version of an old dualism"—that's Gnosticism in its specifically Manichaean iteration—"one always destructive, and now more destructive than ever." The education of which Berry long ago declared himself skeptical perpetuates both heresies, and the result is absurdity and perversion—a perversion that has now become the deadly disease of the world.

When education makes its goal the degradation and obsolescence of the body—and it has—the recovery of the domestic arts becomes all the more urgent. When we take care of things at home, when we work well and to prop-er scale, and when we understand that work as vocation, we have begun to recover a lost wholeness. When we consider to what ancient heresies that lost wholeness attaches, we may at last become aware of how grave our condition is and how high the stakes are.

I acknowledge, again, that there are many people who consider the clash between heresy and orthodoxy, or the decisions of ecumenical councils, unworthy of serious study. But if it takes ecological chaos to recall from exile the Queen of the Sciences, these same sophisticates, many of them with seven letters following their names, will have to admit that what they have been doing is risking correction by disaster. Perhaps a polluted habitat will persuade them of what theology couldn't: that health may depend after all on right praise and right belief—the dual, the instructive meaning of *orthodox*.

Berry says that when he was a teacher, he tried to suggest to his "students the possibility of a life that is full and conscious and responsible."[99] In the unstable and ideologically charged atmosphere of higher education today, such suggesting can invite censure. But for about two decades I've been putting Berry's essays in the hands of undergraduates, and I have found that, although some resist his ideas with all the ignorance they can muster, most students are looking for a vision like Berry's and a manner like his of articulating it. They're pleased to meet him. It is true that these students move by the centrifugal force of a mighty habit, that few will stop or even slow the giant flywheel of execrable change they mistake for inexorable progress. But that "monster, custom," saith the lord Hamlet,

> Of habits devil, is angel yet in this,
> That to the use of actions fair and good
> He likewise gives a frock or livery
> That aptly is put on. . . .
> For he almost can change the stamp of nature,
> And either curb the devil, or throw him out
> With wondrous potency.[100]

I'm not running the tired line that education makes us better, against which stands all the evidence of history. Henry Adams said his own Harvard education "had cost a civil war," that members of his generation "killed each other by the scores in the act of testing their college conclusions." I sympathize enough with Adams—that "man from the beginning [has] found his chief amusement in bloodshed"[101]—to doubt that education can succeed where the Sermon on the Mount has apparently failed. I'm merely placing the heavy but inescapable obligation where it belongs and pointing to culture-borne instruction that is there for the using. And this bit happens to recommend a physical discipline for a spiritual malady.

Notes

1. As paraphrased in Philip Bénéton, *Equality by Default* (1997), trans. Ralph Hancock (Wilmington, DE: ISI Books, 2004), 140.

2. Wendell Berry, "Economy and Pleasure," in *What Are People For?* (San Francisco: North Point, 1990), 138; Wendell Berry, "The Loss of the University," in *Home Economics* (San Francisco: North Point, 1987), 77.

3. Wendell Berry, "Discipline and Hope," in *A Continuous Harmony* (1970; Washington, DC: Shoemaker and Hoard, 2004), 108.

4. Gerald Graff, *Clueless in Academe* (New Haven: Yale University Press), 3.

5. Wendell Berry, "The Long-Legged House," in *The Long-Legged House* (1969; Washington, DC: Shoemaker and Hoard, 2004), 127.

6. "Higher Education and Home Defense," in *Home Economics,* 52.

7. "If the proper work of the university is only to equip people to fulfill private ambitions, then how do we justify public support?" See "The Loss of the University," in *Home Economics,* 77.

8. On commercial education, see Wendell Berry, *Sex, Economy, Freedom and Community* (New York: Pantheon, 1991), xii. On the "cultish faith in the future," see "Feminism, the Body, and the Machine," in *What Are People For?,* 188. Note also: "The Future is one of our better-packaged items and attracts many buyers." See *Sex, Economy, Freedom and Community,* xiv. On the "hysterical rhetoric of change," see "Economy and Pleasure," in *What Are People For?,* 133.

9. This phrase suggesting mutual admiration and approval is Berry's; see "The Work of Local Culture," in *What Are People For?,* 164. On "upward mobility," see Wendell Berry, *Life Is a Miracle* (Washington, DC: Counterpoint, 2000), 136. Berry attributes this observation to Wes Jackson; see Jackson, *Becoming Native to This Place* (1994; New York: Counterpoint, 1996), 3. On "outmoding" parents, see "The Work of Local Culture," 162.

10. A ubiquitous theme in Berry, as necessary for farming as for all human endeavors. See "A Practical Harmony" and "Nature as Measure," in *What Are People For?,* 105 and 209 respectively; see also Wendell Berry, *Standing by Words* (1983; Washington, DC: Shoemaker and Hoard, 2005), 155; and *Sex, Economy, Freedom and Community,* 172.

11. "The Work of Local Culture," in *What Are People For?,* 163. Hannah Coulter's children fall victims to this; see Wendell Berry, *Hannah Coulter* (Washington, DC: Shoemaker and Hoard, 2004), 95.

12. "Word and Flesh," in *What Are People For?,* 199.

13. See *Sex, Economy, Freedom and Community,* xii.

14. "Feminism, the Body, and the Machine," in *What Are People For?,* 185; or again, the sophisticate is someone "who before puberty understands how to produce a baby, but who at the age of thirty will not know how to produce a potato." See "Think Little," in *A Continuous Harmony,* 75.

15. "Discipline and Hope," in *A Continuous Harmony,* 124; and elsewhere: "If you are dependent on people who do not know you, who control the value of your necessities, you are not free, and you are not safe." See *Sex, Economy, Freedom and Community,* 128.

16. *Life Is a Miracle,* 33.

17. "The Rise," in *The Long-Legged House*, 106–7.

18. "Economy and Pleasure," in *What Are People For?*, 129.

19. *Life Is a Miracle*, 123.

20. "The Loss of the University," in *Home Economics*, 93; on the "complicity" of the arts and humanities, see *Life Is a Miracle*, 132.

21. That is, humanists copy the scientists out of "shame . . . that their truths are not objectively provable as are the truths of science." "The Loss of the University," in *Home Economics*, 92–93.

22. See "An Argument for Diversity," in *What Are People For?*, 116.

23. Ibid., 79, 91. On the difference between "about" and "from," Berry is exemplary; see, e.g., *Sex, Economy, Freedom and Community* (135–37), *What Are People For?* (160–62, 197); Jayber Crow is a man who has apparently learned not only about but from Dante; see *Jayber Crow* (Washington, DC: Counterpoint, 2000), 66, 71, 133.

24. On "Michael," see "The Work of Local Culture," in *What Are People For?*, 162; see also *Standing by Words*, 189. On Homer, see *Life Is a Miracle*, 146; this also appears in *What Are People For?* (161) and underwrites the death of Nathan Coulter; see *Hannah Coulter*, 159–64.

25. "Getting Along with Nature" in *Home Economics*, 8; see also *Standing by Words*, 206.

26. "Getting Along with Nature," in *Home Economics*, 8; "Nature as Measure," in *What Are People For?*, 209.

27. "Getting Along with Nature," in *Home Economics*, 15.

28. *Life Is a Miracle*, 23.

29. "Getting Along with Nature," in *Home Economics*, 20.

30. "Out of Your Car, Off Your Horse," in *Sex, Economy, Freedom and Community*, 20.

31. "Word and Flesh," in *What Are People For?*, 201.

32. On science's self-anointing, see *Life Is a Miracle*, 18; on specialization, see *Home Economics*, 76; on limiting our desires, see Wendell Berry, *The Gift of Good Land* (San Francisco: North Point, 1982), 112.

33. "The Loss of the University," in *Home Economics*, 77.

34. John Milton, *Paradise Lost* I, 254–55; "Poetry and Place," in *Standing by Words*, 108, 167.

35. "Poetry and Place," in *Standing by Words*, 167.

36. Ibid., 154; italics Berry's.

37. Ibid., 177.

38. "Notes: Unspecializing Poetry," in *Standing by Words*, 87.

39. Ibid., 87–88.

40. See "The Work of Local Culture," in *What Are People For?*, 154.

41. Wendell Berry, "In Distrust of Movements," in *Citizenship Papers* (Washington, DC: Shoemaker and Hoard, 2003), 47.

42. Aldo Leopold, *A Sand County Almanac* (New York: Oxford, 1949), 158, 209, 178, and 223.

43. "Some Thoughts on Citizenship and Conscience in Honor of Don Pratt," in *The Long-Legged House*, 77; see also "An Argument for Diversity," in *What Are People For?*, 112: "The land and its human communities are not being thought about in places of study."

44. "Two Economies," in *Home Economics*, 67–68.

45. "The most exemplary nature is that of the topsoil. It is very Christ-like in its passivity and beneficence, and in the penetrating energy that issues out of its peaceableness. It increases by experience, by the passage of seasons over it, growth rising out of it and returning to it, not by ambition or aggressiveness. It is enriched by all things that die and enter into it. It keeps the past, not as history or as memory, but as richness, new possibility. Its fertility is always building up out of death into promise. Death is the bridge or the tunnel by which its past enters its future." See "A Native Hill," in *The Long-Legged House*, 204.

46. "Selective bookkeeping" is a favorite idiom of Berry's; see, e.g., "Six Agricultural Fallacies," in *Home Economics*, 128. "Net gain" is another; see, e.g., "Feminism, the Body, and the Machine," in *What Are People For?*, 187; also *Life Is a Miracle*, 21, 70, 136.

47. "Word and Flesh," in *What Are People For?*, 201 (thanks to Tom Banks for the Latin rendition); see also "Thoughts in the Presence of Fear," in *Citizenship Papers*, 21–22: "Education is not properly an industry, and its proper use is not to serve industries, either by job-training or by industry-subsidized research. Its proper use is to enable citizens to live lives that are economically, politically, socially, and culturally responsible. . . . The first thing we must begin to teach our children (and learn ourselves) is that we cannot spend and consume endlessly. We have got to learn to save and conserve. We do need a 'new economy,' but one that is founded on thrift and care, on saving and conserving, not on excess and waste."

48. "The great fault of the selective bookkeeping we call 'the economy' is that it does not lead to thrift; day by day, we are acting out the plot of a murderous paradox: an 'economy' that leads to extravagance." See "Six Agricultural Fallacies," in *Home Economics*, 128. "Neither of us [Wendell Berry and Wes Jackson] believes that either art or science can be 'neutral.' Influence and consequence are inescapable. History continues. You cannot serve both God and Mammon, and you cannot work without serving one or the other." See *Life Is a Miracle*, 127.

49. "Preserving Wildness," in *Home Economics*, 142.

50. "Getting Along with Nature," in *Home Economics*, 15.

51. The Chain of Being "gave humans a place between animals and angels in the order of Creation. . . . Lacking that ancient definition, or any such definition, we do not know at what point to restrain or deny ourselves." Ibid., 15. "Rats and roaches live by competition under the law of supply and demand; it is the privilege of human beings to live under the laws of justice and mercy." See "Economy and Pleasure," in *What Are People For?*, 135.

52. "An Argument for Diversity," in *What Are People For?*, 120. Also, "soil husbandry," for example, requires "acts that are much more complex than industrial acts,

for these acts are conditioned by the ability *not* to act, by forbearance or self-restraint, sympathy or generosity." See "Two Economies," in *Home Economics,* 66.

53. "An Argument for Diversity," in *What Are People For?,* 119.

54. "The Total Economy," in *Citizenship Papers,* 64.

55. "People, Land, and Community," in *Standing by Words,* 69.

56. "In Distrust of Movements," in *Citizenship Papers,* 47.

57. "Discipline and Hope," in *A Continuous Harmony,* 101.

58. "In Distrust of Movements," in *Citizenship Papers,* 47–48.

59. "Poetry and Place," in *Standing by Words,* 198.

60. See "Mayhem in the Industrial Paradise," in *A Continuous Harmony,* 171.

61. "In Distrust of Movements," in *Citizenship Papers,* 51; likewise "farming, animal husbandry, horticulture, and gardening, at their best, are complex and comely arts; there is much pleasure in knowing them, too." See "The Pleasures of Eating," in *What Are People For?,* 151. Berry insists that a life that is "harder, more laborious, poorer in luxuries and gadgets" will also be "richer in meaning and more abundant in real pleasure." See "Think Little," in *A Continuous Harmony,* 78–79.

62. "In Distrust of Movements" and "The Whole Horse," in *Citizenship Papers* (48 and 121), as elsewhere.

63. See, e.g., "The Pleasures of Eating," in *What Are People For?,* 149–51; also *Sex, Economy, Freedom and Community,* 41.

64. See Wendell Berry, *The Unsettling of America* (San Francisco: Sierra Club, 1977), 12; Wendell Berry, *The Hidden Wound* (San Francisco: North Point, 1989), 112; also the title essay in *What Are People For?* The answer to this question is, in part, "work."

65. "My grandson," Berry says, "is now following his father and me over some of the same countryside that I followed my father and grandfather over. When his time comes, my grandson will choose as he must, but so far all of us have been farmers. I know from my grandfather that when he was a child he too followed his father in this way, hearing and seeing, not knowing yet that the most essential part of his education had begun." *Life Is a Miracle,* 151.

66. "Discipline and Hope," in *A Continuous Harmony,* 90.

67. On "a human mind-centered world," see "Poetry and Place," in *Standing by Words,* 179.

68. "To work without pleasure or affection, to make a product that is not both useful and beautiful, is to dishonor God, nature, the thing that is made, and whomever it is made for. This is blasphemy: to make shoddy work of the work of God." See "Christianity and the Survival of Creation," in *Sex, Economy, Freedom and Community,* 104.

69. *Life Is a Miracle,* 130.

70. Ibid. Of the ministers in his own community Berry writes, many "have been 'called' to serve in its churches, but not one has ever been 'called' to stay." See "God and Country," in *What Are People For?,* 97.

71. "The Total Economy," in *Citizenship Papers,* 72.

72. "I owe a considerable debt myself to Buddhism and Buddhists. But there are an enormous number of people—and I am one of them—whose native religion, for better or worse, is Christianity." See "Christianity and the Survival of Creation," in *Sex, Economy, Freedom and Community,* 95.

73. Jayber puzzles over the meaning of this sentence before speaking with Dr. Ardmire, who, at the end of chapter 6 of *Jayber Crow,* advises Jayber on his "calling." See especially 52–54.

74. David Jones, "Art in Relation to War," in *The Dying Gaul* (1972; London: Faber and Faber, 1978), 150. Thanks to Wendell Berry for showing me this passage.

75. So Saint Augustine could soften "the detestation of the flesh characteristic of his Manichee phase" by presenting "body and soul as the two components of a torn and divided self." See Roy Porter, *Flesh in the Age of Reason* (New York: W. W. Norton, 2003), 37. Coleridge's dictum is more precise, here as elsewhere: we may divide in order to distinguish body and soul, matter and spirit, so long as we do not distinguish in order to divide, for the two constitute a unity. See, e.g., Samuel Taylor Coleridge, *Aids to Reflection,* ed. John Beer (Princeton: Routledge, 1993), 114.

76. See, e.g., "Poetry and Place," in *Standing by Words,* 179.

77. "A Secular Pilgrimage," in *A Continuous Harmony,* 4–5; see also Katherine Dalton, "Rendering Us Again in Affection: An Interview with Wendell Berry," in *Chronicles,* July 2006: Berry says, "I was never satisfied by the Protestantism that I inherited, I think because of the dualism of soul and body, heaven and Earth, Creator and creation—a dualism so fierce at times that it counted hatred of this life and this world as a virtue" (33).

78. See Harold Bloom, *Where Shall Wisdom Be Found?* (New York: Riverhead, 2004), 261; also Bloom, *The American Religion* (New York: Simon and Schuster, 1992), 51.

79. "A Secular Pilgrimage," in *A Continuous Harmony,* 7.

80. *The Long-Legged House,* 141.

81. "A Native Hill," in ibid., 200.

82. William F. Lynch, "Theology and the Imagination," *Thought* 29 (1954): 61–86; 61, 66–67.

83. Quoted in Philip J. Lee, *Against the Protestant Gnostics* (New York: Oxford University Press, 1987), 43.

84. Wendell Berry, *Collected Poems, 1957–1982* (New York: North Point, 1985), 207.

85. Lee, *Against the Protestant Gnostics,* 25.

86. Ibid., 200.

87. On individualism, see ibid., 104.

88. "A Secular Pilgrimage," in *A Continuous Harmony,* 9.

89. Lee, *Against the Protestant Gnostics,* 202, 126.

90. "God and Country," in *What Are People For?,* 96. And again: Lee writes of an American evangelicalism so gnostic that it has "no real interest in this world" and conducts "ordinary business life . . . as if the Gospel did not exist" (127). Berry says: "To be uninterested in economy is to be uninterested in the practice of religion; it is to be uninterested in culture and character" (*Sex, Economy, Freedom and Community,* 99).

91. Lee, *Against the Protestant Gnostics,* 214; on marriage and place, see 30.

92. *Hannah Coulter,* 71.

93. *Sex, Economy, Freedom and Community,* 22.

94. "Two Economies," in *Home Economics,* 62, 67.

95. "Enriching the Earth," in *Collected Poems, 1957–1982,* 110.

96. Walker Percy, *Love in the Ruins* (New York: Farrar, Straus and Giroux, 1971). Percy's novel names the conditions of modern dualism "angelism" and "bestialism." Lynch seems to have been the source for at least the former of these terms. See "Theology and the Imagination," 68; also, William F. Lynch, *Christ and Apollo* (1960; Wilmington, DE: ISI Books, 2004), 80. Lynch was tutored by Allen Tate in this; see Tate, "The Angelic Imagination," in *Collected Essays* (Denver: Alan Swallow, 1959), 432–71. Thanks to Ralph C. Wood for directing me to Tate's essay.

97. Lynch, "Theology and the Imagination," 68.

98. "Feminism, the Body, and the Machine," in *What Are People For?,* 195.

99. "A Statement Against the War in Viet Nam," in *The Long-Legged House,* 75.

100. *The Riverside Shakespeare,* ed. G. Blakemore Evans et al. (Boston: Houghton Mifflin, 1974), 3.4.161–65; 3.4.168–70.

101. Henry Adams, *The Education of Henry Adams* (1918; Boston: Houghton Mifflin, 1961), 238, 57, 128.

James Baker Hall

Wendell's Window
and the Wind's Eye

THE SUMMER AFTER Wendell and Tanya were married, before they moved
into quarters befitting his first teaching job at a Baptist college with mandatory daily chapel, they lived in a cabin on the Kentucky River bank—with
kerosene for lamplight and butane for cooking and for heating water, which
had to be hauled in a few gallons at a time. There wasn't enough elbow room
in that cabin for more than a change of clothes, if you could find berth enough
between the bed and everything else to get into them, but it was rendered spa-
cious by the great excitement of their protracted honeymoon. Wendell had
thrown himself into the preparations, repairing the screens and windows and
doors, whitewashing the walls, cutting the weeds, and generally shaping up
the setting. It was called the Camp, a power place from his boyhood in nature,
a locus of his independence from home rule, and for him the perfect summer
hinge into his marriage. For Tanya it was something quite other, a crash course
in just what she'd signed up for, until death do them part. Those of us fortunate enough to be watching joined the newlyweds in delight at the romance
of it all. For his wedding present to his bride, Wendell toppled the old out-
house and built a new one—still without a door, as befitted the view. Until that
summer of 1957, Tanya's idea of rustic was classy Mill Valley, California, where
her professional aunts and uncles lived on a treed hillside a few minutes from
the Golden Gate Bridge. For her wedding present to Wendell, twenty-one-
year-old Queenie—for her striking resemblance to the profiled Nefertiti—
rolled up her sleeves, got out the mosquito spray, and proceeded to figure out
what the situation expected of her—so that she could exceed expectations.
She multiplied that cabin space with fresh flowers and turned the screened-in
porch into a place to be, where everything happened.

Wendell, who'd already made it into the famous *Poetry* magazine and was
on his quick way, wrote out there, on a folding card table in the corner, with a
view of the old brown river. Overnighters slept on a narrow cot out there that
during the day was a bolstered place to sit. And before we went to bed, we sat

out there on the porch with the lamp turned low and watched fireflies and listened to the crickets and the tree frogs and the river, sometimes talking quietly but not always. In Wendell's presence you understood without his saying anything that it was his well-thought-out conviction that there were often better things to listen to than humans, even those so distinguished and interesting as yourself. Owls, for instance. The sound of an owl would shut down conversation at the Camp. A towboat pushing barges upstream, for another. The Camp wasn't just a quiet place; it was a place of quiet, where the click and clack of dishwashing in an enameled pan hung in the trees, sometimes welcome but not always, and where a speedboat was a messenger straight from hell. Shoot the s.o.b. before he reproduces. Before light Wendell got up and put on his tall rubber boots, stealing down the slope to a johnboat tied up to a sycamore tree, and ran his trotlines, in the dark, as any poet for real would want to do. In the middle of the night once, he hauled up a twenty-seven-pound catfish, waking his bride to share in the excitement. Chunks of Ivory soap were used sometimes as bait.

Although that cabin was left standing for another six-plus years, the newlyweds were the old Camp's glorious last hurrah, just as it was their setup and send-off and an emblem of what brought them back. Between that summer of 1957 and their return in 1964 to settle in a house just up the road, they lived on the West Coast, in Italy, and in New York City, where they got to know artists and intellectuals of reputation. Some of those new worldly friends would visit them there on the riverbank in the coming years. Many others, along with the growing number of Wendell's readers, kept track of the now famous story unfolding there through poems, stories, and essays.

Salvage from the original Camp was used in the construction of the new one, which was well insulated and lined inside with six-inch tongue-and-groove, and had the look and feel not of a weekend, like its predecessor, but of a life. No, a *way* of life. Wendell was out to prove that the received opinion of the day about not being able to go home again was seriously wrongheaded, confused, and shortsighted. "The Long-Legged House" was the cabin's literary name, bestowed in his magnificent essay by that title, but no one has ever called his writing place anything but the Camp. The makeshift card table from the old cabin was replaced by a long, deep work counter fastened to the wall and floor, and the vacation view from the old porch was framed before eternity in the grand window above it, the "wind's eye" in those elegant and wise meditations that bear the name of "Window Poems." The old Camp, where you were among the river gods, embraced by a simpler, freer way of life, wasn't gone: trusting birds at the feeder a hand reach away testified to that, the same wildflowers around the door entrance and down the slope, the same ever-changing muddy river rising and falling and swirling and going quiet on the surface as the same blue heron, or his progeny, lifted off upstream and disappeared. The old Camp was very much still in the air, but things were considerably more complicated and momentous now for the still very young writer-man no longer on his honeymoon. A sprawling vulnerability came close to being his base condition, as his conversation and writings testified. There were children in the picture now; history was tightening the ecological and political screws; more people were paying attention to him; more causes needed his voice. In 1957 he'd been a camper on that riverbank; now he was an outspoken citizen of the endangered world. He shook his head in despair often, and stared off into space as though he did not want to talk anymore about what he saw. His trotlines had grown heavy, I find myself saying, and the dark in which he worked them no longer a thrilling challenge, a source of juice, more like a fear now, a dread, a terrible drain. The delightful twenty-seven-pound catfish had been replaced during the intervening years with two-ton tar babies like agribusiness and world population and the fossil-fuel culture.

The artist had good use for ordering devices, and the many-paned window provided him with one, a grid with more than two dimensions, a way to measure and to frame anything of his choosing. "The window has an edge / that is celestial, / where the eyes are surpassed," he sums up at the end of a sequence.[1] What we've been witnessing is the transforming power of the presiding image, from random thought and perception into picture, from time into timelessness. The way these poems move, each within itself, and within the overall—how the flat rock of the voice skips—suggests to me the equal influence of both the grid and the river. How to put this? The other shore is out of reach, but the language aspires there: dramatizing where it settles, commencing its pulsing circles.

He wrote these poems in longhand, probably with a pen, on a yellow legal pad (made dear to him early on by his lawyer father), sometimes with his feet propped up on the desk and a pencil or a Camel cigarette behind his ear. After breakfast every morning that he wasn't off teaching or reading or lecturing, he went to the Camp to write, disappearing out the back door and around the side of the house with a briefcase and a thermos. Depending on the weather, the stove would be the first order of business, and he would be dressed in coveralls, wearing a stocking cap as he swept the floors, often joyfully. Or the doors would get propped open to the delights of the breeze, and he'd be dressed in khaki work pants and work shirt and wearing Red Wings, a tall thin man, six-four, good-looking, with a deep voice and a big laugh and a real mean streak, and an Irish charm that still disarms many who think they aren't going to like him, the self-appointed Jeremiah from Hicksville. In any portrait of Wendell, there hangs nearby a Cézanne calendar—he loves especially the landscapes—and a Vermeer postcard, maybe a Dégas too. Depending on which dog was current, there could be one stretched on the pine floor of the Camp as the "Window Poems" were being written, but he would be the only possible distraction. The birds coming and going at the window feeder weren't a distraction from his work, more likely the other way around. The level surfaces were well-ordered and sparsely populated. To the right of the working counter were deep shelves, with manuscripts, correspondence, journals, tasks, books, and, to the right of that, the door onto the porch with its swing, hoisted to the ceiling in off-season.

I remember many times sitting beside him at that window—he would insist that I take his more comfortable chair, and sometimes I would. One summer evening as the light was fading, we were there talking about William Carlos Williams and Rexroth's translations from the Chinese, when a towboat came up the river, its sound preceding it. The foliage gave one barge and took it back and returned two, until I was wishing I'd counted, and then there the whole rig was with its running lights: sand barges on their slow, flat push upstream to Frankfort, the pilot's cabin of the caboose towboat lighted up. Without comment Wendell handed me the binoculars so that I could watch what was going on, the pilot and another man at the wheel, much as the "Window Poems" hand you access to what's in the author's deepest mind and most eloquent language. I was poised between wanting to say something and not wanting to break the silence, as is the encompassing spirit of that suite of poems. It's at the heart of their wisdom.

From the legal pad he typed them there at the Camp on an office-model Royal, out from under its cover, using twenty-pound Corrasable Bond and making a carbon on yellow seconds or onionskin (this was a long time before copy machines), which he sent to me. In the margins I noted my responses and sent them back—or kept them because I didn't want to part with them, and wrote a fan letter. I loved these poems when I first read them and found them thrilling, and inspiring—he was so far out ahead of the rest of us—already he knew what he had to write about and who he wanted to be and what he wanted to sound like—already he was becoming very accomplished, one good book after another. And I still love those "Window Poems," for the load-bearing freedom they manifest, flying out of the gravities they debate and flying back in, the simultaneous grace and momentousness of their moves transforming their lashings-out and their propositions into notes of a song.

Of all Wendell's poetry, I think I like best the work he did during that period, mid-sixties through early seventies, the first four or five books, when he was still feeling his way, earning each step, testing himself.

The depth of thought and feeling in the "Window Poems" transform the notational style and vice versa. They add up the way a Brueghel does, each little scene intense and absorbing, yielding to its small place in the encompassing community. There's hesitation, self-doubt, vulnerability, life-sizeness here, in and among blazing visions where everything is writ large. There's an ear with perfect pitch, a lightness of touch, which makes for a voice deeply afraid of getting nailed, especially by its own anger and righteousness. In the corner of the forty-paned window at the Camp, feeding from a roofed flat, the nuthatches, chickadees, sparrows, bluejays, robins, cardinals flew in and grabbed something up and flew off, and the poems did and keep doing likewise, hunting for what to trust. All taken together they sound like what they do, not what they say: the author is throwing the dice, the stakes are high: his long wrists are loose, he's on a roll.

Note

1. Wendell Berry, *Collected Poems, 1957–1982* (New York: North Point, 1985).

Barbara Kingsolver

The Art of
Buying Nothing

FOR YEARS AND YEARS, I resisted acquiring a cell phone. When people asked for my "cell number," I always thought that sounded like a prison address, and I was relieved not to have one. I heard how useful these devices were, how handy, but I also saw them turn many ordinary humans into harebrained drivers, antisocial boors, and helpless natterers. I didn't feel I needed technical assistance toward any of those goals. Finally my colleagues became so amused or puzzled by my backwardness, they could not refrain from asking what world-shaking event it would take for me to get one. I said, "I'll get a cell phone when Wendell Berry does." It seemed a safe answer.

But life is full of surprises. My first child became a teenager, prone therefore to nomadic evening socializing, and I became prone to wanting to know where she was. I would remind her as she headed out the door, "You'll never be more than fifty feet from a telephone." How the world can shift under our feet, in order to prove us wrong and our children right. Even as I mouthed that maternal truism, workers were busy removing all the telephones from public restrooms in parks and shopping centers, yanking them out of airports by the hundreds, leaving whole banks of flat metal telephone sockets to stare out blindly like so many enucleated eyes. With all humanity now carrying around personal telephones, these old landlines as they were quaintly called (are we all now at sea?) must not have been busking enough quarters to earn their keep. With or without me, as usual, the world moved on.

We suffered some worrisome missed connections, wasted other people's time, and finally bought an ethereal talking device for our family. I have not concluded that cell phones are good, or that they are bad, only that they warrant both respect and wariness. I was also stung by the prevailing material truth of our times: how the mad dash toward new things predictably creates problems for anyone left behind. So I've turned my vigilance to other skirmishes in the hundred years' war between New Shiny Things and What We Already Have.

All of us have our prophets whose teachings help us navigate the rockier straits of our lives. For me, the thorniest passage is to raise a spiritual family in an overly material world, and the question I often ask myself is: What Would Wendell Do?

I don't mean to imply any great familiarity here. I claim no special insider knowledge of the Wendell Berry domain, except insofar as his writings and life have stood before me longer than I can remember, quietly provoking me toward the humble, rock-solid good sense I hope someday to call my own. I was introduced to his existence, I think, by my grandmother, who referred to him as "that fellow that won't use a tractor." She seemed vexed, but my young mind pictured noble horse versus noisy tractor and became enchanted with an early object lesson in "less is more." Now we are friends, Wendell and I, to the extent that we write each other notes, keeping one another posted on writerly business and shared concerns. I do not call him for advice every time a material decision presents itself; that would disturb his peace to the point of madness, which would not be friendly of me. I just guess. Fortunately, he set out perfectly clear guidelines in his essay "Why I Am Not Going to Buy a Computer," in which he listed his standards for technological innovation, roughly as follows:

1. The new tool should cost less than the one it replaces.
2. It should be at least as small as the one it replaces.
3. It should do better work.
4. It should use less energy.
5. Ideally it should use some form of solar energy, such as that of the body.
6. It should be repairable by a person of ordinary intelligence.
7. It should be purchasable and repairable as near to home as possible.
8. It should come from a small shop that will take it back for repair.

And most important, in my opinion:

9. It should not replace or disrupt anything good that already exists, and this includes family and community relationships.

I have paraphrased here for brevity, and, to take an even greater risk, I will go ahead and argue that these rules can apply more generally. I realize the point of that brief (and now very famous) essay was to question our society's widespread devotion to technological fundamentalism. I know that the author was wisely and manageably sticking to his point. But I tend to wander, and I have found these standards can be used for judging not just technical beasts like cell phones and computers but virtually all the categories of durable goods we bring into our lives.

I might be playing with matches here, since that essay has already been misinterpreted on a grand scale. It was all the talk, for a while, among people who utterly ignored its meaning and invented a different one. Bizarrely, it aroused feminist ire. In explaining his fondness for writing without a computer, the author happened to mention a valued household arrangement in which his wife, Tanya, types and comments upon his handwritten drafts. Many readers sniffed out enslavement there and did not hesitate to browbeat the presumed enslaver.

Oh, how the world (as I've mentioned) can embarrassingly shift beneath a person who is ranting about some sure thing. Labor-saving devices have a way of "saving" us from work we wish we'd held on to: that fact is now bitterly understood by U.S. laborers of every stripe. Nearly two decades after that essay was published, we are a nation whose jobs have massively migrated south, east, and west, and as such we would probably not get so riled up now against Wendell's argument for keeping half his cottage industry inside the cottage. And the charge of sexism was just dumb. My husband also comments on my drafts and provides many other kinds of help, including research and technical support. If I were to state this publicly (which I believe I just did), I can't imagine I'd be hit with a pile of mail about how I'm exploiting my mate. Anyone can figure out he is doing these things because he values the work I do and adds his creative effort to mine in order to help our household economy and promote the general welfare. That people naturally assume such good sense on the part of a husband, but not a wife, only proves that women are still not adequately credited with brains by either gender. It was readers' bigotry, not the author's, that created the furor over "Why I Am Not Going to Buy a Computer." It grieves me to see any words become celebrated for what they did not say, while the real point was missed, rowdily and entirely. I don't want to do that here.

I take the real point—I hope I'm not mistaken—to be this: acquisition of new things, any new things, in a person's life should be subjected to hard standards. Our present cultural imperative is that all new things are better than all old things; in service of this conviction we're racing toward life on a deforested, stinky junk pile. We could reconsider. Anyone can see that a remarriage, however happy, still contains in its history some nugget of death or divorce; we could recognize some smidgen of similar tragedy in the act of marrying ourselves to new possessions. Something is getting thrown into the world's dustbins, which are already groaning. We should quiz the new candidates fiercely, asking them to prove themselves worthy in measurable ways: smaller, kinder, cleaner, more helpful to our communities. Wendell's nine rules apply pretty well to the whole scope of material acquisition in an average person's life, or at least mine.

Now I mean this in the spirit, if not in the letter, of the law. The "smaller than the one it replaces" maxim, for example, rarely applies to clothing. I did hold to that rule for new swimsuits during the course of my youth, but into every sensible woman's life the time does come to reverse the trend. My children, as long as they keep growing, get new clothes only if they're bigger, and for myself I try to maintain body and armor so that another good year may pass in which I've bought no new clothes at all. But the point generally holds: bigger should not be presumed better, but likely the opposite.

The idea is that we ask the right questions as we walk toward every possibility of a new thing in our lives. And believe me, that walk is what most of us call life itself, at least in the country where I live. We don't have to turn on a television or look at billboards to learn how to purchase durable material goods; we need not even leave the house. Catalogues arrive through my door by the dozen, inviting me to buy new clothes or shoes or appliances, toys for my children, tools for my work. Today I sat down to eat lunch, and there across from me at the table sat a tower of glossy catalogues selling sheets and comforters, tableware, handwoven clothing, portable CD players, cameras, potted plants and flowers, and even (I'm not kidding) jet vacations to China with the ostensible goal of protecting wildlife. This I learned just from their covers.

"Get, all of you, skedaddle!" I cried, and threw the whole mess into the recycling basket before the creatures could open their Technicolor maws. I have begged the mail-order companies to spare me. I regret the waste of so much tree life, ink, and hopeful prose, but I don't want to see it. Every picture can plant a seed that starts growing in the brain, unfolding its leaves, curling tendrils around the mind's eye and the heart's desire, growing into a question about one more new thing. That question starts out as, "What will this do for me?" and somewhere in its tender growth it turns into "What will people make of me when I have this?"

And that, of course, is the silliest question in the world. They will make of me what they want, every time, while utterly failing to notice what shoes I was wearing when I made my point. Guests will eat the food but rarely remember the silver or china. They would talk about it later, I expect, if I plopped the mashed potatoes directly onto the table in front of them. Barring that, the vessels are largely invisible. Silliest of all are women who buy things to doll themselves up for men. I know there will be exceptions, and pardon me for bluntness, but in my experience of men on the subject of women's clothing, they notice the categories "off" and "on," and the finer distinctions evaporate. As for men, who can get silly about vehicles, let me state for the record: if you think the car you drive will impress a female with anything beyond the timeliness with which it delivered you to your appointed meeting, guess again. So it goes.

The people who love us are blind to our material trappings, and those who don't will find fault with us regardless—it's just as easy to despise someone for having too much as for having too little. Buying material goods to secure respect and position in the world is delusional. A migratory songbird might as well line her nest with souvenirs and photos of the Sunny South, making a creative statement and settling in. Winter will still come. Only the hard passage can really save us.

I consider it no small part of my daily work to sort out the differences between want and need. I'm helped along the way by my friend Wendell, without his ever knowing it. He advises me to ask, in the first place, whether I wish to purchase a solution to a problem I don't have. Down through the ages we've been threatened with these: ring around the collar, waxy yellow buildup, and iron-poor tired blood were all the products of a fairly unsophisticated advertising industry, and still they sent consumers running for the cure. Now the advertisers are psychologists; they are wizards. They convince us we must zip around and dazzle all who see us, distinguishing ourselves in every possible way from the tedium of peerage. In other words, I can be saved from a problematic life of blending in, listening and learning from others more than I show them of myself, working slowly and humbly at regular tasks, appearing normally human, and being quiet for long stretches—all the basic ingredients of one of my better days. I am offered a solution to the tragedy of being . . . well, let's think about it. Me.

"Virtually all of our consumption now is extravagant, and virtually all of it consumes the world," Wendell says in his essay, and I tell him, "Gosh, you are so right." I need a friend like this, in a world that is getting darn noisy about the things I ought to buy. When I set my table for company and feel the faintest edge of shame that our glasses don't all match, then I set an imaginary place for my friend. I tell him, "Look here, you see? They all still hold water. I'll replace these when they've all gotten broken." We raise a toast to old things.

A new purchase, he insists, "should not replace or disrupt anything good that already exists, and this includes family and community relationships." That is the wisest, hardest lesson. That is a risk with most replacements, period. Every time we throw out an old thing and put in its place a new one, however simple or beautiful or innocuous, that act has cost us something. In some small or large way, the purchase nicked at family, community, and self-worth.

It cost us money, for one thing. Working for and spending money take us by increment away from the sacred core of our lives: our children, our time, our grace. And that new thing extracted a price from the world, too, scooping right out of its belly some share of its minerals or fibers, its fuels burned black-ly for the energy of manufacture, packaging, and transport. However "green" or earth-friendly a new product may be, it is still a flat-out moral waste of goodness if we did not really need it in the first place.

Some may dismiss all this as a specious concern, believing that the prob-lem of trying not to buy things is a rare privilege of the upper classes. They would be wrong. It's a grievous truth, I agree, that too many U.S. citizens gen-uinely lack shelter and food—people who work full-time and still can't be sure of a roof over their children's heads. But the great majority of us have more than any sentient being needs, and still we plot to buy more. Lack of money is no obstacle to consumption, evidently. Consumer debt for luxuries such as TVs and vacations is now common.

The siren song of needless want inflicts internal damage on people of ev-ery class. Buying new things accosts our stability, our satisfaction with our-selves and one another as we already were. It's the most insidious harm of a materially obsessed culture: that the mad dash toward new things, whether it's cell phones or this year's hemlines, contrives an injury upon those left behind with the old. I have known poor people to buy fashionable new clothes for their children instead of food, preferring hunger to having their children judged. Every one of us who participates in the fundamentalism of fashion is participating in that brutal conspiracy.

I have also known people to describe themselves as "poor," to actually think of themselves this way, while leading lives in which they eat well, have secure shelter, dress warmly, avail themselves of good health care, and stand in possession of more material goods than many a whole village in Peru or China. But finer things exist somewhere, exquisitely imagined goods and ser-vices that richer people can afford, and so the self-titled paupers deplore their lesser condition or else they go into debt. It breaks my heart to see it. It breaks my heart to know I play a role in this drama somehow, simply by having more than someone else. It's why I throw out the catalogues, don't hang out with the retail-therapy crowd, and despise as cruel those lifestyle programs about the super-rich; these things can only teach us dissatisfaction. It's a dreadful, hun-gry cycle, and I hate it. I want to shove something large and whole in its mouth so all this craving will stop.

I have such respect for the art of buying nothing. It is honorable work to be happy just as we are. To see without coveting, to want without taking—

these disciplines have dropped out of nearly every religion practiced in our land. To "consider the lilies" nowadays would only lead to buying them. We tell ourselves that buying is healing, self-expression, graciousness, duty, even "thrift" when we get two for the price of one. We take pride in these so-called virtues while our hearts cave in with the dread that we are still poor, no matter what we own. Modesty and compassion obviously got dumped by the side of the road, and frugality is pilloried in the town square. Our country has distinguished itself for its bizarre material contradictions: widespread child hunger and rampant adult obesity; unparalleled debt and unbridled consumption. I can only understand it as mental illness on a grand social scale. But it isn't a nation, per se, that is behaving this way—it is ourselves, one elective purchase at a time. We love to tell ourselves and everybody else: it's a free country. So, then, whose fault is this mess?

Mine, if I let it happen in my own house. I've lived years of my life with scarcely any money, and years with plenty, but what a body needs remains constant, or so it should seem. So I'm troubled when household purchases fluctuate as they do with the tides of our fortune. I try harder to hold a steady course. When material excess begins to look normal, I occasionally reorient myself (and my kids) through periods of work among people whose worldly goods fit in a wheelbarrow and whose wardrobe is the single article that keeps the sun off their backs. For anyone who can do it—through vocational, religious, or volunteer efforts—I recommend this as a permanent cure for the illness of mind that confuses "out of style" with "privation."

But for regular, everyday infusions of clarity, I can just sit down right here and read Wendell Berry. I return again and again to that set of rules, my dependable WWWD. Can I get it locally? Will it do better work? Can I fix it myself? Will it save more energy and utility than it cost the world to produce it? And above all, couldn't I live perfectly well without it? It is sublime capitalist heresy, and also almost always the truth, to say yes, and live without. The people who stand up against a dangerous fundamentalism invariably will be called prophets, fools, or curmudgeons; given the options, I've decided "curmudgeon" is a fair enough aspiration. My kids already know that "because it's ten years old" is not by itself a reason to replace something, whether it's a car or a sweater. All of us hope our children and marriages will surpass that mark without obsolescence. We'd do well to hold the same hope for our cars and sweaters.

The fundamentalism of consumption, the religion in which the consumer becomes the advertiser—this sermon is delivered to me as needed by my minister and consultant, my twelve-step sponsor, the Most Reverend Berry. He makes me laugh.

At the slightest hint of a threat to their complacency, they repeat, like a chorus of toads, the notes sounded by their leaders in industry. The past was gloomy, drudgery-ridden, servile, meaningless, and slow. The present, thanks only to purchasable products, is meaningful, bright, lively, centralized, and fast. The future, thanks only to more purchasable products, is going to be even better. [1]

I picture myself a toad in a chorus of toads. I vow to be something better. A sleek frog, maybe. A salamander. I will wriggle out of this mess, day by day.

Am I making progress? I don't know. I do have a "cell number" now, so I am imprisoned to that extent. I write with a computer, too. I'm scalded each time I turn it on by the essay under discussion—specifically, by the line that blazes boldfaced in my memory: "I would hate to think that my work as a writer could not be done without a direct dependence on strip-mined coal." [2] I hate thinking that too. Here I go. Whatever I write had better be worth that drear price tag.

That equation keeps me focused, I must say. I bear in mind these devices I use are luxuries, not necessities, and set myself on a course toward worthy outcome. "When somebody has used a computer to write a work that is demonstrably better than Dante's," Wendell declares, and when the computer is proven to be the secret of that success, then he says he'll speak of computers with a more respectful tone (though he still will not buy one). [3] Lord have mercy, but I'm not even entering that race. I am just aiming each day for a draft that's demonstrably better than the gobbledygook I wrote yesterday, saddled as I am with a brain that will not, however I might beat my brow, be forced to work like Dante's or Wendell Berry's. To save my life I can't write a book from beginning to end. I seem to write them from the inside out, twisting them around like a dog trying to put on a pair of pajamas, panting and craning my neck until I've finally gotten the thing buttoned up, face forward, right side out. For that organizing miracle I need the help of strip-mined coal and a computer. I've tried other methods. Before I could afford a computer, I handwrote or typed my books for years, dispirited always by my feeble progress.

So I burn the midnight oil, grateful to get it, but aggrieved by my knot of excuses and dependency; I'm aggrieved alongside my mentor, I think, who allows that he burns some strip-mined coal at his house too. "I did not say that I proposed to end forthwith all my involvement in harmful technology, for I do not know how to do that. I said merely that I want to limit such involvement, and to a certain extent I do know how to do that." [4] Good, then. To a certain extent, I do too. I'm not righteous, but fully conscious of my wrongs. I use things I could well do without, possess some things I surely don't need. And I'll yet buy more, probably, before all is said and done. But not many, I hope.

I can survive in a thing-addicted society one day at a time, vowing I will get through today without buying any new stuff. Tomorrow also. Whether or not my small conservation has done the world any good, it will do me some good. I can walk through a week without anything brand-new in my life beyond the likes of these: a hen's fresh-laid egg resting hotly in my palm; a black and brown woolly worm hurrying into my path to deliver his late-breaking forecast. An old poem recited for the first time in my youngest child's voice. The tremble of leaves before a rising storm. The yellow curve of a new October moon. If I can clear the space in my life to seize hold of these, and save my strongest cravings for their ilk, well then, praise be.

Notes

1. Wendell Berry, *What Are People For?* (San Francisco: North Point, 1987), 175.
2. Ibid., 170.
3. Ibid., 171.
4. Ibid., 176.

Katherine Dalton

Fidelity

WHEN I WAS in my twenties I came home to Kentucky to visit one fall and was invited by my father to a supper hosted by one of his old friends. I had then been living in Connecticut and New York City for several years. Everyone else at the party had come straight from riding and was dirty and tired and in a good mood, and as this was my father's crowd I was the youngest there by several decades and hadn't seen most of these people in years. So it surprised me a little to notice, after a half hour or so, that I felt more relaxed there than I had in ages. Partly, of course, it was being home and amidst the courtesy of those people, but I also found that for the first time in a long while I wasn't straining to understand the conversation. I understood both the text and the subtext—what was said and what was meant. I was back among people who spoke my own language.

While I had realized in college that in mores and history I would always be a foreigner up north, I hadn't realized I was a foreigner in language, too. The strain of expressing myself clearly and of understanding accurately people whose words are the same but whose unspoken meanings are different is a subtle one, and I noticed it suddenly that night at the party by its absence. But it was a strain nonetheless, and not so very different from the anxiety felt by an American lost on a French highway, asking painfully "*Où est Paris?*" Only it was Kentucky I was looking for.

There are many books I love, written in many different subtextual dialects of English, but when I read Wendell I am always sinking once again into the ease and pleasure of my most native native tongue. In his stories I hear the voices of my parents' generation, and particularly my grandparents', and all those older Dalton and Baker cousins I have down in south-central Kentucky, in the foothills of the Appalachians. Different people love Wendell's work for different reasons: there are the fellow poets, and the ecological activists, and the liberal patriots, and the conservative moralists, and perhaps to some the appeal of his novels is an exotic one—they are so rural and old-fashioned. But to me he has always been transcendently familiar, and I have wondered if he has a particularly loyal readership of expatriated southerners, who find their grandmothers in his books, too, and a way of talking that is so welcomingly reminiscent as to be a relief.

No artist is sui generis, but Wendell would be the very last person to claim it. Few writers are more evidently indebted to their family and neighbors than he is—his books are full of the voices of those people, many of them long dead but nonetheless alive on paper and in Wendell's memory. In Henry County his characters have an extra dimension, because many of them are drawn from individuals who are still well remembered here. I am not from Henry County myself, but since my husband's family is, he knew some of these people, or his father did, or his eighty-seven-year-old cousin did, and so we talk about them. Those are the kinds of conversations Wendell loves: I have sat in his daughter's parlor and listened to him and a neighbor recall people who died years ago, remembering their names and their families, and who married whom, and the things they did and said. If he didn't love conversations like that, he would not have nearly so much fiction in him.

I never knew either of Wendell's parents, but I have an older neighbor, Martha Carroll, who was good friends with both, and I think they must have been very like her in outlook and manners. And what Mrs. Carroll is, in her quiet way, is a great lady. She is politically minded and clear-sighted yet tactful; she has the kind of manners that are perfectly correct and yet make anyone feel comfortable (which is the point of manners, after all); and she once wrote me a simple note that was as gracious and intelligent a letter as I have ever received. Rural areas are losing all kinds of knowledge as they lose people, but one of the most noticeable losses is in articulateness, and I think the senior Berrys, like Mrs. Carroll, must have been particularly able to express themselves. John Berry Sr. was a lawyer, after all—a small-town lawyer who also spoke with some regularity in front of Senate committees. Some families don't argue about anything over the dinner table, but I think Wendell must have heard a lot of talk at home about community and farming issues, and a lot of what was hashed out over supper or in the field has worked its way into his writing. I have read a few of John Berry Sr.'s speeches, and some of Wendell's phrasing and rhythm is very like his father's, the way a child's handwriting is often very like his parent's. I can even hear John Berry's legal training in the way Wendell argues his essays, logically and unstoppably moving from point to point to conclusion.

Wendell has taken a public stand as a lover of the small and local, and has lived true to that stand, and if this is part of his appeal in other places, it is also appreciated at home. There is a feed and seed / general store in his hometown of Port Royal that Wendell has patronized for years, and he likes to quote the late proprietor, saying, "If William Van Hawkins doesn't have it, you don't need it." He is almost always willing to accept a local invitation to speak, even when he is accepting few other requests, and even though he doesn't like public speaking. As stockholders in a small bank, Wendell and other members of his family (notably his brother, John) have had a large part in keeping United Citizens locally owned, which means that loans are decided locally and that the bank is reinvesting its depositors' money here—manuring its own ground. I think too that there are some longtime neighbors who are not particularly interested in poetry or novels but who value Wendell highly for the man he is, which is really the greater compliment.

Henry County has changed a surprising amount in the ten years I have lived here. Whatever good may also come of it, change is in and of itself an evil, as Dr. Johnson said, and it must be so because it must so often mean a loss of something worth having—youth and strength, loved ones, the world as we knew it and understood it. To a great extent Wendell has been a bard of the lost and of the losers. He is a yellow-dog Democrat in a country tilting more and more Republican; he is an ecologist in an increasingly polluted world; he is a small-scale farmer in a market that wants its vegetables cheap and out of season from Mexico; he is a poet in a land in love with television. For most of Wendell's life he has watched his home state lose both farmland and farmers at a great rate, and that loss is only speeding up now with the end of the tobacco support program, whose guaranteed price paid so many farm mortgages on so many small farms for so long. For many of our neighbors, last year or the year before was their last to grow a tobacco crop, and most of these people have grown tobacco all their lives. Many of them were good at it, and now the need for that particular skill is gone. Nor are the changes confined to tobacco. Farming is less and less a way of life for all of us who live in rural Kentucky. In Eminence, Henry County's largest town, the schools have gone to a year-round schedule with little complaint—so few children are needed at home anymore to work what used to be the crucial summer months. And the twenty-one-year-old son of one of our neighbors told us last year that he is getting out of farming entirely, though he comes from as dedicated and proud a farming family as you could know, with a great capacity for work.

Yet amidst it all Wendell is a remarkably even-keeled man, utterly courteous, deeply happy and positive—a man imbued with such a strong faith that he is at peace even amidst the changes he deplores and has spent his whole life fighting. I cannot think of anyone who has fought harder and yet is more at peace. This is one reason some people revere Wendell: he has that quality of detachment that comes from the very strongest fidelity—from love, real love, for a real place and for real people, weeds and weaknesses and all. If I can see any hint of anger in Wendell, it shows only in the way he will wrestle an idea down to its core meaning, worry it till he has every shred of meat off the bone, and in the way he works and works. I know he is worried that he will run out of time before he has finished saying all he has to say.

"Wendell Berry is the Sergeant York charging unnatural odds across our no-man's-land of ecology. . . . Consider him an ally."—Ken Kesey, in *The Last Supplement to the Whole Earth Catalog*, 1968
Photograph by Guy Mendes, courtesy of Ann Tower Gallery

Patrick J. Deneen

Wendell Berry and the Alternative Tradition in American Political Thought

IN *THE UNSETTLING OF AMERICA*, Wendell Berry described America as a nation with two fundamental "tendencies." These two tendencies were set in motion by the earliest European settlers in America and continue to define the fundamental worldviews of most contemporary Americans—and, increasingly, the modern world. The "dominant tendency" was manifested as a proclivity toward mobility and restlessness that aimed at maximum extraction of resources and accumulation of profits from the bounty of the new continent. Berry acknowledges that this worldview was dominant because it was "organized" at the very inception of the settlement of the new continent. However, Berry also recognizes "another tendency" that characterized a great many other settlers: this "weaker" tradition was marked by "the tendency to stay put, to say 'No farther. This is the place.'"[1]

Berry is almost certainly correct that there have been two traditions in America from the time of its inception, ones that he sees manifested in the respective behavior of America's colonials, whether "colonizing" in an aggressive form or in the traditional sense qua "settlement." Yet Berry is arguably incurious about the *sources* of these disparate patterns. Unless there is a presumption that these respective behaviors were merely instinctual or reflexive, one can rightly take Berry's contention as a point of departure, not only to inquire into the philosophical sources of the behavior of these colonists, but perhaps even Berry's own sources. For it may well be that the colonists were enacting a set of philosophical assumptions that were as implicit in their actions as they are to Berry's thought. Taking those actions as embodiments of certain philosophical traditions that contended for supremacy at the time of the American founding, and remain deeply embedded in the American tradition, one can point to the early modern liberal tradition as a primary source for the "dominant" tradition of colonization qua exploitation, and a contending republican or communitarian tradition that had its deepest sources in ancient philosophy and the biblical tradition. To some—one thinks of Louis Hartz—the dominant liberal tradition has been the *only* tradition in American political history.[2] Berry rejects this monolithic view of American political history, instead joining a number of defenders of the view that the "alternative" tradition, drawn especially from classical and biblical sources, has been present throughout American political history, though in a subdominant tone—one ever less audible—to its more dominant rival.[3]

The Dominant Tradition

America's dominant tendency was drawn philosophically from older sources, such as Francis Bacon and Thomas Hobbes; derived from early modern sources ranging from John Locke and Adam Smith; was articulated domestically by such figures as Thomas Paine, Thomas Jefferson (sometimes), James Madison, and Alexander Hamilton; and was officially instantiated in America's founding documents. At the heart of this tradition is a belief in natural scarcity, of a recalcitrant nature that only grudgingly provides the basic necessities of human existence. The modern age was inaugurated with the effort to increase the offerings of nature by means of the increase of human power and dominion. According to Francis Bacon, science aims above all at the "relief of man's estate." Bacon initiated the modern scientific project of conquering nature with the aphorism "Knowledge is power." According to Bacon, nature is comparable to a prisoner who withholds its secrets from his inquisitor. The modern scientific project seeks to increase our knowledge about those secrets by any means, including, Bacon suggested, torture.

Building on this foundation, liberalism was conceived by assuming that humans are, by nature, self-interested and self-maximizing individuals. Bacon's onetime secretary, Thomas Hobbes, declared that the inescapable motivation of human beings is their endless and restless pursuit of "power after power that ceaseth only in death." Human existence is, by nature, one of conflict and warfare. In this natural condition—one in which human life is "poor, nasty, brutish, and short"—there is no culture or industry, no productive economy of any kind. By means of a "social contract," or an agreement of convention, humans are enabled not only to ensure peace and security but to achieve "commodious living." Comfort, plenty, and culture can only be achieved in a condition that is *unnatural;* "nature," including human nature, is hostile to the goods of human life. As such, it must be harnessed, controlled, and subverted.

John Locke—America's philosopher, according to some—expanded this commendation of "commodious living," arguing in *The Second Treatise on Government* that the fundamental aim of human society is the increase of economic growth. According to Locke, early human societies permitted only the accumulation of an amount of property that was sufficient for the continuity of human life. However, with the invention of money—a contrivance that allowed humans to circumvent the onetime limitation on accumulation—namely, only so much material that would not spoil—unlimited acquisition became both possible and desirable. This unlimited acquisition did not prejudice or fundamentally disadvantage even those who were ill-equipped or even unwilling to increase their holdings, since, according to Locke, the increase of prosperity of some individuals leads to the increase of wealth of the society at large. Thus, Locke argued—anticipating Ronald Reagan's adage that "a rising tide raises all boats"—that the poorest day laborer in England (i.e., in a growth economy) was wealthier and thereby in a more desirable estate than the greatest Indian chief in America (who presided over a subsistence economy). Society was devised in order to secure not only peace but the perpetual and unlimited increase of human wealth based upon the extraction, accumulation, and manipulation of natural resources. The modern liberal tradition commends understanding human beings above all as *Homo economicus*, and economics as the science of increase and growth, of dominion and mastery over nature.

America was conceived largely in light of the aims of this modern project and arguably is the nation par excellence in embodying its belief in the preeminence of individuals who aim above all to harness nature toward the end of increasing material wealth. Its founding documents, the Declaration of Independence and the Constitution, attest to the liberal presuppositions and framework that have guided the nation and formed the citizenry since its inception. The Declaration of Independence enshrines the centrality of natural rights—"endowed by their Creator"—in America's self-understanding. Rights both precede and are retained within political society: they are "inalienable" and inherent possessions of each individual; thus a central presupposition among Americans is that the individual precedes, and in theory and practice is prior to, government and commonweal. In political terms, the theory of liberal rights leads to a stress upon individual liberty and suspicion of if not outright hostility toward government (cf. Thoreau's claim, attributed to Jefferson and similar to statements by Thomas Paine, that "that government which governs best, governs least"). In economic terms, the theory of liberal rights lends itself to a fierce belief in individual agency in the use and disposal of one's property. Liberalism's base assumption that all human motivation arises from self-interest further undermines the claims for a common good and rather privileges the priority of individual choice and economic growth, regardless of the consequences to both moral and economic ecology. It is almost inconceivable to imagine a modern political leader raising doubts about the priority of liberty as a national ideal, or questioning the continued wisdom of growth as the major ambition of our economic system.[4] It would seem that there is simply *no* alternative tradition to this dominant liberal tradition.

Berry contests this supposition, however, both in theory and in his daily practice. He points to an alternative tradition in America, initially composed of settlers who sought to put down roots, to foster community, and create colonies in the original sense of that term. Yet while this has been a distinctive American tradition, Berry acknowledges that over time this tendency was rendered almost invisible, not only because it was not "organized," but because the dominant tendency was actively hostile toward the weaker tendency. "Generation after generation, those who intended to remain and prosper where they were have been dispossessed and driven out, or subverted and exploited where they were, by those who were carrying out some version of the search for El Dorado. Time after time, in place after place, these conquerors have fragmented and demolished traditional communities. . . . They have always said that what they destroyed was outdated, provincial, and contemptible."[5] A more aggressive and hostile form of colonization has displaced its more modest counterpart over time.

This alternative early American worldview, according to Berry, has been subsequently and variously defended in the written work of such figures as the founders,[6] Thomas Jefferson, Henry David Thoreau, and members of the American southern agrarian movement, especially Allen Tate. It has been instantiated in the practices and the worldview of American agrarians and populists.

But its deepest sources are (1) classical political philosophy—particularly Aristotle, with his stress upon humans as political animals who together participate actively in the life of a polity that aims at the common good—and (2) the biblical and Christian tradition, with its call to reverence toward the divinely created order, its injunction against avarice and self-aggrandizement, its insistence upon self-sacrifice, and its commandments enjoining humility and love. At the core of Berry's worldview—one that is primarily drawn from his lived experience as a farmer and member of a small community—lies a set of philosophical and religious assumptions that he occasionally acknowledges but that more often silently undergird his commonsense reflections. Although Berry is rarely inclined to bring more explicitly to the surface the substratum of philosophical and religious belief that provides the foundation of his thought, doing so is not against the spirit of his work.

A Kentucky Aristotelian

Perhaps the most intriguing philosophic source of Berry's thought is only implicit at best—most probably a resemblance not derived from strong first-hand knowledge but nevertheless philosophically sympathetic to it. Remarkably, at various instances throughout his corpus, Berry uncannily echoes the thought of Aristotle. His standard, like Aristotle's, is nature. Nature sets the terms of and establishes limits to human undertakings. Humanity is best positioned to thrive, not through the successful conquest or exploitation of nature, but rather through a respectful heeding of nature's laws and limits. Nature—of which humanity is a part in both Berry's and Aristotle's reckoning—is the whole that governs all of its constitutive parts. While liberalism tends to focus upon and give priority to the various "parts" of nature, including and above all the individual—and hence leads to the foolish belief that those parts can escape the implications of their connection to, and reliance upon, nature—Berry's alternative understanding gives priority to the "whole" and understands all parts within that context. Berry writes:

> We seem to have been living for a long time on the assumption that we can safely deal with parts, leaving the whole to take care of itself. But now the news from everywhere is that we have to begin gathering up the scattered pieces, figuring out where they belong, and putting them back together. For the parts can be reconciled to each other only within the pattern of the whole to which they belong.[7]

Like Aristotle, Berry argues that the whole precedes the parts, that is, that the parts can thrive only when the whole is considered, comprehended, heeded, and cultivated.

In political terms, priority of the "whole" means that less comprehensive "parts" of the city—such as economic life—must be subordinate to the dictates of common good. Like Aristotle, Berry believes that there are two kinds of economy—one that understands acquisition to be without limits, and hence inclines to exploitation, and one that exists within due measure of both human nature and the natural world.[8] Aristotle wrote that some believe in the priority of "business," that is, the idea that economics involves the accumulation of goods "without limit" and is therefore ungoverned by law that enjoins constraint. However, Aristotle contended, such a belief is concerned only with "living," not "living well."[9] To live well, he argued, one must strive to understand the distinction between goods that are necessary for "living well" and those that are superfluous; those that are superfluous, he said, contribute to our enslavement to our desires and appetites.[10] To live well one must subordinate the imperatives that drive the economic logic of accumulation without limit to the governance of political life and a conception of human good and commonweal.[11] Like Aristotle, Berry rejects the view that the market should occupy an exclusive place in considerations of the good life; rather, economics (understood now as "household management") is rightly subject to political life.[12] The "market" occupies space in the city, not vice versa.

While nature provides a standard for judging the good life, for Berry, as for Aristotle, the seemingly simple standard of nature turns out to be a challenging and imprecise guide, one that requires judgment and prudence more than science and logic. Berry rejects the typically polarized contemporary views of the relationship of humankind to nature, one comprised of "nature conquerors" and the purported lovers of nature.[13] The former claim that there is a thoroughgoing adversarial relationship between humans and nature; the latter claim that there is no fundamental disjunction or tension between the two. The former reject that humans are part of nature altogether, while the latter tend toward pantheism. Berry finds both positions to be facile. Instead, in strikingly Aristotelian terms, he advances the "roomy and bewildering" alternative of "the middle."[14] Humanity is at once a part of, and separate from, nature, which is at once "hospitable to us, but also absolutely dangerous to us (it is going to kill us sooner or later), and we are absolutely dependent upon it." The two polarized positions represent fundamentally false choices: humans cannot live wholly as parts of nature, inasmuch as they must consciously decide how to use it for their survival. There is no escape from the necessity of using nature; there is only the choice of how best to establish that relationship, whether as exploiters or stewards. On the other hand, while humans can live for a time in an exploitative relationship with nature, in the long term nature will exact a cost for this alternative extreme and make continued human life increasingly difficult if not impossible. Nature is finally inescapable.

Thus, much like Aristotle, who recognized that humans are "by nature political animals"—that is, it is in their nature to be conventional creatures, albeit ones governed by certain laws, above all by the law of being a human and not a "god or beast"—Berry recognizes that humans occupy an extensive middle ground in which the human relationship to nature must be guided by conscious decision, cultivation, and judgment. Humans cannot be the unconscious "animals" of the pantheists any more than they can be the self-sufficient "gods" suggested by those who would establish human dominion over nature.

Humans uniquely possess the conscious capacity to determine their relationship to nature, but they can determine that relationship reasonably only within the bounds established by nature—both "wildness" and human nature. *Culture* is the inescapable medium of human life and the conduit of the human relation to the natural sphere, as it is for Aristotle: "To take a creature who is biologically a human and to make him or her fully human is a task that requires many years." It is culture, including the acculturation within polities, above all, that makes us "into humans—creatures capable of prudence, justice, fortitude, temperance, and the other virtues." Like Aristotle, Berry observes that, without this cultivation of the human animal into the human being, humanity has an opposite tendency to become worse than beasts: "For our history reveals that, stripped of the restraints, disciplines, and ameliorations of culture, humans are not 'natural,' not 'thinking animals' or 'naked apes,' but monsters—indiscriminate and insatiable killers and destroyers. We differ from other creatures, partly, in our susceptibility to monstrosity."[15]

Above all, humans must exercise prudence, or the Aristotelian intellectual virtue of *phronesis*. Humans must integrate culture and nature, neither assuming their actions to be wholly in accord with or derived from nature *simpliciter,* nor acting as if that they can flourish apart from, or in hostility to, nature. Akin to Arisotelian *phronesis,* judgment must be formed based not on abstraction or "theory" but upon particular circumstance and local knowledge (albeit particularity that is always guided by the demands and limits set by nature). Humans must "consciously and conscientiously ask of their work: Is this good for us? Is this good for our place? And the questioning and answering of this phase is minutely particular: it can occur only with reference to particular artifacts, events, places, ecosystems, and neighborhoods."[16]

Thoughtfulness as a Vocation

Aristotelian thought, and classical philosophy more generally, was almost always an implicit contribution to the "alternative tradition" in America: seeing a vast gulf between life lived in the city-states of antiquity and the nation-state of modernity, relatively few Americans have turned to the Greeks for direct inspiration. The primary conduit of antiquity's main tenets, therefore, was the biblical tradition, particularly the Hellenistic aspects of the New Testament as well as the overlapping beliefs held by ancient Greek philosophers and authors of the biblical texts, both the Old and New Testaments. It is this tradition that is more often the explicit textual source of Berry's thought and that especially undergirds Berry's understanding of an economics based upon *vocation* rather than self-interest. "Vocation," which etymologically reflects an understanding that our work is a "calling," and hence partakes in and contributes to an order that extends beyond our own discrete actions, demands reflection and thoughtfulness. By contrast, modern and liberal forms of work have their origins in self-interest and the imperatives of acquisition and hence have the effect of narrowing our perspective and blinding us to the broader consequences of our actions and our work.

With its stress upon individualism, modern society tends to obscure our acts from their sources and their consequences. In the first instance, modern life puts temporal blinders around our eyes, forcing us to see only the present and inducing blindness toward the past and permitting an exceedingly narrow view of the future. Short-term thinking—the use and destruction of nature for our satisfaction today—is undertaken and justified in light of a blinkered and unjustified belief that any shortages or adverse consequences resulting from our current activities will be solved by technological progress in the future. This restricted temporal horizon severs us from the past. Technological optimism and blind faith in progress can be embraced only if one simultaneously harbors a "hatred for the past."[17] What appears to be our belief in the future—our technological optimism—in fact manifests itself as a free pass to live irresponsibly in the present. It serves as an easy excuse to avoid confronting the consequences of one's current actions. Our seeming future-orientation is nothing more than a deeply constricted form of presentism. Our disinclination to recall the past induces an unrealism about the future and thereby leads us to a drastically constrained short-term time horizon. Berry's work—bound up in the inescapable rhythm of time in which past is present and future is, like agriculture, a seed that will take a certain form under certain conditions of cultivation (or will fail to flourish in the absence of cultivation)—seeks to restore the entirety of the human temporal horizon and thereby restore the possibility of realism.

Our pervasive ignorance of the sources of the basic necessities of human life leads to our inability thoughtfully to understand the sources and consequences of our economy, especially in the forms of our consumption and the production of waste. Berry excoriates the exploitative sensibility of economic agents who most often have no connection to a locality and who see it only in terms of what use any particular place can have for economic growth overall. Calling this the "absentee economy," he notes the way in which local particularities are largely reduced to their usefulness for other parts of the country or the world.

> The global economy (like the national economy before it) operates on the superstition that the deficiencies or needs or wishes of one place may safely be met by the ruination of another place. To build houses here, we clear-cut forests there. To have air-conditioning here, we strip-mine forests there. To drive our cars here, we sink our oil wells there. It is an absentee economy. Most people aren't destroying what they can see. . . . All

the critical questions affecting our use of the earth are left to be answered by "the market" or the law of supply and demand. An economy without limits is an economy without discipline.[18]

According to the assessment of the market—a seeming impersonal force, the collection of individual decisions that transpires without planning or collective intention—there can be no calculable valuation of what is disrupted or destroyed by the extraction of resources, or the exploitation of labor, from various localities. The objections by any such localities that economic logic may prove destructive of long-standing communal forms can have no effect, inasmuch as such forms of life almost never contribute to an increase or improvement in the bottom line. All evaluations are made in terms of whether there is a short-term increase in wealth, prosperity, and efficiency.

Modern economic systems tend toward abstraction, replacing exchange that closely demonstrates the connections between work and its products with complex financial and monetary interactions that obscure those relations. Connections between our actions and their consequences become increasingly difficult to discern and evaluate. Berry writes often of the "estrangement" experienced by modern peoples who are largely sheltered from the activities necessary for life and who do not perceive the costs in that division. Modern consumers—and the word *consumers* is revealing—largely believe that the cost of an object reflects its true "costs." They neglect how modern production incurs severe costs that will be heavily borne by future generations. Thus, for instance, "the cost of soil erosion is not deducted from the profit on a package of beefsteak, just as the loss of forest, topsoil, and human homes on a Kentucky mountainside does not reduce the profit on a ton of coal."[19] An economy that inaccurately calculates the bottom line is an economy that produces vast quantities of waste and necessarily exploits nature. It is an economy without reverence or respect, without a sense of the past or a respect for the future.

Modern peoples confuse the value accorded by the market with *true* value. This is especially true when one considers the degradation of agriculture in the form of the food we eat. "Money does not bring forth food," Berry writes. "Neither does the technology of the food system. Food comes from nature and from the work of people. If the supply of food is to be continuous for a long time, people must work in harmony with nature."[20] Because of the disconnection, in this instance, between our consumption of processed and packaged food and the origin of that sustenance, we consume thoughtlessly and wastefully. By valuing food because of its low price, we thoughtlessly support destructive forms of industrial agriculture, ones that in the present reap enormous crops—and profits—at the cost of future productivity, which will necessarily be limited by the loss of topsoil, the destruction of ecologies due to the pervasive introduction of agricultural monocultures (the agricultural version of our human monoculture, such as most forms of popular "culture"), and the depletion of resources such as water and fossil fuels. Only by full valuation of labor and the fruits of that work can we begin properly to evaluate —to accord proper value upon—our patterns of consumption and waste. Only by accounting for what is lost or destroyed by present practices and the burdens those actions will impose upon our children and future generations can we begin to calculate the true cost of our actions.

Altogether, the narrowing forms of self-interest, the imperative of acquisition, the blinkered temporal view, the rejection of "drudgery" in favor of ease often built on the unmitigated exploitation of natural resources, and the abstraction induced by the modern economic order lead to pervasive forms of thoughtlessness. At the heart of Berry's critique of this thoughtlessness lies a rejection of Adam Smith's assumptions that an economy could work best based upon ever-greater forms of specialization. Berry does not reject the necessity of the division of labor as such; however, extensive specialization takes place in a philosophic context that actively *discourages* thoughtfulness about the connections of all the various forms of work in a complex industrial economy.[21] The whole is understood to be an aggregate of individual choices, an "invisible hand" that spontaneously orients society in the direction it chooses. We are relieved of the duty or obligation to reflect upon the implications of our work: such reflection forms no part of our actual work.

Adam Smith's insistence that narrow specialization would contribute to the wealth of nations represents a rejection of the biblical understanding of a proper division of labor—one in which the aim is not *increase* of material wealth but a proper understanding of the relationships among humans and between God and man. The biblical text that best articulates this proper relationship is 1 Corinthians 12, in which Paul relates that God wishes and intends that humans possess a diversity of gifts in the form of different vocations (1 Corinthians 12:1–11). God allots such gifts diversely precisely so that humans will come to understand their own partiality as parts of the body and thus come to a better understanding of the whole—both the human community and the human part in divine creation. Paul writes, "but now are they many members, yet but one body. And the eye cannot say unto the hand, I have no need of thee: nor again the head to the feet, I have no need of you. Nay, much more than those members of the body, which seem to be more feeble, are necessary" (1 Corinthians 12:20–22). Specialization has a way of divorcing our work from our understanding of its contributions to, and reliance upon, a greater whole. Rather than commending an invisible hand to coordinate our activities—thus rendering us wholly unconscious of, and un-concerned with, the sources and implications of our work—Paul instead in-sists that our work is properly undertaken with awareness of our own partial-ity and with thoughtfulness toward the ways in which our work contributes to the whole. Love, not self-interest, is the proper motivation that underlies our vocation.

In keeping with this biblical understanding, Berry believes an economy that commends narrow and thoughtless forms of specialization does not rep-resent the proper form of work; it is, in fact, bad work.

> Most of us get almost all the things we need by buying them; most of us know only vaguely, if at all, where these things come from; and most of us know not at all what damage is involved in their production. We are al-most entirely dependent on an economy of which we are almost entirely ignorant. The provenance, for example, not only of the food we buy at the store, but of the chemicals, fuels, metals, and other materials necessary to grow, harvest, transport, process, and package that food, is almost neces-sarily a mystery to us. To know the full economic history of a head of su-permarket cauliflower would require an immense job of research.[22]

Not only does the complexity of the modern economy make the likelihood of perceiving the various connections between different kinds of worth exceed-ingly difficult; before even arriving at that recognition, modern economic theory in fact *discourages* such thoughtfulness by its tendency instead to encourage short-term, individualistic, value-based (i.e., relativistic), and resource-exploitative ways of thinking. Thoughtlessness is our default posi-tion and a tendency that is only exacerbated by the resulting complexity of the extreme specialization resulting from the available kinds of work.

In contrast to the modern tendency toward abstraction, Berry calls for *thoughtfulness* in all its forms: thoughtfulness is, above all, our shared voca-tion and constitutes what Berry calls "good work." Good work involves our thoughtful reflection on the sources of life and the consequences of our work. Such work does not entail our full comprehension of all the constitutive ef-forts that go into the creation of a head of supermarket cauliflower or any product of a complex economic system. Good work, rather, entails the effort to see through a glass darkly toward the whole of which we are all constitutive members. Such an effort, in the first instance, acknowledges the existence of an Aristotelian and biblical *whole*: it forces upon our consciousness a recogni-tion that we act not merely as partialities nor as autonomous or monadic in-dividuals but as members of a large living organism of civilization. It forces to our consciousness recognition that, by acting in certain ways, we assent to—

or potentially withhold our assent from—the destruction of that whole. We move beyond thinking that there is an environmental crisis—since the "environment," Berry insists, is a formulation that, unlike "nature," suggests an entity "out there" and separate from us[23]—and instead experience that crisis as "a crisis of our lives as individuals, as family members, as community members, and as citizens."[24] We begin to understand how our actions implicate us in the whole, how we are inextricably linked in the creation of a common culture—or the undermining of that culture—and in the forging of a common good, or, more likely, the neglect of that good in the absence of commonality.

This form of thoughtfulness constitutes the human vocation: in contrast to Adam Smith, who claimed that the wealth of nations is built, above all, on increasing subdivisions of labor that necessarily blind us to the connection of our work to the broader good of society, Berry insists that good work consists in the obligation to reflect thoughtfully upon the connections we necessarily share, not only with one another, but with humans past, present, and yet unborn. Our "human vocation" calls on us to participate in "responsible membership" in the world.[25] Berry chastises participants of the modern liberal economy for "a profound failure of imagination." He continues by insisting that "most people now are living on the far side of a broken connection, and that this is potentially catastrophic. Most people are now fed, clothed, and sheltered from sources, in nature and in the work of other people, toward which they feel no gratitude and exercise no responsibility."[26] Properly understood, vocation results in the widespread invigoration of imagination and would be the necessary component of the one legitimate movement that Berry names "MTEWIID"—the "Movement to Teach the Economy What It Is Doing."[27] Through thoughtfulness and imagination, we can achieve what he calls "practical wholeness."[28]

While modern life divorces us from our sources of sustenance, thoughtfulness by contrast undergirds life within cultures and traditions that cultivate not only our understanding of those sources but a sense of gratitude, wonder, and honor. In such an alternative setting, we are enabled to see more readily our past, in the structures erected with care and thought of permanence by our forebears and the honor we pay them; in the customs and practices that we learn from our parents and from the elders of our community; in the more elementary forms of economy that permit us more closely to perceive the ways that our food and goods of human life are cultivated, produced, distributed, and replenished; and in the fact of our limits, including that ultimate limit of our mortality, evinced at every turn by the constraints imposed by community, lessons of self-control gained through our education, and a variety of traditional "forms," perhaps above all the inescapable presence of memorials to the dead.[29]

Thoughtfulness, from the perspective of liberalism, potentially deprives us of our full-blown liberty. Its consequence is to explode the assumption that we can base our actions solely upon our individual rights and the resulting freedom of choice. It dissolves the supposition that we can and ought to dispose of our property—what we have paid for, using our money—in whatever manner we see fit. Such thoughtfulness becomes a source of support for robust political action—actions that potentially, and likely, will restrict the liberty of individual actors, whether in the economic or personal spheres.[30]

Berry contends that in the end liberalism falsely understands liberty. Thoughtfulness and the understanding that results from it enable a true form of liberty—the liberty that develops from proper choices within properly understood limits. In this, Berry evokes both ancient Greek and Christian understandings of liberty as the free acceptance of proper limits. Ironically, the accumulation of our individual decisions leaves modern liberals profoundly unfree. We are, first and foremost, in the thrall of our appetites; we lack self-control and hence are incapable of the freedom of self-rule. But, further, in ways that become daily more evident to us, our dependence on globalized sources of labor and essential resources subjects us to forces far beyond our capacity to influence or control. America has abandoned the Jeffersonian ideal of economic self-sufficiency as a core basis for political liberty. In developing dependencies upon foreign powers, we are inevitably and inescapably drawn into the vagaries of foreign politics, into concern over the future of often-despicable regimes, and into "foreign entanglements" that have historically led to the transformation of republics into empires.[31] For the sake of cheaply produced goods and the avoidance of "drudgery," the republic increasingly loses its actual freedom—ironically enough, in the name of freedom (now freedom from any form of physical labor and the freedom to buy the cheapest goods): "The United States has chosen (if that is the right word) to become an import-dependent society rather than to live principally from its own land and the work of its own people, as if dependence on imported goods and labor can be consistent with political independence and self-determination. . . . The economic independence of families, communities, and even regions has now been almost completely destroyed."[32] In this sense, Berry seeks to return us to reality—not the fantasy of imagined freedom, but the actual liberty that can be achieved by individuals, families, communities, and polities with an appropriate understanding of limits and the choices possible within those bounds. We will return to reality, either by choice or by the force of natural limits imposed upon us. Berry urges us to take the path of freedom.

Notes

1. Wendell Berry, *The Unsettling of America: Culture and Agriculture* (San Francisco: Sierra Club Books, 1977), 4.

2. See Louis Hartz, *The Liberal Tradition in America* (New York: Harcourt, 1991). See also Vernon L. Parrington, *The Main Currents in American Thought,* 3 vols. (New York: Kessinger Publishing, 2005).

3. For "defenders" of this tradition, alternatively called by some the "republican" or "communitarian" or "civic democratic" traditions, see, e.g., Wilson Carey McWilliams, *The Idea of Fraternity in America* (Berkeley: University of California Press, 1973); Christopher Lasch, *The True and Only Heaven: Progress and Its Critics* (New York: Norton, 1991); Robert Booth Fowler, *The Dance with Community: The Contemporary Debate in American Political Thought* (Lawrence: University Press of Kansas, 1991); and Michael Sandel, *Democracy's Discontent: America's Search for a Public Philosophy* (Cambridge, MA: Belknap, 1998).

4. "Most of [these] concerns are not on the agenda of either major party. It is now impossible to imagine a major politician standing up in public and asking, Why are so many irreplaceable things, from mountains to memories, being destroyed by so-called economic development? Why are so many things we need, from healthy farms to health, being priced out of existence by the so-called free market?" Wendell Berry, "The Purpose of a Coherent Community," in *The Way of Ignorance* (Shoemaker and Hoard, 2005), 72.

5. Berry, *The Unsettling of America,* 4.

6. Berry dedicated his book *Citizenship Papers* (2003) to the signers of the Declaration of Independence. His understanding of the founders differs from that of most contemporary liberals inasmuch as Berry believes these men favored local self-governance.

7. Wendell Berry, "The Purpose of a Coherent Community," in *The Way of Ignorance,* 77; see also "Agriculture from the Roots Up," in ibid., 107–8.

8. See Wendell Berry, "Two Economies," in *Home Economics* (San Francisco: North Point, 1987), 54–75.

9. Aristotle, *The Politics,* trans. Carnes Lord (Chicago: University of Chicago Press, 1984), 1257b42, 48.

10. Berry has similarly argued that people should differentiate between what is required based on "need" and mere desire: "The way out lies only in a change of mind by which we will learn not to think of ourselves as 'consumers' in any sense. A consumer is one who uses things up, a concept that is alien to the creation, as are the concepts of waste and disposability. A more realistic and accurate vision of ourselves would teach us that our ecological obligations are to use, not use up; to use by the standard of real need, not of fashion or whim; and to relinquish what we have used in a way that returns to the common ecological fund from which it came." "Discipline and Hope," in *Recollected Essays* (San Francisco: North Point, 1981), 172.

11. Aristotle writes, "For self-sufficiency in possessions . . . is not limitless. . . .

There is such a boundary, just as in the other arts"(*The Politics*, 1256b30–34). Berry, like Aristotle, regards usury as a dubious economic activity, given that its sole aim is the acquisition of money. Aristotle argues that "usury is most reasonably hated because one's possessions derive from money itself and not from that for which it was supplied" (*The Politics*, 1258b2–4). Berry similarly writes, "Money value . . . can be said to be true only when it justly and stably represents the value of necessary goods, such as clothing, food, and shelter. . . . Humans can originate money value in the abstract, but only by inflation and usury, which falsify the value of necessary things and damage their natural and human sources" ("Two Economies," 61).

12. Berry writes, "Damage [to communities] is justified by its corporate perpetrators and their political abettors in the name of the 'free market' and 'free enterprise,' but this is a freedom that makes greed the dominant economic virtue, and it destroys the freedom of other people along with their communities and livelihood. . . . Because as individuals or even as communities we cannot protect ourselves against these [economic] aggressions, we need our state and national government to protect us" ("Compromise, Hell!" in *Way of Ignorance*, 24–25).

13. Berry, "Preserving Wildness," in *Home Economics*, 137.

14. Ibid., 138.

15. Ibid., 141–42. Compare to Aristotle, who in *The Politics* writes, "for just as man, when he is perfected [when he achieves his telos] is the best of animals, so too separated from law and justice he is the worst of all. . . . Without virtue he is most unholy and savage, and worst in regards to sex and eating" (125a35–39).

16. "Preserving Wildness," 143.

17. Berry, "Thoughts in the Presence of Fear," in *Citizenship Papers* (Washington, DC: Shoemaker and Hoard, 2003), 18. Berry considers modern belief in technology to be a form of "curious religious faith" ("Conservation and Local Economy," in *Sex, Economy, Freedom and Community* [New York: Pantheon, 1993], 10).

18. Berry, "Conservation Is Good Work," in *Sex, Economy, Freedom and Community*, 37.

19. Berry, "A Nation Rich in Natural Resources," in *Home Economics*, 133.

20. Berry, "In Distrust of Movements," in *Citizenship Papers*, 48.

21. As such, "the exploiter is a specialist, an expert; the nurturer is not. The standard of the exploiter is efficiency; the standard of the nurturer is care. The exploiter's goal is money, profit; the nurturer's goal is health—his land's health, his own, his family's, his community's, his country's" (Berry, *The Unsettling of America*, 7).

22. "Conservation Is Good Work," 37.

23. Berry rejects the term *environment* because it suggests that humans are fundamentally divorced from nature. He writes, "The idea that we live in something called 'the environment,' for instance, is utterly preposterous. This word came into use because of the pretentiousness of learned experts who were embarrassed by the religious associations of 'Creation' and who thought 'world' too mundane. But 'environment' means that which surrounds or encircles us; it means a world separate from ourselves, outside us." See Berry, "Conservation Is Good Work," 34. For an instance of

a "learned expert," see Kimberly Smith, *Wendell Berry and the Agrarian Tradition* (Lawrence, KS: University Press of Kansas). In spite of Berry's cautions, Smith unreservedly suggests throughout her study that Berry is concerned with the "environment."

24. Berry, "The Total Economy," in *Citizenship Papers*, 64.

25. Berry, "The Burden of the Gospels," in *Way of Ignorance*, 136. Berry continues, "it is a burden that falls with greatest weight on us humans of the industrial age who have been and are, by any measure, the humans most guilty of desecrating the world and of destroying creation. And we ought to be a little terrified to realize that, for the most part and at least for the time being, we are helplessly guilty. It seems as though industrial humanity has brought about phase two of original sin. We are all now complicit in the murder of creation" (136–37).

26. "In Distrust of Movements," 48.

27. Ibid., 49.

28. Ibid.

29. See "Compromise, Hell!" 23.

30. On the need for robust political intervention in the economic sphere, see "Compromise, Hell!" 25; in the "personal" sphere, Berry would support laws outlawing pornography and abortion, to name two areas of left libertarianism. See "Sex, Economy, Freedom and Community" in *Sex, Economy, Freedom and Community*. Berry is deeply critical of the libertarianism that dominates both political parties, and for that reason rejects the purported Left/Right distinction in modern American politics. See "Rugged Individualism," in *Way of Ignorance*, 9–11.

31. "The global economy is based upon cheap long-distance transportation, without which it is not possible to move goods from the point of cheapest origin to the point of highest sale. And the cheap long-distance transportation is the basis of the idea that regions and nations should abandon any measure of economic self-sufficiency in order to specialize in production for export of the few commodities, or the single commodity, that can be most cheaply produced. Whatever may be said for the 'efficiency' of such a system, its result (and, I assume, its purpose) is to destroy local production capacities, local diversity, and local economic independence. It destroys the economic security that it promises to make" (Berry, "The Total Economy," 68–69).

32. Berry, "Local Knowledge in the Age of Information," in *Way of Ignorance*.

Jack Shoemaker

A Long Shelf

I HAVE LONG THOUGHT that a publisher, if he or she performs properly, ought to be virtually invisible. A publisher's job is to bring forward and to make public the work of a writer. We should stand behind the spotlight, and the light itself ought to be trained on the writer and the book. And I am not myself a writer, so my discomfort here is doubled. But I have decided to think of this short note as simply another act of publication, to make public my profound debt to Wendell Berry, an opportunity too rare to ignore.

In 1969 I sent a friend in Kentucky, David Orr, a copy of the just-published book by Gary Snyder, *Earth House Hold.* Almost by return mail he sent me a book by a young writer I'd barely heard about, *The Long-Legged House* by Wendell Berry. Where Snyder's book celebrated the exotic and otherness of life, from Zen in Japan to working as a merchant mariner and a fire lookout in the Sierras, Berry's book explored and celebrated the familiar, the possible, an American life that I could imagine living. Soon I read a sequence of poems in Wendell's collection *Openings* titled "Window Poems," and I was hooked. A year later, while traveling in Kentucky, I met Wendell and Tanya, stayed a few days at their farm, and we shortly began a collaboration that has lasted now more than thirty-five years. Wendell entrusted me with a small sequence of poems, *The Chinese Painting Poems,* in typescript, which I published with the title *An Eastward Look* as a Sand Dollar chapbook (1974).

In 1979, when I first began to talk about starting an independent, medium-sized publishing company, which became North Point Press, Wendell stepped forward to say that a "medium-sized writer deserved a medium-sized publisher," and he promised his work to our press should we manage to get it off the ground. He pledged his life's work to what was only and barely even an idea.

And so we have been doing this work together, as publisher and writer, for a long time now. When we started, we each had longer hair and shorter children. Wendell's affection and patience for my innocent enthusiasm enabled him to forgive my ignorance and to allow me the time I needed to learn how to do what I had promised to do as his publisher. His only caution has been his constant reminder that neither of us is getting any younger. And that caution has recently made me wake up some mornings to look back on what has transpired and to realize that I have had what some folks like to call "a career" in this business of bookmaking. A career was hardly what I had in mind in the late 1960s when I was dropped from John Tarr's Saturday morning calligraphy class as he declared my letter forms to be "without grace or merit," or when I was trying to learn how to hand-set type, upside down and backward, in Clifford Burke's printing studio on Downey Street in San Francisco. Like most young people, I did not have plans per se, but what I had was a delight in the present moment and a certain measure of devotion. The rest of my adult life I have spent struggling to maintain that simple-mindedness.

As often happens, when ambition rears her head and blocks the view of reality and common sense, I began to have thoughts of leaving my small-press self behind and indulge the fantasy that eventually became North Point. By any measure, North Point was an impossible thing, and to make matters even more difficult for ourselves, we were determined to do this from Berkeley. At our first national book fair, where we exhibited the first North Point catalogue, the then director of Yale University Press stopped by to say, "Thank god you don't know you can't do this anymore." And in that catalogue were titles by writers who took the greatest risk and paid us the highest compliment by pledging their work to this unproven company. When we signed those contracts, the only thing we had actually printed was stationery.

Wendell Berry was first, and his early commitment in fact made the press possible. We knew right off that we would be publishing books by at least one writer booksellers would have to buy. And as I slowly approached the other founding authors (M. F. K. Fisher, James Salter, Gina Berriault, Guy Davenport, Gary Snyder, and several others), each was persuaded to come along at least partially because Wendell Berry had already stepped aboard. A part of the profound debt I owe Wendell's life and work is the very fact of what I can only now look back upon as a career.

In the time since North Point, my career has had some disruptions and relocations, not to mention some company name changes, but always Wendell Berry has been the first one to stand up and say, "Go ahead now and I'll come along and we will just continue." And so I have, and so we have, and somehow against the grain of what has become publishing in this celebrity culture we have managed to make—can it be?—more than three dozen books together.

And I should say that publishing is a political act. I have been privileged to publish a writer of such clarity and passion for all things complexly political and cultural. I am in this business because I believe books can change people's lives—and the books of Wendell Berry have profoundly changed my life, the way I walk through the world, by myself and with my family. It is worth my discomforting awkwardness to be able to say, "Thank you."

In 1958 and 1959, in a shed in Mill Valley, about thirteen miles from where I sit this afternoon, Wendell Berry composed the drafts of what became his first novel, *Nathan Coulter.* As he said later, he had no idea then that he would spend his life writing about the small town of Port William and five generations of the families who lived there. The long story of the Port William membership has become one of the great accomplishments of modern American literature. A recent book in this work brings us to Nathan Coulter's widow, Hannah Coulter. Hannah is, as this book begins, in her late seventies, widowed and alone. She has the time now to look back on her life and on her community. She sees, as she says, "the old fabric, pulling apart, and we know how much we have loved each other."

The years of our friendship and our association in publishing have been times of cultural and political turmoil and distress, when the nation's fabric has been stretched and to some people's minds torn beyond repair. One lesson of Wendell Berry's work is the solace of community. It is a blessing to recall how much we have loved each other.

George Core

Afterword

> The man of letters "must recreate for his age the image of man. . . . He must distinguish between mere communication . . . and the rediscovery of the human condition in the living arts."
> —Allen Tate

THE MOST GENERAL statement that one can make about Wendell Berry and his literary accomplishments is that he is a man of letters. He is a southern writer, of course; and in his lifetime there have been many men of letters in the South. I instance the leading Vanderbilt agrarians in this connection: John Crowe Ransom, Donald Davidson, Allen Tate, Andrew Lytle, and Robert Penn Warren, all of whom wrote successfully in several modes. All but Lytle were good poets. All were superb essayists and their essays, like Berry's, were not only literary but polemical, and they forged not only formal pieces of argumentation and of literary criticism but informal pieces such as reminiscences. All of them but Ransom wrote fiction, and Warren, at his best, created first-rate novels.

The twentieth century in the South also witnessed the careers of important women of letters, especially Katherine Anne Porter, Caroline Gordon, Eudora Welty, Flannery O'Connor, and Elizabeth Spencer. Anyone who knows the literature of the South knows the close connections of these women of letters with the agrarians, and these connections extend far beyond the matter of Caroline Gordon's having been married twice to Allen Tate.

Why so many greatly talented men and women of letters have derived from the South is not a question that can be confidently answered, but it is obvious that many of them were influenced by such figures as Ford Madox Ford and T. S. Eliot, who were not only men of letters but editors of great distinction. Tate, writing five years after Ford's death in 1939, declares, "His influence was immense, even upon writers who did not know him." Tate writes of what he calls the Masonic tradition, especially in the novel, passed along by Ford in "the living confraternity of men of letters." In speaking elsewhere of Ford and his *English Review,* Tate observes that Ford gave "the conviction of being a part of literature to at least half the distinguished writers who survived the war. . . . He, more than any other modern editor, enrolled his contributors in the profession of letters." Tate saw Eliot as continuing that tradition in the *Criterion*. These magazines served as models for the *Southern Review* under Brooks and Warren, the *Kenyon Review* under Ransom, and the *Sewanee Review* under Tate and Lytle, as well as later the *Hudson Review* under Frederick Morgan. These are among the magazines to which Wendell Berry has contributed some of his best work.

In all likelihood nobody, especially now in a time of specialization, sets out to be a man or woman of letters. He or she achieves this status after a sustained commitment to the profession of letters that results in work written in several modes that run from fiction and poetry to the letter itself. Writing, as E. B. White observes, is "not an occupation. . . . It is more an affliction, or just punishment." A real writer cannot evade this affliction: she or he has to deal with it as the urge comes, carrying the author along. Often the writer is not spared from this urge or seizure, as Coleridge was, by the appearance of a man from Porlock. The writer more nearly careers as though on horseback, following the course that a spirited horse chooses, rather than follows a career in the usual sense of that bureaucratic term (as in career *path*). The results of a series of rides into the rough country of the imagination can add up to the work of a lifetime that is seen in retrospect as what would seem to constitute a career as a man or woman of letters. "Having begun in public anonymity," Berry writes in "To a Writer of Reputation,"

> you did not count on this
> literary sublimation by which
> somebody becomes a "name."

Moving from one kind of writing to another—from, say, fiction to essay to poetry—enables a writer to remain fresh and not burn out in any given mode. You can see this pattern unfolding in the work of such contemporary men of letters as Joseph Epstein, George Garrett, and of course Berry himself, just as it did with Warren for decades. For Garrett and Berry writing poetry must be a wonderfully refreshing surcease from the struggle to forge an essay or the toil to create a long novel. Let us consider the final lines of Berry's "How to Be a Poet":

> Out of the little words that come
> out of the silence, like prayers
> prayed back to the one who prays,
> make a poem that does not disturb
> the silence from which it came.

Berry would agree with White that "poetry is the greatest of the arts": "It combines music and painting and storytelling and prophecy and the dance." The music of poetry echoes in part 6 of Berry's "Sabbaths 1998":

> The day ends
> and is unending where
> the summer tanager,
> warbler, and vireo
> sing as they move among
> illuminated leaves.

The music of this poem, like many others that Berry has struck, reminds us of what he has written of "the technical means of poetry"—"its power as speech or song . . . the play of statement with and against music."

Wendell Berry studied under a distinguished man of letters and teacher at Stanford University, a man who found the dance to the music of time in what he wrote and in what others wrote. In "Wallace Stegner and the Great Community" Berry quotes Stegner on that community—a passage in which the author says that thought "thrives best in solitude, in quiet, and in the company of the past, the great community of recorded experience." In describing Stegner's effectiveness as a teacher of writing, Berry tells us that Stegner's students felt in him "the authority of authentic membership in the great community."

That community of writers has other names, especially the Republic of Letters, which is what Allen Tate always called it—the ideal community that exists only in the minds of those who believe in its significance. It is a community of authorship, as Stegner and Berry believe, that derives from the committed members of the profession of letters. The republic of the arts, Ford Madox Ford declares, is "the only republic that has ever lasted." Malcolm Cowley, writing about Tate, describes this realm as "a loose federation composed of many dukedoms and principalities." Among these are the various regions in the United States—the West in Stegner's case, the South in Berry's. Each man is comfortable in writing about his region and is by no means defensive that it is not New England, especially metropolitan New York City. Cowley comfortably worked in many literary beats, and his included Stegner's writing program at Stanford on four occasions. Cowley, another man of letters, describes the Republic of Letters as well as anyone ever has.

In general the committed writer works in solitude and does not perform as a member of a clique—no Algonquin Round Table of wits and witticisms for him or her. Despite Wendell Berry's wide range of literary friends and acquaintances, many of whom have written for this occasion, he is the sole member in a party of one. This should also be emphatically said of the rugged individualists whom he has admired, from Henry David Thoreau to Edward Abbey, Harry Caudill, Wallace Stegner, and Donald Davie. E. B. White calls Thoreau a "regular hairshirt of a man," a description that aptly applies to Abbey, Caudill, Stegner, Davie, and Berry. "Hairshirt or no," White continues, "he is a better companion than most, and I would not swap him for a more reasonable friend."

As the reminiscences in this book of essays skillfully acquired and edited by Jason Peters reveal, Mr. Berry is not only a literary man but a social being who is blessed with a wife who complements him within the society of their family and friends. He has not removed himself from the everyday world, even though much of his time and energy is spent on the solitary pursuits of farming and writing. Like many men of letters he is an ambassador to the wider world and has lectured and read at many campuses and other places. He not only understands but embodies the significance of what Allen Tate deems "the full participation of the man of letters in the action of society." "To act, in short," Berry himself declares, "is to live. Living 'is a total act. Thinking is a partial act.'" And, he adds, "Living is a communal act." In the same essay, "Writer and Region," the author observes that "the context of literature" is not "the literary world"—that "its real habitat is the household and the community"—the community of "common experience and common effort on common ground." He says that in securing his point the "test of imagination, ultimately, is not the territory of art or the territory of mind, but the territory underfoot." The writer, walking or riding through the country of the mind, does not ignore its actual terrain and rise, unchecked, on a balloon into an abstract and idealized literary imperium, the country of the blue. We recall that Henry James's balloon of experience is firmly tethered to the sullen earth, "and under that necessity we swing . . . in the more or less commodious car of the imagination."

It makes no difference what form of literature that the author is pursuing —fiction or poetry or essay or something else. Wendell Berry says of Wallace Stegner that "one of the pleasures of reading him is to see how many kinds of writing he has done well." These include biography and history and criticism in addition to his forte, the novel. Berry's own accomplishments as a writer are more varied. Neither writer can be measured by an old saw that is often dismissive—jack-of-all-trades but master of none. The jack-of-all-trades often thought—wrongly—that he could do everything. When it comes to Berry, he can turn his hand to practically any literary mode, as this book about him abundantly demonstrates. He has written fiction, long and short, of a high order; his poetry has earned him an Aiken Taylor Award, among other prizes; his critical essays are distinguished; and his essays or polemics devoted to environmental matters have won him a wide and devoted audience. For his work in concert he has earned the T. S. Eliot Prize. It is difficult to decide what Berry's forte as a writer is. Any serious reader of his work would be hard-pressed to say in which mode he most excels. Of course we do not have to make such a determination. My point, as you have discerned, is that nothing he writes is merely passable, the standard for the jack-of-all-trades.

"Works of art participate in our lives; we are not just distant observers of their lives." So begins Berry's "Style and Grace," in which he compares Hemingway's "Big Two-Hearted River" with Norman Maclean's *A River Runs Through It*. Works of art, the critic continues in laying out his argument, "are in conversation among themselves and with us. This is a part of the description of human life; we do the way we do partly because of things that have been said to us by works of art, and because of things we have said in reply." Berry compares Hemingway's restrictive style (which, "like a victorious general, imposes its terms") with Maclean's less limited and more submerged style, a style that enables him to reveal "the failure of a man to live up to his own grace, his own beauty and power." Berry's description of Maclean's virtues as a writer is a good description of the subtleties of his own fiction, which we read as he does *A River Runs Through It,* "rejoicing in the end." As he makes plain, a writer often tells a story "because he takes an unutterable joy in telling it and therefore has to tell it."

The best stories often come out of such an urge in which the story more nearly chooses the author, as Robert Penn Warren used to say, than the author chooses the story. Wendell Berry's "Mike" (*Sewanee Review,* winter 2005), which has been selected for Algonquin Books' annual *New Stories from the South,* is a superb instance of such a piece of fiction. "Mike" springs from a story or series of stories told to the author by his father. Mike is an uncommonly intelligent and well-trained English setter. He and his master at their best—at one—work as a team hunting birds. "I think he regarded his partnership with my father as the business of his life," the narrator tells us, "as it was also his overtopping joy." The narrator's father was a man of many passions, including "bird-hunting with a good dog, which had no practical end but was the enactment of his great love of country, of life, of his own life, for their own sake." And later he says, "I am thinking now with wonder of the convergence, like two birds crossing as they rise, of a passionate man and a gifted, elated, hard-hunting dog."

I could consider more of Wendell Berry's fiction but will confine myself to this representative example of his accomplished ease as a maker of fiction. This is but one example of how his "works of art participate in our lives." "Mike" becomes part of our lives, whether or not we hunt. I confess that I am not a hunter but that I relish hunting stories, both oral and written, especially involving dogs; and "Mike" is one of the best of the many I know, such as Caroline Gordon's "Old Red and Old Whiskey." The success of "Mike" depends in part on its voice: the story, as it unfolds, could be read or told in company—at a hunting lodge or anywhere else at which people of like interests gather. Although beautifully written and told, it is not, in the pejorative sense, literary.

The fiction centering in and around Port William, Berry's fictive country, has reminded many people of the stories and novels that are placed in Faulkner's Yoknapatawpha County; but, as an acute Australian critic, George Thomas, has observed of late in *Quadrant* (March 2006), the novels and stories laid in Port William bear "a greater similarity . . . to Thomas Hardy's Wessex." He explains, "Hardy's Wessex stories had the common theme of attachment to and estrangement from a rural community." Such an astute critic as Thomas could make an essay—or even a book—based on this illuminating parallel, which isn't to say that the Faulkner analogy is defective, merely less revealing than the one between Hardy and Berry. But, were one to consider comedy in Berry, Faulkner would provide the better parallel.

The novelist, Ortega y Gasset says in *The Dehumanization of Art,* imprisons the reader "in a small, hermetically sealed universe—the inner realm of the novel." In contrast the poet presents a world viewed from the outside rather than from within. The essayist posts himself differently than does the fiction writer or the poet, addressing the reader more directly—and in his own voice, whether it is that of the literary critic, remote and reflective, such as John Crowe Ransom or Lionel Trilling, or in the shriller tone of the polemicist and reformer such as George Orwell. The latter, as White says of Thoreau, is torn "between the desire to enjoy the world . . . and the urge to set the world straight." We see these impulses in Berry in such essays as those collected in *Another Turn of the Crank.* He sees the crankiness in himself and enjoys dealing with the seriousness of our terrible situation as human beings living on a planet that is rapidly being exhausted of its natural resources and the humor of his attempts to correct a world gone mad. Berry is, as Wallace Stegner says to him, "one of the most provocative and thoughtful essayists alive." To address his work in this vein, we can do no better than to study White's "A Slight Sound at Evening" and Stegner's "The Sense of Place" and "A Letter to Wendell Berry." In so doing, we would be constantly reminded of White's observation that "all writing is both a mask and an unveiling, and the question of honesty is uppermost, as in the case of the essayist." And we would find Berry's work, fiction and poetry and nonfiction, is what White, the presiding spirit of this occasion in addition to Wendell Berry himself, calls "an invitation to life's dance."

Chronology

1934	Born Wendell Erdman Berry, August 5 in Henry County, Kentucky, to John and Virginia Berry. John Marshall Berry is a lawyer and official with the Burley Tobacco Growers Association
1936	Berry family moves to New Castle, Kentucky
1948	Enters Millersburg Military Institute
1952	Graduates from Millersburg Military Institute and enters the University of Kentucky
1955	Meets Tanya Amyx, the daughter of a University of Kentucky art professor
1956	Earns AB (English) from the University of Kentucky (Lexington); enters graduate school at the university in the fall
1957	Earns MA (English) from the University of Kentucky; marries Tanya Amyx on May 29; begins teaching English at Georgetown College (Georgetown, Kentucky) in the fall
1958	Enters Stanford University as a Wallace Stegner fellow; daughter, Mary Dee, born May 29
1959–60	Teaches creative writing at Stanford University
1960	*Nathan Coulter* (novel)
1960–61	Farms in Kentucky
1961–62	Lives in Europe, principally Italy and France, on a Guggenheim Fellowship
1962	Awarded the Vachel Lindsay Prize; son, Pryor Clifford (Den), born August 19
1962–64	Teaches English at New York University (University Heights campus in the Bronx) and directs the freshman English program
1964	*November Twenty-six Nineteen Hundred Sixty-three* (poem) and *The Broken Ground* (poems); begins teaching creative writing at the University of Kentucky (Lexington) in the fall
1965	Moves to Lanes Landing Farm, Port Royal, Kentucky; awarded Rockefeller Foundation Fellowship
1967	*A Place on Earth* (novel; revised, 1983); awarded the Bess Hokin Prize from *Poetry*
1968	*Openings* (poems) and *The Rise* (nonfiction); appointed visiting professor of creative writing at Stanford, 1968–69
1969	*Findings* (poems) and *The Long-Legged House* (nonfiction; reprinted, 2004); earns first place, Borestone Mountain Poetry Awards; receives a National Endowment of the Arts grant

1970   *Farming: A Handbook* (poems), *The Hidden Wound* (nonfiction; reprinted 1989 with a new afterword), and *Ralph Eugene Meatyard* (coauthors, Ralph Eugene Meatyard and A. Gassan); earns first place, Borestone Mountain Poetry Awards

1971   *The Unforeseen Wilderness: An Essay on Kentucky's Red River Gorge* (nonfiction; photographs by Ralph Eugene Meatyard; revised and expanded as *The Unforeseen Wilderness: Kentucky's Red River Gorge*, 1991); named University of Kentucky's Distinguished Professor of the Year; receives National Institute of Arts and Letters Award for Writing

1972   *A Continuous Harmony: Essays Cultural and Agricultural* (reprinted, 2003) and *Civilizing the Cumberland: A Commentary* (nonfiction; bound with James Lane Allen, *Mountain Passes of the Cumberlands*); earns first place, Borestone Mountain Poetry Awards

1973   *The Country of Marriage* (poems)

1974   *The Memory of Old Jack* (novel; revised, 1999), *An Eastward Look* (poems) and *Reverdure* (poem); promoted to professor of English, University of Kentucky

1975   *Horses* (poem), *To What Listens* (poem), and *Sayings and Doings* (poems); receives Friends of American Writers Award for *The Memory of Old Jack*

1976   *The Kentucky River: Two Poems* and *There Is Singing Around Me* (poems)

1977   *Clearing* (poems), *Three Memorial Poems*, and *The Unsettling of America: Culture and Agriculture* (nonfiction); resigns from the University of Kentucky; appointed writer in residence at Centre College (Danville, Kentucky)

1977–79   Contributing editor for Rodale Press, which publishes *New Farm* and *Organic Gardening and Farming*

1978   Receives honorary doctorate from Centre College

1979   *The Gift of Gravity* (poem; illustrated by Timothy Engelland)

1980   *A Part* (poems), *The Salad* (poem), and *Wendell Berry Reading His Poems* (audio recording)

1981   *Recollected Essays, 1965–1980*; *The Gift of Good Land: Further Essays, Cultural and Agricultural*; and *The Nativity* (poem); receives honorary doctorate from Transylvania College (Lexington, Kentucky)

1982   *The Wheel* (poems)

1983   *Standing by Words* (essays; reprinted, 2005); receives honorary doctorate from Berea College (Berea, Kentucky)

1984   Coeditor, *Meeting the Expectations of the Land* (nonfiction), with Wes Jackson and Bruce Coleman

1985   *Collected Poems, 1957–1982*

1986   *The Wild Birds: Six Stories of the Port William Membership* (fiction); receives honorary doctorate from University of Kentucky

1987   *Sabbaths* (poems), *Home Economics* (essays), and, in England, *The Landscape of Harmony* (nonfiction); returns to University of Kentucky to teach courses in literature and education; receives the American Academy of Arts and Letters Jean Stein Award and the Kentucky Governor's Milner Award; receives honorary doctorate from Santa Clara University; appointed writer in residence, Bucknell University (Lewisburg, Pennsylvania), 1987–88

1988   *Remembering* (novel); receives honorary doctorate from Eureka College (Eureka, Illinois)

1989   *Traveling at Home* (poetry and fiction; wood engravings by John DePol) and *The Hidden Wound* (paperback, with a new afterword); receives the Lannan Foundation Award for Nonfiction; delivers commencement address at College of the Atlantic (Bar Harbor, Maine)

1990   *Harland Hubbard: Life and Work* (biography), and *What Are People For?* (essays); reissues *Sayings and Doings* (poems) with *An Eastward Look* (poems)

1991   John Berry, father, dies October 31

1992   *Fidelity* (fiction) and *Sabbaths 1987–1990* (poems); receives Victory Spirit Ethics Award from the Louisville Community Foundation

1993   *Sex, Economy, Freedom and Community* (essays); receives Kentucky Libraries Award for Intellectual Excellence and the Orion Society's John Hay Award

1994   *Watch with Me: And Six Other Stories of the Yet-Remembered Ptolemy Proudfoot and His Wife, Miss Minnie, née Quinch* (fiction) and *Entries* (poems); receives the Aiken Taylor Award for Poetry from the *Sewanee Review* and the T. S. Eliot Award from the Ingersoll Foundation

1995   *The Farm* (poem) and *Another Turn of the Crank* (essays)

1996   *A World Lost* (novel)

1997   *Two More Stories of the Port William Membership* (fiction); preface, *Waste Land: Meditations on a Ravaged Landscape* (with David T. Hanson, William Kittredge, and Mark Dowie); Virginia Berry, mother, dies January 3; Clifford Amyx, father-in-law, dies July 30

1998   *The Selected Poems of Wendell Berry* and *A Timbered Choir: The Sabbath Poems, 1979–1997*

2000   *Jayber Crow: The Life of Jayber Crow, Barber of the Port William Membership as Written by Himself* (novel) and *Life Is a Miracle: An Essay against Modern Superstition*

2002   *That Distant Land: The Collected Stories of Wendell Berry* (fiction), *Three Short Novels* (contains *Nathan Coulter*, *Remembering*, and *A World Lost*), and *The Art of the Commonplace: Agrarian Essays of Wendell Berry*

2003   *Citizenship Papers* (essays)

2004   *Hannah Coulter* (novel) and *Tobacco Harvest: An Elegy* (nonfiction; photographs by James Baker Hall); receives *Writer* award; Dee Rice Amyx, mother-in-law, dies July 3

2005   *Given* (poems), *The Way of Ignorance* (essays); introduction, *Blessed Are the Peacemakers: Christ's Teachings of Love, Compassion, and Forgiveness*;

receives O. Henry Prize for "The Hurt Man" (short story); delivers commencement address at and receives honorary doctorate from Lindsey Wilson College (Columbia, Kentucky)

2006   Delivers keynote address for the thirtieth anniversary of The Land Institute (Salina, Kansas)

2007   *Andy Catlett: Early Travels* (novel); introduction, paperback edition of Sir Albert Howard's *The Soil and Health* (University Press of Kentucky)

Selected Bibliography

Principal Primary Works (alphabetical by genre)

Fiction

Berry, Wendell. *Fidelity: Five Stories*. New York: Pantheon, 1992.

———. *Hannah Coulter*. Washington, DC: Shoemaker and Hoard, 2004.

———. *Jayber Crow*. New York: Counterpoint, 2000.

———. *The Memory of Old Jack*. New York: Harcourt Brace Jovanovich, 1974. Rev. ed. Washington, DC: Counterpoint, 1999.

———. *Nathan Coulter*. Boston: Houghton Mifflin, 1960. Rev. ed. San Francisco: North Point, 1985.

———. *A Place on Earth*. New York: Harcourt Brace, 1967. Rev. ed. San Francisco: North Point, 1983.

———. *Remembering*. San Francisco: North Point, 1988.

———. *That Distant Land*. Washington, DC: Shoemaker and Hoard, 2004.

———. *Three Short Novels*. New York: Counterpoint, 2002.

———. *Watch with Me: And Six Other Stories of the Yet-Remembered Ptolemy Proudfoot and His Wife, Miss Minnie, Née Quinch*. New York: Pantheon, 1994.

———. *The Wild Birds: Six Stories of the Port William Membership*. San Francisco: North Point, 1986.

———. *A World Lost*. Washington, DC: Counterpoint, 1996.

Poetry

Berry, Wendell. *The Broken Ground*. New York: Harcourt Brace and World, 1964.

———. *Clearing*. New York: Harcourt Brace Jovanovich, 1977.

———. *Collected Poems, 1957–1982*. San Francisco: North Point, 1985.

———. *The Country of Marriage*. New York: Harcourt Brace Jovanovich, 1973.

———. *Entries*. New York: Pantheon, 1994.

———. *Farming: A Handbook*. New York: Harcourt Brace Jovanovich, 1970.

———. *Given*. Washington, DC: Shoemaker and Hoard, 2005.

———. *Openings*. New York: Harcourt Brace Jovanovich, 1968.

———. *A Part*. San Francisco: North Point, 1980.

———. *Sabbaths*. San Francisco: North Point, 1987. Reprint, Frankfort, KY: Gnomon, 1992.

———. *The Salad*. San Francisco: North Point, 1980.

———. *Sayings and Doings*. Frankfort, KY: Gnomon, 1975.

———. *"Sayings and Doings" and "An Eastward Look."* Frankfort, KY: Gnomon, 1990.

———. *The Selected Poems of Wendell Berry*. Washington, DC: Counterpoint, 1998.

———. *A Timbered Choir: The Sabbath Poems, 1979–1997*. Washington, DC: Counterpoint, 1998.

———. *The Wheel*. San Francisco: North Point, 1982.

Nonfiction

Berry, Wendell. *Another Turn of the Crank*. Washington, DC: Counterpoint, 1995.

———. *Art of the Commonplace: The Agrarian Essays of Wendell Berry*. Edited by Norman Wirzba. Washington, DC: Shoemaker and Hoard, 2002.

———. *Blessed Are the Peacemakers: Christ's Teachings about Love, Compassion, and Forgiveness*. Selected and introduced by Wendell Berry. Emeryville, CA: Shoemaker and Hoard, 2005.

———. *Citizens Dissent: Security, Morality, and Leadership in an Age of Terror* (with David James Duncan). Great Barrington, MA: Orion Society, 2003.

———. *Citizenship Papers*. Washington, DC: Shoemaker and Hoard, 2003.

———. *A Continuous Harmony: Essays Cultural and Agricultural*. New York: Harcourt Brace Jovanovich, 1972. Reprint, Washington, DC: Shoemaker and Hoard, 2004.

———. *The Gift of Good Land: Further Essays Cultural and Agricultural*. San Francisco: North Point, 1981.

———. *Harlan Hubbard: Life and Work*. Lexington: University Press of Kentucky, 1990. Reprint, New York: Pantheon, 1990.

———. *The Hidden Wound*. Boston: Houghton Mifflin, 1970. Reprint, Berkeley, CA: North Point, 1989.

———. *Home Economics*. San Francisco: North Point, 1987.

———. *In the Presence of Fear: Three Essays for a Changed World*. Great Barrington, MA: Orion Society, 2001.

———. *Life Is a Miracle: An Essay against Modern Superstition*. Washington, DC: Counterpoint, 2000.

———. *The Long-Legged House*. New York: Harcourt Brace and World, 1969. Reprint, Washington, DC: Shoemaker and Hoard, 2004.

———. *Meeting the Expectations of the Land: Essays in Sustainable Agriculture and Stewardship*. Edited by Wes Jackson, Wendell Berry, and Bruce Coleman. San Francisco: North Point, 1984.

———. *Recollected Essays, 1965–1980*. San Francisco: North Point, 1981.

———. *The Rise*. Lexington: University of Kentucky Library Press, 1968.

———. *Sex, Economy, Freedom and Community*. New York: Pantheon, 1993.

———. *Standing by Words*. San Francisco: North Point, 1983.

———. *Tobacco Harvest: An Elegy*. Photographs by James Baker Hall. Lexington: University Press of Kentucky, 2004.

———. *The Unforeseen Wilderness: An Essay on Kentucky's Red River Gorge*. Photographs by Ralph Eugene Meatyard. Lexington: University Press of Kentucky, 1971. Reprint, San Francisco: North Point, 1991. Reprint, Emeryville, CA: Shoemaker and Hoard, 2006.

———. *The Unsettling of America: Culture and Agriculture.* San Francisco: Sierra Club Books, 1977. Reprint, New York: Avon Books, 1978. Reprint, Magnolia, MA: Peter Smith, 1997.

———. *The Way of Ignorance.* Washington, DC: Shoemaker and Hoard, 2005.

———. *What Are People For?* San Francisco: North Point, 1990.

Interviews

Berger, Rose Marie. "Heaven in Henry County." *Sojourners* 33, no. 7 (2004): 13–16.

Berry, Wendell. Interview. "A Return to the Local: You Stay Home Too." *World Watch* 13, no. 5 (2000): 29–33.

———. Interview. *All Things Considered.* National Public Radio. 24 Dec. 1998.

———. Interview. Bob Edwards. *Morning Edition.* National Public Radio. 20 Nov. 1996.

———. Interview. Jack Shoemaker. *Lannan.* Santa Fe. 10 Nov. 1999.

Brockman, Holly M. "How Can a Family 'Live at the Center of Its Own Attention?' Wendell Berry's Thoughts on the Good Life." *New Southerner* (2006).

Burleigh, Anne H. "Wendell Berry's Community." *Crisis* 18, no. 1 (2000): 28–33.

Dalton, Katherine. "Rendering Us Again in Affection: An Interview with Wendell Berry." *Chronicles* (July 2006): 31–36.

"Earl Butz versus Wendell Berry." *Co-Evolution Quarterly* (1978): 50–59.

Fisher-Smith, Jordan. "Field Observations: An Interview with Wendell Berry." *Orion* (1993).

Healy, Thomas. "Taking Care of What We've Been Given." *Counterpunch* (2006).

Jezreel, Jack. "Care for the Earth Is a Local Call." *US Catholic* 64, no. 6 (1999): 12–17.

McNamee, Gregory, and James R. Hepworth. "The Art of Living Right." *Bloomsberry Review* (June/August 1983): 23–33. Reprinted in *Living in Words: Interviews from the "Bloomsberry Review," 1981–1988.* Edited by Gregory McNamee. Portland: Breitenbush Books, 1988.

Minick, Jim. "A Citizen and a Native: An Interview with Wendell Berry." *Appalachian Journal: A Regional Studies Review* 31 (2004): 300–313.

"The Short Answer: An Exchange with Wendell Berry." *Preservation* (March/April 2005): 49.

Snell, Marilyn B. "The Art of Place." *New Perspectives Quarterly* 9, no. 2 (1992): 29–34.

"Toward a Healthy Community: An Interview with Wendell Berry." *Christian Century* 114, no. 28 (1997): 912–16.

Weinreb, Mindy. "A Question a Day: A Written Conversation with Wendell Berry." *Our Other Voices.* Edited by John Wheatcroft. Bucknell, PA: Bucknell University Press, 1991. Reprinted in *Wendell Berry*, ed. Paul Merchant. Lewiston, ID: Confluence Press, 1991.

Williamson, Bruce. "The Plowboy Interview: Wendell Berry." *Mother Earth News* 20 (March 1973).

Woolley, Bryan. "An Interview with Wendell Berry." *Louisville Courier Journal* and *Times Magazine*, 4 August 1974, 8–10.

Audio Recordings

Berry, Wendell. *All Things Considered*. National Public Radio, 24 Dec. 1998.

———. *Bob Edwards Talks with Author Wendell Berry*. National Public Radio, 20 Nov. 1996.

———. *Christmas Poem*. National Public Radio. 24 Dec. 1998.

Berry, Wendell. Jack Shoemaker. *Lannan Readings and Conversations*. Lannan Foundation, 10 Nov. 1999.

Berry, Wendell. *Natural Gifts*. San Francisco: New Dimensions Foundation, 1994.

———. *The Poetry of Wendell Berry*. New York: Jeffrey Norton, 1966.

———. *Wendell Berry*. Lexington: University of Kentucky, 1986.

———. *Wendell Berry, 3-3-77*. San Francisco: American Poetry Archive, San Francisco State University, 1976.

———. *Wendell Berry, March 3, 1986, Lane Lecture Series*. Stanford, CA: 2006.

———. *Wendell Berry Reading at the New York Poetry Center*. New York: Poets' Audio Center, 1966.

———. *What Are People For?* Berkeley: Baker and Taylor, 1992.

Berry, Wendell. *Spotted Horses and Other Stories*. Berkeley, CA: Baker and Taylor, 1994.

Video Recordings

Living by Words: A Celebration of Fifty Years of Creative Writing at the University of Kentucky. Wendell Berry, Bobbie Ann Mason, Gurney Norman, Ed McClanahan, James Baker Hall, Guy Mendes, Jay Bolotin, and Paul Patterson. Kentucky Educational Television. Lexington: KET, 2002.

Nature as Teacher. Wendell Berry and Satish Kumar. London: Phil Shepherd Production, 1992.

Thoughts in the Presence of Fear. Dir. Herb Smith. Whitesburg, KY: Appalshop, 2007.

Wendell Berry and Gary Snyder in Conversation with Jack Shoemaker. Lannan Foundation, 1999.

Wendell Berry and Gary Snyder. Lannan Foundation, 2001.

Wendell Berry. University of Michigan Film Library, 1975.

Wendell Berry's "The Hurt Man." Kentucky Educational Television, 2003.

Music

(These recordings include texts by or about Wendell Berry.)

Dalglish, Malcolm. *Hymnody of the Earth*. Ooolitic Music, 1997.

Grimm, Tim. *Coyote's Dream*. Wind River Records, 2003.

Larsen, Libby. *Missa Gaia: Mass for the Earth*. Koch International Classics, 1995. Musical Score: Boston: ECS Publishers, 1992.

Laurie Lewis and the Right Hands. *The Golden West*. Hightone Records, 2006.
White, David A. *The Peace of Wild Things: For Voice and Piano*. Boston: ECS Publishers, 2004.

Selected Secondary Sources

Angyal, Andrew J. *Wendell Berry*. Basingstoke, Hampshire, UK: Macmillan Library Reference, 1995.
Freedman, Russell. *Wendell Berry: A Bibliography*. Lexington: University of Kentucky Libraries Occasional Papers No. 12, 1988.
Goodrich, Janet. *The Unforeseen Self in the Works of Wendell Berry*. Columbia: University of Missouri Press, 2001.
Greiner, Donald J. *American Poets Since World War II*. Detroit: Gale Research, 1980.
Hicks, Jack. "A Wendell Berry Checklist." *Bulletin of Bibliography* 37, no. 3 (July–Sept. 1980): 127–31.
Merchant, Paul. Introduction. *Wendell Berry*. Lewiston, ID: Confluence, 1991.
Scigaj, Leonard M. *Sustainable Poetry: Four American Ecopoets*. Lexington: University of Kentucky Press: 1999.
Smith, Kimberly K. *Wendell Berry and the Agrarian Tradition: A Common Grace*. Lawrence: University Press of Kansas, 2003.
Theobald, P. K. *Rural Philosophy for Education: Wendell Berry's Tradition*. Charleston, WV: Clearinghouse, 1992.

Dissertations

Baker, Bernard. "Responsibly at Home: Wendell Berry's Quest for the Simple Life." PhD diss., Case Western Reserve University, 1992. Abstract in *Dissertation Abstracts International* 54, no. 2A (1992): 0537.
Bryson, J. Scott. "Place, Space, and Contemporary Ecological Poetry: Wendell Berry, Joy Harjo, and Mary Oliver." PhD diss., University of Kentucky, 1999. Abstract in *Dissertation Abstracts International* 60, no. 11A (1999): 4008.
Burr, Cornelia A. "Perceptions of Landscape in Twentieth Century American Literature: Landscapes from Four American Regional Writers." PhD diss., University of Wisconsin–Madison, 1994. Abstract in *Dissertation Abstracts International* 55, no. 03A (1994): 0564.
Christensen, Laird E. "Spirit Astir in the World: Sacred Poetry in the Age of Ecology." PhD diss., University of Oregon, 1999. Abstract in *Dissertation Abstracts International* 60, no. 10A (1999): 3657.
Collins, Robert J. "A Secular Pilgrimage: Nature, Place, and Morality in the Poetry of Wendell Berry." PhD diss., Ohio State University, 1978. Abstract in *Dissertation Abstracts International* 39, no. 08A (1978): 4935.
Cornell, Daniel T. "Practicing Resurrection: Wendell Berry's Georgic Poetry: An

Ecological Critique of American Culture." PhD diss., Washington State University–Pullman, 1985. Abstract in *Dissertation Abstracts International* 47, no. 03A (1985): 0951.

Holden, John J. "The Land as Sacrament: Wendell Berry's Prophetic Vision." PhD diss., University of Connecticut, 1998. Abstract in *Dissertation Abstracts International* 59, no. 09A (1998): 3455.

Howell, Cynthia M. "Rereading Agrarianism: Despoliation and Conservation in the Works of Wendell Berry, Lee Smith, and Bobbie Ann Mason." PhD diss., University of Kentucky, 1996. Abstract in *Dissertation Abstracts International* 57, no. 11A (1996): 4740.

Perkins, Caroline C. "Living Responsibly in Community: Wendell Berry's Port William Fiction." PhD diss., University of Texas–Dallas, 2000. Abstract in *Dissertation Abstracts International* 61, no. 10A (2000): 4055.

Quetchenbach, Bernard W. "Back from the 'Far Field': Speaking of (and for) Nature in the Work of Three Contemporary American Poets." PhD diss., Purdue University, 1993. Abstract in *Dissertation Abstracts International* 55, no. 03A (1993): 0568.

Roorda, Randall K. "Dramas of Solitude: Narratives of Retreat in American Nature Writing." PhD diss., University of Michigan, 1994. Abstract in *Dissertation Abstracts International* 56, no. 01A (1994): 0194.

Schimmoeller, Katrina. "Humor in the House: Wendell Berry, Rachel Carson, Edward Abbey, and Louise Erdrich." PhD diss., University of California–Davis, 1998. Abstract in *Dissertation Abstracts International* 59, no. 11A (1998): 4145.

Schueter, Luke C. "The Ground Sense Necessary: Mining the Domestic in Gary Snyder and Wendell Berry." PhD diss., Kent State University, 2000. Abstract in *Dissertation Abstracts International* 61, no. 07A (2000): 2721.

Taft, Edward D. "The Land and Moral Responsibility in the Work of Wendell Berry." PhD diss., University of Rhode Island, 1991. Abstract in *Dissertation Abstracts International* 52, no. 11A (1991): 3931.

Tolliver, Gary. "Beyond Pastoral: Wendell Berry and a Literature of Commitment." PhD diss., Ohio University, 1978. Abstract in *Dissertation Abstracts International* 39, no. 11A (1978): 6767.

Triggs, Jeffrey A. I. "The Well-Tempered Self: Structure and Autobiography in Victorian Sonnet Sequences. II. At Home with Generations: A Study of the Poetry and Prose of Wendell Berry. III. A Controlling Sympathy: The Style of Irony in Joyce's 'The Dead.'" PhD diss., Rutgers, 1986. Abstract in *Dissertation Abstracts International* 47, no. 11A (1986): 4091.

Turner, Brian. "Rhetorics of Assent: A Rhetorical Analysis of 'Good Reasons' Arguments for the Environment in the Non-Fiction of Jonathan Schell, Wendell Berry, and John McPhee." PhD diss., University of Alberta, 1992. *Dissertation Abstracts International* 53, no. 12A (1992): 4324 (University of Alberta).

Contributors

JEREMY BEER is editor in chief at ISI Books. He is coeditor of *American Conservatism: An Encyclopedia,* and his work has appeared in *Touchstone, The American Conservative,* and *Utne Reader,* among other periodicals.

SVEN BIRKERTS is the author of six books of essays and a memoir, *My Sky Blue Trades.* His most recent book is *Then, Again,* a reflection on memoir.

ALLAN CARLSON, president of the Howard Center for Family, Religion and Society in Rockford, Illinois, edits the Family in America monograph series and is a contributing editor to *Touchstone.* His books include *The New Agrarian Mind: The Movement toward Decentralist Thought in Twentieth-Century America; The "American Way": Family And Community in the Shaping of the American Identity;* and *Conjugal America: On the Public Purposes of Marriage.*

HAYDEN CARRUTH, a former editor of *Poetry,* is a backcountry New Englander living in upstate New York. He has published dozens of books of poetry, essays, fiction, and miscellaneous arabesque.

GEORGE CORE taught English at Davidson College and was senior editor at the University of Georgia Press before becoming editor of the *Sewanee Review* in 1973. He has edited several books and has written regularly for the periodical press. He and his wife, Susan, go to London every summer and occasionally report on the theater there.

DAVID CROWE is associate professor and chair of English at Augustana College (Illinois). Hemingway's early works have been his principal interest, together with works by such novelists as David Lodge, Jon Hassler, and Tim O'Brien.

KATHERINE DALTON lives with her family on a beef-cattle farm in New Castle, Kentucky. A former managing editor of *Chronicles,* she is now a freelance editor and writer.

PATRICK J. DENEEN is associate professor of government and holds a chair in Hellenic studies at Georgetown University (Washington, D.C.). He is the author of *The Odyssey of Political Theory* and *Democratic Faith,* as well as coeditor of *Democracy's Literature.*

ERIC T. FREYFOGLE has written widely on nature and culture. His most recent books are *Agrarianism and the Good Society* and *Why Conservation Is Failing and How It Can Regain Ground.* Much of his work has dealt with private property and the ownership of nature, including *The Land We Share: Private Property and the Common Good.* He is also editor of *The New Agrarianism: Land, Culture, and the Community of Life.*

MORRIS A. GRUBBS is editor of *Home and Beyond: An Anthology of Kentucky Short Stories* and of *Conversations with Wendell Berry.* He has written about Eudora Welty, William Faulkner, Nathaniel Hawthorne, Bobbie Ann Mason, and other writers. He is associate professor of English and chair of the American studies program at Lindsey Wilson College (Kentucky).

JAMES BAKER HALL, a native of Lexington who has been a Kentucky poet laureate, taught creative writing at the University of Kentucky for over thirty years. He is the recipient of numerous awards, including a National Endowment for the Arts Fellowship in poetry and a Wallace Stegner Fellowship in creative writing at Stanford. He is the author of five volumes of poetry, two novels, and four collections of photography.

DONALD HALL has published fifteen books of poetry, most recently a volume of selected poems entitled *White Apples and the Taste of Stone.* He is poet laureate of the United States.

STANLEY HAUERWAS is the Rowe Professor of Theological Ethics at the Divinity School of Duke University. His many books include *Truthfulness and Tragedy; A Community of Character: Toward a Constructive Christian Social Ethic; The Peaceable Kingdom: A Primer in Christian Ethics; After Christendom?; A Better Hope; With the Grain of the Universe: The Church's Witness and Natural Theology,* and *Cross-Shattered Christ: Meditations on the Seven Last Words.*

WES JACKSON is president of The Land Institute in Salina, Kansas. He is the author of *New Roots for Agriculture* and *Becoming Native to This Place.*

BILL KAUFFMAN is the author of six books, including *Dispatches from the Muckdog Gazette, Look Homeward, America,* and the novel *Every Man a King.* He lives in his native Genesee County, New York, with his wife, Lucine, and their daughter.

BARBARA KINGSOLVER is the author of twelve books of fiction, poetry, and essays. Her novels include *The Bean Trees, Animal Dreams, Pigs in Heaven,* the prize-winning *The Poisonwood Bible,* and *Prodigal Summer.* Her newest book is *Animal, Vegetable, Miracle.* Her numerous awards include the National Humanities Medal.

DAVID KLINE, the editor of *Farming Magazine,* lives and farms in Fredericksburg, Ohio. He is the author of *Scratching the Woodchuck: Nature on an Amish Farm* and *Great Possessions: An Amish Farmer's Journal.*

P. TRAVIS KROEKER is professor and chair of religious studies at McMaster University (Ontario). He is the author of *Christian Ethics and Political Economy in North America* and coauthor of *Remembering the End: Dostoevsky as Prophet to Modernity.*

JOHN LANE is a writer, painter, and educator. He was chairman of the Dartington Hall Trust, is art editor of *Resurgence,* and was instrumental in the creation of Schumacher College. His ten books include *The Living Tree: Art and the Sacred; Timeless Simplicity: Creative Living in a Consumer Society; Timeless Beauty in the Arts and Everyday Life;* and *The Spirit of Silence.* He lives in North Devon in southwest England.

JOHN LEAX is poet in residence at Houghton College, where he has taught for thirty-nine years. His recent books include a collection of essays, *Grace Is Where I Live,* and a collection of poems, *Tabloid News.*

GENE LOGSDON is the author of twenty-four books, including the novel *The Lords of Folly* and the cultural study *The Mother of All Arts.* He lives with his wife, Carol, on their farm in north central Ohio.

ED McCLANAHAN is the author of *The Natural Man* (a novel), *Famous People I Have Known* (a seriocomic autobiography), and other books. In 2003, he edited *Spit in the Ocean #7: All about Kesey,* a collection of tributes to Ken Kesey. McClanahan and his wife, Hilda, live in Lexington, Kentucky.

BILL McKIBBEN is the author of ten books, including most recently *Deep Economy: The Wealth of Communities and the Durable Future,* which is dedicated to Wendell Berry.

JASON PETERS is associate professor of English at Augustana College (Illinois). His work has appeared in the *Sewanee Review, American Notes & Queries, Explicator, South Atlantic Quarterly, English Language Notes,* and *Christianity & Literature.*

SCOTT RUSSELL SANDERS is the recipient of several prizes, including a Lannan Literary Award. His books include *Staying Put, Writing from the Center, Secrets of the Universe, The Force of Spirit, Hunting for Hope,* and, most recently, *A Private History of Awe.* He lives in Bloomington, Indiana.

JACK SHOEMAKER is an editor and publisher. He recently returned to his native California after a dozen years in Washington, DC. He lives in the Bay Area with his wife, the novelist Jane Vandenburgh.

KIMBERLY K. SMITH is associate professor of political science and environmental studies at Carleton College (Minnesota). She is the author of *Wendell Berry and the Agrarian Tradition: A Common Grace,* as well as *Dominion of Voice: Riot, Reason and Romance in Antebellum Politics* and *African American Environmental Thought: Foundations.*

ERIC TRETHEWEY is professor of English at Hollins University (Virginia). He has published six books of poems, most recently *Songs and Lamentations* and *Heart's Hornbook.* His work has appeared in numerous magazines and anthologies in Canada, Britain, and the United States, among them the *Atlantic Monthly, American Scholar, Canadian Literature, Encounter, Georgia Review, Gettysburg Review, Hudson Review, Iowa Review, Kenyon Review, Missouri Review, New Letters, New Republic, North American Review, Parnassus, Paris Review, Ploughshares, Poetry,* the *Sewanee Review,* the *Southern Review, Stand,* and the *Yale Review.*

NORMAN WIRZBA is professor and chair of the philosophy department at Georgetown College (Kentucky). He is the author of *The Paradise of God* and *Living the Sabbath* and editor of *The Essential Agrarian Reader.*

Index